The Countess Choir Woman

Eleanor Cripps

ISBN 978-1-64458-655-6 (paperback)
ISBN 978-1-64458-656-3 (digital)

Christian Faith Publishing, Inc.
832 Park Avenue
Meadville, PA 16335
www.christianfaithpublishing.com

This book is a work if fiction, and any similarity with persons, living or dead, is entirely coincidental. Austria is a German speaking country, but almost each province has its own distinct dialect, especially among country people. I tried my best to convey this fact, and if it did not come across properly, it is entirely my fault.

Printed in the United States of America

Dedication

I am grateful to Ruth Maria Stoeckl, my dear friend since high school, for locating important research material.

Prologue

Adala's voice was barely audible. "The window, Wilburgis, will you open it!"

Abbess Cunigunde rose from her seat at the foot of the bed. "Mother, the air is still cool. It is not good for the lungs."

Adala ignored the jussive words, her eyes pleading with the sister kneeling at the side of her bed. "Wilburgis, it is spring. I so long to hear birds sing, and I cannot breathe." Her voice trailed off.

Wilburgis evaded the abbess's frown and rose with the agility of a young woman. A crackling fire overheated the dimly lit room, and the air was heavy from burned herbs. The softly praying nuns paused and anxiously held their breath as Wilburgis pushed open the leaded glass window and wooden shutters. A ray of sun fell brightly upon the rug and carved bed, the fine embroidered linens and the pale features of Adala, foundress of the exclusive abbey at Göss, a small hamlet nestled at the northern fringe of the Alps in the Austrian province of Styria. A gush of fresh air blew into the room, Adala's labored breathing eased, and her sunken gray eyes rewarded Wilburgis with a grateful glance.

It was May in the year of our Lord 1020, the time of year when birds venture their first hesitant songs in prelude to a spring that had scarcely touched the alpine valley.

"Go see whether the messenger has come," Adala whispered after a little while. The abbess made a slight move as if wanting to speak then remained silent until Sister Wilburgis had left the sickroom.

"Mother," Cunigunde said when the door closed behind the young nun, "I shall immediately inform you of the courier's arrival!"

Adala smiled. "I know, Cunigunde. God forgive my impatience, but I do not have much time left, and I so wish to leave you under the emperor's protection. Aribo has a delicate mission."

Adala's daughter Cunigunde and son Aribo had both chosen to devote their life to the church. Aribo held the important position of archdeacon at the Diocese of Salzburg and was shortly to become archbishop of Mainz. To secure imperial protection over the new foundation, Aribo released his inherited land holdings to the authority of Emperor Heinrich II. He was the monarch's father confessor and blood relative, yet Adala knew this did not assure the success of his petition. She had learned that Pope Benedict VIII was visiting Fulda, a place of medieval learning in Germany, and that the ambitious Aribo also sought the pope's personal seal of approval. Aristocratic families greatly coveted such privileges for their religious foundations.

The fresh spring air allowed the ailing canoness, weakened from fasting and lack of sleep, a restful night, during which Wilburgis never left her bedside while the sisters took turns in the cold and drafty little church to pray for the foundress of their abbey.

When the courier finally arrived with the good news, Abbess Cunigunde personally placed the precious document into Adala's hands. It was given at Mainz on the first day of May in the year of our Lord 1020 and bore the two most coveted seals of Europe: that of Emperor Heinrich II and of Pope Benedict VIII. Thereby, the young convent at Göss attained the status of a free abbey of the Holy Roman Realm, placing the sisters under the personal protection of the sovereign and the spiritual guidance of the pope, simultaneously removing them from the jurisdiction of the archbishopric of Salzburg. Such papal certification required payment of a yearly tribute to Rome, but Abbess Cunigunde and her successors were to deem highest spiritual patronage invaluable for their abbey.

The precious document furthermore bestowed upon each abbess the rank of duchess of the Realm with seat and vote in the diet of Styria and entitled the nuns to freely elect their abbess and administrative steward for their land holdings, subject only to the emperor's approval. Adala and Cunigunde well understood the document's immense importance for the prestige and safety of the titled canonesses of Göss. Foundress Adala was clutching the vellum roll bearing the official seals of Europe's two most powerful authorities in her emaciated hands when she died four months later on September 7, 1020.

At the threshold of a new millennium, Count Palatine Aribo and his wife Adala had chosen the tiny hamlet of Göss at the Mur River to find a home for aristocratic women wishing to dedicate their lives to Christ. The margrave presided over a wealthy Palatinate in Eastern Bavaria and was connected to the imperial family through ties of blood and friendship. The count and his wife were deeply involved in the monastic reform movement of the late 900s, and their son Aribo later not only became archbishop of Mainz but also chancellor to the emperor, their daughter Cunigunde the first abbess at Göss. An original document of the abbey's foundation dates from the year 1000, given by the margrave on his deathbed in the wake of a stroke, to which he shortly thereafter succumbed. When initial construction was completed in the second decade of the millennium, his widow took refuge at the abbey. The noble couple had selected Göss, a remote place southeast of Bavaria, because they owned extensive landholdings and tenant farms in the vicinity, the endowment of which secured the new foundation of substantial and continued revenue. Upon the margrave's death, Aribo gifted his inheritance to the emperor in exchange for the monarch's protection. The place was within the domain of the Austrian dukes of Babenberg and became the first permanent home of a religious order in the province of Styria. The abbey was originally not a convent in the strict sense of the word. According to the chronicle, the order was governed by the rule of St. Benedict, but the women technically were canonesses rather than nuns. As such, they lived in chastity within a religious community but were not bound by all the vows associated with Benedictine nuns, such as poverty, uniform habit, and irrevocable commitment.

The canonesses of Göss initially hailed exclusively from aristocratic families and wore their own colorful medieval attire including jewelry, and it was not unusual for them to personally inspect properties that were part of the "dowry" they brought to the Abbey upon entry. And they regularly visited their families or hosted relatives at Göss. Their number was at first limited to twelve to ensure that the original prebend would suffice to support them, their servants, and an appropriate staff to safeguard comfort and security.

As the daughter of a Count Palatine, Cunigunde and the succeeding abbesses were educated noblewomen who frequently played host to important visitors within their walls and remained informed of historic events affecting the area. The emperor's direct protection and papal privileges formed a potent deterrent against outside transgressions, particularly important since Styria was to repeatedly change hands during the following centuries. Moreover, they bestowed the abbey with an exclusivity that induced aristocratic families to select Göss for their daughters. And while many young women undoubtedly followed a vocation to dedicate their lives to Christ, some sought education and others because a suitable husband could not be found. The emperor's protection and the pope's spiritual privileges eventually ceased, but by then, the abbey was firmly established and well renowned. Half a millennium would pass until some of the novices and pupils accepted were daughters of low nobility and even upper class citizenry.

There existed a male equivalent in religious life for canonesses—the canon, a priest living with other priests in a community resembling a monastery. An eighth century bishop of Metz by the name of Chodregang laid down precise guidelines and procedures for such communities. When later canons and canonesses submitted to the strict rules of either St. Augustan or St. Benedict, it became customary to refer to them as "choir men" and "choir women" because of the extensive choir duties Chodregang's rules prescribed. In church, they did not mix with the congregation but occupied separate seats and enjoyed various privileges ordinary monks and nuns did not have. Their choir service, however, was extremely demanding and comprised sung prayers and litanies, Gregorian chants, and the Latin Mass at various hours during day and night. Since so rigid a schedule prevented male members from attending to pastoral and other duties, their order of the day was modified in many cases. Not so the choir women at Göss who remained a contemplative order and adhered to their demanding duties throughout the abbey's existence.

Families from the surrounding countryside provided so-called lay nuns who performed all manual labor. These women worked long and hard hours and were nuns in the strictest sense of the Benedictine rule, which prescribes a life of "ora et labora" meaning, "pray and work." In a spiritual sense, it also applied to choir women inasmuch as their choir duties literally consumed most hours of their days and nights.

The first canonesses of Göss came from a religious order in Salzburg, about a hundred miles to the northwest. They must have considered their new abode extremely remote. The archdiocese of Salzburg at the time was already a sophisticated and worldly place that owed its great wealth and importance to a strategic location and rich salt mines, as well as farsighted and able bishops, who had established Salzburg as a spiritual metropolis. The Göss Foundation too was to attain a status of honor and prestige, albeit in a different way. Well-endowed from the outset, the abbey's wealth increased steadily through substantial dowries of land, money, and the artifacts each new member contributed. Wealthy and educated canonesses and their abbesses in due course made Göss to an economic and cultural bastion that exerted important influence upon the area. The abbey grew extensively over time, comprised an important library and collection of prized objects d'art collected both from dowries and commissioned by the abbesses from outside artists. And the choir women also created exquisite examples of artistic craftsmanship.

They maintained their status as canonesses until the great Benedictine Reform of the late fifteenth century, when under intense pressure by various movements and visitations they forsook the colorful fashion of the day for the traditional black habit and henceforth no longer ventured outside abbey walls. Their vows became irrevocable, and they subjected themselves to most Benedictine rules. The rule of poverty, however, was never strictly adhered to; abbesses administered individual family funds from which a choir woman could draw as needed to pay for small personal luxuries. One unfortunate consequence was a class distinction within the chapter depending on background and family fortune, which during certain periods led to disharmony and the formation of cliques within the chapter. Certain members of the congregation held offices that were time consuming and partially relieved them of choir duty. They were addressed with the title "magistra" and depending on the importance of their office exercised authority and considerable power. Examples were the prioress (second to the abbess), sub-prioress, magistra celleraria (in charge of provisions and wine cellar), magistra portaria (gatekeeper), sacristan (treasurer), apothecary (pharmacist), magistra in charge of aspirants (pupils), novices, and others. The magistrae formed part of the "abbess's court" that shared her table and certain other privileges. In order to devote the necessary time to their administrative duties, they were unable to perform regular choir duty. The others spent their few leisure hours creating exquisite embroidered vestments, canopies, antependia (altar cloths), and other handicraft.

As far as is known, the status of "abbey of the realm" and direct spiritual protectorate by the pope endured for about two centuries. The emperor designated a steward with the title of "Vogt" to assist the abbess in administering the foundation's holdings, though she retained the privilege of important decisions. In later years, the Habsburg Court in Vienna appointed regional noble men to that function, together with a "Sub-Vogt" to manage more scattered estates. The monasteries of Admont and Seckau assumed spiritual guidance. Regular priests read the daily masses under the direction of a Supremus Capellanus (known simply as the "Supremus"). He heard confessions of the choir women and was in charge of important religious ceremonies. Jesuits for a time manned the positions until the bishops and abbots of Salzburg, Admont, and Seckau delegated Benedictine monks to Göss. These bishoprics also conducted visitations and supervised the electoral process for a new abbess, but distance and difficult travel conditions limited the frequency and lasting effect of such visits.

The choir women maintained a school for titled young girls who became an important source for new novices. A pharmacy dispensed herbs and medicines to the local populace, and there was a small hospice for the poor. On special feast days, they distributed bread and alms to anyone coming to the gate, but they did not engage in charity work outside their walls. The fact that they always remained a purely contemplative order was used as reason for their eventual dissolution.

All buildings were originally constructed of wood, and even after the whole complex fell into ashes during a devastating fire in 1336, the church alone was rebuilt in stone. During one of their numerous forays, a Turkish army in 1480 moved within dangerous proximity of the poorly protected abbey. Tradition has it that the fervently praying nuns "walked" on their knees for about a mile to the ancient Lamberti Church that overlooked the Mur River in sight of the Turkish camp on the opposite bank. Saint Lambertus is said to have come to their rescue by flooding the river and with his arrows foiling the invaders' efforts to cross over in rafts; the enemy finally withdrew, and the abbey was spared. The Turks were the most serious and imminent threat Göss had ever faced, and the incident was an awakening jolt that prompted subsequent abbesses to devote themselves toward improving internal and external safety. Over the next hundred years, all main buildings were reconstructed in stone and masonry with tiled roofs, and the complex was encircled with heavy walls fortified by numerous watchtowers.

Protestantism spread among the local aristocracy during the sixteenth century and severely curtailed recruitment of novices, so that at one time only half a dozen choir women and twenty pupils remained. A vigorous Catholic Counter Reformation revived monastic life, and once again aristocrats, initially from Italy and Bavaria, sent their daughters to Göss, soon to be followed by indigenous families. Even though intense reform movements enforced strict cloister rules and confined the women to within their walls, Göss would never again suffer a shortage of candidates. And while one function of convents was to provide a refuge for young women unable to find a suitable match, many came to follow their spiritual vocation, and some even joined in defiance of their Protestant families' wishes. Often, young girls became inclined toward monastic life while spending time as "aspirants," as those pursuing an education were called. Rules demanded that final vows only be taken by the free will of the individual, though some might have felt they had little choice. There are no records of any nun leaving prior to the abbey's dissolution in the late eighteenth century. And while these daughters of aristocracy missed none of life's necessities in their sheltered existence, their daily routine was not one of leisure. Obedience to abbess and prioress was unconditional, and the harsh schedule of prayer and service to God allowed for minimum privacy and demanded considerable physical endurance as it dominated their lives day and night.

Abbess and choir women remained well aware of events outside their walls as the history of the region unfolded. Family members periodically visited with news from the secular world, and it was the abbey's often onerous and costly duty to host traveling monarchs and their parties. According to the Chronic, a grossly negligent member of the retinue of visiting noble woman Margaretha of Tyrol caused the aforementioned devastating fire of 1336.

Chapter 1

O ur story begins in Transylvania, which is now part of Rumania, but in the eighteenth century formed the easternmost part of Hungary. It is nestled in the huge crescent of the Carpathian Mountains that curve from Slovakia eastward into Moldavia and Romania then south and west again toward the Balkan and the Alps. To the northwest, the Carpathian Mountains form a natural passage for the Danube leaving Austria and a thousand miles to the east create the famous Iron Gate where the great river enters wide plains on its way toward the Black Sea. Transylvania consists of grand forests towered by snow-covered peaks and a fertile high plateau that descends toward the Alfold, the Great Hungarian Plains. Transylvania means "beyond the forest" and is a rich country, the most scenic and interesting of the Hungarian provinces. Its magnificent forests to this day are an expanse of woods as virginal as they were three centuries ago when many of the trees already were hundreds of years old, as tall and mighty as anywhere on the European continent. They teem with game, and stags and deer grow larger and stronger than elsewhere. It is beautiful country, with gentle green valleys between the dark forests, dotted with picturesque towns and hamlets.

The population evolved from various ethnic peoples attracted to the region, and their diversity resulted in a model of religious and cultural tolerance. Its princes were open-minded and farsighted in their culture and education, less so strategically as they aimed to expand their power to other regions. Largely of Protestant faith, they often played the politics of brinkmanship with both the powerful

Habsburgs of Austria and the Muslims to the east. Especially the Sultans were not inclined to allow anyone to gain much power near their border and taught Transylvania some bloody and costly lessons, depriving it of much of its status and influence.

The landholdings of Zay-Ugrocz, an estate in the northwestern part of Transylvania, comprised a moderate amount of arable fields, forests to indulge the owner's passion for hunting, and pastures for horses and cattle. A few dozen socage peasants and their families tilled the land and supplied servants, and others helped to run the estate. The comfortable mansion, stables, and outbuildings were sited on the slope of a hill overlooking a small hamlet of well-kept masonry houses crowded round a whitewashed Protestant Church. In the clear country air, the tolling of the little bell in the slender steeple sounded as if coming from the estate's weathervane.

The Trauttmansdorff family occupied the mansion in the summer of 1730, and when the young countess entered confinement, the midwife predicted another son since the baby appeared to be quite large. Indeed, labor proved to be especially difficult and exhausting for the frail twenty-five-year-old woman who, during her five-year marriage, had already given birth to two sons and a daughter.

Maria Theresa, nicknamed Miczike, was nineteen years old when she met the dashing young Count Maximilian of Trauttmansdorff at a social gathering in Vienna in 1724. It was love at first sight for the lively, petite girl, though chances of a happy ending to the romance initially seemed remote. Baroness Miczike Zay was orphaned. Her father had been part of Transylvania's gentry and had secured a modestly comfortable lifestyle that could be maintained under efficient management, especially if the young baroness were to choose a husband of some means. Miczike's mother, a Countess Kollonitsch, hailed from an old Austrian family of Southern Styria and, like her husband, was of Protestant faith. Two members of her family, though, in the early 1600s had converted to Catholicism. Johanna Countess Kollonitsch entered Göss as a novice, took her vows at age twenty-seven, and, eleven years later, was elected abbess. Highly educated and intelligent, Abbess Maria Johanna became one of the most prolific leaders for her Benedictine choir women. She dedicated herself to expanding the abbey and commissioned the addition of a beautiful vestry, whose baroque glory remains unchanged to this day. Among her first acts as abbess was to order a renovation of the catacombs below the abbey church, designated as the final resting place for choir women, who previously were buried in various locations on the abbey grounds. She was also responsible for the erection of a new tract of cells for her growing number of choir women. Abbess Maria Johanna loved the arts, pursued the acquisition of valuable items, and repeatedly hosted members of the imperial family passing through the area. Her diplomacy and tact resulted in an active relationship with the secular culture in her time. She died of tuberculosis in 1657, not yet fifty-five years old.

Her younger brother had also converted, and one of his grandsons chose the priesthood, reaching the rank of bishop at an early age. So when Miczike lost both parents, Bishop Count Kollonitsch, as her closest relative, became guardian of the young girl. Their diverging religion strained their relationship from the outset. Miczike had been raised with a Protestant's characteristic disdain for the Church of Rome, and there had been no family contact prior to her becoming the bishop's charge. Of course, he would have liked to see Miczike convert and even choose religious life, but the vivacious young baroness adamantly defied both ideas. Her inheritance allowed her a certain financial independence, and while not beautiful, her small face, framed by curly chestnut hair and dominated by large brown eyes, was of captivating charm. The bishop's best hope was to secure an appropriate marriage, and he brought her to traditionally Catholic Vienna for introduction into society. The Trauttmansdorff family regarded the little Baroness Zay from Transylvania far below their standing and prestige and was not enthused about the match. Maximilian was their third son and following family tradition officer in the emperor's army with nominal pay. To maintain the lifestyle expected of his rank required funds above the modest legacy he received from his not particularly wealthy family. His old name and good looks opened him many doors to families of eligible young women among Austria's wealthy and influential nobility with excellent chances for an alliance that would have solidified his financial situation. He was a daredevil with a passion for horses and dedicated to a carefree lifestyle, both of which called for a wealthy bride. Miczike, as a Protestant, did not meet any of the prerequisites his family expected, but her high spirits and spontaneous charm, so different from the stiffness and formality of Viennese society, captured the young count's heart and had him passionately fall in love with her.

The young couple had their will. Maximilian resigned his commission to assume administration of his bride's estate. His family insisted on a Catholic wedding, and Miczike made the required promise to raise their future children in that faith—a promise she promptly broke after the birth of their first son. After initial weak objections, her devoted husband gave in. It was the last straw for the Trauttmansdorffs, and contacts between Vienna and Transylvania became strained and very rare.

Miczike attended Sunday services in the hamlet's Protestant Church, at first alone, later accompanied by her children as they reached an age at which it was customary to bring them. The nearest Catholic Church was over ten miles away, and the count's attendance at Mass was somewhat haphazard, much to the chagrin of the parish priest.

Miczike and Maximilian were happy together, their lifestyle debonair. The dashing officer knew little about administering an estate, even less about managing money. When their financial situation became strained, he borrowed against the land to satisfy his love for horses and cater to Miczike's every wish. A passionate hunter and excellent rider, Maximilian was happiest on horseback and immensely proud of his thoroughbreds. His first three children resembled him with blond hair and blue eyes, though they were small-boned and delicate like their mother. Three births in as many years took a toll on the countess about to give birth to her fourth child, which, to everyone's surprise, turned out to be a baby girl, stronger and healthier than any of the previous ones. She was named Maria Theresa after her mother, whose dark hair and large brown eyes she inherited. Miczike called her Theresa, but when the little girl learned to speak, she referred to herself as Tessa, and the family adopted the nickname. Miczike took an inordinately long time to recover from the difficult birth, and her physician strongly advised against further pregnancies. Housebound by her fragile constitution, the countess did not regain her former spirits and at times succumbed to depression. She was not a devoted mother to her children and especially the youngest perplexed her. Ferenc and Sigismunda, the two eldest, were both serious and withdrawn, and Miczike clearly preferred her second son Michael born the year before Tessa. The boy knew precisely how to charm his mama when in a bind, most often in connection with his detested studies. He knew that whenever her darling was in trouble, Mama would overrule tutor or husband.

Tessa—intelligent, alert, impetuous, and always ready to play tricks on her siblings—soon elbowed her way into her older siblings' lessons. Learning came quickly and easily to her, and she had a burning desire to outdo her brothers and sister. Cared for by nanny, governess, and tutor, the children at an early age became fluent in Hungarian, German, and French. Tessa was also much more athletic than her siblings, and her adored papa taught her to ride before she was five years old. In his heart, Count Maximilian preferred her company to that of his other offspring.

Family life at Zay-Ugrocz was informal with few restrictions, but the children learned to be considerate and quiet in the presence of their ailing mother. They dutifully visited her boudoir every morning and again to say good night before going to bed. It was customary to only join the parents' table after reaching age seven, and when the older two won that privilege, Tessa did not envy them. If her health permitted and when in a cheerful mood, Miczike would sometimes read to them in the afternoons, but beyond insisting on good manners, she was not involved in their upbringing. She clearly preferred the company of her sons to that of her daughters, often criticizing Sigismunda for being too serious and withdrawn and Tessa for being stubborn and impetuous. She also secretly blamed her youngest child for her poor health. Tessa, in turn, had trouble remaining quiet and sedate in her mother's presence and much preferred hunting with her father or visiting tenant farmers on the estate. The children's elderly ayah, as nannies were referred to, had raised the three Trauttmansdorff boys in Vienna, and Maximilian always had been her favorite. She was summoned to Transylvania a few months after the birth of Ferenc. Miczike at first was reluctant because she feared any Catholic influence on her child, but when efforts to locally find a suitable candidate failed, she gave in to Maximilian's wish. The ayah was originally from Bohemia and by then in her sixties but only too happy to follow the summons. With the Trauttmansdorff boys grown, she had been retained in the Vienna household and assigned other chores, but her heart always ached for children. Upon her arrival at Zay-Ugrocz, the young countess delivered a stern lecture about religion and made it clear that Catholicism had no place in the nursery and all religious teaching of the children was to come from her and only her. The ayah was devoutly Catholic but understood that continued employment depended on compliance with her mistress's wishes, knowing only too well that small children would quickly give away any transgression on her part.

Four difficult pregnancies and births had transformed the vivacious bride into an unhappy and dissatisfied young woman who, even on better days, preferred the seclusion of her boudoir to the company of her brood. Her husband remained attentive and considerate, but Miczike's fear of bearing more children caused coolness in their relationship. She spent her time reading and bemoaning her poor health and left the upbringing of her children to him and the ayah, their education to a governess and tutor. Maximilian wished that his sons were strong and athletic and Sigismunda less serious. But he was a devoted father and loved them all dearly, though his favorite companion was brave little Tessa who rarely cried and, like her papa, loved the outdoors.

She was six when on a mild fall day she accompanied her father on a visit to the neighboring town of Ulmeni. The count was at the reins of two fast horses pulling the smart little chaise. Maximilian attended to a few commissions and then visited the priest who'd sent message reminding his parishioner that he hadn't seen him at Sunday Mass in a while. Mindful of his wife's insistence that their children not come in contact with his faith, he left Tessa in the carriage, firmly instructing her to remain there until his return. It wasn't long, however, before the old church opposite the rectory, and the surrounding cemetery intrigued the little girl. The securely tied horses had their muzzles buried in bags of oats, and Tessa, initially proud of her papa's admonition to hold on to the reins, tied them round an armrest and climbed from her high seat. Strolling through the cemetery, she became aware of haunting sounds coming from the church. Tessa loved to sing and easily and quickly picked up nursery songs as well as the slow and somber Bohemian folk melodies the ayah taught her, and she'd strain to listen to the strings of gypsy violins her parents hired for background music when entertaining. But the present tune had a haunting quality different from anything she'd heard before and seemed to float between the tombstones. The heavy door was partially open and allowed Tessa to slip quietly into the cool dark church, in which the air vibrated with the chant of Benedictine monks seated in exquisitely carved choir chairs of the sanctuary. With their faces almost hidden by black hoods, it took the child a few moments to realize that the haunting sound came from below the cowls. She couldn't understand the Latin words, but what she heard exerted a hypnotizing effect upon her. She'd never seen a church like this, so unlike the one she was used to visiting with her mother on Sundays, where bright light and large windows emphasized an austere interior with plain pews and white walls bare of decorations. The ambience of this stone church was a perfect background for the somber chant. Narrow stained glass windows shut out the afternoon sun, the gothic ceiling reached to dark and lofty heights, and the gilded robes of statues in niches and on pedestals shimmered mysteriously in the dim light. Tessa did not know that the red light in the hanging lamp near the sanctuary signified the presence of Christ and that she was expected to genuflect in reverence. Too young for devout piety, the voices evoked in her an infinite tenderness and sense of peace and longing she more felt than understood. All she knew was that she wanted to stay and forever listen to these sounds. She tiptoed on the stone floor down the nave, mesmerized by the chanting voices and unaware that she had begun to join in the singing with a simple "Aaaa." Tessa had an excellent ear for music, and with a voice of unusually low pitch for her age, she sounded like a choirboy singing an upper part in perfect key. Becoming aware of her intonation in these unfamiliar acoustic surroundings fascinated her and increased her boldness. The monks gave no sign of being aware of her presence, perhaps taking her for a young member of the church choir. The child was spellbound and lost all sense of time until she felt her papa's hand on her shoulder, firmly directing her toward the door. There the count turned, dipped his hand into a stone basin with water, genuflected and crossed himself, then—with a moist fingertip—traced the sign of the cross on his daughter's forehead.

"Tessa, what were you doing in the church?" he asked sternly as they emerged into the sunlight, but the child could not contain her curiosity.

"Papa, who were the men in the black cloaks? What was their song? Why is it so dark in there, and who are the figures in the golden clothes? Papa, why did you bend your knee when we left? And why did you dip your hand into the water? Can we please go back and listen some more so I can learn how to sing with them?"

Questions were tumbling from her mouth and continued as he lifted her into the carriage, grasped the reins, and started on their way home. Maximilian had not uttered another word and carefully considered his answers. With the keen perception of the very young, the child sensed his uneasiness.

"Mama will be cross with me," she finally said. "But please tell me, Papa, what was their song, and can I learn it?"

"Their song, Tessa, is called the Gregorian chant, or choral, and usually is sung during services by monks or nuns, men and women who have devoted their lives to God."

"Why does Mama not take us to listen to them in our church so I can sing with them?"

"Tessa, you and Mama and your brothers and sister belong to the Protestant faith, that does not have monks and nuns like the Catholic Church, of which I am part and where the Gregorian chant is practiced. You do sing beautiful hymns at your services, don't you? They're just different, that's all." He tried to sound casual, but Tessa was stubborn.

"I like the Gregorian chant," she said after a slight hesitation, repeating the unfamiliar term. "And I want to sing it. Can you teach me? Or can the ayah? And why does Mama's church not have people who devote themselves to God?"

Maximilian uneasily noted that the child was saying "Mama's church" instead of "our church" but thought it wise not to make an issue of it.

"You're too young, Tessa, to understand what it means to give up life as we know it and become a recluse behind the walls of a convent or monastery. Just think of not being able to ride horses, run through the woods, play with other children, or wear ordinary clothes! Protestants believe that you can serve the Lord in other ways."

"But I want to sing like the monks, or do nuns also sing the Gregorian chant?"

"They do, my child, but you're much too young for it, and besides, you don't know the Latin language! It is sung only in Latin, the language of the church that priests use."

"Papa, may I come with you to your church next Sunday? Perhaps, monks or nuns will be singing! May I please?"

Maximilian found it hard to resist his daughter's pleading eyes, but he also knew Miczike's ardent dislike of the Catholic Church. She'd never forgive him for satisfying the child's curiosity about his faith. He had no intention of ever leaving his church, though he had not been sufficiently devout to insist that his children belong to it, in spite of the solemn promise he and his bride had made prior to their nuptials. Tessa was likely to grow up and marry into the overwhelmingly Protestant Transylvania gentry, and he hoped that the child would soon forget the whole episode.

"You may not," he answered firmly. "Mama does not wish it, and neither do I," he added meekly. "There are beautiful hymns sung during Protestant services, and now I don't want to hear another word about it. You did not obey when I told you to stay in the chaise and watch the horses! Your poor mama would get a bad headache if she knew, do you understand?"

Tessa understood only too well, and Miczike never learned of the incident. The ayah, however, found out that same evening. As she put the child to bed and straightened the room, she heard the little voice hum, at first refusing to believe her ears when she thought she detected notes of the "Salve Regina." She herself had been left at the steps of a convent as an infant and nuns had raised her until she ran away to go to Vienna. Having spent many hours of her childhood in church, she had picked up various Latin prayers of the Mass together with the Gregorian chant. It did not take her long to extract the events of the afternoon from her young charge, including the count's orders not to talk about it. As the child bubbled forth her questions, she patiently answered them, explaining that the figures in the gilded robes were saints, how one became a saint, and that the red light in the hanging lamp by the altar meant that Christ was present in the tabernacle. Tessa could not hear enough about it and would not rest until she had the ayah's reluctant promise to teach her the words and complete sequence of the "Salve Regina" the next day. Only then would she go to sleep while the faithful old woman turned and tossed half the night for fear that her promise might cause her to be sent back to Vienna in disgrace. She need not have worried. Tessa was mature for her age, and the children spent but a few hours each day with their mother. When she was tired of them, Miczike would often dismiss them abruptly. Especially the count's remark that Tessa's disobedience was likely to give Mama a headache was a threat all four children dreaded. Tessa tried hard not to arouse her mother's displeasure, having learned early that she was more often singled out for criticism and reprimand than the others. It especially hurt her that Michael—a year older but at seven, the same height, and a much poorer student than she—usually won with Mama. Not that Tessa was always innocent; well aware of her physical advantage, she often bullied Michael. He would cry easily and run to his mother to complain, assured of her support, especially when the perpetrator was Tessa, who outdid him in just about anything. Still she and Michael were playmates but only to a certain extent. The older Sigismunda was shy and a scholar, and Ferenc was of an age when girls were considered a nuisance one politely tolerates.

Tessa did not forget her church experience, nor did she rest until the Ayah made good on her promise. The old woman too had a good ear, and while she did not remember many Gregorian chants from her youth, she knew the Latin words to the slow, haunting tune of the Salve Regina antiphon. Tessa had been taught that Mary was the Mother of Jesus, but since the Protestant Church does not accord special veneration to the Mother of God, the prayer's deeply devotional words of hope in despair evoked many questions that demanded answers and explanations. The ayah gave them to the best of her ability, and the prayer's notion that "the Mother of mercy look with compassion upon the children of Eve in their valley of tears" held a strange fascination for the child. As she memorized the words and began to understand their meaning, Mary turned into an idealized mother figure, the mother so distant in her young life. Not that she had been raised without love—she'd received affection from both her parents, the devoted ayah, and many others—but Mama had been in poor health and need of special consideration for as long as she could remember. And while the ayah was strict and always insisted on good behavior and impeccable manners, Tessa, the child of nobility, knew that the old woman was but a servant and would never exert major influence on her life. Her beloved papa was wonderful, but there were many days when she barely saw him, perhaps only at the dinner table when children were not expected to speak unless spoken to. Yet she could always talk to Mary, Mother of God, by raising her eyes toward the sky and singing the "Salve Regina." In her vivid imagination, she thought she saw the Virgin smile from the clouds and felt as if touched by a loving hand. The little girl learned to take her troubles to Mary, especially when sent to her room in punishment for a transgression. She would then climb onto the wide windowsill to sit and peer at the clouds and sing the haunting chant of the "Salve Regina," over and over repeating the closing supplication, "Oh gracious, oh merciful, oh sweet Virgin Mary." All the tenderness and ardency of the prayer is expressed in the music of these closing words, and they would console Tessa for whatever troubled her at the time.

By her seventh birthday, she had learned to read both German and Hungarian and sometimes stole into the library with the tall bookcases made of wood from indigenous forests. Working at his desk, the count gladly tolerated his little daughter and would find her an illustrated book to hold her attention. She'd huddle in a corner and become totally absorbed, from time to time asking questions, though only when no one else was present to occupy her papa's attention. If there was, the child remained perfectly quiet and unnoticed, knowing full well that interrupting conversations with visitors would bar her from future visits. Neither did the count mind finding her alone in his library, considering her too young to understand subjects unsuitable for children. He remained unaware when Tessa discovered a low shelf with books from his childhood, including a well-worn small volume titled *Catechism*, a word with which she was unfamiliar. On its first page was a colorful illustration of the Virgin Mary in a white gown and blue cloak, standing on what resembled the large globe in a corner of the library, pointedly placing one foot upon the head of a snake. The Virgin was not holding Baby Jesus in her arms and that made the picture all the more attractive for Tessa, who considered herself Mary's child and was not anxious to share attention with anyone else. The book with many colorful illustrations was written specifically for children and dated from the count's early days of schooling. It thoroughly fascinated Tessa, as did little notes and doodles in her papa's childish handwriting. Knowing it would not be missed, she took it from the library to hide among her own books in the nursery, where even the watchful eyes of the ayah did not spot it. The catechism's simple presentation and lively illustrations provided Tessa with a powerful impression of the Catholic religion. She attended Sunday school and was familiar with the basics of Christian faith, but what she read here sounded quite different. Being aware that she was not supposed to have this book made it all the more attractive to the precocious child who was particularly anxious to learn more about the mysterious monks and their solemn chant. She came across a chapter explaining that Jesus had founded His church by selecting twelve apostles from among his followers and designated Peter to be their leader, which was why Peter was considered the first pope. Tessa knew that the Protestant Church did not recognize the pope and Mama never failed to voice contempt when the church of Rome came up in conversation. She also knew that two centuries ago a man by the name of Martin Luther had decided that the Roman Church was wrong and corrupt and only his own ideas of salvation through Jesus Christ the right ones. Not knowing what had led to the Reformation, it seemed to her that if Jesus wanted Peter to be pope, how could Martin Luther decide that was wrong? The little book explained that all Christians had to belong to the Catholic Church whose teachings they were to embrace and follow or face damnation and hell. She'd been taught that if she behaved well, she would live in heaven someday, but would that be a different one from that of her beloved papa who was Catholic? If the teachings of this book were true, would not what Mama and the pastor said set Protestants on a path to hell? It was all terribly confusing, and Tessa spent long hours thinking about it, afraid to ask anyone to explain.

Miczike's health did not improve over the years. The once charming and lively young woman and loving wife blamed her pregnancies and difficult births for her suffering and over time began to resent her children. They, after all, were the reason why her pretty face had begun to fade, why she no longer was the center of attention at parties and felt tired all the time. She longed for the carefree days of her adolescence, the passionate time of her early marriage. After all, her husband was responsible for the birth of four children in quick succession and the strain it had been on her frail body. Fearful of another pregnancy, she denied herself to Maximilian, who initially understood but grew increasingly frustrated in his marriage, for which he had given up his beloved officer's career. Administering the estate was a boring chore, the only purpose of which was to extract money for a comfortable life and the acquisition of yet another thoroughbred.

Zay-Ugrocz could not support extravagancies. The land was fertile and the peasants hardworking and devoted. With prudent management, it could yield a good return, but the count rarely listened to advice. His main interest was horses, and he sought diversion from his domestic difficulties by spending many hours in the saddle. He taught his children horsemanship at an early age. Ferenc and Sigismunda preferred other activities and complied only because of Papa's insistence. Michael's skills improved with time, but only Tessa really enjoyed the sport. By the time she and Michael were twelve and thirteen, they joined their father at foxhunts and outdid older youngsters from neighboring families.

The four had few contacts within their age group. There was a certain resentment among the Protestant gentry toward Miczike's Catholic husband, and as her visits to Sunday services with the children became less frequent because of her illness, rumors spread that Maximilian was converting them to Catholicism. It was far from true. The count was not a pious man, and the broken promise about his offspring's religious upbringing did not weigh heavily on his mind. But he never felt particularly at home in Transylvania and longed for the Austrian army's camaraderie and Vienna's social life. By the time his children were in their teens, he was making plans to introduce them to Austrian society as soon as they were ready but did not share such thoughts with his wife. He hoped to mend the estranged relationship with his own family and was confident that Viennese society would readily accept his sons and daughters. He was secretly disappointed that his two sons so far showed little interest in becoming officers. If only his headstrong and daring youngest child had been a boy! Tessa continued to outdo her older siblings in anything athletic, but she also learned easily and quickly, though other than Michael, all were excellent students. Much as she liked to read, Tessa still preferred the outdoors and loved to roam through the woods. The only danger facing her during her strolls were wild boars or perhaps a bear, but game was fairly shy due to extensive hunting. Tessa could easily forget that she wore a dainty dress and would climb a tree, humming to herself as she perched in the branches and enjoyed the view. She loved the smell of moss and needles in the dark Carpathian woods, the call of bird or game, or the soft gurgling of a little brook and happily spent summer afternoons in her favorite places. And the ayah would always think of an excuse for yet another ruined outfit stained with sap or torn by a branch. Besides, when Papa was away, Mama would rarely ask for her, and the ayah trusted the good sense of her youngest charge to be careful and return safely.

Chapter 2

Tessa was thirteen when on a pleasant May afternoon, she settled down with a book at the edge of the forest. Beyond the sweeping meadow resplendent in the tender green of spring and dotted with bright wildflowers, she could see the white stucco mansion, the servants' quarters and stables, and hear the faint sounds of country life. Papa and Ferenc had gone away for a few days visiting a breeding farm to inspect a stallion the count hoped to acquire; Mama, Michael, and Sigismunda were in the house.

Tessa read awhile then leaned back on the trunk of a spruce to dream of the world beyond the Carpathians, a world she could only imagine. Papa often spoke of Vienna, and her natural curiosity yearned to see places beyond the familiar dark woods and green slopes. She loved Zay-Ugrocz, though, knowing she'd always return here.

Her interest in the Catholic Church and her fascination with the Gregorian chant had not waned, but in view of her mother's attitude, her knowledge was limited to the dog-eared little catechism and the "Salve Regina." She had learned a few German hymns from the ayah, who could remember various parts of the Latin Mass but no other Gregorian chants. She had never visited the old church at Ulmeni again, but in her imagination, the mystical attraction of the somber ambience and the colorful windows and figures of saints had only grown. She knew that Vienna was predominantly Catholic and wondered whether the city had more churches like that. Papa said that the time would come when she was presented to Viennese society; she'd be a big girl then and explore the city on her own!

Tessa spotted a man on horseback emerging from the hamlet and gallop up the hill toward the mansion and, with the experienced eye of a horsewoman, noticed that the animal appeared tired, yet its rider repeatedly used the whip to spur it on. Couriers were a means of communication among nobility, and the eager man was probably anxious to deliver an important message for her papa. She observed him being met at the entrance by the chief housekeeper and watched him enter the house. She'd picked up her book again when she heard the ayah's shrill voice calling her name. What did she want? Her history lesson wasn't due for another hour, and Mama had announced earlier that she was suffering from migraine. Then she saw the old woman struggling up the slope in an effort to find her. For a moment, she considered hiding, but her affection for the ayah, who had trouble walking on her gout-plagued legs, got the upper hand.

"I hear you, ayah," she yelled, gathering up her book and strolling across the meadow.

It sounded as if tears were choking the ayah's voice when she called, "Hurry, child!" and getting closer Tessa saw that the old woman was indeed weeping.

"Ayah, what is it?" she cried. "What's happened?" There was no answer, but one look at the distressed, wrinkled face told her that something was very wrong. It had to do with the arrival of the courier, and with the rest of the family safely at home, it could only concern Ferenc or Papa!

"Come, my poor child, and be with your mama," the ayah managed to say, opening her arms and hugging the girl. "A terrible thing happened. Your poor papa, he's had an accident, he fell from the horse."

Tessa tore herself loose and ran toward the house, leaving the old woman behind. Rushing across the courtyard, she barely noticed the servants' distressed faces; the housekeeper tried to stop her in the hall, but she flew up the stairs to Mama's boudoir. The door was closed, and when Tessa bolted into the room, her mother sat upright in her chaise with Michael clinging to her and an ashen-faced Sigismunda standing by her side. Miczike stared at her daughter with unnaturally large eyes as if expecting someone else. Her features seemed frozen, her lips pressed together, and the room was deadly quiet until Michael began to sob. At that instant, Tessa knew that her beloved papa was dead and her mind raced back to the church in Ulmeni and the Gregorian chant. For a few moments, the monks' voices seemed to drone unbearably loud in her head then abruptly stopped as her mother said in a toneless voice, "They say Papa fell from his horse and broke his neck, and now I am alone!"

Miczike started to weep, and Tessa moved toward her, but her mother buried her face in Michael's hair, oblivious of her surroundings. Choked with tears, the girl stood rigid until Sigismunda walked over and whispered, "Come with me, Mama has forgotten about us." The two sisters quietly went to their room, finally allowing their composure to dissolve into tears.

Sigismunda was almost sixteen, a slight blond girl with regular but plain features. She loved to study and was the most religious member of the family. She had been confirmed the previous year and very proud of being a full member of the Protestant Church. The two girls were physical and temperamental opposites and not particularly close. Sigismunda was the most mature of the four siblings and instinctively felt it her duty to take charge. She'd been with Miczike when Baron Takats arrived, a neighbor who had accompanied Maximilian and Ferenc. Sigismunda described how he searched for words trying to break the terrible news. The count, he said, insisted on riding a temperamental black stallion he considered acquiring and confidently swung himself into the saddle. Takats and Ferenc watched as the count galloped down a slope when the animal, spurred on to jump across a brook, lost footing in the soft bank, and caused the rider to take a vicious fall. Takats and Ferenc ran to help and at first thought Maximilian only unconscious. But his neck was broken, and seconds later, his heart stopped beating. A young family had lost husband and father.

The Baron left the stunned Ferenc behind and immediately embarked on the long ride to Zay-Ugrocz to deliver the devastating news. Sigismunda tried to comfort her mother, but Miczike did not respond and angrily dismissed the Baron, asking that her eldest son return home immediately. Then Michael, curious to find out about the horseman's arrival, walked in. His mother had opened her arms to him, and it became painfully obvious that he was the only one Miczike wished to remain by her side.

A wailing ayah joined the two girls, and Sigismunda rose to summon the housekeeper and send word to the family physician. The elderly man hurriedly arrived to administer a potent sedative to Miczike that mercifully left the countess asleep.

As word about the tragedy spread, the neighboring nobility gathered with the bereaved family. A hearse drawn by four horses brought the count's body, and a pier was set up in the reception hall. It became evident that the countess was not capable of taking charge of the necessary arrangements. She was reluctant to summon the priest from Ulmeni, but as soon as Father Nagy heard the news, he came without invitation to administer last rites, and the countess did not dare to refuse him. Ferenc had returned to recount the terrible accident. Miczike listened to the crestfallen lad's story once then dismissed him along with the girls and only tolerated Michael's presence. The two sisters tried to console the distraught Ferenc who felt that his mother was blaming him.

The personalities of the Trauttmansdorff children revealed themselves during the traumatic days following their father's death, especially in view of their mother's adamant withdrawal from reality. At seventeen, Ferenc had suddenly become head of the family but was too distressed by the experience of witnessing his father's death to focus on anything. Sigismunda's composure and mature efficiency surprised servants and neighbors alike. Baron Takats and his wife came to stay with the family and lend support and advice, but there was no doubt that Sigismunda was in charge. Everyone was astonished when the young woman, so proud of her recent confirmation in the Protestant Church, insisted that her father receive a Catholic burial. Miczike had an outburst of temper and accused Sigismunda of forsaking her religion.

"I am not breaking with my faith, Mama," came the calm reply. "But you have no right to deny our papa his."

After consultation with Father Nagy and the Protestant minister, a compromise was reached to which Miczike reluctantly agreed.

The priest would conduct the funeral and the minister the memorial service since the family's Protestant friends, notwithstanding Transylvania's spirit of tolerance, would have refused to set foot into a Catholic Church.

Michael was content to stay close to his mother during those days, realizing that he was above the competition of his siblings. As the one closest to her father, Tessa was the most devastated of the four. She could not stop crying and spent most of her time in the black-draped reception hall hiding among the tall plants placed along the walls. As befitting an officer, Maximilian was dressed in his Austrian Cavalry uniform, and Tessa—used to seeing her papa in his elegantly informal hunting garb, alive and laughing and always with a tender word for her—was at first terrified of the figure on the pier. She put out her hand to touch his folded fingers as if expecting that he would respond and reach for her as he used to. But those fingers did not feel like her papa; she'd never touched death and could not think of what they felt like. A shiver ran through her young body as she withdrew her hand, and the ayah gently led her from the room. She returned unnoticed and found a hiding place among the greenery. Sitting on the floor with knees drawn to her chin, she fixed her eyes upon the shiny tips of his boots, the only part of the body visible from her place. Time and again, she thought of the somber Ulmeni church resounding with the Gregorian chant of the Benedictine monks. How she wished she had been able to persuade Papa to return there with her and listen to the monks! Over and over, she hummed the "Salve Regina, Mater Misericordiae" in a barely audible voice, and more than ever, she looked toward a merciful Mother of heaven for love and consolation. With each passing day, Tessa missed her father more desperately, and when not holding watch by his pier, she roamed the estate for places that held special memories. One such favorite spot was by a stone fence at the edge of a pasture where Papa had supervised her first endeavors on horseback and the place from where many a fox hunt had started. It was a rather level, open area on a small plateau above the mansion with a wide view toward the valley, bordered by the beautiful, centuries-old forest he had taught her to love. So when Sigismunda brought up the subject of where their father should find his final resting place, Tessa quickly suggested that spot. Miczike had rejected the Catholic cemetery in Ulmeni, and it was not unusual for landowners to be buried on their estate. Sigismunda supported the suggestion, and Tessa, having felt very much excluded, was glad she had been able to do something for her papa. There was a discussion about it being a bit distant from the mansion, but Father Nagy offered to consecrate the grounds.

The Trauttmansdorff family buried their husband and father on one of those rare spring days when nature enchants with the delicate palette of May filled with the promise of summer's rich beauty. A few puffy clouds accentuated the deep blue sky, the larches' tender chartreuse brightened the somber green of spruce trees on the wooded slopes and wild primroses and gentian dotted the pastures. The joyful spirit of a world resounding with renewal was a singularly strange background for the final act of life prematurely ended.

Four horses were harnessed to a simple black-draped wagon used as hearse due to the steep and uneven path to the burial site. The bright sun reflected on their polished gear and the count's sword atop the casket. Groomsmen had their hands full to control the restive thoroughbreds unaccustomed to the crowd of black-clad people milling in the courtyard. They were servants, dignitaries from neighboring hamlets and peasant tenants with their wives and children. The low murmur ceased abruptly when family and noblemen emerged from the mansion.

Five days had passed since the accident. The funeral had been delayed for a day because of the countess's inability to recover. Two close relatives who lived on an estate a day's journey from Zay-Ugrocz escorted her. Irma and her brother Tibor were middle-aged unmarried cousins of the countess. Miczike had often compared her daughter Sigismunda's personality to that of Cousin Irma.

A messenger had been dispatched to Vienna, but the distance of several hundred miles did not permit anyone to arrive in time for the funeral.

Two young ministrants flanked Father Nagy standing by the hearse with a prayer book in his hands, uneasily waiting for the procession to form. The priest was deeply sorrowed over the loss of his most prominent parishioner and felt unwelcome among the Protestant nobility; he had not been invited to join family and friends earlier in the reception hall.

The church bell in the hamlet began to toll. Father Nagy and his ministrants stepped to the head of the cortege and groomsmen on foot led the horses. Irma and Tibor supported Miczike, dressed in deep mourning with her face covered by a long veil. The children, also in black, walked behind her. Officially an adult since confirmation, Sigismunda too was veiled and walked stiffly holding Michael's hand as if expecting a need to control him. Ferenc's sad eyes were dry. He was deeply hurt that his mother had asked to be escorted by her cousins and not by her eldest son.

Tessa was still unable to control herself; her shoulders shook with sobs, and tears blinded her eyes as she stumbled up the hill. Behind her walked the neighboring gentry followed by village dignitaries and common folk. Tessa knew that somewhere among them was the ayah who had known her papa since birth and was as devoted to him as any member of the family. She wanted to hold the old woman's hand and cry and pray with her—in her papa's faith. Her lips silently recited the "Salve Regina" in the hope that the Virgin in heaven would open her arms to her father. Looking up to the bright sky, it seemed to her that there could only be one heaven above and that Christ's mercy would embrace all good people, whether they worshipped in a plain Protestant or a mystical Catholic Church.

Wreaths and bouquets surrounded the open grave. Father Nagy and the ministrants took their place behind a simple wooden cross that had temporarily been placed there. The casket was lifted from the hearse and immediately lowered into the ground. The priest recited the customary Latin prayers, unfamiliar to most of the assembled crowd. Tessa noticed her mother wince when a ministrant handed Father Nagy an aspergillum and extended the font with holy water to sprinkle the casket. Tibor stepped forward and spoke briefly about Maximilian—brave officer, devoted husband, and loving father. One by one, the mourners expressed their condolences to Miczike, her cousins, and the children. They shook the black-gloved hands, murmured a few phrases, and reached for a small shovel to drop three small heaps of soil into the open grave as the customary farewell. The immediate family was first to do so, but Tessa could not bear the hollow sound of the dropping soil and, from a bouquet, picked a few white flowers that softly settled on the casket. Then it was the house servants' turn, and she finally felt the ayah's arms embracing her. She could barely endure the long wait until all the villagers and socage peasants had curtseyed and kissed the countess's hand and just wished everyone would go away so she could be alone by her papa's grave. Finally, Miczike, the family, and gentry friends started back toward the mansion without even a nod to acknowledge Father Nagy's presence. Only the ayah watched Tessa approach the priest and utter in a choked voice, "Please pray for my papa!"

He smiled. "Bless you, child, he is now with our heavenly Father."

Through her tears, Tessa didn't notice the expression on his face when she added, "And with the Blessed Mother!"

The following days and weeks revealed a cruel reality to Miczike. Several among her late husband's friends as well as a string of moneylenders showed up at the mansion with demands for money owed and the sum of their claims disclosed a precarious financial situation. The count had borrowed heavily to finance his passion for thoroughbreds, and it became painfully clear that the family had lived beyond its means. Various members of the gentry gallantly offered to accept a valuable horse in lieu of cash. Miczike had never been interested in the costs of everyday life. Prior to her marriage, her parents and later the bishop had attended to such matters. She found herself completely overwhelmed by the situation and just wished for it to go away. Paying scant attention to advice from her steward, she quickly acceded to demands by her friends but refused to deal with or even listen to ordinary creditors and persuaded Tibor to come to Zay-Ugrocz to take over. He was shocked when he realized the gravity of the family's financial situation. The only solution he could envisage was to sell the estate in order to satisfy the debts, which would leave the family with just a modest legacy.

The children remained unaware of the situation. Their lessons had resumed, and while they saw strange people come and go, they paid no attention. Their mother was withdrawn and rarely called for them. Miczike was consumed by her own grief and refused to acknowledge her children's suffering. Even Tibor was unable to effectively communicate with her and summoned his sister for help. In the midst of all this, a message arrived from Miczike's uncle offering to assume guardianship and financial responsibility for the children provided they moved to Vienna. Kollonitsch had become cardinal; his words were firm and explicit and left no room for negotiation. Irma and Tibor conferred about it at length prior to discussing the matter with Miczike. Her demeanor made amply clear that she was loath of making decisions and more likely to consent to a concrete plan. The two had never been close to the youngsters but were prepared to accept Miczike into their household while she adjusted to life as a widow. The children's needs, they decided, would best be served in Vienna at the expense of the cardinal. They abhorred the prospect of a Catholic environment and a cleric's guardianship yet were not prepared to extend their invitation to the youngsters. Moreover, the four had reached an age that called for a more formal education and social contacts that Miczike could not provide lacking proper funds. Irma and Tibor thought through all aspects of their proposal and were prepared to answer their cousin's objections.

They met little resistance. The tragic event and her fragile health had overwhelmed Miczike, and the prospect of being both mother and father to four youngsters loomed an impossible task. She was also aware of her inability to manage money or administer property. Tibor did not reveal the full extent of her dire circumstances but stressed that the situation demanded immediate steps. He proposed hiring an administrator for Zay-Ugrocz and to use all income to service debt obligations, vaguely hinting that an eventual sale might be inevitable. Miczike was to receive a small monthly stipend for her personal expenses, and in order to keep these to a minimum, Irma and Tibor offered her their home. They diplomatically avoided mentioning that her brood was excluded from this invitation by emphasizing the children's educational and social opportunities in Vienna in the charge of their influential uncle. The boys could both enter the military academy with Ferenc almost eligible to begin a career in the

Austrian army. The cardinal would likely send the girls to a finishing school, and the Vienna Trauttmansdorffs would surely step in with appropriate contacts to find them suitable husbands, hopefully of sufficient means to perhaps even redeem Zay-Ugrocz from its creditors. It all sounded like a reasonable solution to Miczike's pressing problems, except, of course, that she resented relinquishing control of her children to her detested uncle. He had never been unkind to her, but she recalled the stern and condemning letter he wrote upon learning of her broken promise about the children's religious upbringing. However, she convinced herself that it was unlikely they would live with him. Once the boys were in military academy and the girls in educational institutions, they would quickly escape his influence. She did not care for her husband's family but thought that her daughters might well end up living in the household of Maximilian's eldest brother.

Miczike was a selfish woman without particular affection for Irma and Tibor whom she considered stuffy and boring, but they were her closest relatives. She persuaded herself that an able administrator could pay off her debts, and once she recovered her health, she would soon be on her own again. Neither she nor her cousins gave much thought to how the children might feel. As minors, they were not expected to have a voice in the decision. Indeed, it was agreed that not their mother but Tibor should be the figure of authority to break the news to them. And so on a rainy summer afternoon that bore little resemblance to the beautiful spring, they were summoned to the library to face their uncle across Papa's carved desk. Tibor came right to the point. He spoke about their mama's poor health and her need for rest and quiet to cope with illness and sorrow, which would not be possible while they all lived at Zay-Ugrocz. He and Irma could provide a better environment in their home, but as teenagers, they were in need of more formal education than their governess and tutor offered. The place to be at this point in their lives was Vienna, and their generous great-uncle, the cardinal, had offered to take them into his care. Tibor stressed that the boys would soon enter a military academy and took pains to describe life among boys their own age in favorable detail. He was less specific about the immediate future of

Sigismunda and Tessa but impressed upon the older girl the responsibility of spiritual guidance for her younger sister who had not yet been confirmed.

The children reacted with stunned consternation. They had never traveled beyond Transylvania and knew Vienna only from what their parents and especially their father had told them about the big city. Unfavorable remarks of their mother had formed a negative image of the cardinal in their mind. Yet what concerned them most was the prospect of leaving Zay-Ugrocz. It was hard to imagine life anywhere but here, the only home they had ever known. They had grown close since the death of their father, and the idea of being separated seemed unbearable. Sigismunda was the first to break the silence.

"Where shall Tessa and I live, and how often can we see Ferenc and Michael, Uncle Tibor?" she asked.

"Child, I cannot answer such details," he demurred, "but you shall all be in Vienna under the care of your uncle, and that should speak for itself. And do not trouble your poor mother with undue questions, but be considerate of her frail condition. She suffers infinitely more by all this than you do."

Sigismunda and Ferenc were not convinced that this was so, but respect forbade them to voice their thoughts. Tibor considered the matter settled and dismissed them by mentioning that a message was being sent to Vienna announcing their imminent arrival.

The four silently went to their study room where the ayah awaited them. The alert woman was aware of rumors about the estate's financial straits, and a maid had overheard a conversation between the countess and her relatives. She knew of a message by His Eminence, the cardinal, and that a drastic change in the lives of her charges might take place. So what she now learned from the children did not come as a complete surprise to her, and she valiantly tried to cheer them with stories about the big city, how they would return to Zay-Ugrocz for vacations, and that surely she would be allowed to accompany them. Her devoted love and common sense helped a little to deflect the shock, and her tales of the famous city, seat of Empress Maria Theresa's Court, stimulated their curiosity. There'd be no language problem since they had always spoken German with the ayah and their papa, nor did new teachers intimidate them, knowing that their basic education was solid. But what was their uncle, the cardinal, really like? The ayah had no answers but as a Catholic knew that he held a position of great prestige and that they would have to address him as His Eminence and kiss his ring as a sign of respect to the high office he held. Sigismunda found that prospect objectionable, Ferenc said nothing, and Michael was too preoccupied with the fear of leaving home to pay much attention; he insisted that he would not leave his mama and showed no curiosity about Vienna.

"Does the cardinal know how to sing the Gregorian chant?" asked Tessa and, when noticing Sigismunda's raised eyebrows, explained that she had once gone to Ulmeni with Papa and heard it there in the church. In her imagination, Catholic clergy likely spent most of their time with this beautiful music, so consoling and infinitely more beautiful than the hymns sung in her church on Sundays. The ayah was quick to change the delicate subject lest her complicity in teaching Tessa the "Salve Regina" were discovered and talk returned to what life in Vienna might be like. The woman knew that the old countess had died and the count was in ill health. She well remembered the objections of the family to Maximilian's marriage but could not fathom that the old man would not want to see grandchildren he'd never met. After tragically losing his youngest son, he surely would wish to take charge of their lives! Anxious to ease their fear about the future, she talked about the glamorous Trauttmansdorff city palace and the hunting lodge in the mountains, where their father had spent his vacations as a youngster and shot his first deer.

Her words restored hope in the anxious hearts of her charges and eased their fears about leaving home and familiar surroundings. Miczike contributed nothing in this regard and instead dwelled on the half-truth that she was unable to care for them, though their alert young minds detected a note of falsehood. Ferenc was too polite and perhaps shy to ask questions, knowing that he in any event had been due to leave for military academy soon, even though he felt little inclination toward that career. Michael reverted to pouting when his efforts to talk his mother into allowing him to stay failed, and the usually spirited Tessa was still grieving too deeply for her papa to object, apart from knowing that she was least likely to win an argument with Mama. Sigismunda barely suppressed the urge to ask why their mother was not coming with them to Vienna since she could no longer live at Zay-Ugrocz, but her pride was aroused by the idea of assuming responsibility for her younger siblings. She'd know how to parry that clergyman if she felt he was forcing his religious views on them!

Tibor urged Miczike to arrange for a celeritous departure of the children, arguing that a drawn-out farewell would only make the situation more painful for everyone. The girls' modest wardrobe was mended and replenished with a couple of altered dresses of their mother's, the boys received new suits, and everything was packed into a couple of trunks. They'd outgrown toys, and with lives oriented toward the outdoors, there was little else to bring along. The two older ones chose some favorite books, Michael insisted on his tin soldiers and Tessa on her collection of little wooden animals that one of the groomsmen had carved for her in years past. They were creatures of the Carpathian forest—a family of deer, a bear, wild boar, fox, rabbit, and badger. With the ayah's help, the catechism was included among her things. It would turn out that the little book had prepared Tessa better than her siblings for life in a Catholic city under the guardianship of a cleric.

It was decided that the boys' tutor Imre and the ayah would accompany them as chaperones. Imre's father was in government service in Budapest, where the tutor planned to remain. As for the ayah, Miczike welcomed the chance to rid herself of the woman who stirred her conscience each time she laid eyes on her. Let the cardinal worry about her future! That the ayah's presence made leaving home just a little easier for her children was of minor importance to her.

Irma returned home, and Tibor dedicated himself to solving the estate's most pressing problems. Miczike occasionally did wonder whether she had acquiesced too easily and quickly to the cardinal, and anxious to avoid questions from her children, she saw them as little as possible. She'd pretend that a migraine or other ailment prevented her from seeing them and, when they did, would admonish them to be on their best behavior in Vienna and not give the cardinal an excuse to criticize their upbringing. She now painted a more favorable picture of her uncle. He was stern, she said, but surely would look out for them, and since he was unfamiliar with Transylvania, it was up to them to convince him of what a place of culture and fine manners it was. And under no circumstances were they to ever deviate from the Protestant faith! Reminding them of her own steadfastness in this respect while under his guardianship, she overlooked that she had been both older and financially independent. The self-centered Miczike lacked insight of what it meant for four youngsters between ages thirteen and seventeen to be under control of a powerful cleric who, by nature of his chosen life, viewed Protestantism as heresy.

Tessa paid a daily visit to her father's grave. A modest memorial headstone had replaced the wooden cross and a border of small boxwood and other shrubbery been planted. Transylvania climate was moderate, but winter lasted many months, and Tessa knew it would be years until the plants grew to appropriate size. She could only hope that whoever lived at Zay-Ugrocz would care for the grave until she could visit again. She asked the housekeeper and other servants to do so, but they were unsure whether they'd remain on the estate.

On their last day at home, each of the four siblings pursued a favorite activity. Ferenc and Sigismunda spent time in the library, Michael patiently sat outside his mother's boudoir hoping for a few more hours with her, and Tessa visited the grave to bid farewell. She cried bitterly and promised her beloved papa that she would never, ever forget him no matter where she lived and how old she was and would return as soon as she could. She finally tore herself away and one last time savored the scenery: woods of giant spruce and tender larch and pastures abloom with wildflowers that would soon fall under the scythe of the season's second mowing, the view of houses clustered round the simple church steeple of the hamlet. The mansion was just beyond a ridge but in the bluish haze below stretched the Alfold Plain, where she had only rarely ventured during her young life. They would head west toward the setting sun the next morning, and she tried to imagine the many horizons to cross until they reached Vienna. In the library hung an old lithograph of the city showing steep roofs behind heavy fortifications, towered over by St. Stephen's Cathedral. She wondered what the interior of the large church was like. The ayah said it was more beautiful and larger than any other in Christendom, but the ayah knew only Vienna and Prague, the city of her birth. Papa had once said that the church at Ulmeni would fit many times into St. Stephen's. Tessa tried to imagine how a Gregorian chant might sound in so large an edifice. Her reveries came to a halt when the chime from the village church reminded her that it was almost dinnertime. She tenderly kissed her papa's headstone, adjusted the bouquet of wildflowers she had brought, said a little prayer, and hurried back.

The ayah was waiting and quickly helped her change. Dinner was to be with their mother and Uncle Tibor, and by the time Tessa entered, everyone had already assembled in the dining room. Tibor's brow was furrowed, and Mama gave her an impatient look, but nothing was said as she took her place. Michael appeared the most content, having coaxed a secret promise from his mother that he could return within a year at the latest. Everyone listened quietly while Miczike nervously talked about the exciting time awaiting them in Vienna, and Tibor silently wondered how he and Irma would tolerate their verbose cousin. The butler and maid had sad faces because they were fond of the children and feared for their dismissal after the countess's departure.

After dinner, the family went to the library, where hot chocolate, a drink that had recently become fashionable, was served for the special occasion. Everyone was ill at ease, and Miczike nervously tried to bridge pauses with inconsequential chatter. Tibor finally rose and announced that since the stagecoach was to call at dawn, they should seek an early night and the four dutifully kissed Mama's cheek and hand, bowed to their uncle, and withdrew. Emotional exhaustion and youthful fatigue had them soon fall asleep, and when a new dawn sent its first rosy arrows across a clear sky, the ayah had difficulty getting them up. They donned the gray traveling outfits, and the girls wore straw hats with gossamer scarves tied below the chin.

Tessa thought her hat cumbersome, but her feeble protests went unheeded as the ayah explained that roads were dusty and young ladies needed to protect their hair.

The stagecoach from Ulmeni was waiting under the porte cochere, trunks were loaded, and Imre and the ayah took their seats. Miczike said farewell to her children in the reception hall within ear-shot of the horses' nervously shifting hooves and clicking harnesses as they shook their manes. The woman secretly welcomed these messages of impending departure. She'd tossed and turned all night fighting her nagging conscience. Suddenly overcome with motherly love, she persuaded herself that the responsibility of their upbringing without a husband was more than she could cope with; she had rarely been in situations calling for courage and determination. Arriving in the big city after her parents' death had been exciting, and falling in love with her future husband and defying her uncle's objections were challenges to her stubbornness. She'd left it to the infatuated Maximilian to fight with her guardian and his family and that their marriage set an end to her husband's career did not concern her nor that their union meant a rupture with his family. Kollonitsch could perhaps have prevented the wedding, but the obstinate young girl had become a burden the untimely death of his sister had placed on his shoulders. He was a deeply spiritual man of the church and unprepared for her tearful outbursts. His efforts to have her convert had failed, and the prospect of marrying a Catholic count coupled with the solemn promise to raise their children in that faith assuaged his mind.

Miczike had naively imagined that she and her husband would bring glamour to rustic Transylvania, and as Countess Trauttmansdorff, she would play an important role in local society. It never happened; Hungary's gentry harbored resentment toward Austrian rule, and the prestigious Trauttmansdorff name did not impress them, much less that the count was Catholic. And of course, four pregnancies in short succession and her ensuing frailty had con-fined the young wife to the house. The children's daily care was in the hands of the ayah, a governess and a tutor. Michael spent more time with her than the others; he was a cheerful boy and quick to understand the advantage of flattering Mama. And it was much easier to cope with just one child at a time! She'd miss him, but he was growing up, and she'd see him again when he was a responsible adult. She realized that her promise to have him return within a year was an empty one; she had only given it to quiet his persistent pleading. Ferenc and Sigismunda often felt like strangers to her; their plain features and dedication to learning made her wonder how she and Maximilian came to have two children so different from them! The birth of Tessa had been her most difficult, and she unreasonably blamed the child for her failure to fully recover. Moreover, the girl was physically stronger with more vitality and spirit than the others, and her presence made Miczike uncomfortable. Observing the closeness between Tessa and her father had even aroused her jealousy; why, the girl went riding and hunting with Maximilian, activities that she no longer felt able to pursue!

But however selfish and irresponsible, that morning, Miczike did feel badly toward her children. Ferenc and Sigismunda showed little emotion as they embraced and kissed her. Michael shed tears, but his mother's promise and the pending adventure of the trip raised his spirits. Tessa's eyes were red from tears shed for her beloved papa and for leaving Zay-Ugrocz, not the mother she stiffly embraced. Normally, the most impetuous of the four, she lightly kissed Miczike's cheek and hand then turned abruptly and walked away. As the youngest and last to say farewell, the gesture served as a signal for the others to curtsey one last time and follow her to the coach. Miczike sank into the arms of her cousin and wept hysterically, but the heavy wheels rolling across the courtyard gravel drowned the sound. The coach crossed the village and began its descent toward the valley.

Ferenc sat with Imre and the ayah, the two girls opposite with Michael between them. Upon reaching the main road, the carriage picked up speed and its rattling, the horses' hooves and occasional commands by the coachman were the only sounds. The passengers were deep in their own thoughts. The ayah anxiously watched her charges and was glad to see Michael dozing, his head resting against Sigismunda, who stared at the fleeting landscape. Ferenc pulled out a book and tried to read as the vehicle swayed on the uneven road, and

Tessa looked at the meadows and villages, sadly remembering the last time she had been riding here with her papa. They were headed toward the wide Alfold Plain stretching across the central part of Hungary. There was a brief stop at a way station in late morning to water and feed the horses, and the ayah produced food the cook had packed for them. They all alighted to stretch their legs and cupped their hands to drink from a bubbling well that fed into a wooden trough. The next stop was to change horses in late afternoon; after which, they again picked up speed to reach the estate of a distant relative who'd agreed to accommodate the party for the night. The elderly owners gave them a friendly reception, but all four were exhausted from their long day. They washed up and were served a simple dinner. Hospitality did not include the company of their hosts who'd withdrawn to their library, but the children were happy to go to bed early. Imre was annoyed to find himself, and the ayah relegated to servant quarters. The old woman did not retire until she had brushed and pressed their clothes.

The countryside changed the next day with hills and mountains fading in the east as they passed the Alfold Plain's endless wheat and rye fields waiting to be harvested. They watched the unfamiliar scenery unfold with interest. The two younger ones provided most of the conversation with Michael chatting and Tessa chiming in. Ferenc still tried to read, and Sigismunda stared outside, contemplating for the hundredth time how to convince their uncle that their Protestant faith was an unshakeable core of their lives. As the most spiritually inclined and mature among the four siblings, she felt a keen sense of responsibility toward the Protestant faith.

Larger settlements fascinated them. They had never ventured far from the estate, so even modest-size towns were a new experience, and the ayah had to answer many questions about how these places compared to Vienna. Experiencing new and different parts of their country temporarily pushed the pain of leaving Zay-Ugrocz into the background. They listened with glee as the ayah and Imre argued which city, Vienna or Budapest, was more elegant and sophisticated. When they stopped in a more sizeable town for the night, they took a walk through the cobblestone-paved streets. It was late afternoon, and there was great commotion on the central square where market stalls were dismantled for the night. People were dressed differently and spoke with an accent, houses and shops were unfamiliar, but what fascinated them most was the size of the place! The Ulmeni stagecoach had reached its final destination, and they continued in a different, more comfortable one. Roads were smoother and wider as their journey brought them closer to Budapest, and they excitedly talked about the prospect of covering the distance from there to Vienna on a Danube barge.

The Hungarian capital was a prelude to Vienna and surpassed all their expectations. The twin cities of Buda and Pest are sited along both banks of the mighty Danube, and they thoroughly enjoyed standing on one of the huge bridges and watch the busy river traffic pass below. The tutor went to ascertain the departure day of their barge, and they rejoiced when he brought news that their stay would be extended by a couple of days until the next one was scheduled. This allowed the ayah time to retrieve a change of clothes from the trunks and to wash and press their travel outfits. Imre had reached the end of his journey and was anxious to join his family, but they persuaded him to show them around the city. Noblemen were not expected to walk in the streets, and Imre hired a modest carriage to take them round. Even the reserved Sigismunda joined in the animated questions, and the tutor was barely able to keep pace.

Only a few years ago, Maria Theresa had been crowned Queen of Hungary and not until she had made major political concessions and overcome numerous objections. As part of the Habsburg Realm and no longer threatened by the Turks, Budapest experienced a cultural and economic boom. The gallant Hungarian noblemen pledged their allegiance to the young queen in return for a common defense and handsome individual rewards rather than affection for anything Austrian. Acknowledging Maria Theresa as head of state yielded more advantages than obligations, but it also freed the queen's hand to cope with her northern and western neighbors. Her Hungarian subjects paid her little more than lip support and continued to enjoy their leisurely lifestyle.

Sophisticated Budapest made Ferenc and Sigismunda acutely aware of their provincial background. They visited the main Protestant

Church, and when they passed the Catholic cathedral, Tessa surprised everyone by asking that the carriage halt for her to go inside. Sigismunda objected, but the tutor, a nonpracticing Catholic, who'd managed to hide his religion for the sake of his job, saw no harm and ordered the coachman to stop. A stony-faced Sigismunda remained with Michael in the carriage, but Ferenc was also curious and followed Imre and Tessa through the heavy oak doors into the church. The boy continued talking in a normal voice until Imre told him that one should only whisper in a Catholic house of worship in deference of Christ's presence. For the same reason, he said, they would all have to genuflect. Tessa and Ferenc did not want to offend and complied, but the boy was glad that Sigismunda had stayed behind, unsure of how she might have reacted. It had been many years since Tessa's visit to the church at Ulmeni, but she sensed the same somber and mysterious ambience in the cool darkness of these walls. There were no chanting monks present, yet she could almost hear the sound coming toward her from the tall ceiling, the niches along the nave, the small eternal light near the main altar, and the golden glow of the tabernacle. The girl felt transposed back to Transylvania and with closed eyes began to hum the "Salve Regina." Surely, she would feel Papa's hand on her shoulder at any moment! The tutor was familiar with the chanted prayer and suspected the ayah as teacher, but since his association with the family was to end shortly, he did not pursue the matter. The haunting notes moved Ferenc, who was unable to explain a strange connection he felt. When they returned to the carriage, Sigismunda asked no questions, her siblings volunteered no comment, and Imre never mentioned anything to the ayah. Two days later, they said farewell to their long-time teacher.

They boarded the barge for the final leg of their journey on a gray and overcast day. The distance was less than 150 miles but the trip's duration uncertain because it led upriver against a strong current and depended on weather and time spent in ports along the way. Accommodations for the few passengers were primitive, but Imre had suggested this mode of transportation, persuading Miczike who recalled the poor and unsafe road between Budapest and Vienna. The Trauttmansdorff children were delighted and the novelty of their first trip aboard a boat, however modest, more than compensated for any discomfort. The ayah was in a constant state of anxiety each time they were out of her sight, fearing that one of them might fall overboard and well aware that no part of the deck would remain unexplored. Circumstances were favorable. They picked up a strong wind and made good progress. The hectic activity in the small ports where they watched cargo being offloaded and goods, fresh water, and provisions taken on commanded their rapt attention, and even the monotony of the landscape along the river in Northern Hungary failed to bore them. The flat, marshy banks were teeming with wildlife, and they spotted pheasants, quail, small deer, and an occasional stag. When Pressburg (the modern Bratislava) came into sight, they knew that they were poised to leave their native land and enter Austria, though politically Bohemia to the north as well as Hungary were part of the Austrian realm. Well-versed in geography and history, they were bursting with questions and the captain, who'd taken a liking to his young passengers, explained the historic significance of this mighty fortress above the Danube. Why, Austria's young monarch Maria Theresa had been crowned Queen of Hungary there in a glittering ceremony not long ago! Decades earlier, Hungary had risen in bloody revolt against Habsburg hereditary claims of their country. However, the queen's father had granted far-reaching amnesties, assured Protestants freedom of religion, confirmed Hungary's Constitution and laws, and strengthened the authority of the Hungarian diet. Still Maria Theresa's succession as Queen of Hungary was not assured until one of her first acts upon ascending the throne in Vienna was to appoint Hungary's aging chief justice, Count Palffy, commander-in-chief of Hungary's army. Until then, this position had been held by Austrian generals and the count, who'd known Maria Theresa since childhood, did much to soften his countrymen's objections, though they steadfastly refused to accede to her wish of appointing her husband, Grand Duke Francis, as coregent. It sounded like a fairytale when the captain told of the handsome young queen stepping aboard a magnificently decorated barge at Vienna and sailing down the Danube to Pressburg. Clad in gold-embroidered Hungarian garb, she received the fabled crown of

St. Stephen, the very same the Austrians had taken from Budapest to Vienna and sold back to Hungary three hundred years earlier. The mantle Hungary's first King Stephen wore at his coronation in the year 1001 was draped over her shoulders. The new queen complied with every aspect of Hungarian tradition. She was unfamiliar with horseback riding, but when told that the ceremony demanded this skill, she took lessons despite the fact that only three months earlier she had given birth to her fourth child and first son. Since she was to ride astride, she wore chamois breeches and boots under her dress. The captain said that he was in the crowd that watched the queen after her coronation and solemn rendition of the oath ride in a magnificent carriage drawn by six horses through streets decorated with bright streamers and flags. At the foot of "Royal Hill," the queen—still in crown and mantle—mounted a black stallion, rode to the top, and brandished a sword toward the four corners of the earth while the people cheered enthusiastically. Maria Theresa did not speak Hungarian and delivered her address to the diet in Latin, the universally accepted language of learned persons.

The Trauttmansdorff youngsters were fascinated. Their imagination was aroused by the conjured image of a young queen who, in 1740 at age twenty-three, had succeeded her father as heir to a powerful realm. Now that they were to live in the city of her court, the captain's story transformed Maria Theresa from a distant monarch into an intriguing person of flesh and blood. Was the queen beautiful? Yes, they were told; she had large blue eyes, blond hair, and a lovely complexion. Resplendent in her magnificent robes and speaking in a clear, unwavering voice, she had indeed left a regal impression. Wedded at age nineteen to her first and only great love, Grand Duke Francis of Lothringen, at twenty-three, she had already given birth to four children, and after three daughters, her first son was cause for great celebration in Vienna. Little Prince Joseph would eventually succeed his mother as Joseph II and four decades later would play a decisive role in Tessa's life.

For now, the youngsters' eyes were focused upon the eleventh century belfry above the fortress, and their thoughts were dominated by the realization that they had left behind the country of their birth.

The landscape now changed. The mountains visible to the north were the westernmost slopes of the Carpathians, a modest version of the high elevations and majestic woods of Transylvania, but the four waved them a fond farewell. They had crossed the border into Austria.

The remaining distance was to be covered during the night, and they were expected to dock at Vienna in the morning. Tepid winds delayed progress, and it was almost midday when the ayah excitedly called for them. A misty rain was falling, and through its veil, the city's massive fortifications rose like a menacing mirage in the distance. After the threat of yet another siege faded with the dawn of the eighteenth century, the city began to expand beyond the heavy walls, even tearing some of them down. Yet the first impression they had was that of a foreboding citadel. Steep, crowded roofs of houses peaked over the massive walls with St. Stephen's Cathedral towering over everything. As the boat slowly sailed upriver, a hesitant sun broke through the mist and made the church roof glisten in silvery shimmer. They knew from their history lessons that Hungarian King Matthias Corvinus, after conquering Vienna in the 1480s, had offered to pay for the roof of the cathedral, whose foundations had been laid around the year 1200. The bankrupt but proud citizens at first refused because the king insisted that the tile reflect the colors of his red, white, and green banner, but an approaching winter with its ravages on an exposed interior in the end forced them to agree. Weather had long since blended the bright colors into a soft gray that almost matched the sandstone walls. The youngsters had never laid eyes on a church of such size and stared in silent awe while the ayah quietly wept tears of joy at the sight of the beloved shrine. It had been her fond hope to see it again before her death, and her joy was only marred by her revered master's cruel fate.

Only hours now separated them from meeting their uncle and the curiosity about the city their papa had loved and often talked about was tempered by uneasiness. Tessa reached for the ayah's hand, and Sigismunda put her arm round Michael's shoulders. Even the reserved Ferenc drew close, and the siblings felt united by the shared uncertainty of their future. They knew that their childhood had ended and the carefree days of Zay-Ugrocz would never return. The ayah hoped to find work in the cardinal's household, which at her advanced age offered the only prospect for a decent living and to remain with the children.

Chapter 3

The boat finally docked amidst hectic activity of the port. The captain sent a sailor ashore to see whether anyone had come to meet his passengers. No one was located, leaving the little party in a quandary since they had no money to hire a carriage. The boat was due to leave port by evening and their story touched the captain. He gave the sailor a coin to go find the cardinal's house and deliver news of their arrival. Their clothes had become damp standing on deck in the slight rain so the soggy little group huddled by their trunks in a warehouse. The afternoon wore on, and they presented a sorry sight to an approaching man in splendid red livery. A stevedore pointed him toward the group, and the lackey's face mirrored astonishment. Apparently, he had expected offspring of the noble Trauttmansdorff family to look more distinguished.

"I come from the household of His Eminence, the cardinal," he said stiffly. "You were expected two days ago. Kindly follow me to the carriage."

The relieved youngsters paid no attention to his raised eyebrows and haughty manner. They were most anxious to leave the inhospitable harbor and hastily followed the lackey.

Four splendid horses pulled a carriage of highly polished mahogany, trimmed with shining brass. They had never before seen one so elegant and hesitantly took their place on the cushioned seats. The liveried man mounted the back, and the coachman smacked the whip. The sun was setting in clear skies as they crossed the flat marshes between river and city. Vienna had experienced an enormous building surge after the victory over the Turks in 1683, and the ayah explained that they were passing through "Leopold Town," named for Maria Theresa's grandfather Emperor Leopold. Another district to the west was known as "Joseph Town" in honor of her uncle Emperor Joseph, who was stricken by smallpox and died a young man without sons to be succeeded by his brother Charles, Maria Theresa's father. He too had no sons and spent most of his twenty-nine-year reign with efforts to ensure the succession of his eldest daughter Maria Theresa. The youngsters' eyes were wide with wonder as they soaked in the new impressions. Reaching the fortifications, the carriage rambled over a wooden bridge across a canal that had once served as moat through the Red Tower and into a street ending in a large square, where the magnificent cathedral rose in the summer dusk. A bell tolled for vespers and throngs of people pushed through the doors to attend the service. At the near corner of the square was an expansive and elegant building.

"The archbishop's palace," said the ayah, her voice almost drowned by the bell.

"What's the difference between an archbishop and a bishop?" Ferenc wanted to know.

"The archbishop is head of the archdiocese of Vienna and has several bishops under him," the ayah explained. "Your esteemed uncle is a cardinal, which is an even higher rank, for he and cardinals from other countries are directly below His Holiness, the pope."

"Does our uncle live in this palace with the archbishop?" asked Tessa, who was anxious to visit St. Stephen's and would have been pleased to live nearby.

"He does not," answered the coachman. "His home is several blocks away, but we'll be there soon."

They passed the cathedral and turned into a long and narrow square, which the old woman explained had once been an inner moat for the protection of the imperial castle, long ago filled in but still referred to as the "graben" (ditch). What impressed the youngsters most was the height of the buildings in the inner city, some six or seven stories high and elegantly decorated in a style they would later learn was known as "Viennese Baroque." They passed a couple of smaller squares until the carriage turned into a narrow lane and halted in front of an elegant and graceful portal. They quickly alighted, and the ayah held Tessa's and Michael's hands as she led them to the entrance. A liveried doorman motioned them toward a side alley, apparently the entrance for servants. The ayah tried a feeble protest.

"These are the young counts and countesses of Trauttmansdorff," she said, "grand nephews and nieces of His Eminence."

The doorman eyed the sad little group and cast an inquiring look toward the lackey who'd met them at the harbor. Without another word, the man ushered them to a side door in the alley where they entered a long dark hallway. Ferenc and Sigismunda felt insulted, and the girl silently resolved to complain to her uncle about it.

The hallway opened into a spacious larder, where a nun in black habit and white headdress with stiffly starched wings met them. They'd later learn that this was the attire of the Ursuline Order. The wimple below the voluminous wings framed a round face with pink cheeks dimpled in a broad smile.

"Welcome in the name of our Lord, and my, do you ever look hungry and tired and wet," she added, touching Sigismunda's sleeve. "Come with me, I have a meal ready for you. You're much delayed and will want to go to bed early. His Eminence will see you tomorrow when you're rested." And she thought, cleaned up, and changed.

"I am Sister Constanze," she continued, "and you'll be under my care. Do tell me your names! I take it you all speak the language since your papa came from Vienna, right?"

Sister Constanze's friendly demeanor and easy chatter dissolved some of the fears the arrogant lackey had evoked. Too tired and hungry for questions, they followed the nun into a room with a plain table and benches that appeared to be a dining room for servants. A barefoot young girl placed dark bread, butter, ham, cheese, and cold fowl on the table. They were unaccustomed to eat from pewter plates and used to being served, but the food looked tempting, and they eagerly reached to help themselves. Sister Constanze resolutely held out her hand and said firmly, "Before eating, we thank the Lord for this food and ask Him to bless it. Bow your heads and pray with me! In the name of the Father and the Son and the Holy Spirit! We ask

Thee, Lord, to bless the food Thou hast given us and beseech Thee to make us worthy of the many blessings we receive each day. Our Father—"

They all knew the Lord's Prayer but though not familiar with the Ave Maria that followed kept their weary heads bowed. When she had finished, they hesitantly chimed in with their amen. The nun did not join them but watched as they heartily ate a meal that tasted better than anything since home.

"Why can't we see Uncle Kollonitsch now?" asked Michael.

"Because His Eminence has no time for you this evening, son," came the answer. "And we'll talk about it some more in the morning, but he is to be addressed as His Eminence, not ever as uncle," said the sister, and again, the friendly yet firm tone of her voice made clear that her words were not subject to discussion.

"Now come along, I'll show you to your rooms, your trunks are already upstairs. Ayah will sleep with the girls, and there's an adjoining room for the boys. In the morning, there'll be hot water available to wash, and I'll come and see that you are properly dressed and groomed for your audience with His Eminence."

The two rooms on the top floor of the palace contained only the most basic furniture, and again, it was obvious they had been assigned servants' quarters. But the bed linens were spotless and inviting, and the ayah quickly retrieved their nightclothes from a trunk while they shed their damp garb. The rooms had dormer windows, and in spite of being tired, they looked out over the dark city.

From their recessed windows, they couldn't see the narrow street below, but the crowded rooflines with their alcoves and mansard balconies and dormers fascinated them. A faint pink glow stemming from many lights lay over the city to silhouette gables, spires, and cupolas. It was all so different and much grander and more awe-inspiring than Budapest. Their journey had been a succession of new experiences and adventures, and there'd been little time to be homesick. Now fatigue overwhelmed them, and neither excitement nor anticipation could keep them awake. Even the tense and anxious Sigismunda had trouble keeping her eyes open. She and Tessa shared a double bed, and the sisters held hands as they fell asleep. They barely stirred until the ayah gently shook them awake.

"Time to get up," she said. "There's water for you to wash real good, and I'll help you with your hair. Come now, sister's waiting, and His Eminence may wish to see you soon!"

While the girls rubbed their eyes and tried to take in the unfamiliar surroundings, she went next door to rouse the boys. The water in the large pitchers was only lukewarm and the earthen wash basin small, but they helped one another with the most thorough scrub down since leaving home. The boys required more prodding, but the ayah was determined to have her charges neat and respectable for their first meeting with the man who henceforth would be the most important person in their lives. Anxious that their appearance would meet approval, she'd laid out their Sunday clothes. She braided Sigismunda's blond tresses and smoothed the boys' hair into place, only Tessa always wore her brown curls freely falling upon her shoulders.

With their ablutions completed, some of their exuberance returned and rested as they were after a good sleep. They eagerly pounded down the stairs until confronted on a landing by a hooded monk.

"Quiet!" said the stern figure in a low, firm voice. "This is a cardinal's palace where one does not create such racket!"

Sigismunda thought, *But these are servant's stairs, and we haven't seen much of a palace.* But she bit her tongue, and they sedately proceeded to the room of the night before where milk, bread, butter, and honey awaited them. Sister Constanze entered and again led prayers before and after breakfast. With the dishes cleared, she announced that His Eminence would see them soon and that she was about to instruct them of their required behavior.

"You shall always address the cardinal as 'His Eminence,' and when he extends his hand, the boys will bow, the girls curtsey, and you will kiss his ring!"

"Why not his hand?" Sigismunda wanted to know.

"Because the ring is the symbol of the high office you honor and through his office Christ, the Lord," came the answer. "When a priest is cardinal, he becomes successor to an apostle, which is both a high honor and obligation."

"We're Protestants and don't have cardinals," said Sigismunda in an effort of defiance, nurtured by her secret resentment of the nun's prayers. The girl was determined to explain all this to their uncle and obtain his assurance that they would live and worship according to their Protestant faith. Sister Constanze's voice became a shade more firm.

"You are now in a Catholic home and under the care of His Eminence who has assumed responsibility for you, and you will act as instructed. Remember also that you are not to speak unless addressed by His Eminence and to answer his questions with respect and deference."

Her voice again assumed its warm, motherly tone, and were it not for their religious background, they would have thought her quite likable. It did not escape their attention that Sister Constanze rarely spoke to the ayah except when she had an order for her, which was delivered calmly but with the unmistakable authority of mistress addressing servant. They began to worry about this pillar of their childhood, the person they had known for as long as they could remember and to whom they felt closer than to their mother. What would happen to her when they left for boarding school?

Sister continued her instructions about behavior. They'd been raised well and because of their mother's fragile health and limited tolerance had learned restraint at an early age. They also were used to treat adults of social standing with respect. Their father, unfamiliar with Hungarian serfdom that regarded socage persons more or less as slaves, had taught them to be kind and considerate toward everyone. Only the spoiled Michael could occasionally get away with bad behavior. The spirited Tessa with her mischievous streak most often found herself in trouble. Her feeling that Miczike resented her was reinforced by a casual remark she overheard the housekeeper make that the countess had been in poor health since the birth of her youngest child. Tessa was the only one not to resent Constanze's prayers, which impressed and curiously touched her, especially the one to the Virgin. She was also dying to see the great cathedral and attend a Catholic service but for now carefully hid such ambitions, especially from Sigismunda.

Sister Constanze was still speaking when the monk entered. Surprised and a little frightened by the encounter on the stairway, they'd not registered his face and now saw that he was fairly young with dark hair and deep-set eyes below bushy brows, his chin framed by a cropped beard. The brown hood no longer shadowed his features that bore a serious but kind expression.

"God be with you! I'm Brother Sebastian," he said in a sonorous voice, which instantly reminded Tessa of a Gregorian chant.

"His Eminence wishes you to attend Mass in the chapel prior to receiving you. It will begin shortly. Sister Constanze and I will be with you, and you will closely follow our example and instructions since you may not be familiar with Catholic worship."

Sigismunda gathered her courage. "Today is Saturday, Brother Sebastian. We're Protestants and would like to attend our Sunday service tomorrow. Mama does not wish us to enter Catholic churches and would be very angry if we did as you say," she added defiantly.

The monk looked at her evenly. "Sigismunda—I believe that is your name—you and your brothers and sister need to understand that you are no longer in Transylvania. Your mother has given up her parental rights and formally appointed His Eminence as your spiritual and de facto parent. She did so of her own free will when she surrendered you to the cardinal. Surely, she did not expect that you would be educated in the Protestant faith in his household."

He spoke matter-of-fact and without severity or rancor, neither raising his voice nor displaying signs of anger, yet the tone of his voice foreclosed argument. His words had a profound effect on the two older children. "She did so of her own free will," he'd said whilst their mother had stressed that she did not have a choice and that the arrangement was temporary until her health was restored and Zay-Ugrocz past its present financial bind. They sensed a finality in what the monk had said, and at that moment, Ferenc and Sigismunda both realized that they would not return home for a long time, at least not until they were of age and had the means to do so on their own. The statement affected Tessa less harshly perhaps because she had sensed from the beginning that her mother had not found it hard to give her up and because of her curiosity about St. Stephen and Catholicism. Michael was not concerned. He had Mama's secret promise to return home soon, and he did not doubt that she would find a way to bring him back. His faith meant little to him. He was always bored during Sunday service and religious instruction, as he was with most of his lessons. He didn't care which denomination's service he attended and hoped that Mass on Saturday would replace Sunday service.

Tessa piped up, "What kind of prayers should we say during Mass?"

Brother Sebastian smiled, showing his strong white teeth. "My child, you need not pray on your own during Mass, you experience and live Mass, which is not a prayer service, but a bloodless renewal of Christ's sacrificial death for us on the cross. We begin by confessing our sinful behavior to God and beg for His forgiveness and mercy. Thankful that God has allowed us to appear before Him, we glorify Him, His Son, and the Holy Spirit in a special acclamation. We then learn the Word of God by listening to scriptures from the Old and New Testament and sing a psalm, following which the celebrant will read a passage from one of the four gospels, sometimes followed by a sermon. When he has finished, we affirm our faith anew by reciting the credo. Now we come to the central part of our celebration, the offertory, during which the priest offers bread and wine—fruit from earth and vine and work of human hands—as our sacrifice, solemnly asking God to accept it to be transformed into the flesh and blood of Christ. Following ancient tradition, the priest symbolically purifies himself by washing his hands, asking the Lord to wash away his iniquities and cleanse him of his sins. He then prays for the church and appeals to the saints for intervention on our behalf. We kneel in deep devotion as he raises first the host and then the chalice, repeating the very words Christ spoke to His apostles the night before he was given up to death. At that very moment, His presence descends among us, and the bread and wine actually become His flesh and His blood. Christ Himself is our sacrifice, and together with the priest, we say the Lord's Prayer, followed by a prayer for peace. The priest then eats from the bread and drinks from the wine. Those among us who have repented our sins, confessed them, and were granted absolution are permitted to join in communion, acknowledging that we shall never be worthy of His grace but that His word releases us from the darkness of evil. Following communion, we say a prayer of thanks and receive a blessing from the celebrant, who sends us out into the world to sin no more, to do good and spread His peace."

Brother Sebastian's words, spoken in a spirit of simple piety, impressed his young audience. It was a far cry from what Mama had always described as the sanctimonious pretense and hypocrisy of the Catholic Church. Sigismunda and Ferenc were firm Protestants and considered their convictions unshakable. On the other hand, they were intelligent, well-read adolescents, raised in tolerant Transylvania and well aware of their mother's trend to exaggerate. They knew she was fervently opposed to the point of being contemptuous of the Catholic Church. Could it be that she had been less than honest with them? Perhaps, their late papa's faith was not so corrupt and hypocritical after all!

After a brief silence, Brother Sebastian asked whether they had any questions. Even if it meant revealing her secret, Tessa could no longer contain what was foremost in her heart, and she asked hesitantly, "Do you know how to sing the Gregorian chant, Brother Sebastian?"

"I do indeed," was the answer. "Where did you hear about it, child?"

"Oh," she said, "my papa once took me to Ulmeni, and the monks sang it in the church there, but it was a very long time ago. I liked it and want you to teach me, will you please, Brother Sebastian?"

"I shall be happy to, child. But first, all of you must study Latin, the universal language of the Catholic Church, Mass, and the Gregorian chant. Indeed, we shall have our first lesson this afternoon. I know that you already speak more than one language, and if you study earnestly, you should be able to learn it quickly."

Tessa was tempted to show off her Latin by reciting the "Salve Regina" when her eyes met those of the ayah and she caught herself fearful that Sigismunda would easily guess whence such knowledge stemmed.

"Why," Sigismunda wanted to know, "is the service not in the language of the congregation like in our church?"

Brother Sebastian ignored the phrase "our church" and answered, "Because *Catholic* means 'universal,' for all and everyone. As a Catholic, you may attend Mass in France, Italy, Spain, Hungary, or anywhere in the world. And the priest's words shall be precisely the same, and you will always feel that you have come home to Christ. For the same reason, when His Eminence, the cardinal, travels to Rome to visit the Holy Father and to converse with other cardinals, they do so in Latin, the language they all speak. I very much doubt whether an assembly of Protestant clergy from different countries would find a way to communicate so readily."

Sigismunda did not have an answer to that, and there was a brief silence until Sister Constanze returned with two small white veils.

"Women cover their heads in church, and these are for Sigismunda and Tessa. But first, we must tidy your hair, child," she added with a stern glance in the ayah's direction as if to inquire why this had not already been done. A look of resentment came into Tessa's eyes, but Sister Constanze lost no time in braiding her brown locks into a thick plait. It changed the girl's appearance. Tessa had strong features dominated by large brown eyes, a distinctly chiseled nose and a wide mouth with strong, regular teeth. She was tall for her age—already Sigismunda's height—and Mama had more than once remarked that she could be mistaken for a boy. The chestnut locks that fell across her high forehead and framed the narrow cheeks softened the impression. With her hair tamed into a braid, she looked older than her years. She missed the familiar feeling of hair falling over her shoulders but did not dare to object. Sister Constanze placed the veils over the girls' heads, and she and Brother Sebastian escorted them toward the main vestibule.

Perhaps, Cardinal Kollonitsch's residence did not quite deserve the term "palace," though homes of noblemen and high clerics were commonly referred to as such. The structure predated the baroque period and was actually a multistory townhouse, wedged between similar buildings but separated on one side by an alley to allow for deliveries and access for servants. Indeed, the residence formed only the front part of a complex from which single-story wings extended on each side, joined in the back by stables and a carriage house. The lofty vestibule was a center hall that traversed the palace from the front portal to jalousie doors leading into a courtyard garden abundant with flowers. The vaulted ceiling and the walls of the hall were whitewashed, and the floor consisted of highly polished stone tiles laid in an intricate pattern. Along one wall were placed chairs and a carved bench. On the other hung a life-size crucifix, below which a niche harbored a brass bowl filled with a large bouquet of fresh flowers. The priest led the way to the chapel entrance next to the large cross. The sanctuary apse faced the garden, and a bright sun shone through the Gothic stained glass windows, reflecting a rainbow of colors through the nave. The few tight rows of carved pews almost reached the steps separating the nave from the sanctuary. To one side of the altar was an elaborate chair upholstered in red velvet and flanked by two smaller ones of plain wood. The chapel reverberated with the sound of an organ too powerful for the small expanse. Above the railing of a rear loft, one could see rows of peaked cowls and white headdresses revealing a choir of monks and nuns.

Sister Constanze and Brother Sebastian dipped their fingers into the stone basin with holy water near the door and crossed themselves while reverently genuflecting toward the altar. Both watched the children who, fearing disapproval, followed their example. The monk motioned the boys to join him on the right side of the aisle, and Constanze and the girls took their place to the left. The chapel quickly filled with lackeys and servants. Sister Constanze knelt in prayer as they waited for Mass to begin. Everyone rose when the choir joined the organ for the entrance hymn. A ministrant carrying a cross, followed by two other young boys, entered through a door near the altar. Behind them appeared a tall man they assumed to be their uncle. He wore splendid green vestments over a white robe hemmed with lace and made a formidable appearance with a miter adding to his height. He handed his cardinal's hat to a ministrant, and the service began as he slowly ascended the steps to the altar reciting a Latin prayer. He spoke in a low voice and from time to time turned toward the nave and opened his arms uttering a Latin phrase to which the congregation responded in the same language. The four Trauttmansdorffs could not fully follow the proceedings but dutifully joined the others in standing, kneeling, and sitting. The only German words spoken where when Kollonitsch stepped to a carved lectern and read from the New Testament—the Gospel, as Brother Sebastian had called it—and this was the only time they were reminded of services at home.

At communion time, the monks and nuns descended from the choir and filed through the nave then knelt at a railing by the altar steps, joined by Sister Constanze and Brother Sebastian and a few lay people. As confirmed members of their congregation, Ferenc and Sigismunda had participated in communion at home but understood that they were excluded here. The two followed the service with grudging fascination. The splendid ritual of the traditional Catholic Mass, a mysterious proceeding they did not fully understand despite the monk's explanations, the incense, the beautifully trained voices of the choir, and the powerful organ captured their young impressionable minds. The contrast between this splendid ritual and the bland interior of their church without statues, pictures, or organ music, and a pastor in his plain black garb conducting a simple service could not have been greater. The cardinal's private chapel was richly decorated with colorful paintings and statues in gilded robes. The tabernacle above the marble altar glistened golden and so did the accoutrements—the chalice for the wine, the small plate on which the host was placed and especially the magnificent object he repeatedly held up high while a ministrant rang a cluster of small bells. Later, they would learn that it was called a monstrance and that Christ in the form of a host was encased behind a small glass window in the center. Flickering candles and the fanciful light through the stained glass windows heightened the solemn ambience. Ferenc and Sigismunda were unprepared for this spectacle and found themselves unwillingly enraptured, and their curiosity aroused. Michael had a short attention span, became bored, and was ready to leave. Tessa was the most profoundly touched, particularly by the beautiful singing voices, and looking up became enthralled by a statue of the Virgin Mary. The life-size figure stood on a pedestal in the alcove of a side altar opposite her pew. The slender, curved body of an idealized woman holding the Christ Child embodied typical Gothic style. Some of the statue's colors had faded but not the golden crown atop the graceful head with long brown hair. A faint smile illuminated the beatific face. Her gaze met that of the beholder, and Tessa could not avert her eyes. After years of perceiving the Virgin as a mother, her heart and mind easily bonded with the statue. "Do not be sad, my child, I am by your side, and all shall be well," the Virgin seemed to say, and the girl's lips silently moved to say the only prayer to Mary she knew, the "Salve Regina."

A rousing hymn concluding Mass brought her back to reality, and everyone stood as the cardinal turned to bless the congregation. He exited through the side door, and they remained in their pews until the others had left. Now that they finally were to face their guardian and spiritual parent, as Brother Sebastian had referred to him, their uneasiness returned. Tessa reached for Sigismunda's hand, and the older girl made a brave effort to hide her nervousness, as did Ferenc. Michael was the least concerned, he craved to leave and explore the new surroundings. Moments later, one of the young ministrants, who'd shed his white cassock, appeared and whispered something to Brother Sebastian, who rose and motioned them to follow him across the vestibule. They entered a large room with walls of bookcases that reached the ceiling. A narrow ladder on coasters was hooked onto a railing for access to upper shelves and thick oriental rugs covered the floor. The library was flooded with sunlight through clear, leaded windows facing the garden. The cardinal, now in long black cassock except for red collar and skullcap, stood behind a lectern. He was a dignified, tall figure with gray hair and clean-shaven, handsome features that bore an air of authority. He took a couple of steps in their direction but made no move to embrace them, yet there was warmth in his voice as he extended his hand and said, "I welcome you to my house."

As instructed, they approached one by one to kiss his ring, the girls curtseying, the boys bowing. He addressed each by their name then asked in a slightly different tone, "How is your mother, my niece?"

"She is not well, Your Eminence," said Ferenc then fell silent not knowing what else to say.

"I trust her health will improve," remarked the cardinal dryly. And he continued, "You will be in the good care of Sister Constanze and Brother Sebastian whose instructions you are to obey. Starting this afternoon, you will begin to study Latin, and I am confident that you will readily apply yourself to learning. Brother Sebastian will also instruct you in catechism and other subjects of which your education is wanting. It is my understanding that your German is fluent, so you should have no difficulties. You will, of course, not leave the palace except in the company of those in charge of your care, but you are free to frequent the garden for recreation. Today is the feast of a saint, which is why we celebrated Mass later than usual. On weekdays, it is read at six in the morning, and you are to attend daily before breakfast. Brother Sebastian will report to me on the progress of your studies, and I shall periodically inform myself as I meet with you."

His voice never changed its calm, even tone, making the speech sound less harsh than his choice of words. The four listened in silence, and when he had finished, Sigismunda glanced at Ferenc, but the boy made no effort to speak.

"Your Eminence," began the girl, "Mama said that Ferenc and Michael are to enter a military academy to become officers like our papa. When will that be? And for tomorrow, Sunday, we ask your permission to attend service in a Protestant Church."

Kollonitsch's face and voice did not change.

"Your mother has entrusted you into my care. I am now your spiritual father, and as such, it is my duty to see that you lead a life pleasing to God. This is only possible for those of Catholic faith, and therefore, you must first convert to the true religion before other decisions can be made. I trust I have made myself very clear."

It had taken all of Sigismunda's courage to ask her question, and without support from her older brother, she did not dare to challenge this man who held their fate in his hands. There was a brief silence, and then Tessa piped up, "I would like to sing with the nuns and monks in church. When may I do that?"

64

An expression of faint surprise crossed the cardinal's face, and he said, "Soon, you will all become familiar with our hymns and chants and have ample opportunity to sing in church."

"And I already know some Latin, a prayer that is," Tessa continued.

The cardinal smiled. "That is very good, who taught you?"

She began, "My"—then caught herself to protect the ayah— "my papa," she finished and now the cardinal's brows went up in surprise.

"I am very glad to learn that," he said. "You will have ample occasion to learn Latin prayers and sing Latin chants. And now you may go into the garden until midday meal is served. Your lessons will begin this afternoon."

He extended his hand, and they again kissed his ring, received his blessing, and left the library while Brother Sebastian stayed behind.

The courtyard garden was bordered on two sides by slender colonnades sheltering open hallways where a few monks and nuns quietly paced with missals in hand. Cowls hid the monks' faces, and the heads of the nuns were lowered toward their breviaries.

The garden was meticulously kept with meandering walkways paved in brick. Shrubs and plants were in full bloom and had apparently been chosen to yield new blossoms throughout the season. There were lilac bushes—Papa mentioned that Vienna was famous for its beautiful lilac—forsythia for early spring, a few elder bushes and fruit trees. Interspersed was an abundance of flowers, especially roses in shades of yellow, and sister explained that His Eminence preferred these. She also showed them a small section exclusively dedicated to herbs. This was her domain, she explained, and while some were raised for flavoring and preserving in the kitchen, most served medicinal purposes.

"These can cure many ills, and our selection is the best in the city. Why, even the archbishop sends for our teas or a tincture if there's need in his palace. We also dispense them to sick people who come to our door with their ailments. I'm trained as an apothecary and decide what should be used from case to case. Some of my herbs are rare and precious and these I transplant into small pots to keep in my cell during winter for replanting in spring."

Sister Constanze obviously took great pride in her expertise and work, though modesty prevented her from dwelling on it.

A few narrow benches along the walkways offered space for only one person each. This was a garden amidst a busy city meant for quiet contemplation, not frolicking or noisy chatter, and when Michael spoke up in a loud voice, sister quickly put a finger on her lips and motioned to the pacing figures.

This manicured enclave of nature was a novelty for the children accustomed to the untamed beauty of their land of mighty forests, green pastures, and murmuring brooks lined by wild filbert and elderberry bushes. Miczike had little interest in flower gardens, and mostly, vegetables were grown at Zay-Ugrocz during the season. This fragrant, picturesque courtyard, where every square foot was meticulously planned and cultivated, resembled a tiny piece of blending nature with religion, as witnessed by various saintly statues. Sister Constanze explained them. St. Florian pouring water from a bucket on a burning house protected from fires. St. Francis of Assisi presided over a birdbath; St. Anthony invited prayers for the retrieval of lost goods; St. Urban, a Viennese favorite, held a bunch of grapes and was patron of good wine. And then there was the holy family—Joseph, Mary, and the Child Christ—leaning against her knee. The figures were hewn from either plain stone, pink granite, or marble and apparently dated from different time periods. The hierarchy of saints was alien to this Protestant family, but with the penchant of youngsters savoring good stories, they listened to the nun talking with loving devotion. Ferenc and Sigismunda were tempted to question some of what she said, but the day had taught them that their queries did not go far, and they remained silent. Tessa listened intently; butterflies soon distracted Michael who was beginning to get very hungry.

The stables in the back section of the complex faced another wider street. They had a second story with quarters for lackeys and grooms. When the youngsters saw six horses in the stalls, they wondered about riding but did not have the courage to ask. Next to the stables was a carriage house for chaises and coaches, including the one that had met them at the dock. A groom pointed to a splendidly ornate carriage reserved for special occasions.

The chapel bell tolled the noon hour. Moments later, others throughout the city chimed in, and the midday air reverberated with their sound. Despite the distance from the cathedral, the sonorous bell of St. Stephen's, nicknamed "Pummerin" by the Viennese, could easily be recognized. Sister led the way back toward the house, and the ayah joined them for their midday meal. They were happy to see her and anxiously asked what she had been doing.

"Washing and pressing your clothes," was the answer. At home, a laundress had done such work since the ayah's primary duty was to care for them and involved few manual tasks. But she was grateful she'd not been sent away and willing to do any work. Anxious to hear how they had fared during the first meeting with their uncle, she nevertheless restrained herself until she'd be alone with them at bedtime.

Brother Sebastian led the prayers before and after lunch, in Vienna, the main meal of the day. The food was different from what they were accustomed to, but it was well prepared, and they enjoyed it. While they ate, Brother Sebastian spoke about the pending lessons. For the time being, Latin and Catechism would take precedence over other subjects, and he made clear that he would regularly report to the cardinal on their progress. Sister Constanze was to teach them prayers, such as the rosary or litanies, and sing with them. He mentioned the cardinal's expectations of quick progress and the importance of showing their gratitude and appreciation through diligent studies. Michael wrinkled his nose at the word *diligent*. At home, he'd always managed to charm the tutor, and when that failed, his mama would get him out of trouble. He'd think of ways to charm Brother Sebastian. Tessa was excited. Ever since the ayah had taught her the Latin "Salve Regina," as well as the German version of the prayer, she had often pored over the two sets of words, trying to reconcile Latin and German syntax and grammar. She was anxious to learn this new language, especially as it pertained to chants and hymns. Although their musical education at home had been limited to the flute and a little violin, they could read music and were familiar with the basics of harmony.

Ferenc and Sigismunda listened silently to the monk's words. The girl remained determined to adhere to her faith, but her coolly reasoning mind told her that open resistance was bound to fail. They had no choice but to live in the care of their uncle, and he did not give the impression of a man with whom she could win an argument. Though dedicated, she and Ferenc were not passionately religious and well aware that their mother was less of a devoted Protestant than an ardent anti-Catholic. Even Sigismunda had sometimes thought their pastor rather bland and boring. Attending services and being confirmed was something one did because it was customary, not out of deep piousness. She and Ferenc expected to soon leave their uncle's house for further schooling in a likely less stringent religious environment and in their hearts hoped that their grandfather would ultimately welcome them all as members of his family. Surely, the cardinal would appreciate to be relieved of their burdensome presence! In the meantime, the best strategy was not to make waves and to nurture the Protestant faith in her heart. Ferenc had similar thoughts; he was a bookworm and had never been anxious to embark on a military career. Studying Latin interested him, for he knew that it was not limited to the Catholic Church, but the language of learned men as well as Roman poets and philosophers.

Their dining room became the classroom. Immediately after the meal, Brother Sebastian produced writing material, opened a book, and started their first lesson. He was a good teacher and succeeded in holding their attention while he explained basic rules of Latin grammar and declination. Only Michael quickly lost interest and, at the end of the lesson, could not repeat much of what they'd been taught. His mind had wandered to the butterflies in the garden and his tin soldiers upstairs, which the ayah in the meantime surely had unpacked. The monk never lost patience and insisted he repeat a word or phrase as many times as it took for it to be correct, and the boy soon discovered that what had worked so well with Imre was lost on this teacher. Instructions in catechism followed Latin, and it turned into a long afternoon for the boy.

Tessa surprised everyone with knowing some basic Catholic teachings. She was too impulsive to hide her knowledge when

Sebastian touched on subjects with which she was familiar from Papa's catechism. Sigismunda and Ferenc repeatedly looked at her in astonishment, at which time she would quickly say, "Papa told me about this." They had all received Bible lessons, but they were now taught strictly Catholic teachings, most of which unfamiliar. Brother Sebastian suspected that someone besides the late count had talked to the child about Catholicism and assumed that it had remained a secret for good reason. He finally dismissed his class for a little recreation, reminding them to head for the chapel as soon as the bell rang for vespers.

The garden quickly became their favorite place, and this tiny piece of nature provided the only however small link to home. Faced with the reality of their new home a feeling of abandonment set in. Michael clung to Sigismunda and, with tears in his eyes, asked how long they had to stay here. The girl was mature beyond her years and, since Papa's death, especially since leaving Zay-Ugrocz, had become the person to which they would turn in distress. Even Ferenc, though he would not admit it, sought out her calming presence. The impulsive Tessa had rarely felt close to her well-behaved and sedate older sister in the past. Sigismunda's slight air of superiority made her feel inadequate, but now she and the ayah were the only lifelines in a sea of uncertainty. Walking behind her older siblings, she listened to Ferenc and Sigismunda discussing the future. Both expressed hope that the message their mother had promised to send to the Trauttmansdorffs with news of their arrival in Vienna would soon result in contact with their relatives.

Vienna's August air was stifling hot, and not the slightest breeze moved between the densely stacked buildings. The heavy walls soaked up the sun and during the night radiated intense heat. There were hot summer days in Transylvania, but the immense forests always brought relief, and a gentle wind was usually blowing from the mountains. Not so among these tall buildings and the youngsters were uncomfortable in the formal clothes the ayah had insisted they wear that day.

"Just think how sister must feel in those black woolen robes and tight headdress!" remarked Sigismunda. "And she looks so serene while always busy with something. Mama used to talk about how stern and cruel nuns are, but I think she's actually quite nice."

"I wish she wouldn't make us pray all the time," Michael piped up. "It's boring and Mama would be very angry if she knew about all those prayers to the Virgin!"

"Michael," said Ferenc, "it was Mama who sent us into the house of a Catholic cleric. I think we just have to put up with it and not make them think we're uncouth common folk when we're really Transylvania nobility! Sigismunda and I expect you two to give these Austrians no reason to look down their noses upon Hungarians," he added and turned to address Tessa, but the girl was not there. She'd stayed behind as they passed the statues of the holy family and sat on the stone bench beside it. Of the four siblings, Tessa most loved the outdoors, and while least concerned about the religious aspect of their environment, she felt like a caged bird in this city. The pretty flowers and manicured paths of the courtyard were no substitute for pastures and forests and wide views. It felt tight and confined and gave her an oppressed feeling that had begun during their ride through the narrow streets the night before. If she were to climb one of the taller trees in the courtyard, perhaps, she could see woods beyond rooftops. Then she remembered the view from their mansard window that revealed only more roofs and church spires! Somewhere beyond the walls of the town, there had to be meadows and big forests, not just the marshy, flat stretch of land between the Danube and the fortifications!

Tessa sensed her siblings approaching and rose to meet them. Before they could ask what she was up to, the bell started ringing for vespers, and they all headed into the chapel. The brief service had such beautiful music that Tessa forgot her depressed musings. When it was over, Sister Constanze motioned them to remain in their pews, handing each a rosary of wood beads with a silver cross.

"We shall stay to say the rosary," she said quietly, explaining that it started by reciting the credo followed by repetitions of the "Our Father" and "Ave Maria." "I will lead you in prayer, and you will soon learn to love this beautiful ritual."

Hungry and tired at the end of this eventful day, they obediently knelt to murmur along with the nun. They quickly and easily memorized the words of the "Ave Maria" and, of course, already knew the "Lord's Prayer." A bored Michael bowed his head low over his folded hands, and sister failed to notice that the sleepy young lad was dozing. The others wondered how many times the same prayers were to be repeated, and the quarter hour that it took to complete the rosary seemed very long. When it was over, they went to the room that served for classes and dining and eagerly devoted themselves to a simple but ample and tasty meal.

After a final prayer, Sister Constanze dismissed them into the care of the ayah. They climbed the stairs to their rooms below the roof and were delighted to find that the old woman had spent the day unpacking and arranging their things in an effort to give the bare rooms the resemblance of a home. Michael's tin soldiers were marching on one of the wide windowsills and Ferenc's books neatly lined up on the other. Sigismunda found her books and embroidery conveniently arranged, and Tessa's carved animals of the forest awaited her. Best of all, the faithful servant had secretly brought two miniature paintings of their mother and father from the nursery and hung them on the wall. All their clothes had been washed and pressed. Since the next day was Sunday, they'd again have to wear their good apparel; lighter cotton garments more suitable for hot weather were ready for weekdays. They hugged and thanked the ayah and tenderly touched the few personal belongings that had become all the more precious. Tessa bravely held back tears looking at the little creatures that made her long desperately for her beloved forests. Overcome by fatigue from the excitement and emotional experiences of the day, they went to bed. The sun burning all day upon the tiled roof had rendered the air in the mansard rooms stifling hot, but regular breathing soon told the old woman that her beloved charges were asleep. Only then did she climb into her narrow cot in a corner of the girls' room. She had worked hard all day and was very tired, but though she had learned nothing about her own fate, anxiety about her future had eased a little. At least no one had asked her to leave.

*****

Miczike's message had indeed reached the Trauttmansdorff Palace, a larger and more elegant mansion than the cardinal's residence. It was not received with enthusiasm. The old count was frail and on the verge of senility, and there were days when the death of his third son mercifully escaped his mind. He lived with the family of his eldest son Franz, for whom Ferenc had been named. The middle son had married a wealthy young woman of excellent background and quickly advanced in his military career. Count Franz and his wife had three children and little inclination to assume responsibility for four more. Baroness Miczike had been regarded as a poor choice for Maximilian for more than one reason. Transylvania gentry were not considered equals. The young baroness possessed no family wealth and had evidently persuaded Maximilian to break his solemn promise of raising their children in the Catholic faith, and Franz was not inclined to bring four young heretics into his household. The old count had never met his Hungarian grandchildren and in his confused state did not even show much interest in those of his other sons. Franz told his father about the pending arrival in anticipation that the news would quickly be forgotten. Prior to her death, the old countess had established a modest legacy for each of her third son's children as they reached age eighteen. She'd added a proviso that the funds could never be transferred to Hungary or paid to her daughter-in-law, Miczike, who had no knowledge of the arrangement. Franz decided to take no initiative; the cardinal had volunteered custody, let him handle the situation! Besides, the count and his family spent the month of August at their comfortable summer hunting lodge in Upper Austria, and only a small staff of servants and the old man remained in town.

Chapter 4

The first rays of sun reaching into the mansard rooms found the ayah awake. Sister Constanze had told her that they were all to go to St. Stephen's for High Mass this Sunday. The ayah dressed and went downstairs to fetch water. Carrying the heavy pitchers several flights of stairs left her breathless, but she would never have dreamed asking the boys to help. When all was ready for their morning toilet, she helped the girls and braided their hair in spite of Tessa's objections, and the child reluctantly complied after being reminded that Sister Constanze insisted on a neat coiffure.

The sister again led prayers. She reminded them to bring along their rosaries and the girls not to forget their veils.

"Saying the rosary is boring," said Michael, and before sister could comment, Ferenc cut in, "Why do you repeat the same prayer so many times—it's not possible to pay attention to each word over and over, which makes it all rather mindless! Why not just say each prayer once and concentrate on what you say?"

The sister smiled calmly. "Repeating the beautiful words of the Ave Maria is an exercise in contemplation by itself, Ferenc. You think of the Virgin, her unquestioning obedience to the Lord, her own Immaculate Conception, unblemished life and boundless love toward us all. With time, Ferenc, you will understand that the mind better concentrates and our thoughts tend to wander less when one goes through the exercise of reciting a beautiful, familiar prayer over and over. Besides, we distinguish three different themes for the rosary— the joyful rosary, the dolorous rosary, and the glorious rosary. The joyful contemplates the life of the Virgin, the dolorous the suffering of Christ, and the glorious His triumph over death, resurrection, and sending of the Holy Ghost. For each sequence of ten Ave Maria, there is a specific thought to contemplate and meditate on. As you become more familiar with what these are, you will soon recognize the special grace bestowed upon those reciting this beautiful prayer sequence! Also when we say the rosary after vespers this evening, I want you to think of the many blessings the day has brought and how fortunate you are to be under the protection of His Eminence. Just imagine what would have happened to you without the Virgin Mary watching out over all of you!"

"I'd be home with my mama at Zay-Ugrocz," Michael blurted out, and a faint flash of anger crossed the nun's face though her voice remained even.

"Your mother is with your uncle and aunt and does not live there anymore."

The nun knew that their home was to be sold to satisfy family debts, but it was not up to her to break such news to them. Still her words brought home the stark reality that they were in Vienna indefinitely and there was no alternative but to adjust as best they could. Sigismunda and Ferenc thought of their father's family but decided to raise this subject with their uncle at a later date.

Brother Sebastian and Sister Constanze escorted them to the cathedral with the ayah barely able to keep pace. The youngsters enjoyed walking through the streets and savored the many new impressions. Elegant carriages drawn by sleek horses and occupied by well-dressed people rattled over the cobblestones. Market squares were deserted and shops closed for Sunday, but people emerged from buildings dressed in their finest to head for Mass. Many disappeared behind portals of various small churches they passed. Elderly men pulled clumsy carts to collect garbage or shuffle horse manure from the streets.

They walked along the graben, lined with particularly tall and distinguished buildings. Brother Sebastian stopped at the beautiful monument in the square's center to explain its significance. Nine stone-carved angels with faces of ecstatic adoration joined to form a massive column. At its top, the Holy Trinity appeared to float upon clouds. The monument commemorated the Great Plague of 1679 and was completed in 1693 in fulfillment of a vow made during the terrible suffering of the city when a large segment of the population died a horrible death. People prayed day and night and vowed that if the scourge were lifted, they would erect a special monument of gratitude.

Having passed the graben, St. Stephen's Cathedral came into full view. Its single spire rose several hundred feet into the sky. An originally planned second tower was never completed; it housed the mighty bell that called the faithful with its resounding toll.

Entering the famous shrine for the first time in almost two decades brought tears to the ayah's eyes that only Tessa saw who'd also been aware that the woman could barely keep up with their brisk walk. She reached for the ayah's hand.

"I too am happy to be here with you," she said. "You've told me many times how beautiful it is!"

St. Stephen's deeply impressed them. They knew little about the architecture of cathedrals and stared perplexed at the gargoyles without understanding their meaning. They were bursting with questions about these stone carvings on the cathedral's exterior, but Brother Sebastian said Mass was about to begin and there would be plenty of time later for explanations. The interior left them even more in awe. Gothic walls soared toward a mysteriously dark ceiling, and stained glass windows filtered the sun to a mere twilight barely mitigated by the burning candles in brass chandeliers. The overall impression was one of profound mystery. A heavy scent of incense permeated the air, and except for a faint shuffling of feet from the throngs crowding into the nave, respectful silence prevailed. The ambience of intense faith and reverence instilled them with a new sense of piety. Even Michael stared in silent wonder while they followed the nun to a pew. Their eyes beheld the many statues above seas of votive lights flickering at their feet. The mighty organ began to play, and everyone rose as the archbishop of Vienna made his entrance, preceded by a procession of ministrants, deacons, and priests. Sister Constanze whispered that the cardinal was attending in a secluded alcove high above common folk.

High Mass at St. Stephen's was a grand pageant that bore little resemblance to the sequence of Mass explained to them. Later, they would understand that except for ceremonial details, the structure of Mass always remained the same. Tessa loved every moment, especially the rousing organ music and beautiful singing of an invisible choir. She tried to take in the many strange and intriguing details, unable as yet to appreciate their significance. There were enigmatic saints with enraptured expressions on their faces and marble altars in alcoves along the side naves with intricate wrought iron gates. Then her attention focused on the high pulpit and its steps that circled a massive column. Tan sandstone was carved with such intricacy that railing and pulpit had a weightless, airy grace resembling the lace of an altar cloth. A little sham window carved at the pulpit's base revealed the face of an ordinary man unlike the elegant features of the four apostles sculpted above. The ayah later explained that when the stonemason created this masterpiece, he immortalized himself in that window.

Tessa longed to join in the singing and resolved to learn the beautiful chorales and hymns. Surely, she'd be able to persuade sister to teach her! She was the most musically talented among her siblings, but even Ferenc and Sigismunda could not help comparing the plain hymns they'd sung at home with the glorious music surrounding them here. The magnificent church deeply impressed their receptive minds, as did watching the people, who seemed deeply pious and immersed in prayer. Catholicism had begun to exercise its hypnotic power.

Their lives settled into a daily routine of days filled with intense studies of Latin and catechism, with prayer and church services mornings and evenings and recreation limited to brief walks in the garden. Everyone but Michael made honest efforts to adapt. They studied diligently and helped their brother with his lessons, but the boy found Latin boring and difficult. Brother Sebastian was satisfied with their overall progress and regularly informed Kollonitsch, who received them in his study once a week to praise or admonish.

The cardinal was a dedicated priest who'd followed a strong vocation in early boyhood and never wanted to be anything other than a priest. He did try to understand the youngsters, but his age and dedicated faith limited his empathy. Their efforts did impress him, and especially Tessa's, who loved languages, was an ardent student and full of curiosity and fascination of the Catholic Church. She tried to replace the void in her heart that losing her papa and leaving Transylvania had created with music. When she discovered that the nuns and monks of her uncle's household attended several services during the day during which they sang psalms and litanies closely resembling Gregorian chants, she would sneak into the chapel even if it meant giving up recreation time in the garden. She'd have loved learning to play the organ but was told that this instrument was primarily for men.

On such occasions, only Michael missed her. Ferenc had never been fond of physical exercise and was content to sit and read a book from the bishop's library. Sigismunda liked needlework and would quietly work on her embroidery, but Michael was bored and unhappy that he and Tessa grew increasingly apart. His consolation was the secret hope that his beloved mama would soon send for him, and he repeatedly asked the cardinal for messages from her. There were none.

Miczike became depressed after her children's departure and suffered pangs of guilt about so readily agreeing to the arrangement. In conversations with her cousins, she would indulge in lengthy tirades about undue pressure, yet when Tibor questioned how she would have coped with the responsibility for her large brood, she had no answers and reverted to bemoaning the fate of being a young widow. Her complaints about poor health found little echo with her robust relatives, who devoted their time to administering their estate. The resulting lack of a sounding wall caused Miczike to forget her real or imagined ailments, and she began to feel better. She shed a few tears when signing the papers that finalized the sale of Zay-Ugrocz but was resigned to the fact that it was the only way her creditors could be satisfied. One of the cardinal's conditions for assuming full responsibility for the care of her children had been that half the remaining proceeds from the sale be divided between her children. This would leave each with a small legacy, and Miczike knew that it meant a meager dowry for her daughters and very modest basis for her sons to become officers in the Austrian army. Well, perhaps, they would all marry into moneyed families! As for her, she met a middle-aged widower without children at a social gathering and took note of his admiring glances. Irma made a point of mentioning his extensive land holdings and esteemed social standing, hoping that an eventual marriage would relieve her and Tibor of their difficult guest. Marriage prior to the end of her mourning period that customarily lasted at least a year was unthinkable, but in due course, it became obvious that she would eventually marry her well-to-do beau. And since she blamed pregnancies for her poor health, his desire not to have children was most welcome. She began to write her brief letters to Vienna in which she elaborated on the disadvantages of being a houseguest and her many physical sufferings. Michael's questions about returning home were ignored.

Sigismunda and Ferenc still hoped to hear from their Viennese relatives. Without means of making contact, they wondered whether news of their arrival had indeed reached them. They began to beg the ayah for help. The poor woman knew that she risked both the Trauttmansdorff's displeasure and dismissal from the cardinal's household, until she no longer could resist the pleas of her beloved charges. So one Sunday afternoon in late October, she set out on her mission. The Trauttmansdorff Palace was outside the fortifications of the old city a fair distance from the cardinal's residence, and by the time she knocked at a side entrance, she was very tired. The maid opening the door was a stranger to her, and she timidly asked for servants she'd worked with during her time. The girl became impatient and was about to close the door, when the head housekeeper arrived to find out what was going on. She too had joined the household after the ayah's time, but when she learned that this woman had been her master's ayah, she asked her into the kitchen and served her a glass of cool cider. The ayah's eyes filled with tears at the sight of familiar surroundings, and she gratefully rested while the housekeeper went off to see the countess in her boudoir. October is high season for stag hunting, and the count was at the lodge. Their son was a cadet at the military academy, and daughters Louise and Charlotte were visiting a friend closely related to a lady-in-waiting at the court. Connections such as these were of great social importance.

The housekeeper announced the arrival of an old woman purporting to have been the ayah of the three Trauttmansdorff sons and had come to convey a message from nephews and nieces. The countess was well aware of the situation and knew the ayah. She'd been expecting her first child when a message from Transylvania requested sending the woman to care for a new baby. The ayah had been a household factotum in Vienna, and the young countess knew that she would take charge of the nursery. She had other ideas, and the message from Hungary was welcome news as it relieved her from finding an excuse to engage an ayah of her own choice.

Like the rest of the family, she did not care for Miczike and was happy to see the couple leave for faraway Transylvania. The countess was not an unkind person, but she strongly supported her husband's decision not to establish contact and ignore the arrival of the young relatives. The count did not intend to challenge the appointment of the cardinal as guardian, which he could have done as the closest relative. They agreed that a Catholic cleric was best suited for the task of educating four young heretics and likely bring them to their senses! The countess surmised that the ayah had come without authority from the cardinal and had no desire to become involved.

"Give the old woman this florin for her effort," she said to the housekeeper, "and tell her that his grace is away hunting. We are happy that the children of the late count are well cared for in the home of His Eminence and hope that they appreciate his kindness and live up to his expectations. Their grandfather is very ill and unable to receive them, but I will inform his grace when he returns."

The housekeeper knew this was not the message the old woman was hoping to hear, but when news of the young count's tragic death had first reached the palace, she and the other servants had not been anxious either to see four youngsters added to the household. When the ayah was handed the coin, she knew that her mission had failed without even a chance to plead it, and the message confirmed her impression. There was nothing left for her to do but humbly express her gratitude to the countess and take leave. She cast a last look at the house where she had spent the happiest decades of her life. If the Lord willed it, she might never enter it again. On her way home, she desperately tried to think of a gentle way to break the news to "her" children, and she rehearsed words and phrases that would leave hope that the day might yet come when their uncle's family would welcome them. Knowing how ardently they had anticipated a favorable message, she did not dare to nurture much hope but could not bring herself to end it either.

It was almost evening by the time she returned; vespers were over, and she found the four upstairs playing cards. The ayah had secretly brought along a deck, fearing that His Eminence or anyone else in his household would look askance at "gambling." So the cards remained carefully hidden, only to be brought out when they were safely in their rooms and Sister Constanze and Brother Sebastian otherwise engaged. The four were enjoying themselves, and the ayah heard rare laughter as she climbed the stairs. The bantering stopped abruptly at her entrance, and anxious eyes scrutinized her face. Sigismunda and Ferenc instantly discerned that the news was not good while the ayah laboriously lowered herself into a chair and wiped her forehead with a red kerchief.

"It's mighty warm outside and a long way across town," she said, catching her breath. "Four flights of stairs don't help my old legs either!"

"What did Uncle Franz say? Tell us quickly!" Tessa burst out.

The ayah took her time settling down then related that their uncle was away hunting, their grand papa very ill, and the countess socially engaged.

"But they now do know that you're all here, which perhaps they hadn't been aware of 'til now," she added. "And I think if you're patient and continue to behave well, you may hear from them and perhaps be invited one day."

Ferenc and Sigismunda understood that the ayah herself was not convinced of her words, but they put up a brave front.

"I wish I could go hunting with Uncle Franz," said Tessa, "though I'm sure Austrian stags aren't near as big as ours!"

Michael shrugged his shoulders. "I'm waiting for Mama to have us all come home for Christmas! I know she'll want us to!"

"I don't think we can make the long journey in the wintertime," said Ferenc. "The Danube will be frozen over, and there'll be too much snow on the roads."

Michael was not about to be discouraged. "If the river is frozen, we can use a sleigh all the way, that's much faster! Why are you always against what I want, Ferenc?" he added belligerently.

Sigismunda shook her head. "Don't quarrel! Mama never said we could come home for Christmas. Perhaps, there's no money to pay for our travel, and I'm not sure how much fun it would be anyway to stay with Uncle Tibor and Aunt Irma. I don't think they like us too much."

Michael was not convinced, but to the ayah's great relief, the bell called for supper and put an end to the conversation.

The youngsters had never been asked to join the bishop's table and continued to eat in the room next to the larder that also served as their classroom. They ate with the ayah and sometimes Sister Constanze or Brother Sebastian, but once assured that they faithfully said their prayers before and after each meal, the nun and monk preferred to join their congregations.

The Viennese traditionally loved to eat, which was reflected in their cooking, and the food served to the children was varied and plentiful. Sometimes, they talked about favorite Transylvania dishes, and the ayah pestered the cook to let her cook something special but abandoned such efforts when she sensed resentment. Sister Genevieve was in charge of the Kollonitsch kitchen, a thin, elderly woman quick on her feet and not about to tolerate intrusion in her domain. The cardinal appreciated her culinary talents, and the ayah was anxious to avoid a complaint. The Austrian realm comprised countries of various cultures and traditions, and Viennese cuisine was anything but monotonous. It included dishes of Bohemian as well as Hungarian origin, though not from Transylvania.

The day's main meal was at noon, and they frequently were served meat, except of course Fridays, when it would be fish from the Danube. Supper was simple but adequate, and if one of them felt hungry in midafternoon, Sister Constanze would find them some bread and butter and perhaps an apple from the larder. They were not supposed to help themselves or roam the kitchen as they had at home.

Later that evening, Ferenc and Sigismunda conducted a whispered conversation. Michael and Tessa were perched on the wide sills of the mansard windows in the girls' room, amusing themselves with scenes of everyday life they could see from their observation point, and the ayah was busy getting their clothes ready for the next day. In the other room, the two older ones shared their thoughts about the ayah's mission. They no longer harbored great illusions yet refused to abandon all hope of establishing contact with their father's family, and Ferenc was still confident that Uncle Franz would want to see them upon his return from hunting. They never considered their Protestant faith to be a factor partly because they had undergone a subtle change during the past weeks and now saw Catholicism a fascinating alternative to their own creed, which led them to expect their relatives equally inclined. Much of Hungary and Transylvania were generally tolerant, but sentiments in Catholic Austria differed in the various regions. There was no religious persecution, and people were free to practice their faith, but following Habsburg tradition, the empress was devoutly Catholic as was the overwhelming majority of her subjects. The Viennese had built their cathedral stone by stone through centuries of personal sacrifice and continued to donate time and money to build new places of worship and to beautify and maintain existing ones. There were close to two hundred churches in the city in the eighteenth century! Most people actively practiced their faith, services were well attended, and hundreds of masses said each day. Clergy and especially monks and nuns were accorded high esteem and their prayers considered of special importance. The children had come to appreciate their uncle's exalted position in church hierarchy and the great respect accorded to him. Kollonitsch had achieved his position at an exceptionally early age. He was a highly educated man, the archbishop of Vienna valued his advice, and due to his high rank and excellent family background, Kollonitsch was received at court. Miczike had resented him from the day they met and would shrug off whatever suggestion he offered. Her insistence to marry Maximilian had been strengthened by a desire to antagonize her uncle. Given her antipathy toward him, it was all the more astounding that she so readily agreed to relinquish custody of her four children. He'd made no promise except that he would take care of their physical and educational needs, and Miczike presumed that they would follow her obstinate example and defy his wishes. Two decades later, Kollonitsch well remembered his unruly niece and was determined to avoid a repeat performance. As a dedicated servant of God, he was deeply convinced that forsaking secular life was the only path leading to God. Yet he was also a reasonable man and did not blame his young charges for their Protestant faith, nor did he consider them a burden. God had entrusted him with the mission of saving their souls by guiding them toward the true church.

He would occasionally admonish Michael for his lack of interest in his studies and Tessa for being too impetuous, but he was never harsh or unjust and inflicted no punishments. He tolerated the ayah's presence because he understood that she was their only link to home and that dismissing her would be a terrible blow for both the children and the old woman. He expected that in time she would no longer be needed and intended finding her a place to outlive her life. Had he been aware of her effort to contact the Trauttmansdorffs, he would have been displeased but not inordinately so because he surmised that the count and his family were not anxious to meet their relatives. They had been notified of the pending arrival and knew where to find them yet had made no effort to do so.

His interest in the children went far deeper than they thought. He paid close attention to Brother Sebastian's daily reports about progress in their studies and regularly questioned Sister Constanze about their adjustment to life in his household. He'd watch them in the garden and was particularly intrigued by Tessa, the most enigmatic of the four. He knew that the girl was very intelligent and had a beautiful singing voice but that she was also impulsive and hotheaded and difficult to tame. He noticed that she sometimes withdrew to the holy family statue to sit quietly on the stone bench. Was she praying? Kollonitsch knew little about children of that age, or any age, but he often wondered how she would adapt to his plans for her future. Sigismunda was outspoken in matters of faith and probably the most dedicated Protestant among them, but Brother Sebastian praised her excellent progress in Latin and Catechism and thoughtful questions. Ferenc's whole personality was oriented toward studying and the inattentive, spoiled Michael would eventually fall in line. *Give them time*, Kollonitsch thought, *it's only been a few months, and so far, there've been no major problems.* All were well mannered, and he actually looked forward to the weekly meetings with them. It never occurred to him how much they would have appreciated a small gesture of warmth or empathy.

The first two days of November were important dates in the Catholic religious calendar. On the first, All Saints' Day, the church accords special veneration to its saints and the martyr's death many of them suffered. On the following, All Souls' Day, people visit graves and flock to the churches to light votive candles and pray for the saints' intercession with God for their departed loved ones. Brother Sebastian went to great length to prepare his pupils for these important days and to explain the significance of saints. The special veneration accorded them puzzled the young Protestants, who recognized meritorious religious persons but did not revere them. Brother Sebastian carefully chose special saints and vividly described their good deeds or willingly endured extreme sufferings, usually for refusing to forsake their beliefs. Christ had promised great reward to those forsaking family, possessions and even life for His sake, and it followed that such persons would attain eternal bliss and become intercessors on behalf of the faithful. Sebastian did not state that joining a religious order was a prerequisite to entering heaven or becoming a saint, many of which, including Hungary's first king, had been secular people. Yet he elaborated on Christ's urging his followers to forsake the world for Him and went on to describe the gratification obtained by teaching, studying theology, caring for the sick and poor, or spending a contemplative life. Those devoting themselves to such ideals would surely find themselves blessed.

His words struck a strange cord in Sigismunda. The girl knew that she was not attractive and, with an expected small dowry, had little chance for a good match. Her cool and realistic mind told her that men did not place great value on bookish young women. Teaching had always interested her, and she found a challenge in coaxing her younger brother to devote himself more intently to his studies. She hoped that with the help of her papa's family, she might become sufficiently educated to teach at an institution for girls of wealthy families, but without support, there was little chance to realize this ambition. Unfamiliar with Catholic teaching, Sigismunda had paid little attention to Jesus's call to forsake family and possessions for a life of service to Him. The option of becoming a teaching nun had never occurred to her. Now she found herself respecting and liking Sister Constanze, who mentioned that her Order of Ursuline Nuns was dedicated to teaching children of common folk with little or no money to pay for an education. The intelligent, well-educated sister came from a bourgeois family and appeared perfectly happy and content with her life.

Sigismunda did not share her thoughts with her siblings, nor had she given up her Protestant beliefs. But her young mind was slowly succumbing to the powerful influence surrounding her. Brother Sebastian's explanations for the veneration of saints made more sense to her than their pastor's unilateral condemnation of the practice. Why would someone who had sacrificed his life to the Lord not command a powerful voice in heaven and look with compassion and mercy upon earthly sinners? She was unaware that Ferenc entertained similar thoughts, though his were not oriented toward teaching. Never enamored of a military career, he would have complied only to please his father, nor did the prospect of administering an estate attract him. Reading and studies were infinitely more interesting than the daily problems of dealing with servants and peasants.

Michael and Tessa were spellbound by Sebastian's stories, which brought a welcome interruption from Latin grammar and catechism rules. Brother Sebastian was a good raconteur and spoke to an attentive audience. Saints had intrigued Tessa ever since she first saw statues of them in Ulmeni's little church. She wanted to know more details and was promised a book from the cardinal's library dealing with specific life stories.

At Mass that morning, Tessa saw that before the figure of each saint was a bouquet of chrysanthemum, the only flowers the garden still yielded, and she was sure that Sister Constanze had arranged them. The siblings' outdoor recreation was cut short by the advancing season. During the warm and sunny days of early October, they had savored every minute in the garden and enjoyed the fresh air and walking along the brick paths. Now these were slippery from the fog descending upon the city until late morning, the stone benches were cold and no longer invited settling down with a book. Their rooms were dark and chilly, and the oil lamps did little to brighten them. Fires were started early each morning in the tiled stoves that heated the main rooms of the palace, and they radiated warmth for the rest of the day, but their rooms were not equipped with such luxury. They'd been given additional covers for sleeping, but as it became colder each day, they spent their free time in the warm classroom next to the kitchen.

November is the dreariest month of the year in Vienna, and All Saints' Day was no exception. The fog was extremely dense, and the stained glass windows in the chapel glowed in a deep purple against the dark sky. The somber service did little to cheer them up, and after a hearty breakfast, they were grateful to listen to the monk's stories as a variance in their curriculum.

The midday meal was appropriate for a holy day, and they savored the roast fowl and sweet cakes for desert. They wanted to hear more stories of saints, but Brother Sebastian wished to talk about the importance of the following day, dedicated to All Souls. The Catholic Church teaches that to atone for lesser sins prior to entering heaven, souls had to suffer in purgatory until attaining the perfection required for heaven.

"That is why you should pray fervently to the saints to intercede on behalf of your father and others who have died," said the monk.

He had barely finished the sentence when Tessa blurted out, "No, Brother Sebastian, you're wrong there. My papa is already in heaven, he is not in purgatory! Don't say that he is suffering! He's happy and I know this is so! And you have no right to say otherwise!"

She would have gone on, her voice growing louder and more passionate as she spoke, but Sigismunda put a firm hand on her arm. The monk remained calm.

"Tessa, your behavior is inappropriate. You know that you are not to interrupt or raise your voice. You will go to your room and remain there until you are completely calm and mind your manners. I do not wish to see you here until you have my permission to return!"

Tessa was too excited to obey.

"No!" she cried. "You're all wrong! What you said is not true! My papa is in heaven. My papa—"

Sigismunda quickly rose and, taking her sister's arm, pulled her from the room to hustle her violently protesting and now sobbing sister up the stairs. The ayah heard them coming, and Sigismunda quickly explained what happened, leaving Tessa in the arms of her nanny.

When Sigismunda returned, the monk's voice was very firm. "Sigismunda, your sister is old enough to understand a command, and you did not have my permission to leave the classroom. You both misbehaved, and I shall have to inform His Eminence."

The girl did not defend herself, glad to have prevented the scene from getting worse. She knew her younger sister to be prone to temper tantrums, which until this day had not occurred in Vienna.

The lesson continued, and when the three went upstairs, they still found Tessa agitated. Sorrow about her papa, homesickness, and lack of outdoor exercise combined to precipitate the violent outbreak that the patient ayah had not been able to calm. Tessa did not care what her uncle or Sebastian thought; she longed for her father and home and continued to sob.

"Oh, be quiet, Tess!" Ferenc finally burst out. "You know very well that no one's perfect, we all commit sins, and so did Papa! If he hadn't bought so many horses, there would have been enough money around for us to remain at home!"

He didn't intend it as an accusation; he just blurted out his frustration. Tessa raised her head and stared at him with wide, tear-filled eyes.

"What did you say, Ferenc?" she stammered.

Sigismunda smoothed a lock from her sister's forehead and said gently, "It's true, Tessa, but Papa was not aware how bad things were, and the moneylenders let him borrow as much as he wanted. It wasn't his fault, and if Papa had not died, he could have made everything right again. Now stop crying. You're not allowed to have supper, but we'll all sneak a bite or two into our pockets. Won't it be fun to cheat on Brother Sebastian?"

They all chuckled, and even the distraught Tessa managed a little smile.

"I still think our papa is in heaven, and I'll pray extra hard to the Holy Mother to make sure that it's so!"

Sebastian supervised at the supper table and kept his eye on the ayah, who he suspected would disobey his order and put some food aside for Tessa. He wasn't familiar with the mentality of teenagers, and the siblings stuck together in their little plot. While Ferenc engaged his attention with questions pertaining to the afternoon's lesson, Sigismunda and Michael alternated in "accidentally" dropping pieces of bread, cheese, even ham onto their lap that found its way into their pockets noticed only by the ayah. After final prayer, they bade good night and silently climbed the stairs. Once in their rooms, the ayah put a finger on her lips to warn against someone listening, and they understood, casually chatting about the day while pulling food from their pockets. Tessa had spent the evening staring across the wet roofs trying to imagine them to be the trees she could see from her old room at Zay-Ugrocz. Sobs still shook her body from time to time, but the outburst had released bent-up emotions, and she felt somewhat relieved. She was not really afraid of any punishment her uncle might impose. She was a courageous child frequently disciplined by her mother for transgressions. Papa would be upset when she could not control her temper but knew ways of calming her and then spoke earnestly about it. "Only little kids behave that way," he'd say, "and you are no longer one but a big girl and your papa's precious daughter, who should be sweet and friendly and not be given to such outbursts!" Then she'd put her arms round his neck and listen to his admonitions, though she could rarely bring herself to apologize.

She was hungry now and eagerly ate what her siblings brought. When they were in bed and the oil lamps extinguished, Sigismunda took her sister's hand and spoke to her in a soft and comforting voice.

"Tessa, Papa would have been very sad today about your poor manners. Remember how we promised ourselves we'd make him and Mama proud of us by behaving as noblemen and not like commoners! We don't want those Austrians to think we're Transylvania peasants! We're just as good as any of them, and you didn't act like a young countess today. You'll have to bring yourself to apologize to Uncle tomorrow, like it or not."

Tessa knew in her heart that her sister was right, but pride stirred, and she said defiantly, "No, I won't! The monk was wrong! Ferenc says Papa didn't care how bad things were, but he loved horses. I know he did nothing wrong and should be in heaven now!"

Sigismunda remained patient. "Tessa, I know you've been interested in the Catholic religion for a long time. I saw Papa's catechism among your things. You know that we must repent for our sins to be forgiven and that you are supposed to actually tell a priest that you are sorry. Don't you remember that Papa went to confession a couple of times each year? So think of him looking down at you from heaven, tell the cardinal you're sorry, and imagine how proud of you Papa will be! Promise me?"

The exhausted Tessa was about to fall asleep and gave only a vague little sound, but her body relaxed, and Sigismunda knew she had reached her.

All Souls' Day dawned with more mist and rain, and the ayah had trouble getting them ready in the morning. Special prayers for the dead were said during mass, and the youngsters shed tears for their father. Following the service and prior to breakfast, the girls were summoned to the library. Never before had they seen the cardinal display such stern demeanor as they stood before him and listened to a lecture about obedience and humility. When he had finished, Sigismunda stepped forward, dropped to one knee, and said, "I ask forgiveness, Your Eminence. I was wrong in leaving our classroom without permission." She fervently hoped that her example would induce her sister to do likewise.

Kollonitsch extended his hand, Sigismunda kissed the ring, and he said in a friendly tone, "I forgive you, child. You are doing well in your studies, and until yesterday, no report of misbehavior had reached my ears."

Sigismunda rose and stepped back, holding her breath. She need not have worried. During the service, Tessa had looked up at Mary's figure for a long time, and the Holy Mother's even gaze and enigmatic smile seemed to tell her that her father would want her to apologize. There was a heavy silence, but after a few more moments of inner struggle, she uttered, "I'm very sorry, Your Eminence."

"Kneel!"

She hesitated for another moment then dropped to her knees.

"You have offended God not only with your behavior but also your doubts about purgatory, which all souls must endure! Since it was your first serious lapse, your punishment shall be lenient. Today, you will only have bread and milk in your room, where you shall remain except for saying ten rosaries kneeling on the floor in the chapel, five before and five after noon. In your prayers, you must earnestly ask all the saints for their intercession so God may forgive you! You will also beg forgiveness of Brother Sebastian who has been very kind and patient with you. Do you understand?"

"Yes, Eminence," Tessa whispered, kissed the ring on the extended hand, and rose. He dismissed them, and while Sigismunda joined her siblings for breakfast, Tessa went upstairs for her piece of dark bread and mug of milk. Sister was watching, and this time, there was no cheating.

Apologizing to her uncle and later the monk was much harder for the willful and tenacious child than the bread-and-milk verdict or kneeling on the cold stone floor of the chapel for the hours it took her to say the rosaries under the watchful eyes of sister. Tessa was a proud, defiant girl and in the past had often escaped punishment because of the indulgent ayah and her loving papa, who found it so hard to be cross with his darling. She avoided provoking her mother, which was not too difficult because of the limited time spent in her presence.

God seemed harsh and very distant that dreary afternoon as Tessa knelt and said Hail Mary's, her eyes fixed upon the tabernacle.

She would rather have looked at the Holy Mother's figure, but she had been directed to kneel on the altar steps, and the statue was not within her vision. Only a few candles burned, and the November day's scarce daylight barely penetrated the windows. The small eternal light cast red reflections upon the golden sanctum that looked like drops of blood. She'd bravely gone through the morning session, but now the hungry and tired child was cold and feeling terribly alone, forsaken, and unloved. Would it always be like that? Why had Papa died and Mama sent them away? Even living with Uncle Tibor and Aunt Irma would have been preferable, she could have run into the woods or go to the stables and chat with the groomsmen! Tessa was not given to self-pity, but while struggling through the last of her rosaries, tears welled in her eyes and ran down her cheeks and onto her folded hands. She bravely suppressed her sobs and carried on in a choking voice. Then she felt an arm round her shoulders as Sister Constanze gently pulled her to her feet and into a pew. Holding her close, the nun carried on where Tessa had stopped. "Holy Mary, Mother of God, pray for us sinners, now and in the hour of our death, amen." She buried her head in the nun's black habit that faintly smelled of lavender and listened as the sister prayed the last sequence of her penance. When she had finished, she kept Tessa in her arms and spoke softly to her.

"It's all right, child. You have sinned, but the good Lord heard your prayers and knows that you are very sorry about your transgression."

Tessa thought her punishment had been harsh and unjust and most of all regretted that she had to apologize. She began, "But my papa—"

Sister anticipated what would follow and raised a hand to stop her.

"To receive absolution at confession, child, one must resolve not to commit the same offense, the same sin again. And you will try to obey Brother Sebastian and not make him angry, won't you? Promise that and all will be well! And, Tessa, this coming Sunday, the sisters and I will practice some chants and litanies here in the chapel with Brother Jacob at the organ. You may come and join us an hour before vespers. I know you have a good voice and am sure the sisters won't mind if you sing along with us. Would you like that?"

"Oh yes, I would, Sister Constanze, thank you very much!" Tessa whispered with a smile brightening her tearstained face. She headed for the door then came back to hug the nun. "Thank you, Sister Constanze. I promise I'll be good."

She shyly kissed the nun's cheek, unsure whether it was appropriate to do so, then quickly left without seeing the warm smile on Constanze's lips nor her moist eyes. That evening, there was butter and a generous slice of cheese on her bread, and her mug was filled with hot milk. Tessa did not know whether the ayah had been to the larder for her and the old woman never mentioned that it was Sister who handed her the meal.

The nun knew that Tessa's presence during singing practice would reach the cardinal's ears and was afraid he might think she was rewarding disobedience. Without telling Brother Sebastian, she went to Kollonitsch to plead her case. Constanze had experience in teaching and was very good at it. She told the cardinal that Tessa had an excellent voice and that developing her musical talent through special lessons would channel her energies toward spiritual goals. It would also require a sacrifice because the girl would be deprived of recreation time since lessons were not at the expense of other studies. Constanze felt a twinge of conscience for neglecting to mention how much Tessa loved to sing, but she convinced herself that the Lord would be pleased about a good voice raised in His praise. Kollonitsch concurred and gave permission for Tessa to commence formal music lessons under Sister Agnes, whose reputation as a tough, no-nonsense choirmaster had been important to win his agreement.

Tessa was delighted. After months of missing Transylvania and the freedom of home, her bent-up energies and compulsive nature finally had something into which she could put her heart. She was confident she would please her teacher. After all, she'd often been told that she sang well.

Sister was a tall, somewhat heavy woman in her fifties. She had undergone formal musical training and played both harpsichord and viola exceedingly well. Her vocal cords did not have great range, but she knew exactly how each note should sound and how to further talent. She was not overjoyed when Constanze spoke to her about taking on this teenage student and suspected that she was being used to tame a naughty kid. She had originally welcomed not to be involved with the young heretics. And she had the innate disdain of the musically gifted toward those lacking talent and often prayed for patience when practicing with her choir that comprised members with more good intention than ability. The cardinal's wish, however, was not to be questioned, and she sent for Tessa to come see her.

Tessa had never entered a cell before. She knew that the few nuns and monks belonging to her uncle's household occupied the two side wings of the palace, and she and her siblings had seen them pacing silently in the cloisters, breviary in hand. She enjoyed listening to their singing on the organ loft during services and watched them file through the nave for communion, lowered faces hidden beneath the wings of their white headdress.

When afternoon lessons were over, Sister Constanze accompanied Tessa through the misty garden and down the hall of the east wing. Everything was very quiet and no household sounds audible from the main building. Sister stopped at a narrow door and whispered, "Now remember for next time, Tessa, it's the last door. Don't knock on any of the others and always announce yourself very quietly."

She then tapped just once, and the door opened almost instantly. Sister Agnes's stately figure filled the frame, and she motioned Tessa to enter while her stern gaze scrutinized the girl's face.

"So you want to study music," she said in a melodious voice that belied her formidable appearance. "I am Sister Agnes, and we shall see whether you have talent. Thank you, Sister Constanze, that will be all," she added and Constanze withdrew.

Tessa timidly looked round the bare room furnished with a narrow bed, a prie-dieu below a large crucifix, an armoire, chest of drawers, and plain chair. The only items revealing that this was not an ordinary cell was a small harpsichord in one corner with a tiny stool before it, and she wondered how the big nun managed to sit there.

Sister Agnes lost no time. She asked her to sing something and expected a song or perhaps a hymn. Tessa never hesitated. Of course, she would sing the "Salve Regina!" The ayah had taught her to the best of her memory, and over the years, it had changed some more in Tessa's memory, but her low-pitched voice remained perfectly on key. She put her heart into the recital and concentrated her mind on the Virgin in the hope that Mary would hear this prayer and help her win the heart of the stern-faced teacher. Tessa was a pious child, and it came to light in the way she sang the closing words, "Oh clemens, oh pia, oh dulcis Virgo Maria." And indeed, she touched Agnes more than the nun would admit.

"You're a bit off from the way it ought to be," she said, "but that was not bad and if you work hard, we can do something with your voice!"

Her words began a relationship that became a large factor in helping Tessa cope with her new life, though her studies turned out to be different from what she had expected. Rarely was she allowed to sing chants or hymns; instead, she had to study harmony, musical history, diction, and the techniques of singing—which meant endless, boring scales. She had not anticipated these exercises, but she understood that she was being guided toward doing it "right" and became a dedicated student. The tiny stool disappeared under Agnes's voluminous robes as she sat striking notes on the harpsichord, which Tessa had to identify, write down, and sing. Or sister would dictate scores to her and ask she transcribe them in different keys. Tessa had received basic musical education at home; she knew the notes and would have loved to try her hand on the harpsichord but was not allowed to touch it. Agnes was a strict teacher who dispensed more criticism than praise, but the girl knew she'd done well when the nun said, "Now you're getting close to doing it right!"

For the time being, her hopes of joining the choir did not materialize, but she was allowed to listen during practice in the chapel. These were her favorite times, and she paid rapt attention to Sister Agnes leading the monks and nuns through hymns and chorales, correcting or praising.

Tessa's new activity brightened the dark, dreary month of November, and even though she suffered serious bouts of homesickness, her young life had a new purpose, and she devoted herself to her musical studies with energy and zeal.

The lazy and superficial Michael suffered more than the others did. He and Tessa had been buddies during childhood. The boy always felt safe when caught in some mischief because Mama would excuse him and blame Tessa, knowing that the truth made little difference. Now his younger sister was involved in music studies and had no interest to team up with him on anything he suggested. He did not understand that the events of the past year had matured Tessa beyond her age. Being made to apologize to the cardinal and Brother Sebastian had left a deep scar on her proud mind. Anxious not to jeopardize her music lessons, she promised herself to avoid getting into trouble. Sigismunda was determined to help her younger brother, but Michael never had much in common with his two older siblings and resented her persistence. He would test her patience, and there were times when his only contribution was copying what she dictated. Brother Sebastian guessed the truth, aware that Michael was his weakest student, who'd never develop a love for learning. Moreover, the boy was always bored during free time if Sigismunda was occupied with needlecraft, Ferenc read and Tessa was immersed in musical exercises. Now that the season eliminated use of the garden, Michael did not know what to do with himself. Brother Sebastian understood their need of physical exercise and obtained permission to take them on strolls through the city, which they welcomed with enthusiasm, especially walks in the city's parks.

In December, a pale winter sun broke through the clouds and brought welcome change from the dreary November days. It was now Advent, and their religious teaching focused on the Virgin Mary and her unconditional submission to God's will. They were preparing for the important feast of Immaculate Conception on December 8, but Sebastian allowed them to devote some attention to the day of St. Nicolas on the sixth. They were not familiar with the Viennese tradition of honoring the sixth century bishop who, according to legend, had rewarded pious children with treats. Viennese custom paired the saint with a figure of Beelzebub with chain and whip to punish and frighten the naughty ones; that figure was known as "Krampus," a name rooted in heathen bad spirits. The church looked on benignly, and neither supported or suppressed the tradition. It was customary for adults too to share treats, such as fresh or dried fruit and bread baked with nuts and raisins. The church regards Advent as a time of fasting in preparation for Christ's birth, but on December 6, St. Nicolas Day, Sister Genevieve handed each of the youngsters a small basket filled with prunes, dried apricots and pears, a fresh apple, and candy made of honey and nuts. She had baked the dark bread chock-full with raisins and hazelnuts, and they relished it with their milk. The day happened to coincide with the second Sunday of Advent, and lighting the appropriate candle on the Advent wreath on their table brought home the realization that Christmas was close. Michael complained that he wished he could be with Mama to enjoy traditional Transylvania holiday festivities. He also wanted to know whether lessons would discontinue for three weeks during the holiday season as was the case at home, but no one mustered the courage to ask.

A few days before Christmas Eve, they received a letter from Mama, in which Miczike elaborated on her sufferings and complained about the hardship of being at the mercy of her cousins but said little to touch the hearts of her children. She admonished them to behave and not bring shame upon her. Almost casually, she mentioned that Zay-Ugrocz had been sold to satisfy the creditors and that a small legacy had been placed in trust for each of them until they came of age. It would not amount to much of a dowry for the girls and likely fail to adequately subsidize an officer's career; therefore, they were lucky to be in the care of their uncle. In closing, she lamented how much more difficult her life as widow was compared to theirs, whose future still lay before them. Also that she loved them and was brokenhearted about their separation.

Michael was the only one who did not catch her insincerity, but even he understood that he was not to return to the home where he was born and raised and where a loving Mama had defended his indolence. He shed some angry tears but still hoped his mother would make good on her promise to have him join her wherever she would live in the future. Ferenc was secretly relieved that inadequate funds likely canceled his officer's career; he was a bookworm and hoped that Kollonitsch would arrange for enrolment at one of Vienna's famous universities. Sigismunda understood that a small dowry all but wiped out hopes for a good marriage, whereas Tessa's mind, despite being homesick for her beloved Transylvania, had become totally enthralled by music. She sensed that Sister Agnes was an excellent teacher and worked as hard as she could to assure that her lessons would continue.

Still the loss of Zay-Ugrocz was a hard blow to them, coming as it did just before the holidays. It meant they no longer had a home and Mama made no mention of her future plans. The two older ones knew they would not indefinitely remain in their uncle's house and felt uneasy about the future. Kollonitsch had never revealed his intentions, and they did not dare bring up the subject.

Sister Agnes was very pleased with her student, though she kept up her stern demeanor and rarely offered praise. Tessa could not have been more diligent. She faithfully copied notes, memorized her theory lessons, and practiced scales, which drove her siblings crazy. They did not share her talent, and Michael would tease her, demanding that she at least treat them to songs instead of "do-re-mi" and "la-la-la!" Seasonal confinement and space limitations aggravated the situation since Tessa's voice carried beyond the door when the other three studied in the boys' room. Only the ayah listened and enjoyed every note, grateful that her darling had found an outlet for her energy.

As Christmas drew near, Sister Agnes told her pupil that she had a special reward for her in mind. During the vigil service in the chapel on Christmas Eve, Tessa would be allowed to join the choir on the organ loft and sing a carol in solo performance. The girl was so excited she impulsively jumped up and threw her arms around the nun in an embrace, withdrawing a moment later in fear that the impulsive gesture had ruined her chance. She didn't dare look at sister's face while stuttering an apology and missed the tender expression on the stern features. It had been a very long time since anyone had hugged Sister Agnes, and the girl's joy warmed her heart.

"It's all right, Tessa," she said gently. "But we must always be in control of our emotions, and you will have to study hard and not miss out on scales and other exercises if you want to earn this privilege. Remember that you will sing solo and any mistake will be heard by all. Do you think you can do it without bringing shame on me?"

That thought had not entered Tessa's mind; she'd never sung to an audience before but was confident that she could, so why worry?

Sister Agnes chose the simple carol of the Rose of Jesse blooming from a sprig in midwinter, the virgin bearing a child. The tender melody and naïve piety of the text was a good choice; the notes could be interpreted in a lower key to better suit Tessa's voice. It was to be a surprise, but the girl could not contain her joyful excitement and had to tell the ayah who faithfully kept the secret.

Christmas Eve was a day of fasting. Breakfast and the midday meal consisted only of bread and warm milk. Wonderful scents emanated from the kitchen, where Sister Genevieve and her helpers were busy with preparations for the following day, the church year's most important feast. The children were told that they would join their uncle's table for the first time and could expect very special delicacies. They tried hard to concentrate on their lessons, but their mouths watered from delicious whiffs of breads and pies baking in the adjoining kitchen. Tessa could barely contain her excitement and time and again mentally rehearsed the carol. She was glad that Brother Sebastian limited his lessons to Bible readings and was too distracted to join in the discussion why only Luke's narration gave details of the circumstances of Christ's birth and that of other Evangelists did not. At five o'clock in the afternoon, they were sent to their rooms to prepare themselves for chapel service at six. They knew their evening meal would be equally frugal and that there'd be more praying until it was time for midnight Mass at St. Stephen's.

When they entered the chapel, Sister Constanze motioned Tessa toward the narrow circular stair leading to the organ loft. The girl started to bolt up the wooden steps, became aware of the noise, and tamed her exuberance to tiptoe the rest of the way.

The choir of about a dozen monks and nuns was crowded on both sides of the organ. The monks in their cowls took up less space, but the nuns with their wide, crisply starched Ursuline headdresses looked like women huddling below a bizarre snowdrift. Sister Agnes took Tessa's arm and led her to a corner at the front of the balcony overlooking the nave. The girl saw her siblings and would have loved to know why they thought she was not with them. Lackeys, maids, and servants of the palace took their seats, then the door near the altar opened and ministrants with incense vessels preceded the cardinal in his purple vestments, the church's traditional color for Lenten periods. It was a prayer service, and he spoke briefly about how ardently the people of Israel had prayed for a Redeemer, who they hoped would deliver them from the Roman yoke, pleading that He descend like dew from heaven, rain from clouds. When he had finished, Sister Agnes motioned to Tessa, and the organ played a few notes to introduce her carol. The girl's heart was full of joyful piety, and her first notes were a little hesitant and soft, unsure how it would sound in the large room. Brother Jacob at the organ gave her an encouraging nod, and as confidence rushed through her, Tessa forgot about Transylvania, Zay-Ugrocz, homesickness, and even her papa. There was only the joy of music, and her young voice rose above the organ to fill the chapel. "Behold a rose of Judah from tender branch has sprung! A rose from root of Jesse, as prophets long had sung. It bore a flower bright, that blossomed in the winter when half-spent was the night."

She never noticed her siblings turn their heads and Kollonitsch briefly look up. She was happier than she had been for many months, and when she reached the end of the third verse—"By His humility, we live as God's children, in peace and unity"—she wished she could go on forever! There was a brief silence. Tessa looked at Sister Agnes, and the nun nodded, her lips silently forming the word *good*. The choir resumed and fresh incense on the glowing embers sent fragrant whiffs of white smoke from the little vessel. A final blessing concluded the service.

After a frugal meal, they were back in chapel saying rosaries, but Tessa never felt hungry during those long hours until midnight. Sigismunda had given her a peck on the cheek and said, "You sang well, Tessa." Ferenc nodded approvingly, and Michael wanted to know why she hadn't told them and why she never sang songs instead of scales in their rooms. Tessa was elated by a never before known feeling of accomplishment that far surpassed praise for a lesson well learned or anything else in her young life for which she had been commended. For so many years, she wanted to share her singing with others, and now a nun had helped her accomplish that goal and allowed her to sing in a chapel before the most important people in her life and did it well! She wanted to dance and laugh and sing at the same time and had a difficult time containing herself. That evening, they prayed the "joyful rosary" that contemplates the five stations in Mary's life from conceiving Jesus to offering her divine son in the temple. Tessa raised her eyes to meet the inscrutable gaze of her favorite statue and felt that the smile on the pale lips was meant for her alone that evening. Amid the murmuring voices, Tessa mentally prayed, "Holy Mother, help me become a good singer, and I shall sing your praise! Always!"

Snow fell all afternoon, and when it was time to leave for the cathedral, the ayah made sure they were bundled up warmly. They had outgrown their old boots and wore new ones Kollonitsch had commissioned for them. Snow crunched under their feet in the bitterly cold night as they walked through streets and alleys crowded with people with small oil lamps heading to the traditional midnight service held in every church around town to celebrate the good news of Christ's birth. Candles burned in the windows, and the city seemed to glow in anticipation of the joyful event.

The cathedral was so cold that the holy water stoup by the entrance had a layer of ice on the surface. Thousands of candles flickered in chandeliers and at side altars. Tessa wondered how the organist could play so well when surely his fingers must be stiff from cold. The four youngsters huddled together, their breath rising with that of the other singing voices. The singular magic of Christmas cast its spell on all, and the ambience of the beautiful midnight service celebrating the birth of Christ touched them deeply. A sleepy Michael let his head drop against Sigismunda's shoulder; he'd complained all day of hunger and now could not keep his eyes open anymore. The Mass lasted almost two hours because of the large number of people receiving communion. Row upon row stepped up to the railing that separated the sanctuary from the nave to kneel and wait their turn.

When they finally made their way back through snow-covered streets past celebrating crowds, they were tired and cold and longed for their beds. Clerics observed a fast until breakfast Christmas morning, but Sister Genevieve had a wonderful surprise for the youngsters. She motioned them into the kitchen, where mugs of hot apple cider and thick slices of fragrant warm bread studded with raisins and nuts waited. At that moment, it was the best treat they could have imagined, and their joy and exuberant gratitude warmed the nun's heart and had her forget her own hunger. She would spend the rest of the cold night praying with the others in the chapel, but these kids would enjoy a good sleep. The loving ayah had placed hot bricks wrapped in cloth into their beds to make up for the unheated rooms.

Christmas morning dawned under a bright sun that transformed the snow-covered city into a citadel of glittering beauty. Following an early Mass in the chapel, they gathered round their table for a hearty breakfast of hot milk, yeast cake, butter, honey, and preserves. Good food and the joy of Christmas soothed their longing for home, and they chatted happily. Withdrawn Ferenc and staid Sigismunda joined in the banter with animation. Later, they enjoyed a snowball fight in the garden.

Cardinal Kollonitsch watched them from the window of his library while pondering the past months. When first learning of the count's death, his niece's financial circumstances, and the indifferent attitude of the Vienna Trauttmansdorffs, he was unsure whether he should assume responsibility for four adolescents he had never met. He still had a bitter taste left from the relationship with his obstinate niece and the breach of her solemn promise to raise her children in the Catholic faith. He spent hours in prayerful contemplation asking God for guidance and emerged with a clear vision of what he was meant to do. God had shed His grace upon him by granting him an excellent mind, financial independence, quick advancement in his clerical career, and close friendship with Vienna's archbishop. Now divine foresight presented him with a different challenge— saving four young and impressionable minds from a life as heretics and entrusting him with their conversion to the true faith. It was his conviction that whenever God sent a challenge, He also granted the fortitude to live up to the task, and he never doubted that he would. He had to admit that so far it proved easier than anticipated; the four youngsters were adjusting as well as could be expected with few behavioral problems. He was especially pleased about their good minds and eagerness to learn, at least of three of them. Their progress in Latin was excellent, and he instructed Brother Sebastian to include Austrian history in the lessons. While satisfied with their progress in studying catechism, it was difficult to ascertain the extent to which Catholicism was replacing their Protestant convictions. Were they as yet able to appreciate the error of their creed, as he saw it? He could only hope that God's grace and exposure to Catholic rituals would lead them onto the right path. Today, they would share his table for the traditional Christmas Day feast. He had declined an invitation to join the archbishop and wondered whether his charges realized that he was rewarding them with his invitation. The happy banter in the garden reminded him dimly of his own youth, though he'd been a serious child never in doubt of his destiny. Was there a vocation to religious life in the hearts of these youngsters? Reality dictated that their financial situation left them few alternatives, but even monasteries and convents required dowries. The devoutly Catholic empress insisted that becoming a monk or nun had to be entirely voluntary, and he agreed that a forced decision only resulted in a poor servant of God. He intended to apply his influence and authority to stir them in that direction. An important first step would be to send them to different institutions and deprive them of supporting one another. He did not think it wise to give them advance warning of his plans and decided to begin contacting various religious orders. First and foremost, it was necessary that they formally convert to Catholicism and be properly baptized and confirmed, and after consultations with Brother Sebastian, he thought that they'd be ready by Easter, a time when the church traditionally accepted converts. Today's festive meal seemed an excellent occasion to informally ascertain their progress.

He watched as the ayah slowly and painstakingly made her way into the garden, apparently to call them inside to prepare for the festivity. He had not yet decided on her future. Well, he would not turn her into the street, instead find her a place in a convent to spend her last years. He suspected the ayah and not a religiously indifferent father to be the source of Tessa's knowledge and interest in Catholic beliefs. It placed the old woman in a favorable light, even though she was of little use because of her age and poor physical condition.

The ayah had cleaned and pressed the youngsters' clothes as best she could, but wear and tear began to show. Especially Tessa had grown during the past months, and she wondered whether the cardinal would notice that her skirts reached only mid-calf. Tessa's broad-shouldered, lanky frame was no longer the scrawny body of a child but was beginning to blossom into that of a young woman. The girl had resigned herself to her sedate hairdo but still looked forward to unbraiding her tresses each evening. She would not turn into a beautiful woman. Her chiseled nose and wide mouth were too pronounced to be pretty in a conventional way, but her large, expressive eyes, immaculate complexion, and beautiful teeth combined to make her the most attractive among her siblings. Sigismunda had always been plain. The shy Ferenc recently seemed to have acquired a slight stutter. Michael resembled his handsome father but lacked Maximilian's engaging charm and always looked bored.

The ayah's careful scrutiny of their appearance irked Sigismunda.

"It's all right, ayah, we're as presentable as we shall get and perfectly capable of dining with our uncle without disgracing ourselves! Let's go now. And, Michael, don't keep asking when you can see Mama, it won't lead anywhere. We'll be here as long as it pleases him, and that's that! And, Tessa, please don't start an argument, no matter what anyone says!"

Sigismunda asserted authority over her younger siblings but never criticized her older brother, for whom she felt a little sorry, though she wasn't quite sure why. The two younger ones, albeit grudgingly, accepted her admonitions.

Kollonitsch wore immaculate black robes with red collar and skullcap. His critical eye caught the shabbiness of the youngsters' clothes, and he made a mental note of asking Sister Constanze to have new outfits made. In view of his plans, he did not wish to replace more than was necessary.

"May God shed His blessings upon you on this glorious day of His Son's birth," he said with a smile brightening his stern features. "It is the most joyous day of the year, and we shall celebrate it together!"

The thought crossed Sigismunda's mind that for Protestants, Good Friday took precedence over Christmas since that was the day on which Christ redeemed the world. Next was October 31, the day Martin Luther nailed his ninety-five theses on the door of Wittenberg's church, but she kept silent and bowed her head for the blessing. Sister Genevieve appeared to announce that the meal was served, and for the first time, they stepped into their uncle's elegant dining room. Here too the walls were paneled in oak and the tall ceiling exquisitely carved. Religious paintings decorated the walls with one opposite the cardinal's chair depicting the magis' adoration of the holy family. The table was set with beautiful Viennese china and silverware and laden with platters of food. There were capon and wild fowl, roast pig, ham and rack of deer, vegetables, and freshly baked breads. The food was more varied than anything they knew, and the opulence surprised them. They had anticipated that nuns and monks would join the cardinal on this day, but there were only five settings. Kollonitsch had deliberately reserved this occasion for them; they had lived in his house for four months, during which time, he had never seen them for more than an hour at a time. He thought that the privacy and relaxed atmosphere of the holiday meal would help to win their confidence and lay the groundwork for the future. Michael naively let slip an exclamation of surprised delight at the sight of the beautiful table, and the cardinal smiled.

"Let us hope that you will enjoy your first Christmas dinner in Vienna," he said. "But first, we must thank the Lord for sending His only Son into the world and for the bounty He bestows upon us. Let us pray."

The youngsters responded to the lengthy invocation with their "amen" and took their seats—the boys to his right, the girls to the left. They had excellent table manners and politely waited until their host had helped himself from the various platters. Ferenc and Sigismunda ate moderately, but Tessa and especially Michael were still growing adolescents and demonstrated a healthy appetite after fasting during the long Advent and particularly the previous day. Kollonitsch opened the conversation with a comment on Tessa's singing.

"You did very well, child. Sister Agnes tells me that you work hard and have a talent for music. Did you ever sing to an audience before?"

The girl flushed with joy at his praise. The subject of music made her drop the withdrawn demeanor she had displayed since his reprimand.

"No, Your Eminence," she answered. "Never. And I like Catholic hymns much better than those we sang in church at home, but what I'd really like to sing is the Gregorian chant. When I was little, I listened to monks in a church at Ulmeni, and I've been wanting to learn it ever since. I really would, Your Eminence!"

Kollonitsch did not show his surprise and asked, "Ever since you were little? Tell me about the visit to the church?"

Tessa was unaware of her older siblings' puzzled expression and proceeded to tell the story of the afternoon in Ulmeni.

"And when I walked through the cemetery and first heard voices coming from the church, I went inside, and it was all around me and came from everywhere, and everything was resounding with it! At first, I didn't even know that it was monks singing in the pews up front 'cause their faces were hidden under hoods. And it didn't sound anything like songs or hymns, I didn't know what it was, but I just loved it, and my papa later said it was called 'Gregorian chant' and that it was only sung in Catholic churches. I so wanted to hear it again, but I knew Mama wouldn't like it and Papa made me promise not to tell anyone."

Tessa caught herself just in time before revealing that the ayah had shared her secret and taught her the "Salve Regina," unaware that this would have greatly enhanced the old woman's standing in the cardinal's eyes. She was afraid having already said too much and cast an anxious eye upon her sister. Sigismunda looked at her plate and wished that Tessa wouldn't talk so much and Ferenc shared her thoughts. Michael was too involved with his food to pay attention. Kollonitsch had listened intently.

"That must indeed have been a wonderful experience," he said, "and I'm very happy to hear that you like the Gregorian chant so much. I too prefer it to any other music. I shall speak to Sister Agnes, or does she know about it? Have you been studying chants, and do you already know one, Tessa?"

The girl hesitated then said quietly, "Only the 'Salve Regina,' Your Eminence."

The cardinal decided not to question her further and casually remarked, "You must sing it for me soon," then changed the subject to include the others in the conversation. He asked Sigismunda whether she also liked music, and the girl answered that she enjoyed hearing it but would rather read and one day perhaps teach. Back in Transylvania, she had occasionally taught the children of house servants to read and write and had loved doing so. She'd also taught Sunday school in the Protestant Church. Kollonitsch again listened carefully then directed himself to Ferenc.

"And what is your favorite pastime, son?"

Ferenc flushed. "I, I l-like to read b-books," he stuttered. "History, mostly about the T-Turks." His voice trailed off, too embarrassed to continue.

"Ferenc," Sigismunda said resolutely, "is very smart and the best student among us! He's especially good at Latin, but he's too shy to say so!"

Ferenc, his cheeks a bright scarlet, wished his sister would keep quiet, but help came from an unexpected source. The diplomatic Kollonitsch empathized with the lad's embarrassment and—determined to make each of his young guests feel good—said warmly, "I don't think your brother is shy, Sigismunda, only modest, which is a Christian virtue. I'm well aware that you are a good student, Ferenc, Brother Sebastian has told me so, and you should be proud of your progress. The church needs good minds, serious men devoted to study and contemplation!"

Sigismunda caught the gentle reprimand, and Ferenc gave his uncle a grateful look. The cardinal had won an admirer with his remark. Both Ferenc and Sigismunda were too occupied with their thoughts to pick up the phrase "the church needs."

Kollonitsch next turned to Michael who was busy with his third helping.

"And what do you like to do best, Michael?"

The boy swallowed and replied spontaneously, "I want to go home and be with Mama! I don't like the big city, and I don't like Latin! Mama needs me, and she promised I could come back to Zay-Ugrocz after a year!"

The other three held their breath, but Kollonitsch remained friendly, though the warmth of a moment ago was missing in his voice as he said, "I'm sorry that you don't like Vienna, Michael, but I think you may change your mind as time goes by. I don't know what your mother promised you, but as you all know, she no longer owns Zay-Ugrocz, so you could not possibly live there with her. She is still with your uncle and aunt, and there's no place for you in their home at this time. But then let's not discuss unpleasant things this festive and holy day, but trust in the Lord, who will guide us and give us the strength to cope with whatever the future brings! Vienna is a famously beautiful city and our cathedral one of the most revered in Christendom. Tomorrow is the feast of St. Stephen, the church's first martyr, which will be celebrated by a special Mass. Also there will not be any lessons until after New Year's Day, and you may suggest to Sister Constanze and Brother Sebastian how you would like to spend your free time, and they will help you. With the beginning of the New Year, you will need to study extra hard, for I have great plans for you. Now about the Cathedral's history."

He proceeded to tell them how the citizens of twelfth century Vienna had resolved to build the greatest church in the world and how for centuries thereafter every man, woman, and child made great sacrifices of money and time.

The youngsters had never seen their guardian so relaxed and friendly and buoyed by the excellent meal enjoyed the time in his presence. After the plates were cleared, Sister Genevieve brought trays with small sweet cakes and bowls with preserves, and when Tessa asked permission to bring some to the ayah, the nun said they would find more treats to share with her in their rooms. Returning there later, they felt more content than at any time since leaving Transylvania and, in spite of a little homesickness, were proud that they had lived up to their stern guardian's expectations. They shared their experience with the ayah who heaved a silent prayer of thanks that everything had gone well. She'd had a good meal with the servants in the kitchen and indeed was handed a large platter of sweet treats to take upstairs, though Michael was the only one who kept on eating. It wasn't long until nature took its course; they'd been up the better part of the previous night, and the heavy meal left them drowsy. They settled down to read but quickly dozed off, and the ayah covered them with blankets, wrapped herself in a warm shawl, and listened to their even breathing. She'd wake them in time for Evensong. The lack of any message from the Vienna Trauttmansdorffs deeply saddened and convinced her that there was little hope they'd ever establish contact. The old woman had a good notion of what the future held and had prayed long and hard that the youngsters would be given a choice but whether they did solely depended on family assistance. She couldn't understand why Maximilian's brothers would disassociate themselves so completely from their nephews and nieces and attributed this attitude to their wives' influence. Perhaps, the countess had never told her husband about her visit in the fall. The old count likely was too frail and forgetful to remember that he had grandchildren in dire need of a helping hand. There was nothing the ayah could do except pray that God would watch over them.

They enjoyed the holiday from lessons, and only Tessa anxiously looked forward to resume her studies with Sister Agnes. She faithfully practiced her scales, much to the dismay of Michael, who missed no chance to tease her, sometimes in a mean way. The boy felt like a spiritual outcast among his siblings. He resented the fact that they apparently enjoyed their studies, especially Tessa and her singing. With little to occupy his mind, there was nothing to compensate for the loss of his easy life, and as a consequence, he also was more homesick than the others. Of course, they all missed Transylvania and the freedom and comfort of home. Most of all, they missed their late father. Ferenc and Sigismunda channeled their energies into subjects such as Latin and theology. That they were subjected to strictly Catholic training no longer disturbed them. It was Sigismunda's nature to be dedicated to whatever task she embraced. Her reasonable mind appreciated that certain aspects of the catechism were logical, such as the tradition of recognizing the pope as legitimate head of the church because Christ Himself had explicitly appointed Simon Peter as such. The deeply pious Brother Sebastian was a good teacher who easily answered her objections to the practice of indulgences, one of the factors leading to the Reformation movement. He argued that it was only natural that people wanted to alleviate the suffering of loved ones in purgatory by making sacrifices on their behalf, which they perceived as giving money to the church. Without such donations, there would have been no Sistine Chapel, nor the magnificent sculptures Pope Julius II commissioned Michelangelo to create, why, even the greatest church in Christendom, St. Peter's, might never have been built! But in the end, the mysteriously beautiful and elaborate ceremonies of the Catholic Church cast the greatest spell. Even the small chapel with its beautiful golden statues made any Protestant Church feel cold and impersonal by comparison. Moreover, they instinctively knew that survival depended on their adjustment.

From a religious aspect, Tessa suffered least. She'd been interested in the Catholic Church for years, a fascination suppressed only by necessity. She also was at an age when a young mind tends to dedicate itself with passion to whatever catches the imagination. Their always sheltered lives had become even more so, they knew so little about what the world had to offer! Their sense of security cruelly shaken by the loss of their favorite parent, they felt expelled from home, forsaken by their mother. The initially resented uncle became an anchor of stability, and while they did not love and almost feared him, they respected his fairness and apparent wisdom and knew that obeisance to him was their only option. And if this meant conversion to Catholicism, so be it! Ferenc and Sigismunda now viewed the differences between Protestantism and Catholicism as rather circumstantial and mainly philosophical. Both creeds were based on the Bible and Jesus Christ, the Redeemer. After all, Catholicism was the faith of their beloved papa and should have been theirs from birth had not their mother broken a solemn promise, a step she'd justified with wishing to save them from the spell of an arrogant and pompous clergy. In spite of often professing her desire to preserve their minds in the purity of the Protestant faith, she had not hesitated to "forsake" them to the care of a cardinal! How could she feel so deeply about Protestantism and decide on such a course of action? These were the thoughts of Ferenc and Sigismunda; Michael did not trouble himself with anything beyond the immediate present, and Tessa had long ago felt rejected by her mother.

The days between Christmas and the New Year brought beautiful winter weather, and Sebastian took them on sleigh rides to the outskirts of the city, which they thoroughly enjoyed. They had not set foot beyond the fortifications since their arrival and seen little of Vienna other than the route between palace and cathedral and a couple of parks. Brother Sebastian was a knowledgeable guide and enjoyed being with them. He appreciated the importance of winning their goodwill, perhaps even some degree of affection. The cardinal expected him to have them fully conversant with catechism and possess a solid knowledge of Latin by Easter, and there was still an extensive curriculum to cover prior to their formal conversion.

Until then, they had not really appreciated the gracious beauty of Vienna, overwhelmed as they were by the hectic bustle of many people crowded together. The tall buildings had awed and street noise repelled them. There was the clattering of horses' hooves and rattling wheels of elegant carriages, hand-drawn carts or wheelbarrows on the cobblestones, shrill female voices marketing goods, coachmen shouting commands, and people carrying on loud conversations. It was too abrupt a contrast to their accustomed life in the country. The bustling and noise prevented them from becoming aware of the city's exquisite architecture. Vienna had undergone a striking transformation and become a truly beautiful place after the death and destruction caused by the great siege of 1683. When the Turks arrived at her gates to threaten the town's existence and in effect Western culture, Vienna had barely recovered from a horrible bout with the plague a few years before. But the people's heroism and endurance during the summer of 1683 against an enemy outnumbering them tenfold prevailed, albeit in the end with the help of a hastily assembled relief army, joined by every European sovereign except Louis XIV of

France. Even this army was less than half the size of the one under the command of Grand Vizier Kara Mustapha, yet the intruders were decisively defeated and their leader killed. Vienna, Europe's most important eastern bastion, was saved. And when shortly thereafter the Turks were finally expelled from Hungarian territory they had occupied for a century and a half, nothing could suppress Viennese energy and exuberance. From ashes of destroyed medieval houses rose six- and seven-story buildings with exquisite baroque façades. Space was at a premium, so construction had only one way to go—up—and when there was no more room in the inner city, sections of the fortifications were torn down to allow for expansion. Peripheral settlements destroyed by the enemy rose again. It became safe to live outside the walls, though a ring of open space, referred to as the "glacis" (smooth area), was preserved vacant between fortifications and new construction so as to facilitate defense in case of a future enemy. Beyond the glacis, the local aristocracy built a string of magnificent private palaces seldom equaled elsewhere in Europe. During the decade following the siege, Vienna endured yet another albeit briefer and less devastating outbreak of the plague. Emperor Charles VI, Maria Theresa's father, vowed to build a large church, and the following year laid the cornerstone. The project took more than twenty years to complete and became known as "Karlskirche" (Charles's Church), the only one in Vienna in pure baroque. A first glimpse reminded the children of St. Peter's in Rome, which they knew from a drawing that Brother Sebastian had shown them. The Karlskirche, they felt, almost didn't look like a church when they first laid eyes on it across a large open square. A huge cupola topped the main structure, and the lower façade resembled a temple with Greek columns and arched side wings. Two tall, freestanding obelisks replaced steeples. Their astonishment increased viewing the interior. The opulent, colorful, downright cheerful and happy ambience of this place of worship was in stark contrast to the Gothic mysticism of St. Stephen. They'd never visited a baroque church before and felt it conveyed none of the piety inherent in the gothic style. Bright light streaming through large clear windows added life to the colorful paintings and frescoes, figures that seemed to move and sing God's glory and burst with exuberant joy. Their praise to the Almighty was not in awe and fear but joyful and without inhibition.

Another excursion brought them to Belvedere Palace, summer residence of the late Prince Eugene, Austria's arguably greatest general and strategist. As a young man and fugitive from his native France, the prince fought in the relief army against the Turks and subsequently rose to lofty heights in Austrian military service. His monarch rewarded him generously for his great victories, and Eugene, a lifelong bachelor, spent lavishly on exquisite buildings, collections of objects d'art and especially priceless books that would later become the core of the Austrian National Library. Belvedere Palace was built at the turn of the sixteenth century on a slope just beyond the glacis overlooking Vienna, designed and executed by the city's foremost architects. The youngsters were especially captivated by the magnificent formal gardens between the two main buildings, known as "upper" and "lower" Belvedere, and spent joyful hours trudging along the paths between snow-covered, meticulously trimmed hedges and mythical figures carved of stone.

On New Year's Day 1744, Kollonitsch received them in his library and informed them of his goal: Easter would be celebrated in mid-April that year, at which time they were expected to formally convert and be accepted into the Catholic Church, provided they passed their examinations. He left no doubt that failing to do so would have serious consequences, though he did not elaborate as to what these might be, nor did he tell them what his intentions were after that date. They knew better than to ask. Michael could only think of more boring studies, especially Latin, but hoped it would be just another hurdle until his return to Mama in the summer, and he wondered how he would hide from her being Catholic. The others harbored no illusions about returning to Transylvania. Ferenc and Sigismunda still hoped to attend institutions of higher learning; the boy wanted to study philosophy, the girl to become a teacher, and Tessa's dreams were fixated on singing. All were anxious for Michael not to fall behind and especially Sigismunda did her best to help him along, a constant challenge to her talents and patience. She blithely ignored her younger brother's pouting excuses and spent her leisure time tutoring and helping him with his assignments.

Their daily routine became even more rigorous in the New Year and left them with little free time. Outings again were limited to the weekly pilgrimage to St. Stephen's for High Mass and, weather permitting, a Sunday afternoon walk in a park or visit to a different church. During the week, their days were consumed by church services, lessons, meals, and more studies—except for a couple of hours—which Tessa devoted to her music lessons and practicing her assignments. The singing lessons saved her from getting into trouble. Sister Agnes was an ideal teacher who recognized talent and knew how to direct her student's passion and energy. Back home, the mischievous girl had often played practical jokes on her siblings or the servants. Vienna's tightly controlled environment allowed no leeway for practical jokes, but Tessa had a vivid imagination and often dreamed up little schemes that the ayah usually anticipated and managed to diffuse. Then Tessa would pout at her, convinced that she'd never have been found out, but the old woman knew better and feared that discovery would suspend musical studies and precipitate another passionate scene.

Sister Agnes suspected an insecure and somewhat unstable personality and feared that these did not bear well for the cardinal's plans. Tessa's temperament could be provoked by failing to meet her own expectations; she'd turn red, furiously stamp her foot and become deaf to reason. When this happened, sister would immediately interrupt the lesson and ask her to kneel before the cross. Tessa would shake and weep and clench her teeth while the nun kept a firm hand on her shoulder and recited prayers. It took time, but sister always succeeded, and when the girl finally calmed down, Agnes spoke firmly but without anger, "Tessa, you must learn to control yourself. If you do not, I shall have to speak to His Eminence, and it will mean the end of your music studies. An angry voice cannot be beautiful! And I refuse to teach you if you behave like a naughty child. Rather would I spend my time praying for your soul!"

Her words always had the desired effect on Tessa, who found it so difficult to apologize and loathed to admit wrongdoing but readily asked the nun's forgiveness and beg for more lessons. Sister often took the weeping child into her arms and allowed her to find relief crying on her shoulder. As a young child, Tessa had gone through many tantrums in the ayah's arms and knew herself that her outbreaks were immature and childish. They made her ashamed of herself, yet there were times when she simply lost control. She had become genuinely fond of Agnes and hoped that the nun would not tell anyone about these scenes. Her instinct was correct. Tessa's talent had initially just roused the nun's interest, but as time went by, she developed motherly feelings and an understanding for the loneliness of the girl. Sister Agnes knew how much music meant to her student and did not intend to share behavior problems with the cardinal. Trying to stimulate Tessa's enthusiasm and perhaps to demonstrate her teaching success at the same time, she thought of another incentive. March 25 was the Feast of the Annunciation, and sister told Tessa that if she continued with her progress, she'd allow her to sing the "Salve Regina" during that day's special Mass. The girl was ecstatic and devoted herself with even more passion to her studies. What the ayah taught her long ago was not quite the correct version of the chant, and she discovered that it was more difficult to relearn something than to study a new piece. Agnes was continuously amazed how eminently suitable the girl's voice was for the Gregorian chant, how exquisite her timbre in the lower keys. Studying Latin had improved her comprehension and diction and imbued her singing with a sincere piety that sister hoped sprang from devotion, not just musical talent and the desire to do well. Again, she wished Tessa's performance to be a surprise and invited her to practice in her cell. The gesture delighted her pupil who, like all children, loved surprises and that way also escaped Michael's teasing.

And Tessa excelled. She sat with her siblings during Mass on Annunciation Day until just before Communion then quietly slipped away to tiptoe up the narrow stairs to the organ loft. Sister Agnes motioned her to begin, and this time, the organ remained silent as Tessa sang with tender fervor. A mesmerizing tension descended upon the chapel as if everyone held their breath not to miss a single note. The ayah's cheeks became wet with tears of pride and happiness and she thanked God for allowing her to see this day.

Tessa was elated as never before. Her frustrations, homesickness, even Transylvania were forgotten as she concentrated on the chant, eyes focused upon the statue of Mary in the nave below, and in her heart, she spoke directly to the gentle Virgin. When the prayer's final words—"Oh merciful, oh pious, oh sweet Virgin Maria"—resonated through the chapel with loving piety, she touched every heart in the audience, and the faces of nuns and monks on the choir reflected their admiration. Sister Agnes put an arm round her.

"You've done very well, child," she whispered, and Tessa saw a tear in the nun's eye. She barely heard the final prayers and the concluding hymn. Nor did she rush down the circular stairs as she had at Christmas. An emotion never before felt filled her heart, and she longed for it to stay, afraid that it would vanish if she moved. Finally, Sister Agnes took her hand.

"Come, Tessa, it's time to leave," she said and gently led her away.

Chapter 5

Their formal examination prior to being accepted into the church took place the day before Palm Sunday. Kollonitsch personally conducted it in his library, and though the two older ones wouldn't admit it, they were all pretty nervous. Sigismunda worried about Michael because her family pride did not want to see him disgrace himself. She'd mercilessly drilled her younger brother and ignored his sulking resentment. Michael really didn't care much what his esteemed uncle thought of him. As soon as he was back in Transylvania, he'd be a Protestant again anyway, if only to please his mother.

Their dutifully penned letters to her became increasingly formal over time. Aware of her distaste for the Catholic Church, they decided it was wiser not to mention the pending conversion. Ferenc and Sigismunda no longer objected to changing their faith, resigned that they likely would remain in a predominantly Catholic country ruled by a devoutly Catholic monarch. They had discovered that many of the negative things Miczike had said about Catholicism and the clergy were untrue or at least highly exaggerated. The formal solemnity of Catholic ceremonies, the splendid vestments of the cleric, and the mysterious lure of the richly decorated churches enraptured their young minds, and the timelessly beautiful prayers of Mass won their hearts. The constancy of these prayers conveyed to them a feeling of permanence and soothing continuity after the cruel interruption of their lives. Studying Latin with its perfectly structured grammar helped them appreciate the wisdom and beauty of the Mass, its profundity and eternal meaning. They knew that religion was based on faith, and that faith rested on mystery. Protestant services, of course, were also based on faith in God and Christ but practiced in the cool brightness of an austere church and by a pastor with little emotion and a penchant toward moral philosophy fell far short of a solemn Mass! Had not their papa steadfastly refused to convert, much as Mama had pressured him? He'd adhered to his faith and always been the more admired parent. They had long discussions on the subject and became convinced that he would have wanted them to convert and thereby offer him a gift of love, perhaps even help him attain eternal bliss. They prayed for him daily at Mass during the part when the church remembers the dead but rarely remembered Miczike during prayers for the living.

Kollonitsch questioned them thoroughly and was pleased with their understanding and detailed knowledge of catechism and structure and history of the church. Brother Sebastian had discharged his tutorial duties very well indeed! The cardinal was well aware of Michael's shortcomings and lack of scholarly interest but did not intend to exclude him from his plans and consequently gave him the easiest questions. Michael still missed out on a couple, but the cardinal declared himself satisfied, and all four breathed a sigh of relief.

Their official conversion would occur on Easter Sunday, and they were told to prepare themselves during Holy Week for the sacrament of reconciliation—their first confession. Only after formal absolution from their sins could they complete their conversion by receiving the Eucharist.

Confessing sins orally to a priest had been the subject of Miczike's particular scorn. How could some cleric presume to sit in judgment over anyone? One should confess to God and to Him alone! Only He could look into one's heart and forgive transgressions. Tessa, with her dislike of apologies, was perhaps the most skeptical, and Brother Sebastian devoted special attention and empathy toward convincing these young Protestants of the necessity to orally confess their sins. In the New Testament, Christ gave His apostles the discretion and power to absolve from sin with the words, "Those, whose sins you forgive, they shall be forgiven, and those you retain, they shall be retained." As mere humans unable to read thoughts and look into hearts, how

117

could the apostles exercise this power without being told what sins had been committed? To be absolved from past transgressions was an infinite grace, and to formulate sins into words and actually say them to a priest was part of penance. It called for a much more thorough examination of the mind than just sitting in church and telling God that one had sinned. Also priests imposed a formal penance, a small price to pay for forgiveness! The four understood the argument but anticipated their first confession with great trepidation just the same. Unlike young Catholic children at their first confession, when sins consisted of an occasional lie or other insignificant mischief, they had to examine many years of conscience. They hadn't committed any mortal sins, but the church was strict and considered many of the transgressions young adolescents commit as serious. Tessa was conscious of her lack of temper control and penchant for mischievous pranks and was troubled about the required resolve to avoid these in the future. What if she was not able to do that!

They were much relieved when Brother Sebastian explained that the priest hearing their confession at St. Stephen's on Good Friday would be a stranger and that he could not see their faces in the confessional. He also instructed them to state their age and explain that it was their first confession due to being raised Protestant. Still the idea was intimidating, and they lived in fear of Good Friday. Brother Sebastian asked them to seek quiet contemplation in the chapel and time and again went over the Ten Commandments, the seven deadly sins, and the laws of the church. Ferenc and Sigismunda had no trouble pinpointing their transgressions; Michael cared little and picked what sounded easiest to admit, without wasting much thought to explore his faults and shortcomings. Tessa truly suffered. She had convinced herself that the chance for continued voice training depended on a perfect confession and worthy conversion. The more she meditated, the more "sins" she felt she had committed. The practical jokes played on her siblings, the lies told her mother to avoid punishment, the temper she could not control, the harsh words she was apt to say when angry—notably to her siblings and the ayah—all weighed heavily upon her. What if the priest would not grant her absolution because she was too great a sinner? What if he emerged from the confessional to announce to one and all that this girl was not worthy to become a Catholic? Would the cardinal show her the door, and was she to beg in the streets of Vienna like the women dressed in rags and huddled in the doorways? Even the regimented life in this stern household was preferable to such an existence! If only she would be forgiven for her terrible transgressions, she promised herself never to rebel again! She was so consumed by fear that she was inattentive during her music lesson with Sister Agnes on Wednesday of Holy Week. When the nun asked her to concentrate, she started to shake and broke into tears. It took a little prodding, but Tessa finally admitted that she lived in fear of being refused absolution. The wise Agnes interrupted the lesson and spoke to her pupil like a mother, explaining that Christ had sacrificed Himself on the cross so that sins would be forgiven, even serious crimes, provided the sinner repented and resolved not to sin again.

"But that's just why I'm so afraid," said Tessa. "I'm not truly sorry that I don't love my mama or that I get angry so much! How can I make myself love her as I should, and how can I be sure I'll never be angry again?"

"You can't," replied the nun. "None of us can be sure we won't sin again, for deep down, we know that we're far from perfect. But we can concentrate on our most serious faults and resolve to become better people, and that is what Christ expects from us. He knows our frail mind and how easy it is for the devil to tempt us. Tessa, the Lord gave you a unique gift, the gift of your voice with which to praise Him. Thank Him for this gift every day of your life, and remember that He has the power to take it away also. So be worthy of your talent and raise your voice to His glory! And pray, child, pray that you may be accepted into the true church!"

Her tender voice calmed the girl's fears. "We'll continue with our lessons after Easter," Sister continued. "Now go to the chapel and think of what I have said. Pray and recite the psalm of the Merciful God Brother Sebastian taught you. I'll be rejoicing on Sunday when you and your sister and brothers affirm your faith and receive communion for the first time."

Tessa spontaneously reached for the nun's hand to kiss. "Thank you, Sister Agnes," she whispered. "Thank you and I do so love you!"

The quiet chapel had a mournful ambience with statues and paintings shrouded in black for Holy Week, reminding Tessa of the black draping at Zay-Ugrocz after Papa's death, and a new fear grasped her—the fear of death. A shiver ran down her spine, but thinking of her father brought peace. She felt his love surrounding her and remembered the priest at Zay-Ugrocz after the funeral saying that he was in heaven. Surely, Papa would put in a good word for her now that she was about to embrace the true faith!

Good Friday was a day of fasting and praying; only one meager meal was served at midday—water and plain bread morning and evening. After breakfast, they were allowed to spend quiet time in their rooms. Sigismunda had gone to help Sister Constanze with a chore, and Tessa sat at her favorite place on the wide windowsill that seemed smaller because she had grown quite a bit during the past months. She pulled her knees toward the chin and was lost in thought gazing across rooftops under a gray and overcast sky when she heard a deep sigh and whimpering sounds. The ayah had been sitting in a corner doing needlework but now was crumpled over. The girl rushed to her side.

"Ayah, what is it, are you ill?" she cried, wrapping her arms round the thin old body. It took a few moments until the old woman could answer.

"No, love," she finally gasped. "I have a cough, and it's been hurting my chest a bit, but it's getting better, and I'll be just fine!" Her contorted features belied her words and failed to alleviate Tessa's concerns. She knelt down beside the chair and held the bony old hands in hers.

"Ayah, I didn't know you were sick! Did you talk to Sister Constanze and ask for herb tea? You know how clever she is with medicines!"

The ayah shook her head. She was afraid her frailty might render her useless and bring her dismissal but wouldn't admit such fears to the youngsters.

"It's nothing, Tessa, just a bad moment, and I'm better already! Would you fetch me a little water for my scratchy throat, dear? And you all have to get ready for the service in the cathedral. I think I'll rest a bit. I might cough in church and disturb everyone, so I'll stay right here. Just remember to make a good confession and see how good it feels when your sins are forgiven!"

It took her a great effort to talk that much, and she tried to distract Tessa, though the girl noticed that the ayah had to gasp for breath between words, and she suddenly realized how thin and wrinkled the old woman had become in recent months. She'd never seen her sick and could not imagine life without her. She rushed down to the kitchen for water, and when she returned, the ayah had stretched out on her narrow cot and appeared to be breathing evenly. She sipped a little from the beaker held to her lips and urged Tessa to remind her brothers in the next room that it was time to leave and not to mention a word of her illness to anyone. The girl put a blanket over her and, feeling the ayah's ice-cold hands, went to fetch another cover from her own bed.

"You rest and sleep, dear ayah," she whispered, kissing the lined forehead. She heard her brothers' footsteps and quickly joined them. Sigismunda was waiting for them.

"Where's ayah?" she wanted to know.

"She's resting," said Tessa. "Her gout is pretty bad, and she's afraid she can't keep up with us on the way."

"But it's early," Michael protested. "We have lots of time, and I want her along, I'm scared!"

Something in Tessa's voice had alerted Sigismunda. "Well, you're a big boy, Michael, and you'll just have to learn to get along without being nursed and cuddled all the time," she said in a matter-of-fact voice.

Brother Sebastian appeared, and they went on their way. The city was unusually quiet. No church bells rang—legend has it that their souls traveled to Rome on Good Friday for renewal. No beggars were in the streets, no musicians at the corners with fiddle or music box. The cathedral was silent and dark with statues and altars shrouded in black and the nave immersed in semidarkness. All of Vienna's prominent clergy was in attendance as the archbishop conducted a somber service commemorating Christ's death on the cross. It culminated in the congregation one by one approaching the altar to kiss the feet of a large crucifix held by a priest. Then the dreaded moment arrived when Sebastian led them toward one of the confessionals located in a side nave. Sigismunda bravely went first, Ferenc followed, then Tessa and Michael was last. Brother Sebastian remained by his side, or he might have ducked and later pretended he'd visited another confessional.

They did not know that Brother Sebastian had briefed the priest about their circumstances and were much relieved to find compassion and understanding, albeit paired with a stern admonition to mend their ways. Afterward, they knelt together in a pew to say their penance of several rosaries. But their knees barely felt the hard wood, and the somber church was less intimidating than before, though they weren't sure what made them happier—being absolved of their sins or having brought the dreaded moment behind them! They instinctively felt that each one had come through well and that this most feared aspect of becoming Catholic had not turned out as terrible as imagined. Their father confessor had not berated them for being Protestants as expected. The wise old priest knew of the archbishop's plans for these young candidates for conversion and did not intend to plant fear into their young minds.

On their way up the stairs, Tessa whispered to Sigismunda that the ayah had felt quite ill and the girls tiptoed into their room. They found the old woman peacefully asleep and her features no longer distorted in pain. And next morning, she woke them with a smile and again seemed her old self.

Fasting on Saturday was less stringent than on Good Friday but continued until resurrection was celebrated at dawn Easter Sunday. They were served fragrant, freshly baked white bread and milk and eagerly devoured the thick slices piled in a basket. Tessa and Sigismunda each brought their second slice to the ayah who'd remained upstairs saying she had to tidy their rooms. In reality, she was afraid that her painfully slow movements and frequent rests between minor chores would attract unwanted attention. The old woman felt her life nearing its end. Concern for the four youngsters had sustained her, for who would look after them when she was gone?

They were still children in need of loving care, and she'd lost hope that such love would ever come from the Vienna relatives. Perhaps, she could make one more effort to see Count Franz personally and move his heart. Being a devout Catholic, she received the sacraments regularly and was at peace with herself. Each day, she asked God to take care of her charges, but motherly instinct told her that they needed a loving heart in this world.

Later, the four enjoyed themselves in the garden, where budding trees and green tips of plantings breaking through the soil announced the first signs of spring. That was when it happened. The ayah felt a sharp pain in her chest and suddenly could not breathe. Sensing that the end was near, she did not even try to reach the door or call for help but, with a prayer on her lips, released the grip on a chair and let her slight body sink onto the floor.

"Dear God, don't let the kids find me," was her last thought, and a merciful God listened. Having missed her at breakfast, Sister Constanze came to investigate and found her lying on the floor with no heartbeat. She summoned servants to carry the slight body into the vestry adjoining the chapel. The nun was well aware how attached the children were to their ayah and felt deeply saddened that this should happen the day before their formal entrance into the Catholic Church, which was to be a day of celebration and joy. Kollonitsch was in the library when she told him, and relieved not having to convey the sad news, she went to the courtyard to summon them. Only Sigismunda caught the grave expression on her face and wondered what had happened. Kollonitsch rose when they entered and, contrary to his usual demeanor, met them halfway across the room.

"Tomorrow," he said, "will mark your formal acceptance into the true church. You have studied hard for that day, and I trust have made good confessions and done your penance. Today, though, the Lord has deigned to test your new faith through a sad affliction, but I know you are strong at mind and heart and will submit to His will."

He hesitated and they sensed that he found it difficult to continue. They thought of their mother and that perhaps some terrible accident had befallen her, and they held their breath in fearful anticipation. After a pause, he added quietly, "God has called His servant, your ayah, to His side. She seems to have been overcome by a sudden illness and had passed on when she was discovered in your room a short while ago."

Tessa's gasp broke the silence. "No!" she cried. "It can't be! Where is she?"

The girl made a sudden move as if she wanted to run from the room, but Kollonitsch took her arm, gently pulled her toward him, and held her to his chest. With his other arm, he drew the others close, a gesture they had never before experienced from him. And all four became but children clinging to a father figure in distress. The last link to their childhood was gone, and they would have to face whatever fate held for them alone. Ferenc and Michael tried to be brave, a deeply moved Sigismunda forced back her tears, and Tessa seemed in shock. Her body was trembling, but the cardinal's strong arm around her shoulder felt like Papa holding her during one of her many passionate moments of real or perceived grief. There was nothing the cardinal could have done or said that helped them more than his spontaneous and simple embrace revealing empathy and human warmth.

After a long silence, he released them and said quietly, "Let us now all go and pray for her soul. Death is but a step toward heaven, and your ayah died in the state of grace. The more fervent our prayers, the more merciful Christ's judgment of her will be!"

They followed him in dazed silence into the chapel, where an afternoon sun filled the nave with gentle light. It was as if God told them that He was opening His heaven to receive their loved one and Sigismunda, who'd worried about the faithful old servant's future once they no longer lived in their uncle's residence, thought that perhaps God had been merciful to take her at this time.

They could barely eat their sparse evening meal and immediately afterward went to their rooms, where their composure gave way and tears began to flow. The older ones wept quietly, Michael and Tessa cried bitterly. The ayah had been the most constant presence in their young lives; she'd held them in her arms from the moment they were born and with unfailing, loving kindness dealt with their laughter as well as their tears. No matter what they did, she never lost patience, listened to the joys and sorrows of their young lives, and surrounded them with a motherly love their mama failed to give them.

It was a sad night, and after a brief and exhausted sleep, they woke in a somber mood. The ayah's absence was felt beyond her kind and encouraging words each new day, her gentle reminders that it was time to get ready. No warm water waited in the large pitchers, no clothes were laid out. All their lives they'd taken such services for granted, and even Sigismunda was unprepared. She persuaded Ferenc to fetch the water while she busied herself preparing their clothes. The cardinal had ordered new outfits for the occasion, and they had looked forward to wearing them. The materials were of fine quality, but the girls' clothes were plain, and they had been a little disappointed, having hoped for something other than austere gray dresses, which made Sigismunda look even more pale and did little for Columba's brunette looks. That morning, though, it made no difference, exhausted as they were from lack of sleep, eyes red and swollen from many tears. Without the helping hand of their beloved nurse, they moved aimlessly until the practical Sigismunda took charge, but even she had trouble collecting her thoughts. She helped her confused sister, ordered a sleepy Michael to wash and get ready, and then quickly twisted her blonde hair into the usual neat bun. Only a couple of days earlier, the ayah had come up with a blue silk ribbon, and the sisters' eyes filled with tears when Sigismunda braided it into Tessa's brown locks. Ferenc helped Michael, and they hurried downstairs and into the chapel. Prior to the solemn Mass of resurrection, they stood before their uncle at the altar rail to formally recite the creed. He asked them to forever forsake the devil and affirm that their conversion was voluntary, after which he baptized and welcomed them into the church. They were to receive their first Holy Communion from the hands of the archbishop during High Mass at St. Stephen's. Kollonitsch wished it so to forever impress upon them the great importance and solemnity of the occasion. On their way to the cathedral, they were all very hungry after fasting for the better part of three days. Brother Sebastian had explained that abstaining from food was but small suffering compared with what Christ had endured for them on the cross. Now that they were Catholics, they'd have to accept that fasting was repeatedly required during the church year. The monk never noticed that Michael fell slightly behind and chewed little bites from a piece of hard bread he'd saved earlier in the week. Moments before they went to the chapel, he remembered retrieving it to put into a pocket of his new trousers. He knew he was supposed to fast prior to receiving communion and was oblivious of the embarrassment it would have caused his uncle and siblings if he were caught. To Michael, it was now Easter Sunday, Christ had risen, and he had been deprived of food long enough; the transgression did not bother his conscience.

The ayah's death dominated their minds during the solemn yet jubilant Easter service. Tessa found consolation in the beautiful organ music and the soaring voices of the cathedral choir. She and her siblings were seated in a front pew, and when it was time for communion, Brother Sebastian escorted them to the altar rail where they knelt to receive the host. In Latin, they recited the words an ordinary man spoke to Christ as He came to heal his young daughter: "Lord, I am not worthy that you should enter under my roof, say but the word and my soul will be healed."

Placing the wafer on their tongue, the archbishop responded, "May the body of our Lord Jesus Christ preserve you soul for eternal life, amen!"

Sigismunda could not help but recall the simple service at home when she and Ferenc had participated in communion for the first time. Ferenc wondered what Mama would say if she knew that her children had abandoned her faith. Michael suddenly feared that his snack might land him straight in hell, and Tessa's heart was with her Papa and the ayah, the two people she had loved most, who were now forever gone from her life. Only the beautiful music sustained her.

Kollonitsch joined the archbishop's table this Easter Sunday. Everyone at the palace had fasted during Lent and even more strictly since Good Friday. No wonder Sister Genevieve had prepared a very special meal to celebrate the joy of Easter Sunday. Following an old tradition, people ended the long fast by eating small portions from a basket of food that had been blessed in church. It contained bread, eggs, butter, ham, and horseradish, the only fresh vegetable available at that time of year and a traditional condiment eaten with ham. The idea behind the custom was that since everyone was very hungry at the end of the Lenten season, blessed fare would be consumed more slowly and thoughtfully. The daintily arranged foods were wrapped in white linen napkins and the baskets decorated with ribbons. Sister Genevieve distributed small portions onto their plates. After prayers and dutifully nibbling little bites, a festive meal of baked ham, pickled cabbage, fowl, and cooked eggs was served. There were loaves of soft white bread studded with raisins, called Easter stollen and a specialty of Genevieve's. For a brief hour, they forgot their grief and indulged in the hearty meal. Sebastian and Constanze had planned to eat with their congregations that day but had decided not to leave the youngsters alone in the hope that joining them would be a distraction from their grief. Easter Sunday, the day of Christ's resurrection that fulfilled His promise of redemption from sin, was not a time to be overshadowed by death. They were chatting about Viennese Easter traditions when during a brief silence Tessa said, "Where did you take our ayah, and can we say goodbye to her before she is buried?"

Constanze had anticipated the question. "Of course, you may, child. There can be no burials during Easter, and as you know, Easter Monday is also a holiday. I've not been told of the arrangements, but her body has been placed into the vestry where you may visit."

And so after the meal, a subdued little party headed for the vestry, where candles flickered by an open coffin. Death was no longer unfamiliar after having mourned their papa, but the count had been in the prime of his life and appeared more like sleeping, whereas the old ayah looked strangely unfamiliar. Until then, they had barely noticed her age because her plain face and kind eyes were always brightened by a smile. Now these same features had a bluish-gray color and the deep lines set in an expression of suffering and grief. Her closed eyes had sunken deep into the sockets, and the thin lips pulled into a toothless mouth. They touched the bony hands that clutched a rosary, but the tender woman they'd loved all their lives had become a stranger in death. It was not the farewell they'd anticipated. Tessa began to shiver, and Michael expressed everyone's feelings, "I'm scared, let's leave."

No one objected, and they quietly climbed the stairs to their rooms. The ayah's clothes and few belongings were in a small trunk, and Sigismunda went through them to see whether there was anything they might want to keep. Other than a few well-worn garments, they found a frayed Bible and a missal with faded pictures of saints tucked between the pages. At the very bottom of the trunk was the black pompadour the ayah carried on special occasions. It felt heavy and revealed several gold pieces, apparently the savings of a lifetime of servitude. Sigismunda summoned her siblings and told them of her find. They had been without money ever since their arrival in Vienna, and while unsure of the coins' exact value, they knew that their discovery could be important. What to do? They suspected that if they disclosed their find, they might not be permitted to keep it, and since the ayah was without relatives, they decided that the money was theirs. Michael immediately suggested, "Let's use it to travel home to Mama!"

Sigismunda knew better. "You don't know how much such a long trip costs, Michael! Besides, Mama has not asked us to come home! And how could we ever leave here without being found out?"

Michael was not convinced, but the other two agreed.

"Let's think about it," the practical Sigismunda suggested. "In any case, don't anyone breathe a word about it, hear? If ayah had known that she was going to die, she would have given the money to us, and I think it belongs to us alone. Tell you what might be an idea. Now that we're all Catholics, perhaps, our relatives no longer despise us. Ayah said that the Trauttmansdorff Palace was not too far from here and one of the coins would surely pay for having us taken there. Perhaps, if we ourselves talk to Papa's brother, he'll change his mind and send us to school or even invite us to move in with his family."

They all thought it was a good idea but, after some discussion, decided that only one of them should embark on the mission. Well aware that they were not allowed to leave the confines of the palace without supervision, it was agreed that their levelheaded sister was best suited for the job and the absence of only one less likely to be discovered. They were excited about the plan and briefly forgot their grief as they focused on the opportunities that might open in their lives. Sigismunda carefully hid the little pouch under the girls' mattress.

Their chance presented itself the very next day, Easter Monday. Sister Constanze announced after the midday meal that they were free to enjoy the afternoon. The cardinal had been absent all day, monks and nuns joined their individual orders, and the servants had the day off.

"You'll have to guard the palace," the nun said jokingly, "but if you feel uneasy, you may bolt the side entrance since the portal remains locked as usual."

As soon as everything was quiet, Sigismunda took the smallest gold coin and slipped out to get on her way. Markets and shops were closed, and people in their Sunday best promenaded the streets. Sigismunda did not know the way and became aware that she was attracting some unwelcome attention walking alone in the streets. Empress Maria Theresa was a sternly virtuous woman and had appointed a "morality police" to spot unsavory elements, especially prostitutes. One of these agents promptly spotted the girl.

"Where're you headed, Mam'selle?" he asked.

Sigismunda mistook him for a guide and said rather haughtily, "I wish to visit my uncle, Count Trauttmansdorff, who lives in a palace by that name, but I'm new in the city and don't know the way! Can you take me there?"

She tried hard to appear confident, but the man knew that no young countess, especially not one with such a well-known family name, would be walking the streets of Vienna alone. Sigismunda reached into her pocket and showed him the coin. The man hesitated and thought hard. He did not believe the girl to be a noblewoman, more likely a young woman from out of town wanting to visit someone other than a family member in the count's household. He was on the lookout for women of ill repute, but the girl's clothes and looks did not fit that type of female. What was wrong with earning a generous reward for the small service of showing her the way to the palace? He'd disappear as soon as they had reached it, and the rest was up to her!

"Let me have it," he demanded, "and I'll take you there." But Sigismunda was cautious.

"When we've arrived at the Trauttmansdorff Palace," she said with all the aplomb she could muster. The man thought that her manner of speaking and demeanor were not those of a servant girl and decided to take the risk.

"Follow me," he grumbled, "but if you try to go back on your promise, you'll regret it!"

It turned out to be quite a distance, and Sigismunda paid careful attention to the streets through which they walked. She was sure that her relatives would provide a carriage for her return, but if no one were home, she'd have to find her own way back, having brought only one of the ayah's coins. Imre had pointed out in Budapest that aristocrats lived in "good" areas of the city that were distinctly different from those where common folk dwelled, and she was prepared to bolt if he were to take her to a shabby neighborhood. They finally turned into a wide street lined with trees, and the man stopped in front of an impressive mansion.

"That's the Trauttmansdorff Palace, but I'd knock at the servants' door down that alley if I were you! Now pay up!"

Sigismunda ignored his rough tone, too excited and happy to finally stand before the house in which her papa was raised. She handed the man the gold coin and barely noticed how quickly he disappeared.

She looked at the carved doors with their elegant, highly polished brass locks and decided that it might indeed be wiser to try the side door. Recalling their arrival at the cardinal's palace and aware that to gain access she had to convince whoever answered the door of her identity, humbleness seemed the better option. She walked down the alley and noticed the wall that surrounded a complex evidently much larger than the cardinal's. Even the side entrance was impressive, and after another moment's hesitation to gather her courage, she gave it a slight knock. There was no response. She knocked harder, but again, nothing happened. Sigismunda had not come that far to return without results, so she knocked again and again and, when her knuckles felt sore, used a fist to make more noise. She was not aware of approaching footsteps when the door suddenly opened to reveal an angry lackey in a brown-and-black uniform.

"The servants are all off this afternoon," he said gruffly, "and Mam'selle should be ashamed of herself for creating such a racket!"

The girl quickly recovered her composure and said in a tone in which she'd heard Mama exhort a domestic, "I am Sigismunda, Countess Trauttmansdorff, the eldest daughter of the late Count Maximilian. I'm here to see my uncle, the count. Kindly announce my visit!"

The lackey, who happened to be the count's personal valet, was vaguely familiar with the circumstances of his master's younger brother and had served nobility long enough to know that the young lady before him was not a servant.

"Wait," he said gruffly and—after a moment—added, "you may step into the hallway, Mam'selle, but stay there 'til I return!"

Sigismunda decided that the most important part was to get access, so she entered and patiently waited while the lackey disappeared. The man hadn't said whether her relatives were in town, but someone presumably was home or he wouldn't have asked her in.

He was gone for so long that Sigismunda wondered what happened when the lackey finally reappeared.

"The count will receive you in the orangery, Mam'selle," he said curtly. "But you better be who you say you are, or you'll be in lots of trouble!"

Sigismunda did not deign that remark worthy of a response and followed him across a wide and richly furnished hall with magnificent stucco moldings through a reception area and into the charming orangery, as the newly popular winter gardens were called. The bright room earned its designation from exotic plantings in large ceramic pots and several sets of tall French doors leading to a manicured garden. Sigismunda had never seen such a variety of unusual plants, especially orchids in bloom. Comfortable chairs of white cane with chintz cushions were grouped at small tables between the plants, but even though tired from the long walk, she did not dare sit down. She'd been taught from childhood that one did not sit in a stranger's home until invited to do so.

Minutes passed, the silence broken only by the slow ticking of an alabaster and ebony mantle clock in the adjoining reception room. There was no one in the garden, but then it was a cool overcast day. Would she get to meet her cousins? Sigismunda was not given to vivid imagination or wishful thinking, but unaware of what actually had transpired during the ayah's previous visit, she had thought that not hearing from her relatives was because they'd never really become aware of their arrival. Perhaps, Mama had been too embarrassed about giving up custody of her children to inform them, or they didn't know how to contact them. She was admiring the fragile beauty of an orchid when a voice behind her said, "Do not touch the petals or it will wilt!"

Turning around, she looked into the cool eyes of a tall man whose likeness to her father was unmistakable.

"Oh, Uncle Franz, you look so much like Papa!" she exclaimed. "I'm his eldest daughter Sigismunda. Perhaps, you didn't know that my brothers and sister have been in Vienna since last summer! We've been living with Mama's uncle, Cardinal Kollonitsch. And," she added, "we've become Catholics, all of us, this Easter. We're so anxious to meet you, dear uncle, and the countess, and our cousins, and—"

The usually withdrawn Sigismunda got carried away and would have continued chatting had not the count stopped her with a gesture. She'd taken a couple of steps toward him expecting him to embrace her, but he made no move.

"You may sit there," he said, pointing toward a small stool, while he settled himself into one of the comfortable armchairs. When she timidly sat down, he said, "I am well aware of the arrangements your mother made after my brother's death. She declared herself unable to care for you and made you exclusive charges of the cardinal, and you are indeed fortunate that His Eminence accepted you into his household. It is a great honor and privilege to live under the guardianship of so prominent an official of the church, and I hope that you are demonstrating your gratitude. I have no inclination to interfere with these arrangements and want you and your siblings to clearly understand that. I know that you were preparing yourselves to be accepted into the true church and for a spiritual life. His Eminence in fact has approached me for dowries appropriate for entrance into religious orders, and although I am under no obligation, I have agreed to make funds available for this purpose only. I'm sure that His Eminence, who by the way may soon succeed the ailing archbishop of Vienna, a very high honor indeed, had spoken to you about this matter. As far as my family is concerned, there is no desire to establish a relationship, which your mother ended once and for all when she broke her solemn promise and refused to raise you as Catholics. Indeed, your visit here is rather uncalled-for, but I'm willing to forgive the inconvenience because you seem ignorant of the circumstances. I presume your ayah persuaded you to come, although she had been clearly appraised of the situation when my wife received her several months ago. I shall complain to the cardinal about her lack of discretion!"

Sigismunda lost her composure, and her face revealed open shock.

"Our ayah died three days ago," she whispered and tears welled up in her eyes. "We're indeed grateful to His Eminence, but I thought that because of our poor papa—"

"Your father chose to break relations with our family when he reneged on his promise to raise you in the church," was the cool reply. "And now that you know the facts, I trust you will all act accordingly. My lackey says that you seem to have come by yourself, which I attribute to your ignorance that decent young women of standing do not walk alone through town. I shall, therefore, have my valet hire a guard to escort you back home. God be with you!"

With that, the count rose and stiffly walked from the room. The stunned Sigismunda had no time to recover as the valet immediately appeared and motioned her to follow him. Again, they crossed the splendid hall and walked down the corridor. An elderly man was already waiting outside, and the lackey handed him a small coin with instructions to escort the girl to the palace of Cardinal Kollonitsch.

Sigismunda suddenly felt mentally and physically exhausted. Mechanically setting one foot before the other, she could not comprehend that her mission had failed so sadly when she and her siblings had set so much hope into it. Papa had never spoken of his relatives with anything but great affection and respect, usually when Mama was not present, since she was not fond of the subject. He had never left any doubt that the girls would meet their uncles and aunts and cousins and would be introduced to Viennese society while the boys attended the military academy. Instead, her uncle treated her like an outcast he would not even touch. He even considered them unworthy of meeting his family!

Sigismunda could not control the tears running down her face. The loss of the motherly ayah and the cold rebuff by her uncle were more than she could bear. She had never had much hope to return home. During that long walk, Sigismunda forced herself to accept the cruel truth and wondered how to present it gently to her siblings. She knew she could talk to Ferenc but was afraid Tessa might make a scene and that it would be hard for Michael to accept that his dream of joining Mama remained one. Still how would even Ferenc take the news? Hopefully, she'd be able to sneak back into the palace and find a quiet minute to talk to him alone prior to facing the others.

She was in luck because Ferenc had been anxiously standing guard near the door, prepared for an excuse if anyone returned home and asked for his sister's whereabouts. The two younger ones were upstairs, tired from the emotional strain of the past two days. Ferenc was listening for horse's hooves on the cobblestones, expecting that his sister would return by carriage. Instead, the agreed signal of short knocks announced her, and he quickly opened the door. Not knowing whether anyone from the household had returned, Sigismunda put a finger on her lips. He turned to the staircase, but she motioned toward the garden, and the two hastily went there. After they had reached it, he noticed that Sigismunda was shivering in the damp cool air and that her eyes were red from tears.

"Let's go upstairs," he suggested. Sigismunda shook her head.

"I must talk to you first, Ferenc," she pleaded and he caught the urgency in her voice. With a sinking heart, he guessed that the outcome of her endeavor had not been good.

"Ferenc," began Sigismunda, "the Trauttmansdorffs don't want anything to do with us. I think they still have not forgiven our papa for marrying Mama and raising us Protestant. We have no one but

Kollonitsch to care for us in this world, and you know what? Uncle said that Kollonitsch has approached him for a 'dowry' for each of us to enter religious orders! Ferenc, do you want to become a monk?"

The young lad looked past his sister, his eyes focused on some distant point and his forehead furrowed in thought as he tried to work through what he'd just learned. After a few moments, he put his arm around Sigismunda's shoulders, looked into her eyes, and said calmly, "Yes, I think so, Sigismunda. I never wanted to be an officer. As you well know, I like a quiet life of study and contemplation, and I'm deeply impressed by Catholic philosophy and thinking. I don't know whether I'd make a good priest, but I might become a good monk. Tell me, dear, hasn't it occurred to you during the past months that this is what Kollonitsch had intended for us all along? But what about you? Do you object to becoming a nun?"

"I guess not," replied the girl slowly. "I know I'm not pretty and have no money and brains don't count much when it comes to finding a husband. And, Ferenc, I'd rather be a nun and teach children than be forced into a marriage with someone I couldn't love, and that's the truth! But Michael and Tessa? Can you imagine Michael as a monk or Tessa throwing one of her tantrums in a convent?"

Ferenc couldn't suppress a smile. "No, hardly, but they're both much too young for final vows, and perhaps, they'll not even be accepted into an order. I hate to think, though, what the alternative would be since from what you said, any financial support from the Trauttmannsdorff side will depend on it."

Sigismunda nodded and they sat silently for a few minutes.

"It's getting late", she finally said. "We must go upstairs and tell the others. How I wish I could rest awhile before having to do that! But they'll want to know. I'm really exhausted, so you've got to help me, most of all to keep them from making a big scene. God knows what might happen if Kollonitsch finds out I went there without his permission!"

On the way in, Ferenc offered a thought, "Tell you what. Let's not say anything about the religious order part for now, just talk about the fact that our future is in the hands of the cardinal because the Trauttmansdorffs haven't forgiven our parents and want no part of us. They'll find out soon enough about the rest. And you and I can discuss the other subject further when we're alone."

The tired Sigismunda was glad to be spared part of the anticipated ordeal and followed her brother upstairs where Michael and Tessa anxiously waited for her return. The two had chatted about what the immediate future might bring. Homesick Michael planned to ask his uncle for money to return to Transylvania and his beloved mama as quickly as possible and wasted little thought about whether his siblings might come along. After all, Mama had promised only him!

Tessa anticipated talking with the cousins about music and her singing, but she also nurtured other hopes. Papa had described the hunting lodge his family owned in Styria and how he had roamed the grounds there as a child. And what the girl had been missing most was walking through woods or sitting in a meadow listening to birds and watching clouds. Papa had often said that the countryside in Styria was very similar to that of Transylvania.

When Sigismunda and Ferenc entered, the two younger ones jumped up and in their excitement failed to notice their sister's red eyes and tired face. Sigismunda, after all, always looked pale and a little tired! They brimmed with questions and allowed no time for answers. When would they move in with Uncle Franz and his family? Was it a large palace, and did it have a big garden? And what were their cousins like? Sigismunda quietly shook her head to each question and finally took Tessa's hand while Ferenc pulled Michael close. There was a sudden silence into which Michael said tentatively, "They weren't home! But we've got money, and you can go back in a few days!"

"No, Michael," Sigismunda answered. "I saw Uncle Franz, but we won't be meeting any of them. Mama has 'given' us to the cardinal, and they don't wish to interfere. They just don't want to become involved with us. I'm sorry to have to tell you this, but that's the way it is, and we better make the best of what we have here. By the way, Kollonitsch may soon become archbishop of Vienna, which as you know is a very high honor, and we may all move into the archbishop's palace by St. Stephen's Cathedral. Won't that be exciting?"

Sigismunda's brave attempt to sugarcoat the bad news failed to impress her siblings. Michael could not care less about Kollonitsch becoming archbishop, and Tessa saw her hopes of roaming pristine woods vanish. Michael said defiantly, "I'll go back to Mama even if I have to walk the whole way! Mama promised me that I could be with her after a year, and it's almost up! No one can make me stay here!"

Tessa's reaction was different, though no less passionate. "You didn't plead hard enough, Sigismunda! Let me go there and tell him they just have to take us in! I'll behave real well, I promise! Perhaps, he's heard that I often get mad and that's why."

Sigismunda shook her head. "No, dear," she said. "Uncle barely gave me a chance to talk. He mentioned the ayah's visit months ago and said that she was given the same message. They knew all along that we've been in Vienna since last summer, but they just don't want us in their lives, and that's that. Believe me, no pleading in the world will change his mind! He was so cold it made me shiver, why, he wouldn't even touch me! Poor ayah must have felt so bad that she never told us the truth about her visit. I guess they never liked Mama and cannot forgive Papa for marrying a Protestant."

After a pause, during which the two stared at her in stunned silence, she added, "Now remember that the cardinal is our only support in the world, and he might abandon us if he finds out what I did. Don't raise any suspicion at supper tonight! They'll allow for us being sad because of poor ayah. We'll talk about it some more in the next few days, but remember, I'm counting on you not to give me away. Especially you, Michael, but you too, Tessa!"

Neither one of them was thinking very clearly, but they understood their sister's plea and did not want to get her into trouble. Michael still cherished hopes that Mama would send for him, and Tessa feared for her voice lessons. She forced a brave smile. "You can count on us, big sister," she said, "and thanks for going there, it must have been scary! If it had been me, I might have thrown something at Uncle Franz for being so mean!"

That brought a smile to everyone's face, and at that moment, they heard the bell ring for supper. Sigismunda was so exhausted she just wanted to go to bed, but she pulled herself together, splashed some water on her eyes, and followed the others downstairs.

The ayah was buried under gray, overcast skies the following day. Sisters Agnes and Constanze had petitioned their mother superior to allow interment in a cemetery usually reserved for members of a religious order, and their request was granted. The old woman had been a devoted Catholic all her life, and Sister Agnes knew that she had been Tessa's link to the Catholic faith. The alternative would have been a pauper's grave, and the nuns wanted the Trauttmansdorff youngsters able to accord her last honors. Paupers were buried in unmarked Mass graves, and for good reason, their relatives were not allowed to witness burials.

Sister Constanze and Brother Sebastian accompanied them in the carriage. The two had learned about the pending promotion of the cardinal and weighed the changes this would mean in their lives while the siblings wrestled with their chagrin over the death of their nanny and the outcome of Sigismunda's mission. They'd picked primroses from the garden, first messengers of spring, which Tessa made into a little bouquet and tied with the black silk ribbon the ayah used to wear in her hair on festive occasions. They placed it on the simple pine coffin and watched the petals quiver in the wind as the casket was lowered into the grave. A priest said the usual prayers, and Sister Constanze led them in a rosary by the open grave. She then gave a coin to the impatiently waiting old man with a shovel and gently led them away past graves of monks and nuns marked with simple stone crosses. Back in the palace chapel, a memorial Mass was read for the ayah's soul.

Sigismunda again thought that the ayah was perhaps lucky to die before knowing that her beloved charges would enter religious life. She would have thought them still too young for such a momentous and irrevocable decision. Besides, what would have become of the old woman, who was only tolerated in the cardinal's household to ease their transition? She'd have nowhere to turn and likely face life in lonesome poverty. God had been merciful not to let her suffer, which brought peace to Sigismunda's heart. God would also know what was best for them! She'd fretted over their fate often in recent months and despite a sleepless previous night again lay awake when it suddenly came to her that perhaps things were not as glum as they appeared. The fact that there was a small sum due them from their relatives and from the sale of Zay-Ugrocz meant that they would not enter religious life as paupers. She imagined Mama's face when told of the purpose for which the money was used! Sigismunda had always wanted to teach, but noblewomen did not commonly serve as governesses, unless the employer was a member of upper aristocracy. The alternative was to enter an arranged marriage with a man willing to wed a plain girl whose dowry consisted primarily of a good name. Compared to that, the security and peace of a religious order was an easily acceptable alternative. She now knew that Ferenc was thinking along similar lines if only to escape a dreaded career in the army. Perhaps, Mama would indeed send for Michael and Tessa find a way of life through her musical talent.

Chapter 6

Shortly after Easter, Kollonitsch called them into the library. His stern features bore a kind expression, Sigismunda hopefully noted; the girl still feared repercussions from the visit to her relatives. What if they had reported her? She had no excuse for leaving the residence without permission, especially not alone. The smile with which the cardinal received them relaxed her a little. And indeed, his attention did not focus on her. He asked them to sit on a carved settee along a wall between the windows, something they had not been invited to do during previous "audiences," as they referred to these visits among themselves. There was a letter in his hands.

"Your mother has communicated with me," he began and hesitated for a moment before continuing. "There's news I need to relate, which you'll be anxious to know and which I want you to contemplate in your prayers without undue concern."

Michael felt a surge of elation. *Mama is sending for me,* was all he could think of. His three siblings feared something bad had occurred.

"Has anything happened to her?" Sigismunda whispered.

"No, no, indeed, do not be disturbed," he answered, disregarding the interruption. "Your mama wants you to know that she intends to remarry after the anniversary of your father's death and is happy to have found a kind and considerate man who she feels you would like very much if you were to meet him. He was instrumental in finalizing negotiations with the debtors. Your modest shares of the residual will be placed into my trust to administer on your behalf.

Your mother's future husband has ample means to support her. She is satisfied that you are well cared for in my household and wishes you the very best. There is always the chance that she may travel to Vienna with her new husband at some future date, when she would surely be in touch with you. She regrets that it won't be possible for you to attend the wedding and she—"

While the others sat in stunned silence, Tessa could no longer restrain herself and jumped to her feet.

"No!" she cried. "That can't be true! She couldn't do this to our papa! I want to see for myself what she writes, I want to—"

Such an outburst was likely to cause a stern reprimand, and Ferenc held his breath while Sigismunda tried to pull her sister back onto the seat, but Kollonitsch expected adverse reactions and remained calm, ignoring her implication that he was not telling them the truth. He rose and put his arm around the shaking girl.

"It is so, child. Surely, you do not expect your mother to relate such profound news without reason! She feels she has suffered enough sorrow as a widow and will obey convention by observing a full year of mourning. I know that you loved your father very much and were very close to him. Your mother's decision cannot change these feelings. And think what a great joy it is for him that you have converted to the true faith, of which he surely is aware."

He was about to add "in purgatory" but caught himself so as not to further disturb them. Tessa tried to speak but was choked by sobs and clung to her uncle, who again became a father figure. Ferenc and Sigismunda silently stared at the scene and impulsively grasped each other's hands. Michael stood up, gathered his courage, and asked, "Your Eminence, perhaps, you have not read the whole letter? Mama promised me last year that I would return to her this summer and she wouldn't break her promise! I'm sure that my share of the money will pay for my journey home! Would you please read the letter again, Your Eminence? I'm a big boy now, and I can travel by myself, I really can! I'll behave myself very well, and I—"

Ferenc and Sigismunda were stunned that Michael apparently did not care at all that Mama had so quickly forgotten their beloved papa, as long as he could be with her and never mind what happened

to them. Kollonitsch thought along similar lines. He passed the sobbing Tessa to her sister and put a hand on Michael's shoulder.

"No, Michael," he said. "Your mother makes quite clear that all
of you are to remain in my care as your sole guardian. There never were
any plans for you to join her, and promising you otherwise may have
been an effort to make your departure from home less painful. You
will be sixteen later this year, Michael, and must behave like a young
man. You will all be confirmed on Whit Sunday, about six weeks
from now, when you'll become fully responsible, adult members of
the Catholic Church. You have much to study and preparations will
begin tomorrow. I know the last days have been both momentous and
difficult for you," he added quietly, "but I trust your faith will see you
through. I ask you to pray, pray as hard as you can, and our Merciful
Savior will listen and guide your hearts and thoughts. Remember that
He forgave those who nailed him to the cross. I want you to think
kindly of your mother and include her in your prayers."

He didn't say "forgive your mother," whose anti-Catholic mind-
set was unpardonable in his eyes, but he hoped that they would mentally come to terms with this new development and not be consumed
by resentment. Only Sigismunda remembered the required curtsy as
they left, but Kollonitsch did not seem to notice. She was leading the
sobbing Tessa, and Ferenc pulled Michael by the sleeve. As soon as
the door closed behind them, they clung together and stood crying
in the hall until Sigismunda finally said, "Let's go to chapel and pray
for our papa." And the others followed willingly, though Tessa and
Michael could not bring themselves to stay long. They went to their
rooms and succumbed to their own deep sorrow, albeit for different reasons. Tessa sat on the windowsill, knees drawn to her chest
and looking out across the roofs and gables, longing for a glimpse
of nature. She remembered a word from the Bible that her papa had
often quoted, "I look to the hills, from whence cometh my strength."
She wasn't sure whether those were the exact words, but she desperately longed for mountains and forests and peaceful pastures. Would
she ever be allowed to enjoy nature again or be confined to the city
all her life? She silently vowed to do anything as long as she could
live in the country.

Ferenc and Sigismunda remained in the chapel for a long time. Knowing what the future had in store for them reconciled them with this new development that merely sealed their fate. Both had felt guilty for their lack of affection toward Miczike in the past, but that now seemed justified. While not as devoted to their late father as Tessa, they had loved and respected him very much, and for Mama to wed again after only a year of mourning shocked them. The sheltered security of religious life seemed ever more desirable and a good solution. Both felt reassured, and while they thought it premature to share this knowledge with their younger siblings, they were able to convey to them some of their newfound peace. Michael began to think that once he graduated from military academy, he would be able to do as he pleased and return on his own. Tessa was so chagrined about Miczike's callousness toward Papa that she gave little thought to her future. Her pain was too raw and her heart too deeply wounded to pray for Mama. And when Sister Constanze suggested they write a letter to wish their mother well, she could only be persuaded to sign her name without adding a single word.

Work and study were deemed the best cure for their troubled minds, and Brother Sebastian followed the cardinal's instructions and prescribed a heavy curriculum. In addition to subjects such as Latin and history, he taught them laws of the Austrian monarchy as they applied to the church and spoke in detail about the young queen, Maria Theresa, her consort Franz, and their growing family. The royal couple had recently experienced tragedy losing their firstborn daughter.

Tessa remained the most deeply affected by her mother's pending remarriage. She found it impossible to understand how Mama could ever "replace" her beloved papa and she would not have returned to Transylvania even if that were an option. It occurred to her that marriage apparently was not such a loving experience if a dead spouse could so quickly be forgotten. Singing was her only source of joy, and a patient and understanding Sister Agnes showed great empathy with her grief and encouraged her to talk. She knew that expressing her feelings would help the child deal with them. During such a discussion, Tessa passionately exclaimed, "How could my wonderful papa be forgotten so quickly?"

The nun answered, "You're wrong, child, he is not at all forgotten. Does he not live in your heart as before? What does it matter if others forget him as long as you never do? He is in your heart and in your prayers, and you'll remain close to him as long as you live! He knows that and so does the Lord!"

Her words impressed Tessa, and while she could not forgive Mama, she felt calmer than before.

Ferenc and Sigismunda began to mentally withdraw from their younger siblings, as they inwardly prepared themselves for a future in religious life. They decided to leave it to their uncle to divulge these facts to their siblings. For the present, all were preoccupied with learning. Tessa excelled in Latin and held her own in the other subjects, and Michael, as usual, lagged behind and needed patience and perseverance from his teacher and elder sister to keep up. He remained convinced that he would enter a military academy following confirmation, so why spend all this time learning about popes and the church?

When a late spring finally arrived with warm weather, new leaves and flowers, they again enjoyed precious leisure time in the garden. They sometimes discussed the implications of their uncle's pending move to the archbishop's palace. Formal appointment was to come from the pope, but the frail old prelate had approached Rome on the subject of his successor and received tacit approval. They rarely saw their uncle who was spending most of his time with the archbishop. Kollonitsch now officiated at High Mass in St. Stephen's Cathedral on Sundays and during the week rarely left the ailing prelate's bedside.

Ever since Easter, the four made weekly confessions and received Holy Communion each Sunday. Sigismunda often felt guilty that no matter how hard she tried, it was difficult to come up with sins every week. She and Ferenc studied hard and committed no transgressions. Her greatest challenge was to remain patient with her inattentive, lazy brother and resist the temptation to cover up for him. Perhaps, it was good preparation for becoming a teaching nun, but she felt bad when she caught herself silently wishing not to have him around so she could devote herself to her own studies or reading. Ferenc was remorseful about not being more involved with Michael, yet he too easily became frustrated. Michael was not concerned about sins he might have committed and recited in the confessional whatever came to mind. Tessa dutifully confessed the anger toward her mother that she could not suppress. She managed to control her temper quite well these days but still loved playing practical jokes on her sister or brothers when the opportunity presented itself.

Following tradition, a large number of young lads and girls from prominent Viennese families were confirmed at St. Stephen's on Whit Sunday during an elaborate ceremony. With so many candidates to be individually blessed and have their cheek touched in a symbolic light stroke by a bishop, the exertion was too strenuous for the old archbishop, and Kollonitsch took his place. Everyone had fasted since the night before for communion, and standing still for long hours afterward was a challenge for the young candidates. Sigismunda turned increasingly pale and needed all her self-discipline not to faint. Boys and girls formed separate lines, and a "confirmation godparent" traditionally sponsored each candidate. Kollonitsch had approached Trauttmansdorff to sponsor his relatives, but the count declined, perhaps from a guilty conscience. He and his wife did not wish to become acquainted with their nephews and nieces in any way, and being godparents at confirmation would have involved treating them to a festive meal, token gifts, and continued spiritual involvement. And so Kollonitsch appointed Sister Constanze to sponsor Sigismunda, Sister Agnes for Tessa, and Brother Sebastian for the two boys. The confirmation gifts were new rosaries, delicately carved wood beads for the boys, sterling silver for the girls.

Sister Genevieve had prepared a special meal for the occasion. Initially resentful of the interruption in their daily routine, nuns, monks, and the servants who lived and worked in the palace had all become fond of the youngsters. They expected four young heretics and spoiled aristocrats; instead, the four turned out to be well-mannered adolescents not given to airs and apparently willing to embrace Catholicism. Tessa won everyone's heart with the Christmas carol and her beautiful rendition of the "Salve Regina." Sister Agnes was sometimes asked to allow the girl sing solo again, but the wise nun sensed a certain jealousy from some of her choir members and declined.

The brief letter they'd written in answer to the news of Miczike's pending remarriage failed to mention their conversion. On the eve of their confirmation, however, they wrote their mother a very formal letter, in which they expressed their joy of becoming full "adult" members of the Catholic Church. They knew that Mama would be anything but pleased, but even Sigismunda could not help a certain satisfaction imagining Miczike's ire. Why, none of it would ever have happened had their mother not so readily given them up! She felt that some way might well have been found to keep the family together. Tessa wrote that she finally could devote herself to the beautiful Gregorian chant first experienced as a small child at Ulmeni. Only Michael, who'd still not abandoned all hope for home, scribbled a few affectionate words.

Kollonitsch called them into the library two weeks later, and this time, Ferenc and Sigismunda anticipated the topic of the audience. The cardinal sat in his armchair and did not invite them to sit.

"You are now spiritual adults, fully confirmed members of the true church," he began. "And today, I wish to speak to you about your future. I believe that this future should consist of a life dedicated to God, who so lovingly has watched over you. I shall be moving to the archbishop's palace in due course, and the time has come for you to earnestly pursue your vocations. I have been most fortunate in arranging for Ferenc and Michael to enter the monastery of Melk on the Danube, where after further training, you will become novices of the Benedictine Order. Melk is one of the most exquisitely beautiful baroque monasteries in all of Europe, but more importantly, it is an extraordinary place for ecclesiastic study and monastic life. I trust you shall both prove yourselves worthy of this great privilege."

He paused for a moment while the two younger ones stared in stunned silence then continued, "You, Sigismunda, have professed a desire to teach, and there is no order more suited and providing better training for this worthy goal than the Ursuline nuns. You will find many opportunities to realize your ambition by joining them, and you have been accepted in an Ursuline convent in the town of Graz in Styria. As you know from your geography studies of the monarchy, the province of Styria is southwest from here and known for its abundance of magnificent woods."

There was another brief pause before he continued, "Your strength, Tessa, is not in teaching but singing, and Sister Agnes tells me that you are especially devoted to the Gregorian chant. There's an abbey at Göss in the mountains of Upper Styria, where this type of veneration is particularly valued and pursued. It is one of the oldest abbeys of the realm renowned for its small congregation made up exclusively of aristocratic women. I have communicated with Abbess Maria Antonia, a Countess Uberacker, and she has kindly agreed to accept you as an aspirant, as they call their students, and I trust you will prove yourself worthy of this honor. In fact, during the last century, one of our shared ancestors, a Countess Kollonitsch, was an outstanding abbess of Göss."

Again, he paused, this time longer, giving them a chance to absorb his words. No one spoke. After a minute, Kollonitsch continued, "You may be aware that to enter a monastic order requires a 'dowry,' especially at Melk and Göss, but so do the Ursulines, for they, of course, receive no remuneration for their teaching services. Your Vienna relatives have released a legacy from an inheritance to be added to the money your mother has set aside. These funds shall be your dowry and a monthly stipend your order will hold in trust for future personal expenses. These provisions were acceptable to Melk and the convents, but it remains your duty to prove yourselves worthy and to show your gratitude by diligently following the rules. You also will need various items upon entry, such as clothing, linens, and utensils, for which I shall pay from my personal funds. Consequently, I have instructed Sister Constanze to assemble the required items. I trust that you girls will assist her in any way you can. You will depart as soon as your trousseaus are complete."

Again, his words were received in silence. Kollonitsch watched them for a few moments then said in a warm, quiet voice, "I believe you should now retire to the chapel and pray for your vocations. May God bless you and guide you in your ways. You may leave."

They stepped forward to kiss his ring and left the library without uttering a single word. But no sooner had the heavy door closed with a click of its ornate lock than Michael vehemently spun round and reached for the handle. Ferenc apparently anticipated his brother's intentions and restrained him with uncharacteristic agility. Sigismunda came to his aid.

"I'm not going," cried the boy, but his sister put a hand over his mouth, and she and Ferenc pulled him away.

"Be quiet, Michael!" Her whispered words expressed authority and urgency and induced the lad to lower his voice.

"I'm not going to be locked up in a monastery and spend my life looking at books and pray and go to church three times a day! I don't care what he says—Mama will not allow it! I want to—"

"We'll go to our room and talk about it," suggested Ferenc.

"I want to explain a few things to you, Michael," Sigismunda said. "It's not as bad as you think if you will just listen to me! Come, let's go." And she and Ferenc pulled the boy down the hall. Tessa had not moved an inch.

"I want to go to chapel," she said. "I'll join you later." And she walked away without waiting for an answer.

The others had barely climbed the stairs when Michael protested anew.

"If you'll just be quiet for a minute, Michael," Sigismunda said after the door had closed behind them. She then proceeded to tell him every detail of her visit to the Trauttmansdorff Palace.

"Michael, you're almost sixteen, you're a man, and you've got to understand that we do not have a choice! You need a personal recommendation to enter the military academy, and you're never going to receive one from the cardinal or anyone else! And get it into your head that our mama has relinquished all rights of custody because frankly, she does not want to be bothered with us anymore!"

Sigismunda had never before spoken so harshly about Miczike, and remembering how she had beseeched God to help her not bear resentment toward her mother, she tried to soften her assessment yet help her immature brother.

"Michael, do try to understand! Mama is without money and perhaps had no choice but to remarry and have someone take care of her! Zay-Ugrocz is gone forever, we are poor, and even if you could become an officer, remember Papa telling us that you need personal wealth to make a living! We're on our own, and that is it!"

Michael still was not convinced, and Ferenc came to her aid.

"Michael, I've read about the monastery of Melk, and it's a great place! Besides, the empress issued new regulations saying that boys cannot finally commit themselves to become monks until they're eighteen years old, which means you have two more years to go! Who knows what happens in that long a time! Things could change, and in the meantime, you and I will be together, and I expect it to be a lot better to be in a grand place like Melk surrounded by landholdings than locked up in this palace in the middle of a big city! The monastery owns parks and estates, and living there will almost feel like back home! I'll show you a picture I've seen in a book. The monastery is on a cliff overlooking the Danube, and it's beautiful. Why, if you give Kollonitsch too much trouble, he might put you in jail, who knows!"

Ferenc and Sigismunda both knew that circumstances were unlikely to change in the next two or more years, but they were anxious to ease the prospect for their brother and avoid trouble for everyone. Michael typically heard what he wanted to hear, namely getting away from the strict supervision in the palace, the crowded city, and—most of all—having two years to figure out how not to become a monk. He knew that the cardinal was not likely to change his mind, but he still clung to his hope of returning to Transylvania. If only he could get there, people would surely take him in, even if Mama could not afford to! His last hope was the ayah's money and he would not have hesitated to take it all, but Sigismunda had carefully hidden the coins. There were four gold ducats left, and she and Ferenc had decided that when it was time to part, each of them should receive one.

The chapel was very quiet when Tessa came to kneel before the Virgin. Too stunned and confused to channel her thoughts into a prayer, she looked up into the steady gaze of the statue's eyes.

"Holy Mary, Mother of God," she finally whispered, "please stay with me when I'm all by myself! And please let the nuns like the way I sing the chant and allow me to sing it often, and I promise never to get mad, I really won't! I don't know whether I want to be a nun, but I want to sing, and I want to get away from the noisy streets and big houses and walk through woods again! Uncle says Göss is in the mountains, so there should be big trees and meadows and brooks and deer! If it's all true, I will sing your praise, Holy Mother, every day, as long as I live!"

After a while, Tessa's troubled heart felt lighter, and her mind was at peace. Except for her temper, she was a mature child at fourteen. She'd come to accept that her beloved papa was gone forever and that there was no hope of returning to Transylvania. She did expect to enter a girl's school, but perhaps, her only chance to continue musical studies was indeed in a convent. Perhaps, she was lucky that Kollonitsch had selected Göss, where they cherished the Gregorian chant. She knew she was too young for final vows, and if, when the time came, she refused to take them, the nuns would have to let her go! She didn't want to think of what might then happen but, with youthful optimism, relegated that situation to the distant future. The Holy Mother had rescued her from difficult binds in the past, and Tessa's devout faith gave her hope that the Virgin would continue to do so.

While growing up in a sheltered household in rural Transylvania, she had directed all her affections toward her papa, whom she considered the embodiment of what a man ought to be. She had never been exposed to young lads other than her brothers. Her ambitions and thoughts had been oriented toward nature and hunting, and her heart remained untouched by romantic notions toward the opposite sex. The strictly spiritual atmosphere in Vienna filled with learning, prayer, and musical studies did not change this mental outlook. She had never felt at home in the city and less so since the ayah's death. The abbey of Göss could only be an improvement! Surely, there'd be other novices her age, but most important of all, she'd be among mountains and trees instead of tiled rooftops!

If Kollonitsch had expected Tessa to be the most difficult of the siblings to submit to his plans, he was mistaken. The youngest Trauttmansdorff did not rebel and, an hour later, left the chapel and went to the garden to indulge and sit among fragrant spring blossoms and think some more about her future. How beautiful the woods would be at this time of year! How wonderful to once again walk through forests and listen to birds and watch deer! When she again joined her siblings, they were surprised to see her so serene.

"What's the matter with you, Tess?" Michael blurted out. "You can't wait to be a nun?"

"Michael, I want to get away from Vienna and not live in servants' quarters anymore! I want to see green trees and big skies! Don't you? You want to live in those narrow, smelly streets with their beggars and peddlers for the rest of your life? I'd rather be a nun surrounded by mountains and trees like back home," she added defiantly.

The boy grimaced. "I don't like Vienna either," he admitted, "but I don't know whether I want to be a monk and wear frocks!"

"They're robes, not frocks, silly boy," Ferenc corrected. "And I think they look quite dignified, better than our old outfits, which are getting shabby."

The vespers bell interrupted their banter. Supper was eaten in silence, each busy with their thoughts about the fateful revelations of the day.

After lessons next morning, Sister Constanze produced a long list.

"A great many things are required to enter the monastery at Melk and the convents at Graz and Göss, and together, we'll go over your belongings to determine what needs to be added. Brother Sebastian will take inventory of the boys' clothes. In addition, you will require bed linens, tableware, cutlery, and so on. His Eminence wishes me to acquire items of quality, and I trust you will show your appreciation for his generosity. And if your choices are reasonable, I'll let you pick some of the things!"

Brother Sebastian produced books from the library with historic details and drawings of the monastery of Melk, the abbey at Göss, and the Ursuline convent at Graz. All except Michael were keenly interested.

"You read up on it and then tell me," the boy said to Ferenc.

Apparently, Göss was the oldest foundation, and Tessa instantly became fascinated with its illustrious history. What interested her most, though, was an engraving from the year 1681, titled "The Aristocratic Virgin Cloister Göss," that showed the walled abbey with its watchtowers and church spires, surrounded by wooded mountains and a river in the foreground. The literature emphasized the devotion of choir women at Göss to the Gregorian chant, though the pristine environment galvanized her interest even more. Tessa knew that nuns could only walk in pairs in the city but that might not be the case in the country. And that she would only become eligible for final vows at age eighteen, four years hence. Having felt like a caged bird in Vienna, she would finally be able to get out!

Melk apparently was the most impressive and scenically beautiful place. Perched atop a cliff high above the Danube, it resembled a large and elegant castle. Ferenc's attention focused on the information that the monastery had one of Europe's most extensive and extraordinary libraries. The young bookworm knew that a lifetime of studies could not exhaust such a haven of knowledge, and were it not for the fact that he would miss his sisters and especially Sigismunda, he was ready to leave any time. He tried his best to enthuse Michael, who did spend some time scrutinizing the artistic rendition of the monastery. It was right at the banks of the Danube, which gave him the idea of finding a boat to float down river to Budapest in a matter of days! He wasn't sure what he'd do there but at least he'd be in Hungary and he only dimly recalled the long coach ride between Zay-Ugrocz and that city. Surely, he would be able to get word to Mama, who would not leave him stranded! The more he thought about this plan, the more anxious he too became about leaving Vienna. Sigismunda, who by nature abhorred uncertainty, was happy to learn that the Ursuline nuns at Graz ran an excellent school for young girls. At her age, she was eligible to become a novice as soon as she could pass the required exams and take her final vows a year after that. Her convent was in town, but she preferred books to trees and did not share Tessa's passion for nature.

And so Sister Constanze and Brother Sebastian could report to Kollonitsch that his four charges apparently accepted his directives without resistance and were ready to leave when the time came. What surprised the cardinal most was that they did not object to being separated, which had in fact played an important part in his plans. He knew that eliminating sibling support made adjustment to monastic life more likely and reduced resistance to ascetic rules and regulations. He had considered separating the boys also but in the end concurred with Brother Sebastian's opinion that the immature Michael needed his brother's steadying influence; moreover, a large abbey such as Melk presented opportunities for a variety of talents or abilities. The boy would never be a scholar, but the abbey had extensive landholdings to administer and needed men for a variety of duties. If Michael were unable to pass the difficult exams required, he could become a "brother," bound by formal vows, but not part of the formal chapter of choir men, who were priests.

The two girls enjoyed assembling their "dowries," and Sister Constanze granted them considerable leeway. Sigismunda and Tessa had never before concerned themselves with bed linens and other utensils that had simply been accessories in their lives. They had initially scoffed at the plain pewter plates and cutlery in Vienna that only servants used at home but became accustomed to them. Now each received a silver goblet and sterling fork and spoon, together with porcelain cups for coffee and hot chocolate. A bed would be provided locally, but they needed towels, linens, pillows, and blankets. Since Sigismunda was expected to soon enter her novitiate and formal investiture, only one new set of clothes was acquired for her, three for the younger Tessa, still years away from wearing a habit. Each also received linen shirts, stockings of cotton yarn, and dozens of kerchiefs.

"Why is it called a dowry?" Tessa asked. "We're not getting married!"

"You are becoming brides of Christ," sister answered.

Most exciting were the bridal gowns they would wear at investiture, the very special day on which they entered the novitiate betrothed to Christ and take their preliminary vows. Such gowns were later remade into religious accessories like formal vestments for priests, antependia for altars, baldachins, or other ecclesiastic appurtenances. As their guardian and future archbishop of Vienna, Kollonitsch decreed that the gowns reflect the girls' noble family as well as his own high standing in church hierarchy. The girls were allowed to choose from exquisite brocades interwoven with gold thread and dressmakers were engaged to sew patterns of bridal gowns according to the secular tradition of the time. The sisters had never worn anything so splendid, and even Sigismunda, who normally paid scant attention to her clothes, was excited. The blue silk made her pale features glow, and the fashionable style accentuated her small waist. In a gentle and chaste way, she looked indeed a lovely bride. Tessa had grown quite tall and—with her beautiful brown hair, large eyes, and exquisite skin—cast a regal figure in her gown of green brocade, a shade she chose to reflect her love of nature. When they showed off this finery to the boys, Michael spontaneously exclaimed, "Hey, you two are too pretty to become nuns!"

Ferenc said quietly, "I wish the ayah were here to see you in those dresses."

Tessa thought of her papa and how proud he would have been; no one mentioned Miczike.

Assembling the trousseaus consumed several weeks, and spring turned into summer. When everything was complete, the cardinal decided on a departure date and announced that the boys were to leave for Melk the following morning, which brought on a sudden realization that they might not see each other again for a long time if ever. They were permitted to write and promised to do so often. Michael and Tessa had grown apart during the past year in Vienna, and the girl found it more difficult to let go of Ferenc, who felt like abandoning his sisters. He had always been closest to Sigismunda and was sure that she would be able to take care of herself, but Tessa was another matter, and he vowed to stay in touch with her. The girls were to leave a few days later.

Melk was a shorter distance from Vienna than either Graz or Göss, and a monk arrived that evening in a carriage of the abbey. He had a long, private conference with Kollonitsch during which he was thoroughly briefed about the boys' personalities and scholastic abilities. He was an elderly, portly man with a friendly disposition and quickly won the confidence of both lads. He joined them for their evening meal and afterward sent them to the library to bid farewell to their guardian. Kollonitsch blessed them and once again expressed the hope that they would prove themselves worthy for so venerable an abbey as Melk.

The siblings found no sleep that night; they sat together and talked about their childhood in Zay-Ugrocz and their late father. Miczike and her plans to remarry came up only in passing for even Michael could not bring himself to touch the subject. When the early dawn cast a pink glow across the sky, the two boys washed their faces and donned their traveling attires. They all attended early Mass and silently ate their breakfast, dreading the final parting. When it came, both girls wept openly, and the boys tried to swallow the lump in their throat. The novice master, who'd witnessed many a farewell from family members and was aware of the special circumstances of this case, deemed it best to shorten the agony and pressed for departure with the excuse of the long ride ahead. Their trunks loaded, the boys climbed into the carriage and waved to the girls, who looked small and forlorn below the tall portal of the palace. As the clatter of wheels on the cobblestone-paved street faded into the quiet of the summer morning, Sigismunda and Tessa grasped each other's hands and quietly went to their room, where Sister Constanze joined them a short while later. The wise nun had planned a busy day—extended music lesson for Tessa and various activities for Sigismunda to leave little time for sad thoughts.

Tessa was grateful for the long session with Sister Agnes, though she lacked concentration. The nun understood and exercised great patience. It was to be Tessa's last lesson, and she gave the girl a stack of her favorite music scores, advising her to carry on with her studies. Tessa found it hard to part from this motherly figure that had so well empathized with her difficulties of controlling her temper. She owed Sister Agnes her happiest moments in Vienna during which music compensated for lost freedom.

The girls' departure took place a few days later. They had more trunks than the boys, who would wear what Michael called "frocks" almost from the day they arrived. Sigismunda's and Tessa's trousseaux were more extensive, and the wedding gowns alone took up extra space. The girls would wear secular clothes until their investiture. Two of the new dresses made for Tessa were of brown wool for the cold season, which was expected to be more severe and longer at Göss than in the milder climate of Graz. The color matched her brown locks and eyes and suited her better than gray. The chosen style did not follow current fashion, which called for voluminous, often two-tiered skirts and tight-fitting bodices with sleeves trimmed in lace, a gauzy apron and white or pastel kerchief worn around neck and shoulders. Tessa's skirt was pleated, but her budding young body remained hidden beneath a loosely cut blouse. Each girl received several new aprons and kerchiefs of fine linen but without lace or frills, two dozen shirts, handkerchiefs, stockings, bed sheets, pillows with covers, a quilt of eiderdown, towels, cutlery, and dishes. Kollonitsch was intent that their orders not think him lacking generosity. Tessa's dowry was the most extensive since choir women at Göss came from wealthy aristocratic families, and the cardinal feared that her recent conversion was likely to arouse more prejudice there than at either Melk or Graz.

On the eve of their departure, Kollonitsch called the girls into his library after vespers and invited them to sit.

"You are about to enter a new and most rewarding phase of your young lives," he opened the conversation, "and from your past conduct, I trust that you will both faithfully follow your vocation and appreciate the privilege of entering such outstanding institutions. Sigismunda, I am sure that you will become a worthy member of the Ursuline Order of Nuns and, as a teacher, will contribute much to further the education of children. Graz is a handsome town, and the Ursuline nuns cherish their mission. As for you, Tessa, I cannot help but urge you to work hard on restraining your temper. Lack of control as you have displayed in the past does not become any woman, especially one devoting her life to Christ and the church. Both of you are allowed to write and receive letters from your mother and siblings, but I exhort you to keep such communications to a minimum and instead concentrate on your spiritual education. There will surely be times when you will doubt yourselves and your ability to adequately serve the Lord. Such doubts afflict all human beings, both in secular and spiritual life. But sheltered by convent walls from the distractions and perplexities of the world and supported by the spiritual community of nuns, you will overcome such periods, for you have only to call on Christ's help and He will hear your prayers!"

He paused for a few moments before continuing, "On the day you make your profess to formally enter your religious order, you will receive a gold ring as a sign of being wedded to Christ. It bears the initials 'IHS,' which as you know stands for 'In Hoc Signo.' Choir women at Göss, Tessa, also receive a diamond ring at investiture, the betrothal to Christ, as a symbol of eternity for which they dedicate themselves to religious life. I have arranged for these rings to be made, and you will receive them from the bishop on your special day. Resolve never to cease in your endeavor to be worthy of your vows! And now receive my blessings and that of the church as you begin your journey!"

The girls knelt. And afterward, Sigismunda gathered her courage, looked directly into his eyes, and said, "Your Eminence, we are indebted to you for giving us a home when no one else would. Please allow me"—she swallowed and continued—"allow me to thank you also for guiding us to the true faith." She hesitated again then added what weighed most heavily on her mind. "Your Eminence and esteemed Uncle, my sister is still a child, and it troubles my heart that she should make a serious and irrevocable commitment before she is mature and ready for such a fundamental decision. I beg of you, Eminence—"

The expression on the cardinal's face remained unchanged, and ignoring an instinctive movement by Tessa, he said, "Sigismunda, I am well aware of your sister's age and so is the abbess of Göss. Tessa will not take final vows until she reaches eighteen and maturity. The church forces no one to choose religious life, and each novice, male or female, is required to write a statement why he or she freely and without undue influence wishes to take vows. It is therefore not for you to trouble your heart with such thoughts! Our Lord will guide your sister toward the light of her vocation! Now walk with God and bring honor to your name and the convents that receive you!"

There was nothing more to be said, and the girls curtseyed and kissed his ring. When they had reached their room, Tessa burst out, "You sure were brave to say what you did! I held my breath and was scared to death of his answer! But don't worry, sis, I'm a big girl, and they can't keep me there against my will. It'll be easier to run away from the abbey than it is from this virtual prison in the big city! I'll just—"

Sigismunda put her arms around her sister, who had grown so tall during the past year. She knew that escaping the cloistered walls of Göss would be more difficult than walking from this palace but did not want to make things look too bleak for Tessa. On the other hand, she had a keen sense of responsibility.

"Just promise me, dear, that you will never allow yourself to be forced into something you feel you can't live up to! I'll gladly give up my yearly allowance for you if that's what you need to live in a secular world! You will let me know how you are doing, won't you?"

Tessa did not catch the subtle urgency in Sigismunda's voice. She saw herself in the brocade dress wearing a diamond ring, and the image filled her romantic mind. She returned the hug and said cheerfully, "I do promise, Sigismunda, but don't you worry about me, I'll be just fine! I really can't wait to get out of the city and again live among trees and mountains. I was concerned that your convent is in town. Are you sure you'd not rather come to Göss with me? I've read that Göss is well known for accepting siblings, aunts, or cousins. Wouldn't it be great if we both went there?"

Sigismunda guessed that their uncle had good reason for separating them and that he had only agreed for Michael and Ferenc to enter Melk together because the older boy would prove vital in keeping the younger one under control. And she very much wanted to become an educator and reverted to that reason.

"Oh, Tess, you're making it difficult for me, but you do know how much I've always wanted to teach! I love you very much and would like nothing better than being close to you, but you have your singing, and I want to devote myself to bringing knowledge to the young and poor! Can you understand that?"

Tessa nodded. "Of course, I do, Sigismunda, so let's not talk about it anymore."

The two girls finished packing. Tessa took her little menagerie of carved animals and hid them between her linens, together with a few books and her father's picture. The four had agreed that Tessa, as the youngest and closest to the late count, should have it. Michael had not asked for Miczike's portrait, which remained hanging on a servants quarter's wall in the palace of her despised uncle.

The girls would travel southwest and remain together for two more days. They were to part at a road juncture in Styria, where the River Mur sharply changed from its west-east course to turn south toward Graz. Göss was only ten miles west from there, and a carriage from the abbey was expected to take Tessa to her destination, whereas Sigismunda and Sister Constanze, who chaperoned them, would continue south to Graz.

The first day of the trip was to take them to the Semmering Pass, a mountain range that formed the natural border between the provinces of Lower Austria and Styria. The distance from Vienna was about sixty miles across level territory, and the carriage drawn by four horses was expected to proceed quickly, at least as far as the mountain range. They were to spend the night at an inn and continue the following day to reach their destinations before nightfall.

After supper, the girls said their goodbyes to Brother Sebastian and Sister Genevieve. Sister had prepared a special meal and baked rolls for their early breakfast. She prepared a basket with bread, cheese, smoked ham, and small cakes to eat during the journey since way stations along the road offered little food and time was of the essence. Sister Constanze woke them before dawn, and after a quick breakfast, they climbed into the cardinal's travelling coach drawn by four strong quarter horses specifically leased for the trip. Sister Constanze exchanged her voluminous Ursuline headdress with a small white cap, and the girls wore simple cotton dresses and straw hats with veils that could be pulled over their faces to protect from the dust. Their trunks were tied to the roof of the carriage, Sister

Genevieve's basket and an earthen jug with water stowed under the seats. They climbed aboard, the coachman cracked his whip, and in the early morning stillness, the large wheels clattered noisily over the cobblestones. When they crossed the graben, the rising sun colored St. Stephen's tan sandstone a delicate pink. Near the cathedral, the carriage turned sharply east to roll along Carynthia Street and through a gate of the same name. They crossed the glacis and waved to the cupola of St. Charles Church a short distance away. Soon, the sprawling settlements of the city were behind them, and the horses fell into a stiff trot on the level road. Two hours later, Sister Constanze pointed toward the construction of a large complex and explained that this was the new military academy the empress had founded in the small town of Wiener Neustadt. The girls thought of their brothers; perhaps, Michael would yet enter it and become an officer.

The countryside reminded them of the Alfold Plain—level, fertile land, a checkerboard of fields, and pastures divided by fences. Families were out tilling and cultivating, and children waived to the passing carriage. The girls knew that these peasants were infinitely better off than their counterparts in Hungary, for while they likely did not own the land, their status was that of freemen, who could decide to relocate in other areas. They also had the right to send their children to the towns as domestic servants or to learn a trade, whereas Hungarian peasants were tied to the soil they tilled for their masters.

In late morning, the party stopped at a roadside inn to water and feed the horses, and soon thereafter, they saw wooded mountain ranges towered by a snow-covered peak in the distance.

"That one's called 'Snow Mountain' because it often gets a white cap in the summertime. Remember the recent cold snap when it was cool and rainy—that's when it snowed up there," said Sister Constanze. "That's also the direction of Maria Zell, the Austrian realm's most famous place of pilgrimage. People travel there from all over Europe and often cover the whole distance on foot, the last mile or so on their knees. Maria Zell's a small village in the woods with a very large church that treasures a famous image of the Virgin said to heal people of their ailments. Why, our sovereign Maria Theresa and her husband right after their wedding traveled there to ask for a blessing of their union and a male heir."

By late afternoon, they reached the foothills of the Semmering Pass and began the arduous climb up a narrow, steep road. The horses were tired, and the coachman asked his passengers to alight and continue on foot. The girls actually enjoyed walking. To avoid the dust and have some privacy, they put some distance between themselves, and the portly nun unaccustomed to such exercise. Sigismunda again brought up the subject foremost on her mind and, reaching for Tessa's hand, said, "Once again, promise me something, little sister. You're only fourteen and much too young to make final decisions! I don't know what kind of pressure may be put on you, but remember, no one can force you to become a nun, as we learned in church law and by the cardinal's own words. I don't know what would become of you if you decide for a secular life, but I'll think of something, I really will. Better to live in poverty than fail as a nun! We've been told that we can write each other, and I'm counting on you to tell me how things are going. Do you realize how serious I am, Tessa?"

The younger girl hesitated for a moment then asked, "How about you, Sigismunda, have you definitely decided to take the vows?"

"Yes, Tessa, I have. I abhor the alternative of being forced into a marriage that means nothing to me, and my looks leave me little choice," Sigismunda answered matter-of-fact and without bitterness. "I do love children and believe that education is key to a better life. I want to help those who cannot afford to pay teachers, and that is what the Ursuline nuns are dedicated to do."

Sigismunda stopped to rest. They had outpaced their party and reached a clearing with a wide view east across the land they had crossed. The setting sun cast a golden light over the idyllic countryside at their feet. Sigismunda faced her sister and intently searched her eyes.

"Tessa, I have come to believe that the Catholic faith is the true and only true faith and its ways those Christ wanted the world to follow. I love Mass, which I believe to be the most beautiful and loving way to bring the Redeemer back into our midst each time it is celebrated. Surely, you agree that the ritual commemorating and renewing His sacrifice for us by far exceeds the plain lecture and prayer service of the Protestant Church! I feel the divine presence at offertory and shall not tire celebrating it if I live to be a hundred! Yes, I have decided to enter the novitiate as soon as I'll be allowed to—hopefully soon since I'm past seventeen. But how do you feel about it, sis?"

Tessa thought for a minute then said slowly, "Sigismunda, I've been Catholic at heart ever since I was six years old and went to Ulmeni with Papa that afternoon. When I felt that whole church resounding with the most beautiful and haunting music I'd ever heard, I knew that is where I belonged! Papa wouldn't answer my questions and made me promise not to tell anyone, and I didn't, except the ayah, who ended up teaching me the 'Salve Regina.' From that day on, I wanted to sing the Gregorian chant, and when I later found a catechism from Papa's childhood in the library, I guess I wanted to become Catholic without even being aware of it! Right now, I don't know whether I wish to be a nun, but I want to sing, and if the only way to music is by becoming a nun, so be it!"

Sigismunda wanted to say that love for music alone did not constitute a true vocation to religious life but kept silent. Her faith told her that God alone knew what was best for each of them and all she could do was trust in His wisdom. She smiled.

"And you do sing beautifully, Tessa, and the cardinal said that Göss is the abbey most devoted to cultivating the chant. Raise your voice to God's glory, and you will hear His voice guiding you! Perhaps, I haven't been much of a sister to you, but I love you very much and want you never to forget it!"

She put her arms round Tessa, and the two stood hugging. Presently, Sister Constanze and the carriage caught up with them, and they continued their climb in the summer dusk. The road became steeper, progress was slow, and it was nightfall by the time they reached the inn on the mountain pass. Servants unloaded their trunks, and they were ushered into the kitchen for a simple meal of cold pork, bread, butter, and cider. A carriage with fresh horses was waiting to take them into Styria the next day; the cardinal's coach would await Sister Constanze's return. The tired travelers finished their meal and after evening prayers retired. The two girls shared a narrow cot and quickly fell asleep.

The last leg of their journey again started at dawn, and sister had to shake them repeatedly before they opened their eyes. Together, they said their prayers, washed in a small basin of cold water, and sat down for a bowl of hot milk with chunks of dark bread floating in it. They didn't much care for this unfamiliar, typical Styrian country breakfast but were too sleepy to object.

The ride that morning was less comfortable than the previous day. They rolled down a steep, rough road through dense woods not penetrated by the breaking dawn, and the vehicle swayed and rattled as it negotiated rocks and rivulets washed out by rain. Progress was slow. The girls clung to one another and managed to doze while sister silently said her rosary. They reached the valley and a small settlement for a brief stop to water and feed the horses. The girls stretched, grew fully awake, and had their first look at the Styrian countryside, finding that the nickname "Green Province" was well deserved. Lush emerald-green meadows nestled between dark forests dotted by lighter larches. A gushing little river joined the valley from the north, and they wanted to know whether it was the Mur, which they knew flowed through both Göss and Graz. They were told that these waters were known as the "Mürz," which would join the larger Mur at the small town of Bruck, the place where they'd part. Remembering the map they'd seen and that the distance to that point was not very far, the two girls stared into the rushing green waters, a symbol of the brief hours they had left together. They continued their journey in silence, each deep in thoughts. Progress remained arduous, and the girls, accustomed to thoroughbreds, thought that these heavy, stoic horses were more suitable for fieldwork than traveling. The valley widened with farmhouses and barns dotting the sloping meadows fringed by woods. They passed through several villages where buildings closely lined the narrow streets. In Hungary and the environs of Vienna, houses were whitewashed, but Styrian buildings were different in style. They asked Sister Constanze for the reason.

"Most homes in this province are built of wood," was the answer. "It's easy to see that this is the material most readily available. It also protects best from the cold during long, rough winters."

"But they're so dark and have such tiny windows! I think they look forbidding," remarked Tessa.

"Well, most of them are a hundred or more years old, and over time, the wood weathers to a dark brown color. And the windows are small to preserve warmth. They're really quite cozy inside, as a sister of my order who grew up here told me. The Styrian people are friendly and hardworking. Many of your future Ursuline sisters in Graz will be from this province, Sigismunda, and I'm sure you will enjoy living among them," she added.

"What about Göss?" asked Tessa. "Do the nuns there also come from the local area?"

Constanze shook her head. "No, child, the choir women of Göss are daughters of aristocracy and come from all over the realm. A few even hail from other countries, such as Italy or Prussia."

The girl thought about it and wanted to know, "Why would they choose a convent far away from home and not remain closer to their families and the place where they grew up? Why, I'd surely prefer to join a convent in Transylvania or at least Hungary," she added, remembering that there were no convents in her Protestant home province.

Sister Constanze said earnestly, "Tessa, you know that during and after the reformation, Germany became overwhelmingly Protestant and today has precious few, if any, monasteries or convents. But more important—and I want you to remember this well—Göss is an abbey of great prestige that for more than seven hundred years has attracted candidates from all over Europe. I don't think you realize how very fortunate you are that they accepted you. The choir women also maintain a small school for girls of high standing, which you will first join because of your young age. Most of the pupils grow to love Göss so much that they can't wait to become novices and make profess. I have no doubt that you will feel that way too. There is much to learn to be worthy of becoming a choir woman, and Latin is particularly important, for as you well know, the Gregorian chant and all Masses are sung in that language. But you also need to study the Rule of St. Benedict, who founded the order more than a thousand years ago. And during their leisure hours, the choir women pursue needlework and have created magnificent vestments!"

Sigismunda winked at her sister at the prospect of seeing her struggle with embroidery, and Tessa thought she'd rather roam the woods during leisure hours but knew better than express such ideas. Unlike Sigismunda, she didn't have the patience to spend much time on something as monotonous as needlework. Well, she could always make up for it by singing, which surely was more important than stitching vestments for priests!

A slight drizzle cast a misty veil over the countryside as the heavy carriage continued to roll westward. Their hour of parting drew near, and the girls fell silent. The nun sensed their heartache and reached for her breviary. At times, the road ran along the bottom of the valley, and they watched the Murz turn into a small river. How much farther was it until it joined the Mur at Bruck? It was past noon when a distant tall church spire indicated a larger settlement and the coachmen pointed his whip.

"'Tis the town of Bruck over yonder," he announced.

Sister tucked away her breviary, and they craned their neck for a glimpse. The road was smoother now and less dusty due to the rain. The girls smoothed their crumpled clothes, which showed signs of the long journey. The carriage came to a halt before a tavern on the main square of the little town. A portly, red-faced innkeeper stood in the doorway and greeted them respectfully. Yes, fresh horses were available for sister and the young lady to continue the journey to Graz, and the Göss Abbey had sent word that their carriage was due to arrive in a few hours. The girls were hungry and eagerly followed sister into the tavern, but a noisy crowd of peasants and coachmen filled the parlor room.

"We're not entering this den," sister categorically said to the innkeeper. "Surely, you must have a more private room where we can be served!"

Her words were more of an order than a question, and the man hurriedly fetched his wife. A rotund woman appeared and apologized profusely to the "revered, gracious ladies." Would they grant her the honor of taking their meal and rest in the family quarters? They followed her up the stairs into a spotlessly clean room with pine floors. A rough-hewn table and wooden benches below a simple crucifix filled one corner, and they sat down while the busily chatting woman served hearty soup, bread, butter, and homemade cheese. The young lady who was to proceed to Göss was most welcome to spend her time up here until her carriage arrived and she'd make sure that no one would intrude upon her. Sister Constanze was in a quandary and uncertain whether she should leave one of her charges alone. She was expected to personally entrust Tessa to an escort from the Göss Abbey but now had little choice for the coachman was anxious to continue as soon as possible, Graz still being hours away. Constanze went for a private word with the innkeeper and his wife and reluctantly charged them with the responsibility of keeping the young countess safe and secure.

Alone, Sigismunda and Tessa embraced. The younger girl began to weep, and Sigismunda whispered, "Dear God, child, it's so hard to leave you! How I wish now that we could stay together! I always thought I'd find it difficult to part from Ferenc, but this is much harder. I now feel so selfish about my teaching ambitions when I should have tried to persuade Uncle to let us stay together like Ferenc and Michael!"

A lump in her throat made her voice tremble. Tessa sensed it was her turn to be brave and, pulling away, smiled through her tears. "I'll be just fine, sister, don't fret about me! I'm a big girl now, going on fifteen, and I can take care of myself, you wait and see!"

"But I won't see, and that's just what worries me!"

"Well, you'll read then, for I'll write and tell you all about the high-bred girls and nuns of Göss! If they turn out to be mean, I'll play some prank on them, and I'm pretty good at that, remember?"

Sigismunda's smile faded. "Oh, please, Tessa dear, don't get yourself into trouble. They won't have a sense of humor, and there's no ayah to cover up for you! Promise me."

"Oh, for heaven's sake," exclaimed the younger one. "I'm just trying to cheer you up! No more promises! Everything will be just fine! Let's not waste our last few minutes together with worries!"

They fell silent. Sigismunda thought of the vital part Catholicism had played in Western culture because monks and nuns educated the masses and how fervently she wanted to partake in this mission. Finally, she took Tessa's hand and said, "Beloved sister, God gave you the unique gift of a beautiful voice. Use it to sing His praise but also to find peace and tranquility! From all I've heard and read, Göss will be an ideal place for you. The nuns there are referred to as 'choir women' because all Masses and services are sung. I'm sure your voice will be better than any other. And when the world looks dark and your heart is heavy, go and sing and all will be well!"

The door opened, and Sister Constanze stood in the frame, the innkeeper's wife behind her.

"It is time to leave now, Sigismunda, we need to reach Graz before nightfall. Tessa, you are to stay in this room until the carriage from Göss arrives. If you need anything, just call for Mam'selle, and she'll take care of it. You are not to leave the house because this is an unfamiliar place and you don't know your way 'round. The carriage should not be long, and I trust there'll be a proper escort along. Now say your farewells, girls, and let's get on our way! God bless you, my child, I've enjoyed knowing and teaching you."

The two sisters hugged one last time, Constanze made the sign of the cross on Tessa's forehead, and a moment later, they were gone. The metallic click of the closing door felt terribly final, and Tessa made an instinctive move toward it then stood with hanging arms and stared at the roughly hewn boards separating her from the last member of her family. She heard their steps on the stairway and Constanze's firm voice issuing instructions then the coachman's shouted command and clatter of horses' hooves and wheels. She could not bring herself to walk to the window for a last look; her courage gave way to a forsaken feeling, and she let herself drop onto the bench and sobbed. What had happened to her? A little over a year ago, she had a beautiful home and carefree life, a doting father, siblings, and a mother, albeit a distant one. How insignificant the cares of those days now seemed!

"Oh, Papa," she cried out, "why did you have to die? I need you so much! What am I going to do?"

The tears brought relief, and she became calmer, dried her face with one of the fine new linen kerchiefs from her trousseau, and—looking up at the crucifix in the corner—noticed a picture of the Virgin. The naïve painting portrayed a yellow-blond Mary wrapped in a bright blue cloak floating among clouds. Tessa was accustomed to good art, and the naive image failed to console her.

She took a closer look at the room, which was quite different from how common people lived in Transylvania. Near the door was a large tiled stove encircled by a narrow bench and racks suspended from the ceiling that were probably used for drying laundry or damp clothes in wintertime. She pictured people sitting on the benches warming their back on the tiles. The shape of the stove was unfamiliar too; the shoulder-high square base was made of green concave tiles, topped by a whitewashed dome with little bulges of green tile to maximize the heat surface. Another wall had two beds with linen spreads with red cross-stitching that matched the pattern of the curtains. A couple of roughly made dressers and a trunk completed the furnishing. Other than the crucifix and picture of the Virgin, no decorative items distracted from the scrubbed cleanliness of the room, and yet it was invitingly homey. A thought struck her. What if she asked the innkeeper's wife whether she could remain with their family? She and her siblings had divided the ayah's gold coins among one another before parting, and Sigismunda had insisted that Tessa have hers. Surely, the money would pay for her room and board for a while until she could find a place to live? And all the pretty things in those trunks, would they buy her a new life? But the innkeeper might fear the cardinal's wrath by granting her shelter! Sister Agnes often said that when feeling poorly, she should pray, and she tried to, but God seemed very distant. Overcome with emotional exhaustion and fatigue, her head dropped onto her arms resting on the table, and she fell fast asleep, waking up with a start when someone touched her shoulder. It was a gentle touch but startled her just the same, and she jumped to her feet. The person gave a frightened sound and stepped back. Tessa was facing a small woman in black nun's habit and white apron. A white wimple and veil tightly surrounded a homely face with reddish, pockmarked skin. The scars of the dreaded decease disfigured her nose and mouth and left her almost without eyebrows, but the gray eyes were intelligent and alert. She stared at Tessa with a frightened expression and stammered, "Oh, Highness, I do 'pologize for scarin' you! Please, please, forgive, I don't mean—"

Her fright gave Tessa confidence, and she said, "It's all right, I must have fallen asleep. Who are you? And don't call me 'Highness,' I am a countess. Are you a choir woman from Göss?"

The little nun sank into a courtesy. "Oh no, no, High—countess," she said. "I'm jus' lay sister Maria Hedwig, but I come from Göss. The aspirant magistra is in cloister at Mass 'cause 'tis the eve of St. Mary Ascension Feast. I'm here to help with everythin'. 'Tis a bit late an' if countess don't mind, we leave now." She anxiously waited for a reaction and seemed relieved when Tessa smiled.

"That's very nice, Sister Maria Hedwig, I'm ready. My trunks are downstairs. Have you had something to eat or drink?"

The nun shook her head. "You're so kind, countess, but we fast on the eve of feast days. An' choir women just call us by our convent names 'cause we lay sisters serve them. So 'Maria Hedwig' will be good, countess!"

Tessa wasn't sure what the difference was between a lay sister and a choir woman, for Maria Hedwig sure looked like a nun to her, but she would ask for explanations later. She was also weary and tired.

"Let's go then," she said.

The little nun respectfully opened the door for her and followed her down the stairs, past the curtseying innkeeper couple and to the waiting carriage, which was of fine workmanship, though not as elegant her uncle's. The trunks had been loaded, a coachman in brown livery lowered steps, and she and Sister Hedwig climbed aboard with the nun respectfully settling into an opposite corner. They quickly left the town behind, crossed a bridge, and were proceeding up the Mur Valley, wide and apparently prosperous as witnessed by large and affluent farmhouses.

Tessa was curious and full of questions, but Sister Hedwig was shy and deferential and apparently did not want to talk about the abbey and especially not about choir women. Only when questioned about her family was she willing to get more talkative. She'd spent her childhood on a tenant farm near the abbey of Admont in Upper Styria, a couple of days' journey from Göss. At age ten, she came down with smallpox and was almost given up. She'd wanted to become a nun for as long as she could remember, but her parents had objected because she was needed for work at home. During her illness and in spite of the high fever, they heard the child pray aloud that God save her to be a nun when a turn for the better occurred in her condition. Her almost miraculous recovery changed their mind; perhaps, God did intend her to serve Him, and the disfigured girl was unlikely to find a husband anyway. Admont would not accept her because she was so small, but a relative and tenant farmer of the Göss Abbey intervened on her behalf. Help was always needed for serving the choir women, and Sister Hedwig was strong for her size. She seemed totally content with her life. Tessa had become respectful toward nuns during the past year and could not quite imagine being served by one of them. The servants who took care of her needs in Transylvania were little more than slaves, but that time was past, and since the ayah's death, she and her siblings had become accustomed to rely on each other for everyday chores. With the natural curiosity and impatience of her youth, Tessa continued to press for details about the abbey, but Hedwig would only talk about how much she loved being a nun and the privilege of devoting one's life to God. She would say nothing about abbess or choir women, including what their daily life was like. Soon, they were approaching a substantial settlement.

"Here, countess, see—there's the big churches of Leoben, and we're real close to Göss now," Hedwig said and glancing out the window Tessa saw tall spires rising into the afternoon sky.

"'Tis only a good half hour's walk from Leoben to the abbey. An' that steeple over yonder b'longs to St. Jacob's! Can't see it good behind that wood scaffold. They been workin' on the church forever, an' it took more'n a hunnerd years 'til they got to the tower. And there, up that slope, th' big castle's known as 'Massen Castle' that's been here for a long, long time."

Tessa barely kept up with taking in the views Hedwig pointed out. The nun's country dialect took some getting used to, but the woman apparently had a good mind and was certainly deft in avoiding answers she did not think appropriate or felt capable to give. Tessa recalled Brother Sebastian's definitions of building styles and gathered that the church of St. Jacob was being "renovated" from a previous style to elegant baroque. And those other two tall spires, she learned, belonged to the church of St. Francis Xaver of the Jesuit Order.

The carriage hit upon cobblestones as they rattled into town and crossed the main square dominated by a Plague Column and round stone well. There was the town hall with clock tower and comfortable burgher houses; a particularly pretty one had an elegant baroque façade with a relief of allegoric figures. The dimensions of the square surprised Tessa, who asked why it was that large.

"Don't really know, ma'am," was the answer. "But when there's a siege, country folk come for refuge an' need space for wagons an' horses an' the square is where townsfolk make 'em stay. Nowadays, there's a market here all week 'xept Sunday, but 'tis evenin' now, an' stalls are down. There now, countess, take a good look at the Mur River!"

The carriage passed the fortification walls and turned sharply. The road now ran along the river, which glowed a soft pink. Tessa watched the waves turn red as blood in the setting sun when Hedwig's voice interrupted her thoughts.

"Ma'am, see that stone column with three horseshoes? Long ago, a knight was courtin' a lovely maiden, but her father wanted her have nothin' to do with him. So he comes in the night and takes her with him on his horse, and they's ridin' hard to get away. On this spot here, his horse lost a shoe an' stumbled, an' he fell to his death. The maiden's heart was broken, and in the year of our Lord 1514, she became a choir woman at Göss. Could be our Lord always meant her to be one, but I can't think He'd want a man to die for it t' happen! An' she later even got to be abbess! So the story really don't have a sad ending! And from then on, the knight's family had three horseshoes in their coat of arms."

Tessa looked at the slender, fluted column topped by a gothic spire with three stone-carved horseshoes, wondering whether after the death of her beloved, the maiden really felt called to religious life or chose it out of grief. Hedwig told the story with apparent devotion, and the eloquent nun impressed Tessa.

They silently rode along the river turned slate gray in the dusk; their pace slowed as the road rose steeply up a rocky cliff topped by a small, picturesque chapel.

"'Tis St. Lamberti Chapel," said Hedwig, "an' they say 'tis older even than our abbey! St. Lamberti's the saint that saved our abbey from the Turks."

"I read about that," Tessa interjected. "The saint diverted the infidels' arrows after the nuns had trudged on their knees all the way from the abbey praying for his help!"

"Yes, countess, an' look, the horses halt to rest for a spell an' you can see our abbey church, the prettiest in the whole world!"

You've never seen St. Stephen's, or any of the big Vienna churches, Tessa thought but did not say aloud. Why not let the nun believe that her beloved house of worship was the most beautiful in Christendom?

The coach halted to allow the horses a brief rest, and for the first time, Tessa laid eyes on her destiny.

At the river's edge was a large complex of buildings that more resembled a fortress than a convent. It dominated the valley and towered over the adjoining hamlet. Seven weighty watchtowers punctuated massive walls surrounding tracts of two- and three-story buildings with long rows of windows and steep roofs of red tile contrasting the walls painted in bright yellow with white trim, a typical color combination of the time. Within the walls were two churches of diverging architecture that apparently dated from different time periods. The tracts formed several courtyards but also left open areas for trees and landscaped grounds, apparently gardens. Tessa's first impression was one of apprehension about those forbidding walls, but she reminded herself that they'd been built to defend helpless women against intruding marauders. Her eyes drifted from the abbey toward the wooded hills and mountains that bordered the valley, and she imagined how wonderful it would be to roam those woods.

The carriage moved on, leaving the riverbank and proceeding along the walls toward the gate tower. Their approach had apparently been noticed; two large doors on heavy iron hinges squeaked open, they crossed a small bridge and passed through a low arch into an irregular shaped courtyard.

"'Tis the outer court where people that administer land work an' for farmers to bring supplies," Hedwig explained. "See, countess, that's the bureau of the steward, there's our granary and over yonder the brewery, where they been brewing beer for a long time. 'Course," she added hastily, "beer's only for the help an' lay sisters. Choir women drink wine. An' over there's the Parish Church of St. Andreas. The large one here is the abbey church of St. Mary and St. Margaret. The bell's jus' ringin' for Komplet an' litany for choir women an' lay nuns that's not busy."

Tessa was not listening nor did she notice the mighty cannon in the courtyard. The bell's last toll still reverberated in the air, but her finely tuned ear had picked up a Gregorian chant audible through the open door of the church that delighted her.

"I wish I could go into the church," she said but Hedwig shook her head.

"Can't interrupt service that's goin' on, countess. An' after that, it's litany. You get to see our church in the mornin'. I show you to the aspirants' quarters so you can settle down for the night."

The coachman opened the carriage door and lowered the steps for the women to alight. Hedwig quickly got out to assist Tessa while two maidservants emerged to handle the trunks. Tessa stepped down. For the first time, her feet touched abbey ground.

Chapter 7

Tessa smoothed her wrinkled skirts and followed Hedwig through a low archway and gate into a small courtyard. The nun pulled the chain of a polished brass bell by the door, steps approached, and another lay nun opened the door. She smiled at Hedwig and curtsied to Tessa.

"I'm Sister Maria Martina. 'Tis late, magistra was expectin' you earlier, she's now in church, an' I show you to the dormitory, countess."

Tessa was hungry and very tired. She followed Hedwig and Martina down a dark corridor, up a flight of stairs and into a large room divided into cubicles by curtains of white muslin. Martina parted one, and Tessa saw a simple bed and chair, chest, washstand with bowl and pitcher, and privy stool.

"Magistra Maria Henrica, she watches over aspirants, an' she says 'tis your bed here, countess," Martina explained and lit a candle on the dresser.

"Where are my trunks?" asked Tessa. "I need my nightshirt and clean clothes! And I'm hungry and would like to eat first."

The nun looked embarrassed and exchanged a look with Hedwig.

"We don't eat or drink after supper, an' that was two hours back. Forgive me, but I can't bring food at this hour. Your trunks are with the magistra. There's a nightshirt laid out for the countess an' a towel an' soap too. An' God bless you arrivin' at Göss! Sister here an' me, we go back to work now. I's sorry you missed supper, but aspirants get a meal early mornin', an' we hope the countess will sleep well 'til then."

The two nuns quickly withdrew, and Tessa was alone. The dormitory seemed eerily silent, but she sensed that there were girls in the other cubicles, though she could barely detect a sound. Preparing to settle down for the night, she felt hungry, but fasting periods during the past year had taught her to cope. She was thirsty too and, pouring water from the pitcher into the bowl, drank from her cupped hand, then washed her face, and unbraided her hair. She slipped into the nightgown that was too voluminous for her slender body and was about to climb into bed when she remembered that she had not said her prayers. Kneeling on the floor, she quickly went through an Our Father and Hail Mary, wondering what kind of reception Sigismunda had found with the Ursuline nuns. She added a prayer of thanks for the Gregorian chant she'd heard and was about to blow out the candle when there was a faint rustle. Her curtains moved ever so slightly, a rosy face framed by a frilly nightcap appeared, and a moment later, a very young, chubby girl slipped into the cubicle.

"I'm Josepha Countess Plaz," she whispered with a finger over her lips.

"I heard you say you had no supper, and you must be starving! I couldn't survive 'til morning without eating! Here, I know how to sneak a bite from the pantry to eat in bed, and I'll share with you! What's your name? Can I sit with you for a spell? Just don't make a sound!"

Without waiting for an answer, she sat on the side of the bed and pulled a thick slice of fine white bread and an apple from the folds of her gown.

"I'm Marie Therese, Countess Trauttmansdorff, but I'm called Tessa. And that is so sweet of you, Josepha, but are they really that strict here?"

She gratefully reached for the offered bread, and Josepha skillfully broke the apple in halves. The girls chewed quietly for a few moments. Josepha was not pretty. Her small blue eyes were embedded in fat cheeks, she had an upturned nose, and her smile revealed poor teeth. She seemed little more than a child, prompting Tessa to ask her age, and when Josepha said she'd just had her thirteenth birthday, Tessa wanted to know whether she was here for an education.

"Oh no," came the casual answer. "I'm here to stay and become a choir woman as soon as I'm old enough to make profess! My papa says I'm not pretty and won't find a husband. My brother's handsome, but we're not rich, and he needs to inherit the family estate. I'll get a nice dowry for the abbey, though, Papa promised them three thousand florins. How much will you get? I heard you're an orphan and have an uncle who's a cardinal, is that true? And where are you from? They said you come from Vienna, but you don't talk like the Viennese!"

Tessa shook her head. "I'm from Transylvania, that's in eastern Hungary, and my papa died a year ago. Mama—she couldn't take care of the four of us, so my uncle, Cardinal Kollonitsch, took us in. He sent my two brothers to Melk to become monks, my sister Sigismunda wants to join the Ursuline Order in Graz, and I—I'm here. I'm going on fifteen and don't really know what my dowry will be, but," she added with a little touch of haughtiness, "I'm sure my papa left enough for it to be substantial! I'm bringing a gorgeous bridal gown of green brocade, and I'm so looking forward to wearing it!"

"Well," Josepha said dryly, "it'll be a while 'til then. We get to wear it just once, at investiture when we become novices, but we've both got a way to go! Candidates must study an awful lot to pass all those exams. You also have to behave real well, or they won't even let you try! How's your Latin?"

"I've only been studying it for a year now, but I think it's fine."

Josepha wanted to know why Tessa had not learned Latin earlier like other children of Catholic nobility, and Tessa admitted that she'd only recently converted.

"Oh my," was Josepha's reaction. "I hope the others don't find out, or you'll have to put up with teasing and worse! They really think of converts as half heretics and not respectable!"

"But why?" Tessa wanted to know. "Protestants are Christians too, and I come from a very good family! Besides, my papa was Catholic. It's just that Mama isn't because she was born in Transylvania where everyone is Protestant."

Josepha shrugged. "Hey, I don't mind, but there are some mean ones here, and I'm not talking about aspirants but novices and choir women. Watch out for the Galler sisters, especially Maria Bernarda! You see, Göss has a tradition of encouraging relatives to join, and we have pairs, even groups of sisters or cousins here, and they stick together! You should have had your sister come here too. Believe me, your life would be easier! But our magistra domicillarum, Mother Maria Henrica, is very kind. Everyone likes her, and we say she'll become a saint some day! She's very pious and thinks everyone has to suffer with Jesus and let me tell you what I think—"

Tessa was not to learn Josepha's thought. The curtain was pushed aside, and a young choir woman with stern features and candle in hand appeared.

"What do you think you are doing at this hour?" she almost hissed. "Josepha, I see crumbs on your chin, you've been eating outside of meals again! Make sure you confess your constant transgressions! And you, you must be the new aspirant. You should be on your knees thanking the Lord for the privilege of finding refuge in this distinguished abbey! Gossiping late into the night is a poor introduction, I should say. You probably have been eating too, right? I am Reverend Mother Maria Bernarda, and I'm warning you to mend your ways!"

Recalling that Josepha had just warned her of this particular choir woman, Tessa made a contrite face.

"I'm sorry, Reverend Mother, but I've had nothing to eat since midday, and it's been a long trip."

"We don't deal in apologies here, we follow the rules. It's time you became accustomed to fasting! I'll advise the reverend mother magistra that you need a good introduction to this exercise. Now off to bed, Josepha, and lights out!"

She waited until Josepha had reached her cubicle and Tessa blown out her candle. Through the thin muslin curtains, she watched the figure move away. She lay back on her narrow bed and pulled up the sheet. The windows were closed, and the large room was stuffy in the warm summer night. In the stillness, she could hear the breathing of other girls, though she did not think anyone occupied the adjoining beds. Tessa felt a strong antipathy toward the unfriendly Maria Bernarda, but keeping in mind Sister Agnes's admonitions resolved to be as polite as she could. Her mind again conjured the image of the mighty walls enclosing the abbey, but she was too tired to worry. Her last image before drifting off into an exhausted sleep was lay sister Hedwig's effulgent expression when she spoke of the abbey. She never heard the wake-up bell at a quarter past five o'clock in the morning or the commotion in the dormitory. A hand shook her shoulder, and she looked into Bernarda's face.

"There you are again, sleeping over after chatting away half the night! You have but a quarter hour to get dressed, say your morning prayers, and get to church in time for the prim at six. Hurry up now and don't let me catch you being late!"

She let go of her shoulder, and by the time Tessa was fully awake, only a slight movement of the curtains accounted for the visit. Tessa was tired and would have loved to go back to sleep, but she dutifully rose and splashed cool water on her face. She checked her dresser, but the drawers were empty, which left her no choice but to wear her traveling clothes. She brushed off the dust as best she could and smoothed her wrinkled skirts. She ran her fingers through her hair and quickly braided it. When she heard a shuffling of feet, she emerged from her cubicle and found herself trailing a queue of young girls. The last two were but small children, and as Tessa caught up, one of the little girls looked up at her and whispered, "Good morning to you! My name is Francesca, and I've been here a whole year! This is Helena, she's been here only a few months, and she cries a lot, but I console her! What's your name?"

Before Tessa could answer, Josepha, who was just ahead, turned and placed a finger on her lips. Tessa smiled at her, and she and the two children silently followed the others down the stairs, across a courtyard with a well and through a beautiful Gothic side portal into the church. Their little group of girls settled into pews and knelt while a choir of female voices on the loft behind them sang the Latin psalms of the prim, followed by a litany of saints. Tessa still could barely keep her eyes open and was too tired to appreciate the beauty of the church. A young woman in Benedictine habit with a long white veil was with her group, and Tessa assumed her to be a novice. When the last hymn had faded among the soaring walls, muffled footsteps of nuns leaving the choir loft through a side door could be heard, and the novice rose and silently led them back to the dormitory building. They followed her down an arched corridor into a room dominated by a large crucifix. The solid, richly carved furnishings—refectory table and straight-backed chairs as well as sideboards and credenzas along the whitewashed walls—were darkened by age but highly polished. The girls silently lined up behind the chairs, and the novice led them in a lengthy prayer. Then she looked at Tessa and said, "I am Maria Scholastica of Gabelkhoven. I took my preliminary vows at investiture earlier this year, which renders me a novice. I understand you are Marie Therese of Trauttmansdorff, and I welcome you to the abbey of Göss. Our magistra, Reverend Mother Maria Henrica, is with the other choir women observing silence until after High Mass, which we all hear at nine o'clock. You and the other aspirants are having your breakfast now, but I am fasting until after communion. You are to prepare your mind and soul for High Mass and not indulge in idle chatter."

She turned and left the room, and two lay nuns entered and placed pitchers of milk and baskets of white bread on the table. Tessa found herself next to Josepha who had perfected the skill of talking under her breath while barely moving her lips.

"She's so proud that they gave her the name 'Scholastica' at investiture. That was the name of St. Benedict's sister, the first Benedictine nun! We can't pick our convent names, and some of us get awful ones! You can't—"

One of the older girls tapped a spoon to her pewter mug, and Tessa met a reproachful glance, so she and Josepha continued their frugal meal in silence. When they had finished, they went into the treed garden facing a long building tract, which, Josepha explained, housed choir women's cells.

Of the ten aspirants, Helena at five and Francesca at six were the youngest. Helena was a beautiful, shy child with huge blue, slightly slanted eyes and golden curls. She seemed to be quite taken by Tessa and, in a hesitant little voice, told her that she had learned to read and write but, more than anything else, loved to sing. Before Tessa could answer, the bolder Francesca chimed in, "But I can read Latin, which she can't and cries all the time and prays to the Virgin! That's because her mama, the baroness of Halegg, is always sick, and Helena hopes the heavenly Mother will make her well so she can go back home!"

Tessa bent down to take Helena's small hands into hers.

"Has your mama been ill long?" she asked gently.

"Yes," came the halting answer, "as long as I remember. She coughs a lot, and it hurts her bad, and I pray hard to the Virgin to make her well, but I cannot go home 'cause I want to serve the Queen of heaven! I just miss my mama and papa and my ayah so much, and I can't help it when I have to cry!"

Her frail body started to tremble, and Tessa put her arm round the thin shoulders to hold her close.

"Don't cry, Helena, my papa died a year ago, and I miss him very much. I'm a big girl, and yet I cry when I think of him, I really do."

A shadow fell across, and looking up, Tessa saw Scholastica standing over them.

"Do not indulge her childish notions, Marie Therese. A future choir woman must learn early to bring her sorrows to Christ and Christ alone! We do pray for one another but only for our souls! Helena must learn to find consolation in prayer, that is what the Benedictine rule prescribes."

Tessa slowly released the child from her embrace and was rewarded with a grateful glance from eyes smiling through tears. Tessa felt a motherly affection for the child, and it occurred to her that at fourteen, she was probably the oldest of the aspirants. She'd never spent time with young children, and this was a new experience for her. She soon discovered that all the girls came from titled families and had been sent to Göss in the expectation of taking their vows. Except for the lively, chubby Josepha, they already behaved like little nuns dressed in worldly clothes. Walking among the trees, Tessa pulled Josepha aside.

"When do we get a chance to go outside?" she asked.

Josepha did not understand. "What do you mean? We're outside now, and we'll get some more time in the afternoon after lessons and study period."

"No," Tessa said urgently, "I mean outside these walls! Walk through the woods and climb hills! Our home in Transylvania was surrounded by woods, and I've been looking forward so much—" the bell calling for High Mass interrupted her.

"You're out of your mind," Josepha answered, as they hurried back. "I haven't set foot outside the abbey since I came here over a year ago. My parents have promised to come visit before my investiture ceremony and perhaps might take me for a ride. And after final vows, we'll be cloistered choir women and never leave these walls, not even for getting buried!"

The not very agile girl struggled to catch up with the others and missed the stunned expression on Tessa's face. Surely, she had not heard right or Josepha was mistaken! Sister Constanze had walked with them through the streets of Vienna, though it occurred to her that it was always in the company of others. Oh well, if it meant she had to go for walks with one or the other of the girls or a nun, she'd manage to "get lost" as soon as they reached the forest. She was good at that, and even the ayah had learned to simply trust her. Well, for the time being, this garden with its tall trees and view of mountains was preferable to Vienna's noisy and smelly streets.

Three priests celebrated High Mass. Lay sisters, novices, and aspirants sat in the pews; the choir women remained out of sight, and only their voices from the choir loft revealed their presence. Tessa's trained ear guessed that there were more than two dozen of them. At communion time, a silent row of black robed figures filed down the center nave and slowly approached the altar rail. Each kept her head lowered the same way and walked in precisely the same manner, which except for different heights made them indistinguishable from one another. After a few brief moments at the communion rail, they walked through a side door into the sacristy and from there presumably returned to the choir to sing the final passages of the Latin Mass that ended just before ten o'clock.

Leaving the church, Josepha whispered, "We're having our midday meal now, and none too soon, I'm starving! Eat as much as you can, Tessa, it's all you'll get 'til supper at five! And right after we've eaten, our lessons start and go on most of the afternoon."

On their way to the dining room, the girls stopped at two wash-stands to wash their hands, attended by lay sisters, who changed the water in the basins after each girl and handed them towels. Tessa was drying her hands when she heard a familiar voice, "Your dress is filthy and your shoes dusty! I should advise the magistra that you do not belong in the dining hall attired in such a way!"

Tessa saw herself confronted by Maria Bernarda.

"Reverend Mother," she said, "I've had nothing else to wear since I arrived here last night! I wore these clothes on the journey from Vienna, and the roads were very dusty. It's not my fault they don't look fresh."

"Indeed, it is," was the icy reply. "You could have spent a little time early this morning to brush them and clean your shoes so as to spare the other girls the embarrassment of sharing the table with someone in such unkempt condition. But I suppose," she added with a malicious little smile, "cleanliness is not all that popular in Transylvania, especially among Protestants!"

Bernarda turned to walk away, but Tessa grasped her sleeve.

"You are very wrong, Reverend Mother," she said and her voice was angry. "We always wear clean clothes at home, even though we're Protestants! Cleaner than what I've seen in the streets of Vienna during—"

Bernarda's face barely concealed her rage. "Let go of my sleeve immediately! It seems to me that you're still a Protestant at heart, referring to Transylvania as 'home!' I shall report your unseemly behavior to the reverend abbess, and you'll see what will happen."

"Do calm yourself, dear Sister Maria Bernarda," said a gentle yet authoritative voice with a slight accent. A tall and slender choir woman had approached unnoticed.

"Reverend Mother Magistra," began Bernarda but something in the cool eyes made her bite her lip and walk away with a slight bow of her head. The magistra appeared to be in her thirties, but an expression of suppressed suffering rendered her features older; there was a faint smile on the pale lips as she looked intently into Tessa's eyes.

"I am Mother Maria Henrica, the magistra domicillarum for aspirants, which is what you all are until investiture when you become a novice. You do look a little untidy, Marie Therese. By the way, is that how your family called you?"

The evenly spoken words calmed the girl who'd been close to losing her temper.

"No, Reverend Mother," she said, still hoarse with excitement. "My family and also my uncle, the cardinal, called me 'Tessa.' And I am not a Protestant at heart, Reverend Mother, my brothers and sister and I converted and became Catholics at Easter, and we've all studied the catechism for many months. And Protestants in Transylvania are clean people, and I don't know why anyone would say such ugly things to me!"

Henrica gently pulled her into an alcove away from the intently watching girls.

"Tessa, no one says 'ugly things' here. We worship Christ the Lord within these walls, and Reverend Sister Maria Bernarda only expressed concern. We welcome you here, Tessa, and pray that you will become a devoted choir woman, but you must learn to be respectful and accept criticism! I have inspected your trunks and ordered the items you need until novitiate sent to your cubicle, where a lay sister will arrange them for you. The rest of your trousseau shall remain in my custody. Lay sisters will keep your clothes clean and pressed, but you are responsible to look neat and tidy at all times. I dine at the table of the Most Reverend Mother Abbess but spend time with my aspirants each day, and if you have a question, I shall always listen."

She allowed her words to sink in then added, "You have just attended High Mass in our beloved abbey church. I want you to fully appreciate the beauty of our shrine and shall meet you there after your midday meal to explain some of our treasures. Now go and join the others in the dining room and pay attention to our rules, for there is much you have to learn. God bless you, child, and each of your days here!"

Henrica slightly inclined her head, and Tessa, not sure of what was expected of her, curtseyed then hurried to join the other girls in the dining room. Scholastica and her sister Leopoldina, also a novice, presided at the table, where everyone appeared to have been waiting for her. Her voice joined the others in prayer, and after the "Amen," she took her seat next to Josepha.

Maria Henrica's little speech had soothed Tessa. She was hungry and gratefully noticed the ample and well-prepared food two lay nuns placed on the table. All the girls, except little Helena, ate heartily. There was soup, steamed fish, a stew, vegetables, and bread with sweet country butter that reminded Tessa of home. Conversation was permitted during the main meal, but the girls behaved sedately for their age.

"We have three kitchens here," Josepha explained while eating with gusto. "The 'court kitchen' for the abbess and choir women holding important offices, like the prioress, sub-prioress, Magistra Maria Henrica, magistra sacristan, magistra secretary, and so forth. They're part of what is called 'the court' because our abbess has the title 'duchess of the realm.' They eat the best food. The second kitchen cooks for regular choir women, novices, and us, though we don't get some of the tidbits choir women do. And the third turns out rather plain food for lay nuns and maidservants, there aren't too many of those 'cause the lay nuns do most of the work. There's a choir woman supervising the kitchens, and then there's also the magistra cellarum in charge of the wine cellar. You should hear what the court kitchen comes up with on special holidays! I've been told it's fantastic. We'll find out ourselves once we've made profess and are invited to the abbess's table for a particular feast! I think you'll like Abbess Maria Antonia. She's a Countess Uberacker from Salzburg province and has been abbess for about seven years. They say she was the only one ever elected unanimously 'cause everyone likes her so much. And did you notice the different way our magistra talks? She's from Silesia. I think that's somewhere up north near Poland. They do speak German there, though with a funny accent. I've been told that her papa didn't want her to become a nun because she's very talented and got a very special education."

The verbose Josepha was a great source of information, and Tessa resolved to be friends with the bubbly girl. Everyone was chatting animatedly, and Josepha and Tessa kept their voices low not to be overheard.

"Who was the priest at High Mass?" Tessa wanted to know.

"That's the supremus capellanus, Pater Bernhard Starch. There's several priests living over in that building next to the parish church. Perhaps, you've noticed it when you arrived. But the 'supremus,' as he's called, is special. All the priests come from the abbey of Admont up north in Styria, so they're also Benedictines. The supremus hears confessions of the choir women, for us, it's one of the other priests. We go to confession each week, you know. Gosh, if it weren't for gluttony, I sometimes wouldn't know what to confess. There's not much of a chance to sin here!" She giggled. "I hear that there was big trouble once when a supremus got mixed up too much in the abbess's business, which he's not really supposed to do. Or when he gets too old and senile, like one Pater Petrus some fifty years ago—"

Tessa was amazed. "How do you know all this, Josepha?"

"Oh, I have friends among the lay nuns and others who know what's going on," said the girl. "We don't have much excitement here, and everyone loves to gossip," she added with a little smirk. "You'll find out soon enough. But listen to me, Tessa. Watch out for Bernarda, she's got connections! Her aunt is prioress that's the most powerful position next to the abbess, even though she's very old and quite ill, and they say she might have to resign because of poor health. But Bernarda also has two sisters here, Victoria and Eleanor. Seems Count Galler didn't know what to do with so many daughters, I hear he sent a couple more to a convent at Graz. Good thing they didn't all end up in Göss."

Tessa chuckled. "You're too much, Josepha! From what you're saying, I really do wish my sister Sigismunda had come here instead of joining the Ursulines. She's very smart and wants to teach poor children and was anxious to join an order that educates the poor. How come the choir women don't do something like that? What do they do all day?"

"Believe me, they're busy!" Josepha said emphatically. "Why do you think they're called 'choir women?' Because they sing hymns, prayers, litanies, and Latin Mass 'round the clock, seven times during day and night! And there's one thing I really dread about becoming a choir woman, and that's having to go to church every few hours.

I don't know how I'll be able to wake up in the middle of the night, but I'll have to. If you hold office and are part of the 'court,' you get dispensed from some choir duty 'cause you'd have no time left for your job. The same is true if you're old or infirm. By the way, they do run a hospital here and a really good pharmacy that gives out medicine to common folk. And during recreation time, they all do beautiful embroidery or other handicraft."

Tessa was happy to hear about all the singing, and even that it would be during the night did not concern her.

They finished their meal with a sweet crepe topped with strawberry preserves, and Tessa ingratiated herself with Josepha by switching plates and giving her the better part of her desert. After closing prayers, Scholastica announced that they had a half hour of recreation in the garden until they were to report for class. The girls hurried outside, and Tessa headed across the courtyard into the church. She dipped a finger in holy water, crossed herself, and had barely finished genuflecting when Magistra Maria Henrica emerged from the sacristy.

"I wish to tell you about our church, child," she said very quietly, "so you understand and appreciate its beauty and long tradition. Our abbey has been in existence for more than seven hundred years and was founded by the parents of our first Abbess Cunigunde. We believe the original church to have been in the style of a Roman basilica, and there is a crypt below the sanctuary that reveals at least part of the original footprint. It is where our departed choir women find their resting place. In 1338, a terrible fire destroyed much of the church and buildings, but reconstruction began immediately and a gothic church rose from the ruins, larger than the original one, with three aisles and no transept. Changes and additions were made through the centuries and especially during the baroque, but the magnificent choir sanctuary above the crypt is pure Gothic. When I say 'choir,' I'm referring to the sanctuary of the main altar, not the 'choir loft' where we sing."

Henrica turned and pointed to the rear of the church and an exquisite baroque balustrade with intricate lattice railing concealing the choir from the nave.

"Up there is where we gather to sing God's praise day and night," said Henrica, "and where we experience the most exhilarating and rewarding hours of our life. I recall from the letter by His Eminence the cardinal that you have a good voice, Tessa, and our Most Reverend Mother Abbess was happy to hear that. What other skills do you have, perhaps needlework? I personally enjoy painting and creating designs for vestments and encasement of relics."

Tessa was paying rapt attention and began to like the magistra.

"I've never tried to paint, though I enjoy drawing, Reverend Mother," she answered. "But I do so love to sing! I sang solo at Christmastime in the cardinal's chapel, and the 'Salve Regina' at annunciation. Reverend Mother, when will I be allowed to sing here?"

Maria Henrica smiled. "You can't enter the choir loft until after your profess, child. But you'll have ample chance to practice and work on your technique until then. And now let us continue about the church so you will not be late for your lessons. See these grand pillars supporting the vault? The star pattern of their bases determines their shape. Now look at the front two columns and notice that they are twisted like flames cast in stone. They're a symbol of our prayers rising toward heaven like a fire! Keep your eyes on them when you pray, child, and the Lord will hear your words! Such columns are extremely rare, and we're proud that they grace our church."

Tessa's eyes followed the spiraled columns toward the vaulted ceiling with its intricate pattern of support ribs typical for gothic ceilings. Here, they were shaped like delicate blossoms.

Tessa felt the magistra's cool eyes watch her intently.

"Then came the baroque," Maria Henrica continued, "and with it a wave of alterations. Our ten side altars are mostly in that style, and you will pray at them often. Our abbey church is dedicated to the patronage of St. Mary and St. Margaret, whereas the parish patron is St. Andreas. Do you know, child, that you are related to one of our former abbesses, Maria Johanna, who was a Countess Kollonitsch and like you converted to Catholicism from being raised Protestant. She lived about a hundred years ago and was one of our youngest abbesses, barely thirty-eight years old at her installation. She was a most active leader, who commissioned the construction of the second convent building and designated the crypt as burial place for choir women. Her most important legacy is our magnificent baroque sacristy. The door leading to it had to be broken through the sanctuary wall. That is why the frescoes there are no longer complete."

Brother Sebastian's teaching helped Tessa appreciate the stylistic beauty of the church, and her ears hung on the magistra's every word. She felt a pang of regret though for the lost medieval frescoes along the wall. After a pause to allow Tessa's eyes to wander, Maria Henrica continued, "And now, child, it is time for you to join the other girls for your afternoon lessons. Be diligent and work hard, especially study your Latin well, it is of utmost importance in our daily life. And be humble and ask for Christ's guidance."

Her voice became a shade firmer as she continued, "I hear that you have not yet learned to control your emotions, especially your temper. Your behavior today toward Maria Bernarda was unseemly and inappropriate. You must never grasp a choir woman's arm or address angry words to her! This is your first day, Tessa, which is why I stepped in and helped you, but I won't if you act that way again in the future. We punish behavioral transgressions severely, and I would prefer not to inflict them on you. Do you understand me, Tessa?"

The girl's face had flushed a bright red at Maria Henrica's mentioning of the incident, and she barely held back an impassioned account of Bernarda's callous remarks. Instead, she bowed and said meekly, "I shall try my best, Reverend Mother, and I thank you for showing me the church. I love its beautiful piety."

Maria Henrica slightly inclined her head, turned, and moved away so quietly as if gliding across the stone floor. Her black robes melted into the dark nave below the empore like a fading apparition. The girl stared after her for a moment then left the church.

Tessa surpassed the other girls in most subjects not just because she was older. Brother Sebastian had been an excellent teacher, and they had received a solid education at Zay-Ugrocz. She had a talent for languages and no difficulty with Latin, even though she'd only studied it for a year while her Catholic classmates had been familiar with the language since childhood.

The novices Scholastica and Leopoldina participated in the Latin lessons, and it was obvious that both young women had difficulty with grammar. Josepha whispered to Tessa that though they passed their exams for investiture, the supremus insisted they continue Latin classes, and Tessa was secretly proud about outdoing them. But she'd learned that little was to be gained from irritating anyone senior to her in the hierarchy of the abbey. This included almost everyone and especially novices, soon to become choir women. She didn't mind the two somewhat pompous Gabelkoven sisters but thoroughly disliked Bernarda and sensed that the feeling was mutual. Resolved to keep her distance from her, she wondered whether the two other Galler sisters were equally obnoxious. She did like the magistra and intended to try her best not to give reason for criticism.

The lessons lasted for several hours, and the girls afterward remained in the classroom for written exercises, such as translating a lengthy Latin text. Leopoldina and Scholastica left with a remark that "homework was not for novices" and muttered something about attending to "spiritual duties." Tessa gladly helped the other girls with their work. Helena and Francesca both needed tutoring, and she thoroughly enjoyed working with the two youngest aspirants who, of course, were taught according to their age. Helena obviously adored her, and the little girl asked permission to touch Tessa's braided hair.

"It is so thick and beautiful," she said. "I wish mine would grow that long."

"I'm sure it will one day, Helena." Tessa smiled, looking at the child's fine blond locks and delicately beautiful features. Helena had high cheekbones, a perfectly shaped little nose and deep blue eyes, but her skin was unnaturally pale, almost transparent. *I wish she didn't cough so much*, Tessa thought.

During the following weeks, she tried her best to adjust to the abbey's daily regimen and found it even more structured than in Vienna. She did not mind attending church services three times a day and secretly looked forward to the music. Her fine ear quickly discerned some voices not always in tune, and she longed to join the singing, which was mostly reserved for choir women. Josepha mentioned that Choir Magistra Maria Carolina occasionally taught the aspirants hymns and chants, and Tessa anxiously waited for that moment.

Their studies were strictly oriented toward religious subjects, such as the history of the faith and influential church leaders and saints. Still she much preferred her books to needlecraft, but they were taught that also, since the creation of embroidered vestments as well as the "dressing" and encasing of relics formed an important activity at Göss.

Tessa watched the cloistered choir women quietly stroll alone or in small groups in the garden during their recreation time or sit on benches with faces lowered over a book. She knew she was not to address them unless first spoken to and wondered what went on in the minds of the black-robed figures walking between flowerbeds with breviary in hand, rarely raising their eyes. Had they no longing for the beauty of nature surrounding them? Tessa considered her out-doors time most precious, and the all-too-brief periods in the park helped her cope with her rigid new life.

The abbey complex comprised three distinct park sections other than the courtyards created by the various building tracts. The largest was the cloister garden along the northern wall punctuated by three massive watchtowers, known as hermit, trinity, and recreation tower and bordered to the east by two wings of choir women cells. After threats of strife and siege abated, the cloister garden was extended beyond the northern wall by an area known as the convent garden reached through an open arch and a flight of brick steps. Amidst an abundance of flowers and rosebushes were a well and gazebo. Abutting the southern wall was the small abbess garden that Tessa first had a chance to see a week after her arrival. Scholastica told her that the Most Reverend Mother Abbess Maria Antonia wished to see her in her outdoor refuge and to hurry and not let mother abbess wait. Tessa crossed the courtyard between the school building and the convent kitchens and approached a low inner wall against which were the greenhouse, the icehouse, and the bathhouse, in which the girls took their weekly bath. Tessa had thought it odd that she was firmly instructed to wear her shirt while bathing in one of the small sitting tubs placed in private cubicles. Lay nuns brought warm water and laid out bars of homemade soap and pitchers for rinsing off. When done, a lay nun came and put a towel round the girl, who was expected to pull the wet shirt over her head without exposing any part of her body. Tessa was glad that Sister Hedwig assisted her with gentle instructions about the procedure. Personal hygiene at Zay-Ugrocz had been performed with the ayah's help. In Vienna, they'd only had bowls in their rooms for washing, but the ayah made sure that they cleaned themselves thoroughly. Tessa considered the Göss modesty regulations of the Saturday ablution exaggerated. It was a nuisance to bathe with a shirt on, but she had come to understand that abbey rules were not negotiable.

Between bathhouse and icehouse was an arched gate, and Tessa put her hand on the ornate wrought-iron handle. The gate opened with a squeak, revealing stone steps and a winding brick path. Before her eyes was a narrow but exquisite garden. Sheltered by fortification walls and buildings from view, it was a private little paradise, meticulously manicured and teaming with rosebushes, formally trimmed shrubbery and an abundance of flowers at the height of their late summer bloom. Tessa had never seen such a lovely and thoroughly feminine garden. Ivy and climbing plants such as clematis and wisteria grew on white trellises, all but concealing the rough walls, beyond which one could see wooded mountains. She instinctively reached for a yellow rose to enjoy the scent when a calm voice brought her back to reality.

"Here, Marie Therese," it said, and looking up, Tessa saw the freestanding gazebo. She followed the brick path and approached the charming white structure that divided the refuge into two equal sections. The little pavilion with a hexagonal footprint was slightly elevated and open to all sides. Eves and soffit were delicately carved and a wide overhang sheltered from sun or rain. Tessa had almost reached the steps until her eyes discerned the dark figure in the elegant chair. The stiffly starched white wimple below the black veil of fine, silken material had two pleated corners, which she knew was reserved for abbesses. Maria Antonia was about sixty years old and looked very much her age. Her features had an almost saintly expression, and Tessa recalled hearing that she'd been elected unanimously, a remarkable fact since the chapter was rarely in full agreement. The abbess smiled.

"Welcome to Göss, Marie Therese. I am your Abbess Maria Antonia, Countess Uberacker. We are very pleased to have you with us and trust that you will become a pious and devoted choir woman when the time comes." She extended a thin hand, and Tessa bowed to kiss her ring, as instructed.

"Thank you, Reverend Mother Abbess," she murmured.

"Come and sit with me, child, I wish to speak to you," Maria Antonia said, gesturing toward a small stool. After a pause, she continued, "We choir women have the sole mission of glorifying the Lord. We sing His praise incessantly, and during our brief recreation periods, our busy fingers produce items to beautify His sanctuary and the vestments of our priests. And we lead a life of humble and diligent service and of love toward one another."

She paused and Tessa thought that she would no more be able to love Bernarda than she expected that woman to love her. Abbess Maria Antonia had been told of the hallway scene and read the girl's face like an open book.

"Marie Therese, the path toward becoming a good choir woman is a difficult one, for which good intentions alone do not suffice. You will have to work very hard, and such work is not limited to studying Latin, the Rule of St. Benedict, or the New Testament. Even the holiest scripture contains only words, and it is up to each one of us to practice their meaning. Our choir women hail from noble families, and humbleness is a difficult lesson to learn. But learn it you must, as well as obedience, the most important and rigid rule of religious life! Your character will be tested many times during the years to come, often with intent, and punishment for transgressions is harsh, especially for sins of pride and disobedience. I do not wish to inflict punishment on any of the souls in my care, but I must if called for, for that is what God wants me to do. Do you remember the ultimate act of humbleness to which our Lord Jesus, Son of God, submitted himself? He washed the feet of His disciples and willingly accepted the greatest of indignities, flagellation, and crucifixion. Yet He was without sin and forgave the world! How, therefore, can you bear a grudge because of a perceived small slight?"

Tessa's cheeks were flushed. "But it wasn't small, Reverend Mother Abbess! She accused me of being a filthy Protestant! In Transylvania, we—"

A slight gesture stopped her.

"Marie Therese, would you rather have endured flagellation as our Lord did? The choir woman remarked on your untidy clothes, which justly offended her. She was taught to put aside pride when she prepared for her profess five years ago. Her words were motivated by her wish to help you, and you must love, not resent her for it! This coming Saturday will be your first confession here, and you must tell the priest whatever is in your heart that you know would not please our Lord!"

There was a brief silence. Tessa stared at her tightly clasped hands and felt the woman's gaze upon her. When the abbess spoke again, her voice was very soft.

"Marie Therese, never forget that there is not one woman in our order, choir woman or lay sister, who has not endured your struggles. I've been told that you are blessed with a good mind and a lovely voice. When God endows us with special gifts, He places even heavier burdens upon our shoulders. Carry your load with joy! Pray hard and sing His praise, and He will hear you! Ours is a beautiful and blessed life within these walls, and in time, you will understand that their purpose is not to confine but to shelter and defend us from the evils of the world! Those among us worthy of His grace find that the path we walk toward our Savior is one of infinite beauty. Walk it in joyful humbleness, Marie Therese! And when at times you feel you cannot cope with a task before you, do this. There are three large towers bordering the cloister garden, as you surely have noticed. The middle one is known as the hermit tower. Its stairs lead to an observation room, from where you can observe the beautiful countryside surrounding us. You'll find joy and peace in looking at the sky, the clouds, the mountains and trees. When I first came here as a child of eleven, I would climb the tower whenever I longed for my parents and became homesick. Do likewise and your sadness will go away! Will you remember my words, Marie Therese?"

Tessa's face was wet with tears. Her mind was troubled, but she sensed kindness and compassion in Abbess Maria Antonia. Impulsively, she sank to her knees and kissed the slender hand, not the ring.

"Thank you, Reverend Mother Abbess, I will, and I shall go there right now if I may," she whispered.

Maria Antonia dismissed her with a blessing. She sighed as she watched the tall, lanky girl walk down the path toward the gate and knew in her heart that this latest of her charges faced a rocky future. Did she truly have a vocation to religious life? Raising her eyes toward the sky, the abbess fervently prayed that God might grant Tessa the fortitude she would need. Maria Antonia was well aware of Bernarda's occasionally unkind attitude toward lay sisters, novices, and especially aspirants.

"And let kindness fill your daughter Bernarda's heart, oh, Lord," she prayed, "and not have her test this child too severely."

Closing the gate behind her, Tessa cast a quick glance to the clock tower of the parish church and saw that there was still time left 'til evening service. She hurried through the arch of the dormitory building toward the hermit tower. She pushed the squeaky door open and took the winding stairs two steps at a time. They ended in a circular room with openings to all sides, three of them small and narrow and typical for fortifications, but the one to the north had a wide arch. There were stone benches along the walls, and Tessa sat to catch her breath. The view was indeed beautiful. At her feet was the extended convent garden with the river beyond, and a late afternoon sun made little stars dance on the waves. Chestnut trees and weeping willows lined the riverbank. Lamberti Chapel was to her right, and she tried to imagine the attacking Turks, their arrows held at bay by the Saint. As far as her eyes could see, the peaceful ambiance of a summer evening was descending, and a slight haze rose from between the spruce on the mountain ridges like a sigh mourning the waning day. Tessa had come to the difficult realization during the past week that there was little chance she could venture outside the convent walls. But Abbess Maria Antonia had been right—the hermit tower brought peace to her heart, and she prayed for God's help to cope with her new life.

And God heard her prayer for after vespers when the girls returned to their classroom for another study hour a stately choir woman awaited them.

"It's Reverend Mother Maria Carolina, the choir mistress," whispered Josepha. "It means we're going to sing tonight."

Tessa was delighted, and her first thought was that God had listened to her! Maria Carolina waited until the girls had settled into their chairs then, in a matter-of-fact voice, announced that they were going to learn a new hymn. She pulled the black felt cloth from the spinet in the corner and sat down.

"On September 7, we celebrate the feast of our beloved abbey's foundress, the saintly Adula, who passed away that day in 1020 to join our Lord in heaven," she said. "A special High Mass will be celebrated and afterward bread distributed among those waiting at the gate. While this tradition takes place you will be singing. There are only two weeks left until then, and we shall practice each evening. I will now play while you open the hymnals on the table and turn to page 25 so that you may learn the notes. Let us begin!"

Maria Carolina was an accomplished musician and mastered the spinet with deft virtuosity. Tessa read music and followed the melody with ease. The magistra then played the first note and raised her large hands to direct the little choir. Only Tessa went through the whole hymn without hitting a wrong note while the others struggled with the unfamiliar tune and text. Maria Carolina did not miss the talented addition.

"I believe you are Marie Therese," she said. "Who taught you to sing?"

"Sister Agnes of the Ursuline Order in Vienna, Reverend Mother," Tessa answered. "She gave me lessons throughout last winter and spring. She allowed me to sing solo in the chapel, and—"

"I only asked who taught you," was the dry reply. "You have a good voice, a bit low in timbre, but we'll see what we can do with it. Now let us start again at the beginning."

The enthusiastic Tessa felt chastised but was so happy about the chance to sing that she did not mind spending the next hour repeating over and over what had taken her only moments to learn. Music was back in her life, and she had the attention of the choir mistress who, according to Josepha, was in charge of the abbey's music. She also noticed that Helena's small voice revealed an excellent ear.

That night, Tessa went to bed happier than she had since her arrival. The abbess had been kind despite her admonitions, the tower brought peace, and singing filled her heart with joy. Perhaps, all would be well if she could study music, become a choir woman, and hear her voice resound in the beautiful church. Surely, the other nuns would be glad to have someone among them who sang so well! Maria Carolina seemed rather old from the perspective of a fourteen-year-old, and perhaps, she, Tessa, would become choir mistress one day and be able to devote her life to music! She hoped that her beloved papa could hear her from heaven. Tessa fell asleep with a smile on her lips.

Josepha said that the choir magistra was also deputy sacristan and that some women resented her for her blunt criticisms. Tessa looked forward all day to the evening practice, and her concentration was not lost on Maria Carolina. Like typical children, the other aspirants were anxious to get through the tedious repetitions, but Maria Carolina insisted on each girl's best effort and would not tolerate sloppy performance. She understood that Tessa's alto voice could not reach high notes, so she had her sing in a lower key. The girl effortlessly carried her part and combined with the high timbre of the others the little choir aspired to a new musical level.

The days passed quickly and without major incident. Tessa's travel outfit had been washed and pressed, and she alternated wearing it with her only other dress for the warm season, but it was obvious that her clothes were plainer than those of other aspirants. She had never been particularly concerned with what she wore, but then she had never lived among girls, and now on the verge of becoming a young woman, it troubled her. She told herself that it was only because she did not want them considering her a poor Hungarian. She'd been taught that pride was a deadly sin and dutifully confessed her apprehension about clothes to the old priest who conducted the aspirants' weekly exercise of penance and reconciliation. She was told that vanity was a terrible vice for a future choir woman and given a penance of five rosaries to be said on her knees that very night. The priest then asked which activity brought her most joy. Tessa almost said "music" but caught herself, realizing that he might order her to forego singing in further penance. *Mother Carolina needs me in the choir*, she thought, *and I can't let her down.* So after a moment's hesitation, she said, "Visiting the hermit tower, Father."

It was a truthful answer, for looking out across the river and woods and meadows brought her great joy.

"So between now and your next confession, you will not go near the tower while you learn to suppress your vanity and pride. Instead, thank the Lord for the privilege of being here!" the priest ordered.

It was harsh penance, starting with the tired girl kneeling by her bedside in the dark and murmuring her five rosaries. August days were hot, and windows remained closed day and night. Tessa bravely fought back sleepiness, though her head repeatedly dropped onto the bed and she needed great willpower to remain awake. Avoiding the tower was even harder, and she dared not look in that direction during her walks in the garden. It was also difficult not to resent looks of condescension and little snide references about her clothes from other girls, though such behavior was typical for children that age. Even Scholastica made a point of mentioning the beautiful clothes she had given away at the time of her investiture.

"Leopoldina and I are bringing a dowry of one thousand florins each, which is much more than most other aspirants," she declared.

Her sister spoke up, "But, Scholastica, it was Papa's sister— our generous aunt—who provided the money as well as our bridal gowns!"

"Our papa would have given us an even larger dowry, Leopoldina! I am older than you and know more about our circumstances than you do. I wish you would not argue with me. Now come along, the magistra noviciarum wishes to see us."

She angrily took her sister's hand and walked away, and Leopoldina followed with an apologetic smile.

"That's a pretty apron you're wearing today, Tessa," she murmured. Josepha laughed when they were out of hearing.

"Don't let it worry you, Scholastica's always got to be ahead of everyone else. She's just jealous that your Latin is so good. And your apron really is very dainty, Tessa, much nicer than mine!"

The invariably cheerful Josepha was devoid of vanity, cared little about her appearance, and often drew criticism for a stained apron.

But Scholastica's remark hurt Tessa. She did not know the cash amount of her dowry, but the wound of losing her home and being abandoned because of family debt was still raw and made her overly sensitive. Fortunately, Josepha had a knack of always finding just the right thing to say.

Chapter 8

According to tradition Adala, the saintly foundress of Göss died on September 7, 1020, and in 1744, the day of her feast dawned in cloudless splendor. On this and only occasion, the Supremus wore special vestments designed and in large part personally executed by Abbess Cunigunde II during the thirteenth century. They were a true work of art and consisted of an ornately beautiful set of embroidered vestments in vivid colors, embellished with figures so finely stitched they appear to be painted. These garments have endured to this day and are still admired for their artistic detail. Tessa was so riveted by the elegance of design that she barely paid attention to the ceremonies.

Decorated baskets filled with fresh loaves of bread the lay sisters baked throughout the night were placed on the steps of the sanctuary to be blessed and distributed to the villagers, together with rounds of cheese wrapped in white linen. Lay nuns carried the baskets to the main gate after the service, where the shuffling of feet and murmuring voices of the crowd could be heard. On this rare occasion, the choir women emerged from cloister to hand out the food, followed by festivities for common folk in the outer courtyard. Mother Carolina assembled her aspirants near the gate, and the girls watched the choir women emerging, dressed in their festive habits called "flocke," made of finely pleated wool with wide sleeves that almost touched the ground. The gates were opened, and they began distributing bread and cheese into outstretched hands. The aspirants also wore their best outfits, and Tessa had put on her new brown wool dress, even though it was too heavy for the warm day. She was hot but determined not to show her discomfort and concentrated on Mother Carolina directing the singing. Then she heard the all-too-familiar voice of Maria Bernarda among the choir women nearby saying to her younger sister, "Did you see that new girl from somewhere in Hungary in that brown sack of heavy winter material, Eleonora? Really, our common folk must wonder what we've come to that we accept such poorly clad paupers into our noble abbey! If she ever becomes a choir woman, she'll be a detriment to our reputation!"

Tessa almost choked and missed her cue. Mother Carolina raised her eyebrows, and the girl resumed singing, but the mistake confused the others, and only the choir mistress's expertise managed to bridge the lapse. Tessa was mortified. It was her fault and hers alone that they had stumbled! Worse, Bernarda turned and looked straight into Tessa's eyes, her narrow lips parted in a smile of malicious contempt. Heat and fasting as well as embarrassment about her failure combined with insulted pride were too much for the hot-tempered girl. When the last hymn ended, she stepped forward to confront Bernarda.

"What have I done to you that gives you the right to be so mean to me, Reverend Mother?" she said in a loud and angry voice. "I always thought nuns to be kind and loving, but you are not, and I don't think you deserve to be one!"

Hedwig was passing loaves to the Galler sisters, and from the corner of her eye, Tessa noticed the horrified expression on the lay nun's pockmarked face. She felt a hard grip on her arm and heard Mother Carolina's voice clipped with suppressed anger.

"You will contain yourself and return to the dormitory immediately!"

"No!" Tessa cried through tears. "Not until she admits that she—"

"Be quiet! Your behavior is a disgrace, and you will do as I say!" Mother Carolina's voice remained low, but her tone made clear that there was to be no argument.

"Do as she says or you'll not sing again," Josepha whispered close to her ear, and her words sobered Tessa. She bit her lip, murmured, "Yes, Reverend Mother," and walked through the crowd of lay nuns who had overheard the exchange and silently parted to make way. She felt like running a gauntlet, and the way to the dormitory seemed endless. Once there, she threw herself across the bed and succumbed to a violent outburst, sobbing and pounding the pillow with her fists while twisting from side to side in sheer agony. The frustrations of the past weeks, confinement without the hoped-for chance to roam through woods, the penance not to even visit the hermit tower, all came crushing down on her. This was it! She'd never join a community of women such as Bernarda! She'd leave this very evening! But how? The gate would close as soon as the festivities were over. There was the abbess's garden and the trellis that supported the vines. She could climb to the top of the wall and jump down on the other side! She gave no thought to what might happen next, but the idea of escaping felt great.

The dormitory was deadly quiet. She knew that the aspirants and everyone else in the abbey were attending a festive meal but could not bring herself to join, embarrassed about the public chastisement by the choir mistress. Everyone but the youngest aspirants had fasted since the evening before, yet Tessa was too upset to be hungry. She fell asleep and awoke when someone tucked her sleeve. It was Josepha.

"My, you really got yourself into trouble today, Tessa," said the girl, her face more somber than Tessa had ever seen it. "The magistra domiciliarum wishes to see you at four o'clock in her office over in the main tract, and that's always serious. Please, please, Tessa, be humble and accept whatever punishment she meets out! Believe me, you can't win! You behaved badly toward a choir woman and—"

"But you didn't hear the mean things Bernarda said about me, Josepha! Surely, she must be punished also!"

"Don't be silly, Tess, she's a choir woman, and you are nothing, not even a novice! She'll deny everything, and it was you who ruined our hymn and insulted her! Promise me to ask for forgiveness before you say anything else, will you?"

Tessa was hot-tempered and passionate but not stupid and knew that Josepha's words made sense.

"All right, I will, Josepha," she said then impulsively put her arms around the younger girl for a tight hug. "Sometimes, I think you're the only friend I have here! Why are they all against me?"

Josepha's voice was very serious. "They're not, except perhaps Maria Bernarda. Mother Carolina likes you, and don't you think everyone knows that she created a special part for you in the choir? And then you had to ruin it! Tessa, we're preparing ourselves to become nuns because Christ loves us and wants us to serve Him. When I was little, my papa said I was homely and would never find a good husband, and my ayah would wipe away my tears and tell me that Jesus loved me and chose me to become His bride and that He was a more glorious bridegroom than any king! He loves you too, Tessa, but you must earn His love by humbling yourself. Look how smart God made you! And He gave you a beautiful voice and pretty face, which is so much more than either Maria Bernarda or I can claim."

She spoke without bitterness or envy, and Tessa looked at her friend admiringly. The always cheerful, gossipy Josepha had never before been as serious, and she sensed that the girl meant well.

"Thank you, Josepha, I'll never forget how good you are to me and hope that you'll always be my friend. What do you think my punishment will be?"

"I don't know, but you'll have to accept whatever it is because if you don't, they'll only make it more severe! I've heard of cases when renegade novices or even choir women—" Josepha caught herself not wanting to disclose that punishment could be as harsh as whippings on the bare back in the presence of the full chapter while prayers were recited. Instead, she continued, "Even choir women sometimes were locked up in their cells! But we, aspirants, don't even have cells yet," she continued in a lighter tone, "so that can't happen to you. Now stand up and let me look at you! There, your pretty apron is all wrinkled! Reverend Mother Henrica wouldn't like that, so let's find you a fresh one!"

Josepha's chubby little hands deftly smoothed the pleats of her skirt, handed her another apron, and ran a comb through her friend's disheveled hair.

"There, now you look neat again! Now show me a real contrite face!" And glancing out the window toward the church tower, she added, "It's almost four o'clock! The main tract is across the courtyard, and the door at the very end of the hall is the magistra's office. Hurry up and don't keep her waiting!"

Tessa blew a quick kiss on her friend's cheek and hurried down the long flight of stairs. But her feet became leaden, and her pace slowed, and her courage waned as she approached the magistra's door. What if they sent her back to Vienna in disgrace for being incorrigible? She could never live down such shame! Even her beloved papa might consider her an unworthy Trauttmansdorff! Any punishment was preferable to having her arrogant Viennese relatives hear that she'd been expelled! The thought gave her courage. Twice she withdrew her hand then heard the clock tower strike four and timidly knocked at the door. There was a moment of silence before a calm voice said, "Enter!" The magistra was seated behind a richly carved table. Polished cupboards and shelves filled with books and papers lined the walls, the ceiling had an exquisite stucco design, and gouaches in gold frames hung between windows. Tessa's eyes met the stern gaze of the magistra, and following Josepha's advice, she started to apologize when Maria Henrica said evenly, "Kneel, Marie Therese!" Tessa dropped to her knees, and a long silence ensued.

"I have warned you, Marie Therese, about the serious consequences of misbehaving and do not wish to hear what prompted you to insult Reverend Mother Maria Bernarda today. Nothing justifies disgracing your fellow aspirants, yourself, and our beloved abbey on this our special feast day when we celebrate our saintly foundress! I see that you have not yet earned your place at Göss, and you will begin by prostrating yourself before Reverend Mother Maria Bernarda and apologizing to her!"

The magistra noticed Tessa's shoulders convulse as if stricken by a whip, but the girl's head remained bowed.

"And," Maria Henrica continued, "for the next two days, you will eat your meals of bread and water sitting on the floor! Of course, you must also confess your transgression on Saturday. Do you understand me? Now go kneel by the crucifix and pray for our Lord's forgiveness! Reverend Mother Bernarda will be here shortly, and I trust she will find it in her heart to forgive you."

Tessa rose obediently and walked over to the richly carved prayer stool at the feet of a large crucifix. Her face wet with tears, she knelt on the floor but even in her chagrin understood that the magistra had spared her the additional indignity of having to prostrate herself before Bernarda in front of other choir women or aspirants. Time passed, the silence only broken by the scratching of the magistra's pen. *She's writing to the cardinal*, Tessa thought. Then she heard footsteps, there was a slight knock at the door, and Maria Bernarda entered.

"You wish to see me, Mother Magistra," she said in a hurt voice. "I have been praying to the Lord for strength to overcome my sorrow about the insult I suffered on this our special day of—"

There was coolness in Henrica's voice when she interrupted, "Marie Therese is here to ask your forgiveness, Maria Bernarda," she said. "Marie Therese, you will prostrate yourself before the Reverend Mother and express regret for your inappropriate words and promise never again to conduct yourself in such manner!"

Tessa rose and, without looking at Bernarda's face, walked over to kneel before her.

"I said 'prostrate,' Marie Therese, that means you will lie face down on the floor with your arms stretched out at the sides!"

Tessa thought of the day when she had to kneel before the cardinal to apologize. She'd found it so hard at the time, yet it was infinitely more difficult now to lie on the floor before a woman less than ten years older than she who had intentionally provoked her. For a moment, she did not think she could do it, but the thought of her papa and how sad he would be if she were expelled from the abbey in disgrace prevailed. When her forehead touched the floor and her arms were spread, Henrica spoke again, "Now ask for forgiveness!"

It was the most tortured moment in her young life, but Tessa said haltingly that she regretted her words and asked to be forgiven.

She was staring at the wooden planks close to her face yet in her mind could see the triumphant look in Bernarda's cold blue eyes.

"My heart is so very sad, and I only pray," the choir woman began in a falsetto tone, and again, the magistra interrupted.

"It is seemly for a bride of Christ to forgive as our Lord forgives our transgressions every hour of each day. Marie Therese has expressed regret for her behavior."

Bernarda got the message. "I forgive you, Marie Therese," she said sweetly, "in the name of our Lord Jesus Christ."

"Thank you, Maria Bernarda," said the magistra. "You may leave us now. Walk with God!"

When the door had closed behind her, the magistra said, "You may rise, Marie Therese, and return to your dormitory. Your punishment is light this time, but it will not be should you again lose control, for we cannot tolerate outbreaks of such kind. Look over there by the cross, there's a whip hanging on the wall. It has been used on choir women, novices, and even aspirants in punishment for serious transgressions. Spare me having to use it on you in front of the whole chapter! Will you solemnly promise me to improve your ways?"

Tessa slowly rose from the floor. Her tear-streaked, disconsolate face was ashen, and she missed Maria Henrica's fleeting expression of concern. The girl stared at the whip and thought that never in her whole life had she been beaten in such manner for any offense. Searching for words, she said in a halting voice, "I promise to try my best, Reverend Mother."

Henrica read her like an open book. "You may sit there," she said, gesturing toward a little stool by her desk. "And I now want you to listen very carefully, Tessa. Dedicating your life to Christ and living within a small community of women is not an easy mission but one that our Lord rewards gloriously. Even though we follow a saintly vocation, we remain frail human beings, and our minds and hearts fall prey to darkness and sin. The difference between saint and sinner rests on the strength of our love for Christ who, above all, wants us to obey His commandment to love our God with all our heart and our neighbor like ourselves. Maria Bernarda has forgiven your offense, and you must love her with all your heart for that and for being a bride of Christ!"

Tessa lifted her face and looked into Henrica's eyes. "Reverend Mother Magistra, why does she not like me? I have never—"

She was quickly interrupted. "Maria Bernarda does love you, and it is not for us to question the trials and examinations with which God afflicts us to test the strength of our character. Whatever it was that she said was not intended to offend but to guide you, a lowly aspirant, toward the right path!" Her voice softened as she continued, "Tessa, what you are experiencing is no different from the struggles all of us have fought within ourselves. You must understand, child, that the harder the fight, the more glorious the victory. Overcoming great challenges and dedicating the struggle as well as the victory to Jesus on His cross is the essence of our vocation to religious life. You do feel a vocation in your heart, and that is why you have come to Göss, do you not, Tessa?"

Tessa was exhausted, hot in her heavy woolen dress, and hungry from her long fast. She desperately wanted to leave this place of her humiliation, go to her tower, and be alone.

"Yes, Reverend Mother," she said, willing to promise anything in exchange for permission to leave.

Again, Maria Henrica read her thoughts. Looking at the large mantle clock on a sideboard, she said, "You may go and pray until your evening meal at half past five. And," she added, "Reverend Mother Maria Carolina will allow you to continue singing in the aspirants' choir, provided that you pay attention and dedicate yourself to excellence, so you will be well prepared to join our choir after taking your vows."

That was a ray of sun for Tessa, who had feared that her lapse might henceforth exclude her from this joy. A wan smile brightened her face.

"Oh, thank you. Thank you, Reverend Mother," she said, kissed the nun's hand, and left the room. Maria Henrica had said that she should pray without mentioning the church, and the girl hurried through the deserted garden, glad not having to face anyone. She quickly entered the hermit tower and started to hurry up the stairs but stopped abruptly when she heard singing. Tessa instinctively turned to leave when she recognized the voice as Helena's and climbed the steps to the tower chamber. The little girl was standing by the arched window and turned at the sound of her approach. Her sad little face lit up, she ran toward Tessa and wrapped her thin arms around her.

"Oh, Tessa," she almost sobbed, "I'm so glad to see you! I was so scared what might happen to you or that you would go away, and I didn't know what I'd do without you! I love you so, Tessa, I can't imagine being without you!"

Tessa picked up the slight body and, sitting down on the stone bench, pulled the child onto her lap. She forgot her own sadness sensing the loneliness of this five-year-old, whose only friend until now had been the precocious Francesca.

"It's all right, love," she said, gently rocking the child. "I'm not going away, and I love you too, Helena. After all, you and I have the best voices in the choir, don't we? I can't sing the soprano voice, only you can, so neither one of us can leave, right?"

Helena wiped away a tear, and her smile revealed a missing baby tooth.

"Oh, thank you, Tessa, thank you! Mama used to say that I'd always be her little girl, but then she became ill, and Papa said it was best for me to come here. Please promise never to get sick and always stay here with me, please, Tessa?"

Only minutes earlier, it had seemed to Tessa that she could never be a choir woman and spend her life in the company of Bernarda. Christ, she'd felt, had enough saintly women serving Him and did not need her! Now she knew that this child not only loved but also needed her. Was the Lord sending her a message? Holding Helena close, she looked at the sky with its golden clouds in the late afternoon sun, and it occurred to her that Christ had given her life at Göss new meaning, a task if you will, to love and protect this youngest and frailest of His aspirants. "Oh, Lord," she silently prayed, "I promise you that I will not disappoint this child, no matter what they do to me! And I will become as good and faithful a choir woman as I can, if only they will allow me to. Amen!"

Both girls heard the bell ring for supper and, after a final hug, hurried back. The aspirants proceeded to stand behind their chairs for the opening prayer, and Tessa had forgotten that her punishment was to continue in the dining room. Scholastica lost no time to remind her. When she saw Tessa standing behind her seat with the other girls, she said firmly, "Marie Therese, I find it difficult to believe that you could so quickly forget what Mother Magistra has ordered you to do for the next two days. Leave the table and stand over there by the crucifix! After the blessing, you shall sit on the floor to eat!"

Tessa's face flushed a bright red, there was a lump in her throat, and she felt angry words coming. Then she saw Helena's pleading eyes and remembered her promise to the child.

"Yes, Maria Scholastica," she said hoarsely and walked over to stand below the large cross. The other aspirants had never before witnessed such punishment, but none giggled or snickered. There was a shuffling of heavy chairs when they sat down as the lay sisters served the food. Due to the feast day, everyone in the abbey had enjoyed an elaborate midday meal, yet supper still included cold ham, fowl, cheese, eggs, and milk. The little pockmarked nun Hedwig approached Tessa and placed a pitcher of water, a tin mug, and a pewter plate with a chunk of dark bread on the floor beside her. "God bless, countess," she murmured and Tessa almost laughed out loud at the irony of being addressed "countess" and served bread and water on the floor. She gathered her skirt and sat down, humiliated all over again, this time under the eyes of girls younger and less educated than herself. The lump remained in her throat, and in spite of being hungry and thirsty after the long fast, she could barely swallow her frugal meal of disgrace. There was little chatting at the table during the meal, with Helena suppressing sobs and wiping away tears. Finally, it was time for the closing prayer, and the girls returned to church for evensong and litany. It seemed that this long, terrible day would never come to an end, and Tessa was grateful when everyone was finally in bed and Leopoldina ordered the candles extinguished. She lay exhausted in the dark, every part of her body aching, her heart full of despair. She was hot in her heavy linen nightshirt and pushed back the cover. An ascending moon cast a dim light into the dormitory, and Tessa saw the folds of her muslin curtain move to reveal Josepha. She always marveled how noiselessly the rather awkward girl was able to move in the dark dormitory.

"You're not asleep yet, are you?" she whispered. "I just wanted to give you a hug and tell you not to worry, everything's going to be all right! I know it's tough, but try not to let them get to you. We're all in a pickle now and then. It's just that you chose a difficult woman to annoy!"

"Josepha, don't get into trouble because of me," Tessa pleaded. "I've got enough on my plate already."

Her friend suppressed a giggle. "No, you don't, or rather didn't, I saw the puny piece of dry bread they gave you! You must be starving. That's one good reason why I behave 'cause I couldn't take the fasting. Here, I saved you something from the feast." And she pulled a lumpy piece of cake from her sleeve. It had lost its shape from being carried in the pocket of an apron, but it smelled awfully good to the hungry Tessa.

"Josepha, I don't know whether I should," she said. "Do I have to confess that I didn't follow the magistra's orders?"

"No, you don't, silly! According to Mother Henrica's decree, you are to sit on the floor with bread and water at mealtime for two days, but I bet she didn't say a word about eating in bed!"

Tessa grinned at Josepha's logic and hungrily reached for the crumbly Mass. It was a layered yeast cake filled with almond and pear preserve, and even in its present state tasted well.

"Thank you so much, you're a treasure," Tessa said between bites. "I hope I can help you out sometime!"

"I told you I wanted to be your friend, but now let's go to sleep, and tomorrow, I'll teach you more about handling the Galler sisters!"

Josepha blew a quick kiss on Tessa's cheek and disappeared without a sound. They had not aroused anyone's attention. The children were tired from the long hot day and heavy meal, and only their regular breathing could be heard. When Tessa heard light footsteps a little later, she pretended to be asleep. Through her lashes, she watched someone ever so slightly open her curtain to check whether she was alone, and she thanked God that she and Josepha had not been caught together. Josepha's gesture, however, had greatly heartened her. Much as she'd been touched by Helena's affection, Josepha proved to be a real friend when she desperately needed one. *Perhaps, it'll all work out yet*, she thought but found little rest. The events of the day had upset her too deeply, and Bernarda's cold eyes and hypocritically sweet words of forgiveness haunted her dreams.

Tessa's personality changed during the following weeks, and her spirit seemed broken. She lived in constant fear of arousing someone's displeasure and the image of a whipping before the congregation of nuns haunted her. She found it difficult to concentrate on her studies, and even singing brought less joy. The aspirants now had regular choir lessons and sometimes sang in the parish church for the village congregation. Mother Carolina never referred to the incident on Foundress Day, but Tessa knew that she had to try extra hard to regain the choir mistress's confidence.

Once a month on Sunday afternoon, the girls had permission to write letters to relatives. Tessa had sent a long letter to Sigismunda in Graz, a shorter one to her brothers at Melk and a brief and formal note to her mother in Transylvania. That one took the longest to compose, she just didn't know what to say to Miczike and still felt unable to forgive her for forgetting Papa so quickly. In mid-October, she was called into the magistra's office and handed a letter from Sigismunda. It had obviously been read for the seal was broken and one or two sentences crossed out. Tessa assumed that her messages had also been censored, but since she had not mentioned the scene of September 7 and its consequences and had voiced no major complaints, she was not concerned. She deduced from Sigismunda's words that the stricken passages pertained to Sigismunda's concern about her. Perhaps, her sister's questions of how she was coping with life had been too specific. The older girl seemed perfectly happy at the Ursulines. She proudly wrote that she would become a novice at the beginning of the New Year. Sigismunda would then spend the time until her profess acquiring teaching skills, and Tessa imagined that her intelligence had impressed her order. Sigismunda mentioned casually that she also was required to do various manual tasks, which made Tessa feel a little guilty because even as apprentice, she was being served by lay nuns. She read the letter many times and recalled their last hours together and how close they had felt. Now there seemed a certain spiritual distance, and she discerned that her sister's mind was directed toward her vocation. A couple of weeks later, she received a shorter letter from Ferenc. He already was a novice and seemed perfectly happy with his life, briefly mentioning that Michael was training to be a lay monk to work in the administration of the abbey's landholdings. Ferenc made clear that he would have little inclination toward writing in the future because he wanted to devote all his time to his studies and the education of his brother. He mentioned that the abbey of Melk was truly magnificent and that the extensive library with its many priceless volumes exceeded his wildest dreams.

Tessa could not help feeling that the separation from her siblings had gone beyond the physical aspect. Michael's brief salutation at the end of the letter meant little, but Sigismunda and Ferenc both were apparently fully reconciled to their fate and harbored no regrets about devoting themselves to religious life. Was she different? She no longer considered climbing the trellises in the abbess's garden to escape, but whenever she sat in the hermit tower, her heart still ached for the freedom of roaming through woods and the confines of the abbey felt unbearably restrictive. Would she ever get used to this life? She prayed for strength, but was God listening to her prayers? The beauty of the abbey church still fascinated her, and during services, her eyes followed those spiraled columns that Henrica had said were symbolic flames of fervent prayer reaching into the mysterious heights of the Gothic vault. She would then leave the church consoled but in her heart knew that it was because of the music rather than her prayers. She hung on every sound from the choir loft. Perhaps, when the time came for her to be a choir woman and sing chants she so loved, everything would fall into place. Would her love for music compensate for a life so confined, guided by such strict rules and so rigorous a schedule? Ferenc and Sigismunda seemed not only reconciled but also content, her older brother sounding as happy as she ever remembered him to be. Even Michael apparently had found his niche. Did her doubts and fears mean that she was a lesser person than her siblings were? Tessa had always been outgoing and precocious, passionate and full of life. Perhaps in a few years, when she reached their age and maturity, she would better understand how they felt.

Her father confessor was of little help in her mental tribulations. The old priest kept condemning pride and disobedience as deadly sins and elaborated on the virtues of religious life as the one and only path to heaven. Did that mean that all ordinary people were damned? Tessa had become thoroughly familiar with the New Testament and was impressed by the many instances when Jesus shared meals with ordinary people and their families and healed and blessed them. Why, had He not preferred a humble tax collector, who dared not raise his eyes to the Lord, to a virtuous Pharisee? She did not dare ask such questions in the confessional, but her inquisitive young mind dwelled on them.

Their theological teacher was a kindly, rotund monk in his forties and better able to empathize with his young pupils. He spent time with each of them according to their age and abilities, and his patience seemed inexhaustible. They were reading the passage where a young man asks Jesus what he must do to get eternal life and, after being told to love God and his neighbor as himself, responds that he already followed that command. And Jesus tells him to give all his possessions to the poor, abandon his family and way of life, and come follow Him. The man goes away sadly, for he was very wealthy. Tessa mustered all her courage to ask, "Does that mean that you must be a nun, or a monk, or a priest to go to heaven? What about our empress and her consort and children? Surely, they are very rich. Will they and other kings and queens end up in hell?"

Father Gregory hadn't expected such a question, but anxious to prepare these children and adolescents for life as a religious, he understood the necessity of a good answer.

"It is good that you asked this question, Marie Therese," he said in a friendly tone, though without a smile, "for it is one that may occur to several of you. The answer is that lay people, who follow the commandments, confess and regret their sins, do penance and love their neighbor, may eventually enter the kingdom of heaven. There have even been kings who achieved sainthood, such as Hungarian King Stephan! Yet divine grace rests especially upon those who devote themselves wholly to God and turn their back to a sinful world, which does not protect from the devil, as the walls surrounding this abbey do! What higher goal in life, I ask you maidens, could any young woman achieve than to become a bride of Christ! Taking the sacred vows before God and the world, your souls will grow singularly beautiful, your virtues shine ever more brightly! And in reward for your dedication, God will lead you upon an infinitely more straight and blissful path toward heaven than if you were facing the daily temptations of the devil and the evil ways in which he strives to rule the secular world. Even righteous men and women stumble and fall there but not within these sacred walls where you are close to Christ every hour of the day and night and live among others whose mind is set upon the same goal!"

Father Gregory had become quite passionate and was addressing all his pupils. There was a brief silence, then little Francesca piped up, "Will my virtue shine bright enough so I won't be scared of the dark anymore?"

The girls chuckled, and even Father Gregory suppressed a smile.

"You will be a grown woman when you take your vows, Francesca, and a bride of Christ need not fear anything ever!"

The child was persistent. "But, Father Gregory, I am very much afraid of the dark, and when the curtains round my bed move, I am sure a terrible monster is afoot to harm me! Could you make my virtue shine brightly in the dark now, please?"

"Francesca, I did not say that you will 'glow' in the dark. We have lamps to shed light. I was speaking of a light within you that is visible to God alone, the light of your virtuous soul! You are an aspirant in the abbey of Göss where there are no monsters to attack you, and I wish for you to behave like a future choir woman and not think or speak of monsters! Do you understand me?"

Tessa felt sorry for the little girl, who probably still missed her ayah sleeping close by. Other girls shared her bedroom, but curtains shut out familiar faces and surroundings, and their ghostly white apparently inspired the child's imagination. She resolved to take Francesca and Helena aside and try to dispel their fears.

Father Gregory did not take Tessa's question lightly. The girl was at a crucial age, and he knew about her behavioral difficulties as well as her exceptional voice. He resolved to speak to the abbess about it and did so when next reporting to her and the magistra about the scholastic progress of his pupils. He counseled that Reverend Mother Carolina give the girl individual singing lessons and perhaps even teach her to play the organ to occupy her mind.

"Would that not reward her unruly behavior?" asked Henrica. "She certainly spoiled Foundress Day for Mother Maria Carolina and the other aspirants!"

Abbess Maria Antonia shook her head. "I believe she has been sufficiently punished, Maria Henrica. I am of a troubled mind about the girl because of her background and believe Father Gregory's suggestion may favorably influence Marie Therese's future with us. I shall speak to Maria Carolina. It will be an imposition on her time, but if it helps to bring a young soul closer to God, it is a worthy endeavor!"

The artistically talented Henrica saw the wisdom in what the abbess said. She personally liked the intelligent girl and had fervently prayed that God in His wisdom would help Tessa constrain her emotions. Perhaps, furthering her talents through serious studies would provide an outlet for her troubled mind.

Maria Carolina had been disturbed and angry by the Foundress Day event, but the common bond of music gave her better understanding of the sensitive girl, who she knew was deeply affected by her punishment. She never mentioned the incident and would not admit even to herself how disappointed she'd been about her choir's performance. Teaching this talented girl was a challenge for the energetic woman, and she preferred to spend her time teaching to doing needlework. Obeying the abbess by taking on an individual pupil was not a sacrifice for her.

It was Tessa's happiest moment since her arrival at Göss when Mother Carolina said that in addition to singing lessons, she would teach her playing the spinet and perhaps later even the difficult technique of mastering the organ. The girl could hardly believe her ears and spontaneously kissed Mother Carolina's hand.

"Oh, Reverend Mother," she gushed, "I am so grateful, and I promise I'll never again disappoint you! I will do anything you say and—"

"Playing the organ is difficult, and so is proper voice control," interrupted the nun, well versed in controlling her emotions and careful not to show that she was touched by Tessa's enthusiasm.

"We shall begin by finding out how much you have learned in harmony, transcribing notes, and music theory so far. Sit down and I shall test you."

Tessa was more than happy to comply. It was a sunny fall afternoon, and she had been about to go outdoors, but music was her obsession for which she was prepared to sacrifice anything.

The lesson went well. Tessa demonstrated concentration and skill, and Maria Carolina secretly marveled about her quick and easy comprehension as well as her fine ear. Her fingers needed practice, and her mind discipline to control youthful exuberance, but Carolina felt that Tessa would become a great asset to the community of choir women during their rigorous schedule of seven sung services each day.

Tessa never developed the close relationship with Mother Carolina that she had enjoyed with Sister Agnes in Vienna, but their mutual love for music created a bond between them. Life at the abbey despite walls and rules was still closer to nature than it had been in the large city, and Tessa grew more content than she had been since her father's death. She still treasured every precious minute in the hermit tower, where imagination had her dream of freedom, and she was grateful that there were few other devotees of her retreat. Only little Helena went there on occasion, sometimes following Tessa, who became increasingly fond of the child. The two girls would often sing together. Helena clearly adored her, and it became a new and rewarding experience for Tessa to help her cope with the homesickness the shy little girl rarely dared to admit to others.

As Tessa progressed in her studies, Mother Carolina permitted her to practice on the spinet whenever the classroom was not used for lessons or study time. And when a gray and chilly November limited outdoor recreation, Tessa spent all her free time either at the spinet or singing. Her total dedication caused Josepha to complain of neglect, and Tessa was distressed, being well aware of how precious the cheerful girl's dedicated friendship was. She had never had a relationship with a girl other than her sister before and found that she had more in common with Josepha than with Sigismunda. She also knew that Josepha's well-meant caveats prevented many a misstep. Her friend's inclination to gossip had both amused and sometimes annoyed her a little until she realized that much of what she learned from Josepha was of importance in a life for which she was not prepared.

Those aspirants who came to the abbey in early childhood more easily adjusted to life within a community of women. Göss had always attracted relatives, and often, even sisters arrived to find aunts or cousins. Family ties and familiar faces made life away from home more bearable for the young, but a tendency to form cliques, spin intrigues, and indulge in vicious or cruel gossip also caused bad blood or resentment among those excluded. The three Galler sisters and their seventy-year-old aunt, Maria Bernhardina, who'd held various influential posts over the years, were an unfortunate example. When Tessa arrived, Bernhardina was prioress and had held this perhaps most influential position in the abbey for fourteen years. Were it not for her increasingly poor health, she would have been the obvious choice to succeed the present abbess.

The Counts Galler hailed from a place in Upper Styria and had long been involved in the administration of the landholdings of the famous abbey of Seckau. Josepha would joke about how lucky it was that three other Galler sisters were Dominican nuns at Graz. "Just think what it would be like if we had to put up with seven Gallers!" she'd say. Other than the sisters Scholastica and Leopoldina, who were still novices, several other choir women were closely related. Of course, family influence and wealth also counted, though wealth alone did not equal power. Count Khevenhuller, the father of choir woman Maria Aloysiy, commanded wealth and influence as governor of the province of Carynthia. Her dowry was the princely sum of five thousand florins in addition to jewelry and a yearly stipend of fifty florins from a trust that was to fall to the abbey upon her father's death. Maria Aloysiy was well educated and made profess in 1714 at age seventeen yet, to her chagrin, never was appointed to an office. Tessa, apart from not being wealthy, bore the stigma of a convert.

With few exceptions the aspirants rarely had direct contact with the chapter, as the full congregation of choir women was referred to. They hardly knew their faces, for when they walked to the altar rail in church to receive communion, the bowed heads below black veils revealed little of their features. Josepha's extensive information of what went on in the chapter came from her close relationship with lay nuns, who served the choir women and knew things that otherwise remained within the cloister. Some of the same lay nuns also attended to the physical needs of the aspirants, cooked and served their food, washed and mended their clothes, and related gossip.

Chapter 9

Magistra Maria Henrica singled out Tessa and Josepha to be the next likely candidates for investiture, the solemn ceremony when the girls would take their preliminary vows and become novices. Rumor had it that Empress Maria Theresa was considering to raise the age for final vows to age twenty-four, which would greatly delay the abbey's power to dispose over a dowry, prohibited until investiture or even profess. The monthly stipend paid for aspirants until investiture did not compensate for such loss.

Bishops officiated at the splendid ceremony of investiture, and there were psychological as well as financial reasons for having more than one candidate taking her vows. Tessa and Josepha were the next eligible candidates. The abbess concurred with the magistra that especially Tessa should become a choir woman as soon as possible. The older the intellectually agile girl became, the more difficult she might find it to commit herself to religious life. Her friendship with Josepha was no secret, and since the younger girl appeared firmly committed, it was thought that she would provide psychological support, while Tessa could help her friend to master the extensive curriculum required for their exams. Josepha would only be sixteen in 1748, too early for final vows according to the law, but an agreement was made with her parents to allow for her investiture in 1747.

Maria Henrica took the girls under her wing and spoke at length about what it meant to be a choir woman. The magistra carefully stressed the great self-discipline needed for a life ruled by the clock, which left little time for sleep or recreation. Lack of sleep especially bothered the younger women, and they dreaded hearing the bell calling for services at all hours of the day and night. Choir women began their "day" with the first Mass at midnight, for which the bell awakened them at 11:30 p.m. Sung in its entirety, it lasted a full hour and was followed by the "Laudes" or prayer of praise. At quarter past five, the bell called for morning contemplation in the cell and the subsequent "Prim" at six o'clock, a prayer service sung in church that included a litany of the day's saints. The women then assembled in the chapter hall for daily commemoration of their founders and benefactors. A strictly observed silence followed during which most women prayed their daily breviary. At quarter past eight, the bell rang for the "Terz," another sung prayer service preceding High Mass and the psalms of the "Sext." There was no breakfast; only two meals a day were served. They assembled in the refectory for their first and main repast at ten o'clock. Between eleven and twelve was recreation time, when they were allowed to converse and walk in the garden. At noon, they sang the "Non" and listened to Bible readings then followed another recreational period when many women devoted themselves to embroideries or other handicraft. Vespers was at three o'clock in the afternoon, and silence was once again observed until the evening meal at five o'clock. At seven, the bell called for the "Komplet" or evensong, followed by a special litany. The women then retired to their cells to meditate and examine their conscience, observing silence until midnight Mass.

The girls were well aware of the frequent bell, but their youthful minds paid little attention to how tightly structured their day would become, and they reacted in accordance with their character and concerns. Josepha worried how she could live on two meals a day, but Mother Henrica said that the food served was more than adequate. She did not convince this candidate, who secretly plotted how she was going to assure a steady supply of snacks. Her special "friend" was lay nun Maria Erentrudis who, because of her culinary talents, was on kitchen duty. She had advanced to the refined "court kitchen," which catered only to the abbess and her inner circle of choir women in office. Erentrudis was a deeply devoted nun who, during brief respites from hard work and religious obligations, said the stations of the cross thrice each day. Lay nuns coped with a grueling workload and, by sheer necessity, spent fewer hours in church. Erentrudis was a gaunt woman in her forties with hazel eyes and a long nose in a prematurely aged face that always looked gray below her white wimple. She suffered from various ailments, and during the long winter months, was particularly plagued by bronchitis. Daughter of a small tenant farmer in Upper Styria, she was the eldest of ten children and learned early to give up food for her hungry younger siblings. She too had always wanted to be a nun but was needed to help in the fields and care for a large family. When the youngest was finally grown and most of her siblings married, the eldest brother took over the farm, and there was no longer a place for her at home. Her parish priest intervened on her behalf at Göss. Without any dowry, she might not have been accepted since she was already in her thirties. But Erentrudis had often helped out with cooking in the local rectory when the housekeeper was sick, and the priest's high recommendation as an excellent cook secured her acceptance.

Whether it was because of her hungry childhood or caring for little brothers and sisters, Erentrudis took a liking to the cheerful and always hungry Josepha, who aroused her motherly instincts. She knew it was against regulations to slip the girl treats and prayed God would forgive her this weakness, but she could not resist Josepha. And serving at the "court table" of the abbess, she overheard things that were not even meant for the ears of ordinary choir women. Erentrudis was no gossip and certainly not malicious, but shrewd little Josepha knew how to ask the right questions and counted on her relationship with Erentrudis to survive the frightening prospect of having to live on two meals a day.

Tessa was an altogether different story. Food was of minor concern to her, albeit strict fasting sometimes was a hardship. Her all-abiding love of music and the chance of singing many hours each day alleviated the prospect of having to arise in the middle of the night and again before dawn. The girls were taught the Latin text and scores of the numerous chanted responses and psalms, litanies and hymns of the daily services. Tessa's alto was perfectly suited for this type of singing, and the choir mistress hoped that her excellent voice would lead the other women, many of whom lacked musical talent. Josepha's ear for music was average, but she devoted herself to it with undaunted cheerfulness and was grateful for Tessa's patience and diligence in helping her with all her studies.

Living in the abbey for years exerted a strong psychological influence on aspirants and rarely did one return to secular life after spending time within these walls. Many girls came so young they knew no other life. By the time Tessa prepared for investiture, her older siblings had all taken their vows and mutual contact become infrequent. Ferenc and Sigismunda sounded perfectly happy with their fate; her eldest brother was a scholar and researched Benedictine history, her sister found fulfillment teaching young children. Even Michael rarely complained and seemed reconciled with being a friar. He enjoyed the good food and assisted in the administration of tenant farmers. His initial fervent plans to return to Transylvania had become mute three years after the Trauttmansdorff siblings had left Vienna. Against her wishes, Miczike had again become pregnant and died giving birth to her fifth child, a stillborn son. Her sons and daughters dutifully prayed for her soul, and Masses were read for her at Melk, Graz, and Göss, but few tears shed. Her bereaved husband dedicated her tiny legacy to her four children, and Sigismunda, whose vows included strict poverty, donated her share to poor children. The abbey of Melk added the boy's funds to their treasury. Abbess Marla Antonia called Tessa to her office and advised her that the money would be held in trust for her, and that upon taking her final vows, she was entitled to regularly draw small amounts for personal expenses. The matter was of little concern to Tessa, who had no appreciation for money.

Miscike's death burned the last bridge between her and the world. She had never wished to return to her mother, whom she could not forgive her second marriage, but now every bond to Transylvania and her home was severed. It meant final realization that she had nowhere to go and that Göss was her only choice, though she often experienced doubts stemming in part from her deep faith. Was she a good enough person to become a choir woman? Could she be a dedicated servant to Christ without forever wanting to be free and enjoy a world like the one of her childhood? There were times when a voice in the back of her mind said she could hear the voice of God in the pristine silence of a forest as eloquently as in the abbey church, but she knew that such ideas were inappropriate for an aspiring choir woman.

The aspiring novices were urged to spend much time in prayer and meditation asking for God's help to become worthy, and Tessa did so faithfully. She usually chose one of the seven side altars to pray, and her favorite was the foundress altar in the rear nave below the choir empore. It was dedicated to Adala but dominated by a large painting depicting the symbolic marriage of St. Catherine to the Child Jesus. Typical for high baroque art the picture was bursting with life. A choir of angels surrounded the Virgin holding the divine child on her lap with one slender hand tenderly around a little foot. The infant was placing a ring on the finger of a richly robed St. Catherine, who stood before Him with a palm branch. Below the group were two female figures holding a book, and on the lower right were the three founders: Adala, with son Aribo, and daughter Cunigunde. Their pose was stiff and formal to illustrate a more somber Middle Age. Mary exuded motherly love and looked wistfully at the beholder, lips slightly parted as if about to speak. Tessa loved this painting, every detail of which became engraved in her mind. In preparation for her symbolic marriage to Christ, she imagined herself in St. Catherine's place, dressed in a rich bridal gown. The idea of Catherine being betrothed to a child had troubled her at first until she understood the timelessness of Christ as a person, born of God and from the moment of birth fulfilled with His mission. The Virgin had long been the mother figure in Tessa's life, and she wondered whether her real mother had ever held her little foot with such protective tenderness. Years ago, the eyes of the carved statue in the cardinal's chapel had fascinated her as meeting her gaze, but Mary's face in this painting bore an infinitely more vivid expression. Was the Virgin telling her, "Trust me, I am your mother, come and dedicate your life to my Son?"

It was dark below the choir, and the gently flickering candles enhanced the mystery. "Oh, Holy Mother of God, what are you telling me?" Tessa prayed aloud, unaware of Maria Henrica's silent approach until the magistra said, "The Virgin speaks the words of her divine son: 'Be not afraid, I go before you always. Come follow me and I will give you rest.'"

Tessa was not startled by the unexpected presence and felt that the Virgin might indeed say words from Luke's gospel.

Henrica continued, "Remember the Prophet Isaiah, child: 'You shall cross the barren desert, but you shall not die of thirst; you shall wander far in safety though you do not know the way; you shall see the face of God and you shall live! If you stand before the gates of hell and death is at your side, know that I am with you through it all!' Be not afraid, Tessa, for Christ will walk before you always and to follow Him will give you peace. Let us pray together now."

Tessa's eyes were riveted on the Madonna, and she intoned with a voice echoing through the empty church.

"Salve Regina, mater misericordiae, vita ducedo et spes nostra, salve! At te clamamus, exules filii heavae" (Mother of mercy, sweetness of life and our hope, we greet you! To you we appeal, the despairing children of Eve).

Maria Henrica had been about to start a prayer but remained silent. She'd thought that the main value of Tessa's musical studies lay in channeling her thoughts and energies into something useful and away from outbreaks of childish temper. The magistra's interests were painting and architecture, but she recognized the quality of Tessa's voice so ideally suited for a choir woman. No doubt, the girl was ready to sing solo, but that might make her overly confident and cause other aspirants or choir women to feel slighted.

Hearing her own voice resound in the large church was a new experience for Tessa. Singing in the Vienna chapel years ago had been wonderful, but now she could feel the strength and timbre of her maturing voice, and a great joy welled in her heart and relegated her fears to the background. When the last sound of the chant had faded, she turned toward the magistra and spontaneously seized her hand.

"Oh, Reverend Mother, will Christ know how anxious I am to raise my voice in His glory? Will singing help me to become a good nun?"

Henrica was moved; she gently freed her hand and stroked the girl's cheek.

"Yes, child," she said, "He will hear you."

"But, Mother Henrica, I also long to walk through woods and meadows and along the river, and these walls make me feel imprisoned! Is that sinful?"

She stopped in fear of having angered the magistra, but the calm features showed no emotion.

"Come with me, Tessa," she said and rising led the way from the church and across the cloister garden toward the reflection tower. "I know you have been spending time in the hermit tower, but I want to show you something."

The two women climbed the stairs and entered a circular room with plastered and whitewashed walls. Between two windows was the fresco of a simple landscape, painted in contemporary style. Tessa had so enjoyed the hermit tower that she never explored the other two and the painting surprised her. It was very different from anything she'd seen, and the haunting scene was fascinating. A wide horizon stretched over flat land, there was a heave of harvested wheat piled at one side and a row of poplars in the distance. Clouds covered a darkened sky, eerily illuminated by the golden light of a setting sun. The message was one of lonesome sadness, almost despair, brightened by only a small ray of hope. The two women were silent for a while until Henrica spoke.

"I painted this more than twenty years ago when I was a novice and very homesick for Silesia. I recognized such feelings as frivolous, regretted them and did penance, but could not banish my longing until I had painted this scene of my homeland. When I made my final vows, I promised Christ to expiate for my longings by henceforth sharing the pain He suffered wearing a crown of thorns."

Henrica slowly pulled back her left sleeve to reveal her upper arm fitted with a metal ring from which thornlike spikes penetrated the flesh, which had swelled and become badly inflamed. Realizing the pain each movement was bound to cause, Tessa shivered and her eyes widened in horror. A strange smile parted Henrica's lips as she watched the girl's face. She dropped the sleeve.

"No one makes us do such acts of contrition and self-punishment, it is of our own choice, but the ecstasy of experiencing a small share of Christ's suffering every hour of the day and night is exquisite and purifies the soul. However, it is not something we speak about because it is a personal sacrifice of love!"

Tessa was too deeply moved and shocked to speak and kept staring in horror at the magistra's sleeve. When Henrica spoke again, her voice was nonchalant as if in a casual conversation.

"I want you to paint the forest, or the meadow, the mountain or the river in Transylvania for which you yearn most because I know it will help you deal with your feelings. I shall have the materials sent to you. Now walk with Christ and pray. Pray, Marie Therese, that you may be worthy to become His devoted servant!"

Henrica turned and noiselessly disappeared down the stairs.

Tessa stared for a long time at the painted landscape. It had never occurred to her that the magistra of all choir women should wrestle with personal feelings unrelated to faith. It brought her realization that the women within these walls remained ordinary human beings subjected to all the pain and torture that inflicted those of the secular world. She'd always imagined that nuns led a life of peaceful bliss and happiness; how childish and immature a notion! She'd heard that Henrica became a nun against her parents' wish and was surprised that longing for one's childhood home was sinful. Tessa had often enjoyed drawing and thought she might be able to draw a Transylvania landscape while the scenery was still vivid in her mind. She would follow Mother Henrica's suggestion, and if she failed, singing would still bring her joy.

When she returned to her cubicle that evening, she found sheets of paper and a wooden box with pieces of charcoal, several brushes, and tempura colors, together with instructions in the magistra's handwriting. Tessa felt a desire to draw right away, but the "lights out" rule was strict, and especially during preparation for her novitiate, she did not want to precipitate a complaint. She hardly slept that night mulling which Transylvania scenery she would paint. She recalled the elegant gouaches on the walls of the magistra's office and imagined Henrica being the artist. The melancholy of the Silesian landscape in the tower touched her in a strange way. The flat fields, distant trees, and wide gray sky were neither picturesque or pretty, but they portrayed home to a woman as far removed from it as Tessa was from her native land. Who but God knew what moved a person's heart the most? Throughout the long night, Tessa imagined painting the white mansion at Zay-Ugrocz or the view across the plains from her lookout at the edge of the woods. Another favorite spot was a little brook edged by moss-covered stones where drops of water glistened in the sparse rays the sun found through thick branches of spruce trees. Insects danced in their path, and as a child, she'd extend her hand to grasp the rays, only to find them vanish between her fingers. She could still hear the bubbling brook and smell the woods, and when the wake-up bell brought her back to reality, she opened her eyes and stared blankly at the white curtains, hoping they'd turn into waving green branches. Then she remembered that she was at Göss at the dawn of another day on which her lessons and the noon litany seemed to last very long. At recreation time, Tessa tucked the utensils under her arm and hurried toward the reflection tower with an apologetic glance in the direction of her beloved hermit. She placed her things on the stone bench and again succumbed to the spell of the Silesian landscape. Then she glanced north through the arched window at the scene she had beheld for the past three years from the hermit tower. It was late spring, and the larches interspersed between the deep green spruce were still a delicate chartreuse, yellow primula known here as "keys to heaven," dotted the meadows and weeping willows dipped their new leaves into the river swelled by spring rains. Transylvania's lush lands had been on her mind throughout the night, but now they paled before this scenery. Tessa chose the wall between windows facing the river and, with a piece of charcoal, drew the outlines of the mountain ridges, pastures, and banks of the Mur. Her composition emerged with quick strokes, and following the magistra's instructions, she wetted the wall with a sponge before applying colors.

"You are doing well, Marie Therese," said a voice behind her. Immersed in her creation, the girl never heard the magistra's approach. "I shall show you how to properly apply colors. There's a technique you need to follow."

Maria Henrica took the sponge and, with a few quick strokes, softened or erased Tessa's efforts of a blue sky then mixed colors for various shades before applying them with a brush to the moistened wall. The girl was a quick learner, and the choir woman enjoyed watching her take over and follow her mentor's directions. Neither one heard the tower clock strike until there were hurried footsteps on the stairs.

"Tessa, Tessa, are you up here?" cried a breathless Josepha appearing at the entrance. "Father is awfully angry." She saw the magistra standing behind her friend and caught herself. "Forgive, Reverend Mother, but our lesson was to begin a quarter hour ago, and I didn't know."

"It is all right, Josepha, I have been instructing Marie Therese and neglected to inform Father that she would be a half hour late. Do go and tell Father that Marie Therese will be in class shortly."

Josepha left and the choir woman gave Tessa one of her rare smiles.

"Artists tend to become oblivious of time," she said. "Now gather your utensils and proceed to your lesson. You may continue during recreation times but only if you promise to limit your time here. Remember that you are preparing for the most significant step of your life and that this present endeavor should serve only to increase your devotion. Everything religious women do should aim to glorify the Lord, whether it is copying a tiny piece of His creation such as a landscape, the portrait of a saint, or designing and embroidering a canopy for procession."

Tessa collected her tools, curtseyed to the magistra, and hurried to her class.

Maria Henrica remained in the tower for a while and gazed upon the tranquil land beyond the walls then at Tessa's artistic effort. She was pleased with what she saw but even more about the fact that the girl had chosen a motif of her present domicile. Well aware of the mental anguish every one of her aspirants suffered longing for home and parents, she hoped that Tessa's choice was an indication of letting go of Zay-Ugrocz and Transylvania. The sketch demonstrated careful attention to detail, and if she mastered the skill of working with colors, this would be a good first endeavor. Tessa concerned her the most among the aspirants, and as she left the reflection tower, Maria

Henrica fervently prayed that God would guide this young woman in her vocation.

Investiture was set for the twenty-first day of July 1747. The two candidates were to take their exams in early July, whereupon the Supremus would formally recommended them to the bishop as well prepared. The prelate came from Seckau with an entourage of scholarly monks for the solemn ceremony and to administer the vows. Investiture still depended on a final interview with the bishop. The candidates had to write a brief essay stating the reasons why they chose religious life. Josepha feared the exams but giggled over the essay requirement.

"I don't suppose they want me to say it's because I'm not pretty enough to find a husband," she said without bitterness.

Tessa laughed. "And I could say it's because no one else wants me around, not even as housekeeper for my esteemed uncle, the cardinal!"

Such lighthearted moments had become rare with pious concentration continuously urged upon them.

"What names do you think we'll get?" Josepha asked. The question baffled Tessa, although she was well aware that since the early baroque all novices were given a new name in addition to "Maria" to emphasize the beginning of a new life.

"Do we have a choice?" she wondered.

"I don't think so," replied the all-knowing Josepha, "but I heard that Maria Bernarda, who hasn't even received her solemn Benediction, was just named Sub-Magistra Noviciarum, which gives her a lot of influence with Maria Caelestina, who'll be our magistra after investiture."

"If that's true," mused Tessa, "I'll wind up with the ugliest name any choir woman ever had!"

She had been carefully avoiding Bernarda, and there'd been no further incidents, though she had repeatedly drawn lesser punishments for her quick tongue or other minor transgressions. She still couldn't totally suppress her love of practical jokes, and Josepha was an occasional conspirator. More than once did she escape detection due to her faithful friend, and Tessa reciprocated by often doing scholarly work for the girl. They did not feel guilty because it helped Josepha to become a novice and dedicate her life to the church.

Tessa collected her Bible, paper, and writing utensil and headed to the reflection tower to pen her thoughts about why she wanted to become a nun. This was now her favorite place, and on this warm day in late June, she sat on the stone bench with an open Bible and a sheet of fine vellum they'd been given for this purpose. Tessa at seventeen was still too young to comprehend all the implications of becoming cloistered within abbey walls for the rest of her life. Mature for her age and with a good mind, she and Josepha realized their limited choices, neither one born into a rich and powerful family nor endowed with special beauty. Tessa gazed at her own and Mother Henrica's painting then raised her eyes to the summer sky with its fluffy clouds, the tranquil river, and the trees untouched by even the slightest breeze. The scene was peaceful and so was Tessa's heart in anticipation of the pending ceremony. Like secular brides, she and Josepha would be the most honored women in the abbey that day walking down the aisle of the church in the most beautiful gowns they would ever wear, radiant brides about to be wedded to Christ. She wrote:

"In the Name of Jesus Christ, I, Marie Therese Countess Trauttmansdorff, solemnly declare that I shall take my preliminary vows to become a novice of the Benedictine Order of my own free will. The Virgin has been my true mother since childhood, she has consoled me and strengthened me, and in my heart, I believe that she wants me to dedicate my life to Christ, her divine Son.

"Just as the pillars in our beloved church rise toward heaven like a flaming prayer, I want to raise my voice to the glory of our Lord. In His honor, I want to sing all hours of the day and night, and my heart is filled with joyful anticipation of becoming a choir woman. I thank God for having given me the ability to sing. Yet when I look at the world He created—the mountains, rivers, and trees—or hear the song of a bird, I know that they attest to His greatness more than my humble voice ever could.

"It is the goodness of the Lord that has brought me here and given me an asylum I cherish and for which I am deeply grateful. I pray that He shall give me strength and piety to be His devoted servant all the days of my life. Amen."

"My papa and mama have sent message that they will come to my profess," Josepha said and, with her usual little smirk, continued, "and Papa will lead me down the aisle. They also will bring part of my dowry 'cause they want to make sure I'll remain forever ensconced here. Poor Tessa, since both your parents are dead, who will lead you into church to present you to Christ? The cardinal?"

Tessa shook her head. "I don't believe so. He's too important a man to travel that far and hasn't witnessed any of my siblings' taking their vows either. What happens to a candidate with no one to escort her?"

As usual, Josepha had an answer. "It's happened before, of course. A secular official is appointed since it can't be a member of the clergy. We're being given to the church, actually not until profess, but investiture is the first step, and I don't think there's ever been a novice who refused to take final vows!"

Tessa had given little thought to that aspect of the ceremony, but it brought home that she was indeed alone in the world, for surely no member of Papa's family would make the effort to travel to Göss! Did anyone in the outside world even care what happened to her? It was one of those moments when loneliness overwhelmed her and she needed refuge in a tower for consolation and perhaps some singing. This time, it wouldn't be chants but songs from her childhood, Hungarian melodies the ayah had taught her in the nursery. Josepha was watching her and put an arm around Tessa's shoulders, her usually carefree voice soft.

"Don't be sad, dear. Like I mentioned, my parents only come to make sure I'll never again be a burden for them! I'll be glad to see them, but I'm sure it'll also be the last time. I hear that a very wealthy bride has been found for my brother, and since the letter said nothing about her looks, I bet she's ugly as sin! Wouldn't you rather live here to love Christ and put up with the 'Bernardas' of the abbey than sleep in the bed of some creep your parents picked just because he was rich?"

Tessa recalled Sigismunda's abhorrence of an arranged marriage and readily agreed. She knew nothing about married life and, with the wisdom of her seventeen years, saw things only in black or white; therefore, life with anyone but the perfect knight on a white horse was bound to be awful and a sheltered community of nuns a desirable alternative.

Tessa easily mastered her studies and helped an appreciative Josepha. As novices, they would no longer sleep in the dormitory but, until profess, share a cell. Choir women occupied individual cells furnished with their personal belongings. Novices were not cloistered and expected to assist with teaching and supervising aspirants. This greatly reassured young Helena, who was extremely fond of Tessa and sought her out as often as she could. The girl was still frail and often ailing and her persistent cough a worry for Tessa. Helena was an exquisite child with pale but perfect skin and beautiful features, generally withdrawn but always happy in the company of Tessa, who often sang with her. The child counted the years, months, and days until she was eligible to become a choir woman and was mortified by rumors that the empress sought to raise the required age to twenty-four. She was less homesick now and still ardently prayed for the health of her mother, who lay on her deathbed. No longer the youngest among the aspirants, Helena was universally loved for her gentleness and patience and took special care of two new little girls. Helena never refused a favor and even felt guilty for what she considered her selfish affection for Tessa. The two girls had not been able to spend much time together because of the older one's intensive studies. Helena missed her friend dearly but never complained.

A festive mood always prevailed in and around the abbey prior to an investiture or profess. Even the abbess found herself caught in excited anticipation albeit for reasons other than merely spiritual since new novices meant dowries and much-needed cash to bolster the budget. Maria Antonia had been under continuous financial pressure since her installation in 1737, even more so than her predecessor. Special assessments by the crown to finance costly wars as well as papal demands for the yearly "decima" tax increased from year to year. Emperor Charles had needed money to fight the Turks and suppress revolts in Hungary. His daughter Maria Theresa was challenged in her succession during a seven-year war instigated by Frederic the Great, whose armies invaded the Austrian lands of Silesia, and the Bavarian king followed suit. The Viennese Bank holding the abbey's deposits was short on cash and ceased paying interest, and the state demanded a "loan" of twenty thousand florins that had no chance of repayment. Poor harvests and floods destroyed crops and fishponds, and the abbess distributed free grain for bread and seed to her tenant farmers and families besides spending large sums to repair damaged silos, barns, and trout ponds; the latter were an important source of food for her table. Maria Antonia had been her predecessor's secretary and administrative assistant for a decade and possessed excellent business sense, coupled with generosity and empathy for her suffering tenants, who never found a deaf ear for their needs. All this increased the importance of cash dowries from new candidates and played a vital part in the abbey's financial position.

Except for her secular clothes and beloved carved animals, Tessa's trousseau was in the custody of Abbess Maria Antonia. Now she and Josepha were summoned to the seamstress shop, where two lay nuns laid out their bridal gowns. Both girls had grown since their arrival, which had been taken into account at the time the dresses were made. In a letter after her investiture, Sigismunda had mentioned how strange and inappropriate she felt wearing such earthly splendor. Tessa, however, loved the touch of the silky brocade, and her artistic mind reveled in the rich colors of the material. Adjustment to her gown was mainly in length provided for by a deep hem.

"My, you look like a queen!" exclaimed Josepha. "Dressed like that you'd outshine any princess at court!"

Noticing the shocked expression of one of the nuns, Josepha quickly added, "And what a beautiful bride of Christ you will make!"

Tessa indeed cut a striking figure in her exquisite gown. She was tall and slender, and while not beautiful, her high forehead and cheekbones, the slightly prominent, straight nose, and determined mouth were well proportioned even if a little large for the ideal of her time. Her most remarkable feature were her brown eyes below distinctly arched brows, eyes that could laugh with mischief, become tender when she was with little Helena, reflect piety during singing, but glitter with defiance as well.

Tessa looked forward to wearing her gown together with a necklace of gold and pearls from her mother that had been sent to the abbey after Miczike's death as part of her dowry. Wearing jewelry was a novelty, and she held the necklace in her hands for a long time, her fingers feeling the sensual touch of precious metal and pearls. Papa had given the necklace to Mama and Tessa remembered her mother wearing it on special occasions. The children would say good night to their parents prior to formal occasions, and Tessa would compare Mama to a fairy princess. Josepha's chatter interrupted her thoughts.

"Oh, dear, I've really become a bit heavy," she was saying to the nun examining how much room there was in the seams to let out. "Do you think you can make it fit, Maria Justina? Look here, Tessa, what do you think?"

The nun nodded. "Yes, countess, 'tis plenty material, but you need try it one more time. You'll be a lovely bride fo' our Savior, countess," Justina added and Tessa joined in.

"Oh yes, Josepha, the blue matches your eyes, and you do not look heavy at all! Besides, we'll get thin enough fasting during the days before the ceremony," she added jokingly, causing Josepha to grimace.

"You know how I hate to fast, and I don't know for the life of me why a growling stomach serves the Lord better than a full one!"

Tessa chuckled but Justina said gravely, "'Tis 'cause we needs ne'er forget Christ sufferin' for us."

The girls exchanged looks and did not answer, changed back into their secular clothes, and headed for another class.

Chapter 10

J uly 21 was a Sunday. At the earlier examinations, Supremus and
abbess deemed the candidates' answers to the many questions
satisfactory. Tessa's singing lessons had been suspended to allow
preparation for this most solemn day in her life. She sorely missed
her musical studies but consoled herself with the knowledge that she
would have ample opportunity later.

The bishop of Seckau and his entourage arrived on Thursday, as
did the designated secular witness to any investiture, profess, or election of a new abbess. He was Count Saurau and held an official position with the government. Regulations prescribed that as a representative of the crown he personally interview aspiratnts or novices and
question their motives for choosing religious life so as to eliminate
any appearances of coercion or undue pressure. He was accommodated in the abbey's guest quarters and shared meals with the parish
priest in the rectory while the bishop joined the abbess's court table.

Josepha's parents arrived from Brixen in South Tyrol, where
Count Joseph Anton Plaz was ducal equity master, a highly ceremonial position that carried little influence but great prestige, which
pleased his proud and ambitious wife Maria Anna. They too occupied guest quarters, and Josepha invited Tessa to join her and her
parents at supper. It was the eve before the girls' strict fasting and
secluded meditation began, and Tessa was thrilled. She couldn't
remember when she had last shared a meal with secular adults and
was curious to meet her friend's parents.

"Don't let Mama scare you," Josepha said, as the girls walked
hand in hand. "She's become more distant and severe than she was

when I left home five years ago, and I bet she only came to make sure I take my vows!"

"Josepha dear, don't say that! From what you told me, it's a long and uncomfortable journey from South Tyrol to Göss, and she surely wants to wish you well on your great day!"

"You don't know, Mama," replied the girl dryly. "You'll notice she's beautiful and to have a plain daughter with no chance of catching a wealthy or important husband was a terrible blow to her! I told you that my family's not rich, and three thousand florins are a big chunk of money, but now that my brother's found a wealthy bride, Mama delights in telling everyone about my big dowry."

Tessa couldn't think of an answer, but they had reached the quarters and climbed the stairs to the Parlatorium, where aspirants, novices, and even choir women were permitted to receive visitors, though cloistered choir women traditionally remained separated by a screen.

Count and Countess Plaz entered, and watching them embrace their daughter, Tessa understood her friend's feelings. The countess was a slender woman in her forties, taller than her husband and still quite beautiful. She was well dressed and her dark blond hair meticulously coifed. She bent stiffly to kiss her daughter's cheek in response to Josepha's respectful curtsey and kiss on the hand. Josepha clearly took after her father, for the count was short, chubby, and jovial. He warmly hugged the girl and heartily kissed her on both cheeks.

"I am so happy to see you, my little Sepherl," he exclaimed, using a childhood nickname. "You've been so much on my mind these past days thinking about that momentous step you are about to take and whether you're really ready at fifteen years old!"

The countess jerked back her head and said quickly, "Josepha has wanted to be a nun all her life, have you not, dear?" Without waiting for an answer, she continued, "And, Josepha, where are your manners? Do introduce your guest to us, will you?"

Josepha pulled away from her papa. "Forgive me, Mama, this is Marie Therese, Countess Trauttmansdorff, who will take her vows on Sunday also. We are friends and Tessa has helped me with my studies, I don't think I could've done without her!"

Tessa dutifully kissed the hand of the countess, who seemed annoyed about her daughter belittling herself. "Well, now it is nice that you are close, but you certainly have enough intelligence to learn, Josepha. Now shall we proceed to the table."

Lay nuns served an excellent meal in a small but formal dining room. Tessa would always remember this meal, not just because it would be her last one in the company of secular persons. It fascinated her to watch the couple that seemed divided between guilt of committing a young child and being relieved of her care. The count could not take his eyes off his daughter, but his efforts to explore how she felt in her heart were foiled by his wife. *I wonder what it would be like if my papa and mama were here in their place,* Tessa silently mused. While Miczike might have empathized with Countess Plaz, her papa would have insisted on speaking to her in private. She was brought back to reality when Josepha passed her the framed miniature painting of a girl.

"My brother's fiancée, just as I had imagined her to be," she said and Tessa felt a little kick under the table. The countess raised her eyebrows disapprovingly at her daughter's tone of voice, and Tessa pretended to study the plain features of a young woman with small, squinty eyes and a long nose, the narrow face framed by thin dark hair.

"The young Countess Olympia of Caretto is a charming and delightful young lady who will make your brother very happy indeed," intoned the countess. "She comes from a very distinguished family in Naples and is related to his holiness, the pope, and we are honored that our family will unite with so noble and influential a name. The wedding will take place in Naples in October, and I shall write to you, Josepha, about the happy event," she added almost consolingly.

"Thank you, Mama, that is most kind of you," said Josepha and Tessa thought she again detected a trace of irony in her friend's voice.

Both girls were relieved when the meal was over. The count produced a velvet case and handed it to his daughter.

"The abbess told us that you will spend the next two days in intense preparation for the ceremony and that your mind should concentrate on Christ free of worldly distraction. When next I see you, dear child, it will be to escort you into the church as a bride-to-be."

He opened the case, which revealed a magnificent necklace of diamonds and sapphires.

"As you know, this belonged to my mother, your grandmama, who had no daughters. I had always intended for you to wear it on your wedding day, and so you shall, after which it will belong to the abbey. Wear it with pride on Sunday, dearest Josepha, and always remember how much I love you."

His voice revealed deep emotion, which seemed to embarrass the countess, who added quickly, "Your brother and his fiancée have generously consented that this heirloom leave our family." And it was obvious that she would have preferred otherwise.

Tessa thought, *That's one of the few battles the count ever won during his marriage*, and was delighted for Josepha. When it was time for the girls to leave, she quickly excused herself to allow parents and daughter a few private moments. Aspirants were not supposed to walk about the abbey alone evenings, and she waited for her friend at the bottom of the stairs. Josepha soon caught up, her face wet with tears, which Tessa had rarely seen before.

"Oh, Tess," said the girl in a choked voice, "I really think Papa misses having me around! We used to spend as much time together as Mama would allow us. You must have noticed that she doesn't believe in emotions, and he'll be criticized a lot for showing his feelings. But I really don't care what she thinks! I know how precious this necklace is to him close as he was to Grandmama, and I'm so touched that he's sacrificing it. God forgive me, but I do think it'll look better on me than on that ugly Olympia! Poor brother! I don't envy him having to spend his life with that scarecrow, no matter who her precious relatives are."

Tessa chuckled and put her arm round Josepha's shoulders. "There you go, dear! You're a hundred times prettier than Olympia, you'll look beautiful with those sapphires that match your eyes and your gown, and I understand what you meant when you said that being a choir woman beats living with some ugly man or woman picked by one's parents!"

The girls returned to their cubicles in the aspirants' dormitory, and each prayed that the interview with the bishop and Count Saurau scheduled for the following day would go well.

The bishop was a small, wiry man in his forties, and the candidates met him one at a time in the magistra's office that had been specially rearranged for the occasion. Tapestries featuring religious themes replaced Henrica's paintings, thick Persian rugs covered the floor, and the delicate scent of a bouquet of roses was the only softening element, for there was no smile on the bishop's ascetic face as he sat behind the magistra's desk and perused Tessa's examination papers.

"God be with you, my daughter," he said without looking up as Tessa stepped before him. "You have studied your lessons well, and your Latin is good. But I sadly miss humility and profound piety in your reasons for aspiring to the privilege of becoming a choir woman. You need to learn these, and learn you must, for there are painful ways to impress obedience upon members of religious orders. God looks into our hearts and demands dedication to Him and submission to your abbess and sisters in Christ. I trust you understand this and that it was merely youthful carelessness that prompted you to give preference to your wants and needs rather than to the task before you. Do you understand me?"

The harsh words hit Tessa like rocks. She knew that she wasn't humble by nature, but her young heart was full of enthusiasm and love for Christ. She thought that praising Him with the voice He had given her was her way of expressing gratitude for this gift and not pride or vanity of a talent.

"Yes, Your Excellency," she whispered with a lump in her throat.

"In that case, I shall accept your vows as sincere," said the bishop. "But understand that a year from now, when the time comes to affirm these vows and you become a choir woman, I do not wish to hear a single word from your magistra noviciarum about disobedience or lack of humility. It is shameful to remain novice for an additional year or to be expelled from these walls altogether. Therefore, you must work diligently to cleanse your soul of vanity and pride, of jealousy or malicious feeling against anyone, least of all your future sisters in Christ. Make a worthy confession of all your sins and fast and pray until the hour on Sunday arrives. You may leave now to see Count Saurau at the rectory who will ask you a number of questions, the answers to which he will share with me. You may kneel to receive my blessing."

Tessa sank to her knees and kissed the ring on the bishop's extended hand. She left the room in a daze but caught Josepha's startled glance outside the door waiting for her interview. *She's read my face*, Tessa thought, trying to collect her thoughts. Deeply disturbed, she longed to be alone and sort through her emotions. But she knew that the emissary was expecting her and mustn't be kept waiting. She walked across the main courtyard and through the wide arch of the administration building toward the rectory. The parish priest's portly housekeeper stood in the doorway.

"My, my, child," said the elderly woman in a kind, motherly voice, "you look like you need a bit o' consolin' afore you see the count."

Without waiting for an answer, she pulled the hesitant girl into a big kitchen and onto a chair by the table. "Here you sit 'til I fetch you some vittles t' keep you goin'!"

It was the first time a country person had called her "child" instead of by her title, but the motherly woman's tone was exactly what the deeply troubled girl needed. A moment later, the housekeeper returned with a tin mug of cool milk and a thick slice of raisin bread. Tessa shook her head.

"I'm not supposed to—"

"Ah, forget it!" said the woman resolutely, reminding her of the ayah when she wanted her to do something as a child.

"A starved choir woman's no good for servin' our Lord. The count's still talkin' to the granary master and won't be here for a little while yet. Go on an' eat, child, it'll do you a world o' good after all them questions and more t' come!"

Tessa's youthful nature came to the forefront and she relaxed, aware of how hungry she was. The cool milk from the cellar soothed her tense stomach, and the raisin bread was delicious. Under the woman's watchful eyes, she began to feel better, and the simple food calmed her.

"There ya go," the housekeeper said when Tessa had finished. "You look mo' like y'self again, child. You'll make a better novice prop'ly fed an' no one need to know nothin' 'bout our little chat. Now go sit in the father's room 'til the count comes. An' don't you worry y'self, he's a kindly man, he is. I'll tell him you been waitin' there for him all along!"

She led Tessa into a spacious room and pointed to a chair. The open windows faced a garden, and the girl looked out over the neatly planted rows of vegetables, bordered by flowers and honey-suckle. A swarm of bees busily collected nectar. She knew that the priest's housekeeper was responsible for the delicious honey everyone enjoyed, and she watched the buzzing insects making their way back to their beehive by the wall.

They must have found out that they're not working for their young or themselves, she mused. *As soon as they've made their honey, it's taken from them. I wonder what I'll have to show for my life when I'm old and my voice no longer good."*

Her thoughts were interrupted when the door opened, and she turned to face a distinguished elderly man.

"I am Erasmus Count Saurau," he said in a kind voice, "and you are Countess Trauttmansdorff. Please take a seat so we can speak about your future."

He politely held a chair for her and sat down opposite the table, and Tessa instinctively liked and trusted him. He watched her quietly for a few minutes before speaking.

"I am familiar with your background and sympathize with what you have been through in your young life, Marie Therese. It could not have been easy for you and your sister and brothers. Throughout our lives, we are faced with choices, and the greater their importance, the more consideration they deserve. You have now spent three years at Göss and are at an age when most young women in the secular world are already married. So I trust you have given careful thought toward taking vows that bind you forever to religious life. Is this what you wish to do with all your heart and soul, Marie Therese?"

The girl was perplexed. *What is he trying to tell me?* she thought. *Does he want to talk me out of becoming a nun?* But the count's face did not reveal his thoughts; he looked at her steadily and evenly as if trying to read her mind. *Choices! As if I had any choices*, Tessa's thoughts continued. *Does he know what it means to be alone in the world? If I were to decide against taking my vows, I'd be an outcast and a pauper, and what would he say if I appeared on his doorstep asking for help?* The question of becoming a nun was settled in her mind, and it disturbed her to have it brought up at this point. She'd show that harsh bishop and the count what she was made of! The proud aristocrat came to the forefront and ever so slightly tossing back her head she met the man's searching gaze.

"Indeed, I have, count" she said proudly. "I wish to become a choir woman and have wished so for many years. You may tell the authorities that I do this of my own free will because of my love for Christ and religious life, just like my sister and brothers did," she added almost defiantly.

The wise old man read her thoughts.

"I am glad to hear you say that, Marie Therese. It is the explicit desire of Her Majesty, herself a deeply religious person, that so important a choice be made only by men and women of maturity and after long and careful contemplation. That is why she is in negotiation with your uncle, the cardinal, about raising the eligibility for final vows in her realm to twenty-four years. You will be eighteen at the end of your novice year and satisfy the current age requirement. And if this is your true vocation, you have an exhilarating life before you that may well give you more peace and happiness than secular life ever could, and I wish you well. No fewer than eight members of my family have been choir women at Göss since the early 1600s, and I know that most of them, though not all, led a fulfilled and happy existence. May you be among those who did!" He paused to give Tessa a chance to reply then continued, "As you know, it is customary that brides of Christ be led to the altar by a member of their family in symbolic presentation to the church. Since no member of your family was able to make the journey to Göss, this honor has been conferred to me. It is not the first time I do this, for three decades ago, I presented my own daughter Eva Beatrix at the altar of the abbey church for her solemn vows. She died very suddenly a dozen years ago, and I shall mourn her death to the end of my days."

Again, the count fell silent, his face suddenly very tired. He sadly looked down at his hands then—with apparent effort—continued, "I pray that Christ and the Virgin will shed their grace upon you and report to the abbess, the bishop, and the royal authorities that I have found you well prepared, countess."

He rose and extended his hand, and Tessa took it and said, "Thank you, count, but the honor is mine! I shall gratefully accept your arm on this the most important day of my life. Good day, count."

Her heart was light as she directed her steps toward the reflection tower. She wondered briefly how it was that two people of the secular world, a kindly country woman and a member of the aristocracy, had restored her peace of mind after it had been deeply disturbed by a member of the clergy. Should it not have been for the bishop to calm any doubts she might harbor and make her look forward to becoming a nun? Tessa had long ago decided that she could not afford doubts. She had made a choice that would permanently bring music into her life. She would convince the other choir women that the Gregorian chant was the most beautiful form of music and rejoiced in anticipation of hearing her voice resound within the soaring walls of the church. Halfway through the park, she turned and headed back. Her important hour only days away, she wanted to be close to the Virgin. Just before reaching the south portal that always delighted her with its Gothic beauty, there were hurried steps behind her, and Helena called, "Tessa, oh, Tessa, please wait!"

She knew that exertion always made the child cough and stopped to say that she needed to pray by herself. Catching up, Helena's frail body indeed shook with a severe coughing spell, and Tessa held her close until she gained back her breath.

"I was waiting for you in the tower," she finally gasped. "I heard Mother Bernarda say to Mother Eleonora that she hoped the bishop would not approve you to become a novice, and—"

Another coughing spell interrupted the stammering, and for a moment, Tessa was too shocked to respond. Did Bernarda really dislike or rather hate her that much that she did not want her to be a sister in Christ, and had she perhaps expressed such sentiments to anyone other than her sibling? Helena cleared her throat and went on in her urgent little voice still hoarse from coughing.

"Oh, Tessa, tell me that you won't leave here, please? I love you so much, and if you go away, I will die, I really will! Tessa?"

She looked up at her friend and saw that Tessa's face was wet with tears.

"Tessa, did I make you sad?"

The girl shook her head. "No, Helena, your love makes me very happy because it tells me I'm here for a purpose! And don't you worry, love, both the bishop and Count Saurau have approved my candidacy, and I will take my vows in just a couple of days. I will never, ever leave you, Helena, I promised you that a long time ago. Soon, you too will be a choir woman, and we'll be singing together day and night! But you really mustn't run because it makes you cough and that's bad for you and for your voice! So just as I promise, I'll never leave you, you promise me that you'll drink your herb tea and obey to what infirmary magistra prescribes. Will you do that?"

A radiant smile brightened the anxious face, and Tessa again was struck by Helena's exquisite beauty.

"Yes, I promise! I'll drink all the bitter stuff she wants me to, and I'll study hard so I can become just like you!"

"I'm not sure that's such a good idea," Tessa said dryly then, before Helena had a chance to question the remark, quickly added, "I'm going to pray to the Virgin and St. Catherine at the foundress altar, and you may come with me if you like."

Helena nodded eagerly. "I won't disturb you, Tessa. I just want to be near to you!"

Tessa took the girl's hand, and they entered the church. It had been a late spring, and the massive stone walls were still keeping the summer heat at bay. This would change by August when the interior warmed and retained some of that warmth until early December, which gratified the nuns during their many hours of singing. But by Christmas, it would become bitterly cold on the choir, and the frigid temperatures lasted well into May. On this hot July day, however, the soothing cool of the nave was refreshing. Tessa led the way to below the choir loft where flickering candles cast their light upon the foundress altar and the painting she liked so much. She hoped the Virgin would communicate with her, but on this day, St. Catherine's humbly bowed head before the child Jesus spoke more eloquently to her than the searching eyes of the Virgin. Will I ever learn to be truly humble? Tessa thought recalling the proud dignity of the abbess. Was Maria Antonia truly humble, or did the abbess remind herself of this virtue through self-torture like the magistra? Tessa did not think she could ever endure such constant pain, and her heart told her that Christ had suffered for mankind to expiate sin and did not insist that his followers suffer like He did. And the magistra had made clear that what she took upon herself was entirely of her own free will.

When Tessa finally rose, Helena gently tugged at her sleeve and whispered, "Please come to the old cross!"

Tessa understood. The crucifix dated back to the twelfth century and was the church's oldest treasure. Elegant gothic statues and colorful baroque paintings overshadowed the simple work, which had been relegated to an inconspicuous place along the apses wall to the left of the main altar and partially hidden from view. The whitewashed wall emphasized the austerity of the crucified Christ's figure. Thorns did not crown the head, and hair and beard were cropped short to reveal smooth, youthful cheeks. The face with its half-closed eyes, short straight nose, and thin, tight lips was that of an ordinary man bearing an expression of extreme suffering. The body was emaciated, arms and legs thin, the feet with their long toes nailed side by side to the wood instead of crossed as on later representations of the crucified Christ. The simple loincloth almost reached the knees, drooping on one side to reveal a bony hip. Body and face were carved with sparse artistic detail leading to the assumption that this was not the work of an accomplished artist but of a simple countryman. Helena's eyes were unnaturally wide as she looked up to the cross.

"Our Lord suffered so much even before they nailed Him to the cross," she whispered. "I always come here when my cough hurts real bad. But when I die and get to heaven, I want to tell Him that I never hurt as much as He did."

Fear raced through Tessa's mind. "Oh no, Helena, you mustn't talk of dying, we have so many years of singing together ahead of us! Come, let's pray and ask that you get healthy and never cough again!"

She pulled the girl close, and both knelt on the floor with Tessa's hands enfolding those of the child.

"Lord Jesus Christ, merciful Redeemer," she prayed aloud, "I submit to you my life and all I am, and I humbly beg you to make Helena healthy so that we can sing your praise and glory together! Dear Lord, this is my greatest wish for which I will sacrifice anything else I ever prayed for!"

Helena slipped her hands from her friend's and embraced Tessa.

"I know He has heard you, and I thank you! But if He does not grant what you ask, I want you to know that since you've come here, I've been happier than I can remember."

Tessa was still shaken. She'd always been concerned about the child's cough, but it never occurred to her that anyone so young could die. Surely, God would not call this beautiful child to His side, and she resolved that praying for Helena's health would remain foremost on her mind. She and Josepha had been told to concentrate on what was most important in their lives, and she knew that the bishop wanted her to most of all be truly humble. But was not a young child more important to Christ who promised the kingdom of heaven to the little ones pure at heart? Was praying for the innocent not more welcome to Him than obedience to the abbess and submission to sisters who did not mean her well?

Josepha and Tessa were wakened at dawn on Sunday. Both had been to confession the evening before and stayed in the church late into the night saying prayers of penance, which had been particularly long and involved. They had also been fasting since Thursday night, eating only bread with a little cheese and water for their midday meal and a small bowl of gruel for supper. The two meals a day were to prepare them for their schedule as novices that were similar to that of choir women, although during their novitiate, they would continue to eat with the aspirants and rarely be invited to the refectory. Now they were on total fast until after High Mass. A select group of choir women would perform the ceremony of investiture in the sacristy and clothe them with the black Benedictine habit and white wimple. They would then present themselves to the bishop to take their vows and receive his blessing. After the ceremony, they were to join abbess and chapter in the refectory for a festive meal.

"My, am I hungry," whispered Josepha, as they made their way toward Maria Henrica's office for final instructions. "My stomach growls so loud, they won't hear me taking my vows! How's it with you?"

Tessa had barely slept all night and was too excited to be hungry. Both girls still wore their regular clothes, which following tradition would be donated to paupers at the abbey gate. Tessa couldn't wait to rid herself of the drab gray and brown garments that had been altered and mended time and again during past years and become threadbare. Her thoughts were centered on her lovely bridal gown. And the habit she would wear from this day on no longer would draw attention to her modest financial background.

Maria Henrica wore her festive flocke. Once again, she briefed the girls in detail about the long ceremony then sent them to be dressed in their gowns. They first put on fine new linen shirts from their trousseaux; two lay nuns brushed their hair, which the girls had washed the day before. On this day of farewell to secular life, they were allowed to wear it falling freely down their shoulders. Josepha's straight blond tresses reached halfway down her back and flattered her round face while Tessa's lustrous chestnut curls fell to her waist.

"My, does the countess have pretty locks," muttered the nun.

The two women helped them into their gowns and carefully smoothed and arranged the rich folds. They were handed their jewels, and the girls assisted each other with the clasps. Both looked radiantly lovely. The sapphires and blue silk complemented Josepha's eyes, and the flowing gown made her appear taller and slimmer. There was a glow of excitement on her cheeks, and Tessa silently wondered why anyone considered Josepha plain. Her necklace and dress were more precious than Tessa's, yet the younger one clapped her hands in admiration and exclaimed, "Tessa, you look like a fairytale queen!"

The tall, slender young woman in the green and gold brocade dress that emphasized her pale golden skin indeed cast a regal figure.

The loose hair softened the lines of her narrow cheeks and high forehead; her face radiated happiness.

The lay nuns had secretly brought a mirror from the seamstress. Because this was not a day to foster vanity, the gesture would not have met the magistra's approval, but the kindly women saw nothing wrong with two young girls admiring their appearance before forever disappearing under the folds of a black habit and veil. Josepha giggled and danced about the room, and Tessa joined her. They were laughing and exchanging compliments when one of the lay nuns put a finger on her lips at approaching footsteps and the other quickly hid the mirror. A young choir woman entered.

"Are you ready? It is time to form the procession, follow me! Everyone is waiting."

She led the way down the hall and into the main courtyard. The girls blinked at the bright sunshine and gazed at the scene of revelry that caught them by surprise. A large crowd of people in colorful festive clothes was gathered, waving flags and banners with the abbey's seal and milling around the waiting procession. A momentary hush fell over the crowd at the girls' appearance, followed by admiring exclamations like "pretty," "regal," and "beautiful." The choir woman took their hands leading them, and her somber black habit was a striking contrast to their gowns with interwoven gold threads glittering in the sunlight. Village children in their finery and, with flowers in hand, led the procession, followed by dignitaries from the hamlet, the nearby town of Leoben and as far away as Graz.

Ceremonies at the abbey, whether investiture, profess, installation of a new abbess, or celebrating a jubilee only occurred at intervals of several years and always were special events for the surrounding countryside. Göss was both economically as well as culturally a focal point for the region, and special occasions invariably turned into festivals. The bishop with his entourage, Josepha's parents and Count Saurau, were not the only distinguished visitors. Ministerial officials from Graz—administrators of the abbey's landholdings as far away as Carynthia and, of course, Count Stubenberg, the official administrative steward, a position his family had held for generations—had gathered. As the day's celebrated honorees, the two candidates walked last in the procession. Josepha smiled at her father as she approached, and Tessa noticed the lovingly admiring look on Count Plaz's face. Count Saurau formally inclined his head in welcome, and the girl gave him a radiant smile as she placed her hand on his forearm. Both were radiant brides with sparkling eyes and cheeks pink from excitement. Cheers rose from the crowd as the procession began to move, and a village band played. Tessa's sensitive ear heard their being off key, and the count, who closely watched her face, suppressed a smile at the involuntary slight grimace passing her features. When they reached the church portal, the village children parted to form a lane for the officials to pass; the procession came to a halt there for a few moments to allow the dignitaries taking their seats. Tessa impulsively turned toward the crowd, did a little curtsey, and waved. Everyone broke into enthusiastic applause, and shouts of well-wishing and approval were heard. Tessa had never before faced a crowd of people and did not know what prompted her to make this gesture of appreciation; she simply wanted to share the joy and pride in her heart with everyone. She'd later remember it as the happiest and most lighthearted moment of her day.

Handel's water music had become popular during the last decade, and the organ was playing it to indicate that the ceremony was about to begin. The aspirants threw rose petals, and people in the nave turned to watch the two candidates walk down the aisle toward the altar. The girls stood with their escorts while the bishop celebrated High Mass and the choir women's voices filled the church. Tessa thought the bishop looked just as cold and stern as he had during their interview. After the gospel reading about Jesus asking his first disciples to leave house and home, mother and father, family and possessions to follow Him, the bishop's sermon dealt with the merits of devoting one's life to Christ.

"Under the auspices of the Holy Order of St. Benedict, as you enjoin yourselves with the Lord Jesus through solemn vows, your soul shall attain such supreme beauty, your virtues shine so magnificently that even the sun and moon pale in comparison! A bridegroom joyfully awaits the bride, King David longed for his betrothed, yet what could be more desirable than to be wedded to Christ, your eternal bridegroom!"

His thoughts expressed the church's conviction that life as a religious was above that of the secular world like heaven above earth. The words were intended to ignite in young pious minds filled with romantic enthusiasm a shining apotheosis that through the centuries had persuaded many an aspirant to take the veil. Yet he more deeply impressed young aspirants than the candidates who, like secular brides during a wedding ceremony, were caught up in the excitement of the hour and later remembered little of the lengthy speech. They humbly knelt before him to receive communion and were formally presented to the church by their escorts, and when they proceeded to the sacristy for their robing, they were received by two circles of solemnly faced choir women, one for each candidate. Jewelry was unfastened and symbolically placed at the feet of a statue of the Virgin, gowns and embroidered shoes removed. In white linen shirt and stockings, each girl was led to a chair. As befitting, Tessa's eyes had been lowered, but she now looked up to see Maria Bernarda stand beside her chair with scissors in hand, a trace of both contemptuous yet triumphant smile curling her lips and sudden realization hit like a thunderbolt. She hesitated for an instant, but firm hands led her on and gently but decidedly pushed her into the seat. Tessa had never given any thought to what would happen to her hair, thinking that the veil would just hide it, unaware that this traditional attribute of female beauty was part of her sacrifice to the church. There was no turning back, only the painful thought, *Why does it have to be Bernarda doing this to me?* She more heard than felt the scissors cutting her thick tresses, first along her neck, then closer and closer to the scalp until the cool metal touched her skin with each cut. Through half-closed eyes she watched her locks fall into her lap and slide onto the floor. But for the slight grating of scissors cutting through hair, not a sound was heard in the room or from the church, where the congregation silently awaited the return of the robed novices. *Dear God, please let it be over*, she thought with a light-headed feeling due to emotional trauma and fasting. Then helping hands brushed the hair off her shirt and helped her stand. Maria Henrica stepped forward to dress her in the black habit, and choir women put black shoes on her feet, girded her waist with a simple rope, and draped the white wimple round her face and neck. Next followed the scapula, a rectangular cloth with an opening for the head that front and back reached the hem of her skirt, and finally the long white veil of novices. One by one, the choir women stepped forward to place the traditional kiss of love and friendship upon her cheek. Were Bernarda's lips actually cold as ice, or was her imagination playing tricks?

When she and Josepha finally stood before the abbess, Maria Antonia said solemnly, "My daughters, with your worldly clothes, you have shed your secular life to enter the home of God as His brides. You have left behind whatever bound you to secular life. Therefore, you shall receive new names by which you will be known henceforth. The first shall be Maria, for it is the Queen of heaven who in merciful love presents us to her divine Son. Josepha, your name shall be Maria Antonia, for I have felt as your godmother since you came here a young child. You, Marie Therese, shall be known as Maria Columba!"

Tessa would later ask God's forgiveness for her disappointment, but all her troubled mind could think of was, why such an odd name? A few moments later, she overheard a whisper, "An apt name after the renegade saint who was punished more than any other!" Tessa would have recognized the voice anywhere.

The two young women stepped before the altar to render their vows of chastity, obedience, and poverty. The bishop placed rings on their finger as a symbol of their betrothal to Christ and laid his hands on their bowed heads for the blessing. Organ and choir erupted in a resounding hallelujah, and all joined in the traditional Te Deum. "Holy God we praise Thy name, Lord of all we bow before Thee, All on earth Thy scepter claim, All in Heaven above adore Thee, Infinite Thy vast domain, Everlasting is Thy reign!"

Abbess Maria Antonia and her court joined the bishop, his entourage, the Supremus Capellanus, and the choir women in the main refectory for an elaborate banquet honoring the new novices. Cloister rules and symbolic separation between secular and religious world barred Josepha's parents, Count Saurau, as well as other dignitaries, who were hosted by the parish priest and dined at the rectory. The two girls entered the refectory for the first time. It was a room of generous proportions that accommodated many more than the two dozen or so nuns that regularly took their meals here. Intricate stucco moldings and exquisite anaglyptas decorated the ceiling, and the bees's wax candles in the three massive brass chandeliers radiated sweet scent. No paintings decorated the plain whitewashed walls, only a life-size crucifix hung opposite the four windows overlooking the park. The bright light of the refectory and the design of the magnificent ceiling surprised Columba and became her most lasting impression of the banquet. The diners were seated along the outer edge of a U-shaped table covered with embroidered tablecloths and set with heavy silver flatware and candelabra and decorated with bouquets of fresh flowers. The abbess presided between the bishop and the Supremus, choir women holding offices were next, and the two novices were placed at each end of the head table. All eyes turned to the crucifix while the bishop recited a lengthy blessing and after the amen, lay nuns entered with silver platters and bowls of food. Novice Maria Columba ate little and felt strangely disconnected from the scene, almost as if observing it from afar. When later she tried to recall her thoughts during this several hours lasting banquet, she was unable to do so. She barely touched the trout, the stuffed bass, saddle of deer, fowl, the condiments, pies, and vegetables. Was it exhaustion after a sleepless night, trauma over losing her hair, or the solemnity of the day? She could not have said, but nibbling from her plate, she desperately longed to be alone. Choir women normally ate their meals in silence and even on this occasion the abbess and her immediate circle carried most of the conversation. Columba responded only with a nod or brief word to the occasional remark of those seated next to her, who decided that the new novice was immersed in pious contemplation.

Novice Maria Antonia ate heartily. The excitement of the ceremony a past experience, her practical, down-to-earth sense prevailed. She'd never cared much about her dull blonde hair, and losing it did not overly chagrin her. Always curious and inquisitive, she'd questioned a lay nun some time ago and already knew that a nun's hair was cut to the scalp. She felt honored that her convent name was the same as that of the abbess, but above all, she was hungry, and this was the best meal she'd had since leaving home half her young life ago! She had generous helpings of everything, heartily drank two glasses of wine and enjoyed the variety of sweet cakes and candied fruit. On the way to the refectory, she had quickly felt for a pocket in her habit and was delighted to find one. Eating in the cell was strictly forbidden, but the new novice could not imagine life without a bite between meals. After all, of what use to God was a servant weak from hunger?

Finally, Abbess Maria Antonia rose to signal the end of the meal, and after a closing prayer, the participants slowly dispersed. Columba headed for the door when Scholastica caught her sleeve and whispered, "You must go thank the abbess and the bishop before you leave!"

Columba gave her a grateful smile and respectfully approached, bowed, and murmured words of gratitude and appreciation. The bishop seemed to have expected more and regarded her for a few moments of embarrassed silence, but Maria Antonia lightly placed a hand on the girl's bowed head.

"My daughter, I understand that you are overcome by the sanctity of the occasion. You may withdraw for quiet contemplation until vespers."

"Thank you, Reverend Mother Abbess," breathed Columba and kissed the extended hand then turned to the Bishop, who was not willing to dismiss her so quickly.

"It is a virtue for a future choir woman to be of few words," he said unctuously, "and I trust that you will take my earlier admonitions to heart. As a convert, you are doubly blessed to be welcomed into the distinguished abbey of Göss. Now it is up to you and you alone to prove yourself worthy!"

Columba more sensed than saw an instinctive gesture by the abbess, who undoubtedly recalled that Maria Henrica was a convert also.

"Yes, Your Excellency, I am indeed most grateful. I beg, Your Excellency, and the Most Reverend Mother Abbess to pray for me," murmured Columba with great effort, kissed the ring on the extended hand, and headed for the door with undue haste.

"Immature for her age and impulsive. I fear that she will cause you sorrow through the years," the bishop said looking after her. "Is her dowry adequate?"

"She's a warmhearted young woman of great piety with a heavenly voice," replied Maria Antonia. "There have been many tragedies in her young life, and she seems to have dealt with them quite well. Her uncle, His Eminence Cardinal Kollonitsch, has forwarded the sum of five hundred florins from his private purse in addition to a smaller sum from her father's family, and there is also a yearly stipend from her mother's inheritance. I am overjoyed that the cardinal guided his four charges to our true faith and that they all chose religious life."

The influential cardinal's name had the desired effect on the bishop.

"Under your able auspices, dear sister in Christ, let us hope that she shall become a worthy choir woman."

Reaching the park, Columba had to restrain herself not to gather her skirts for an undignified run toward the reflection tower. She didn't know why she chose it over the hermit tower for her only thought was seclusion. The little door screeched in its hinges and unaccustomed to her habit's full sleeves one of them caught on the handle for a little tear. It brought her back to reality. "What a way to start religious life by tearing my habit." She sighed then rushed up the stairs two steps at a time. A slight breeze rendered the chamber invitingly cool. Columba stood and leaned her forehead against the rough stone.

"Oh, Papa," she whispered, "if you're in heaven with God, ask Him that my future days here shall not be like today!"

It crossed her mind that it was not her father she should address in her prayers and that this day was to be one of great bliss. Then why was her heart so heavy, why her fear of the future that suddenly loomed dark and difficult? Columba did not question her decision to choose religious life at that hour, yet the bishop's attitude and words left her feeling inadequate and unsure of her ability to live up to what was expected of her. She looked at her painting and that of Maria Henrica, which related to her pain with its desolation.

She sensed the melancholy of the Silesian landscape and wondered how the magistra had felt on the day of her investiture. Transylvania seemed so far gone she rarely longed for it anymore. All she wanted was to cry in someone's arms and talk about her fears. She recalled looking across the table at Antonia, round face flushed with excitement and blue eyes sparkling as she thoroughly enjoyed her meal and animatedly chatted with the choir woman next to her. She seemed a picture of bliss, a feeling both had shared this morning. Why did her happiness not last? Columba felt immensely tired and, dropping onto the stone bench, stared at the now familiar view. At her feet was a perfectly peaceful scene, the gently flowing river, lush pastures, and late blooms on a chestnut tree. She could faintly hear music from the hamlet's festivities and idly watched an old man appear with his scythe to mow the narrow strip between the abbey wall and the river. She could hear the sound of grass being cut and fall with each swing of his arms and wondered whether this peasant had ever sat down to a meal like the one served to her that day. She noticed another man sitting motionless by the river with a fishing rod. Would his family depend on his luck for food on their table this evening? She thought of the bread and cakes distributed for the occasion to anyone coming to the gate and wondered whether the man merely wanted solitude. The two men and their activities eased her somber mood, and she began to feel calmer. When the first bell called for vespers, she rose resolutely and, casting a look at Henrica's picture, said aloud, "I'm no longer sad. I am strong and know I can live up to my vows! I can become just as good a choir woman as any of my sisters in Christ! I am now Novice Maria Columba, and though I do not like the sound of it, I will not be punished like the saint with this name!"

She hurried down the stairs and walked across the empty park to the south portal and into the church. It was soothingly cool and dark inside and only a few candles burned at the various altars. Columba dipped her fingers into holy water, genuflected and headed toward the pew for novices when she felt a hand, and faced the choir magistra.

"Sing vespers with us this evening, my daughter," Maria Carolina said with a smile. "Here's your text. And rejoice, Maria Columba, for soon you will be with us on the empore joining your voice with us to the glory of the Lord, whose bride you became today!"

She placed a hymnal with a bookmark at the appropriate page into the novice's hands and walked away before the girl could thank her. Columba took her place beside Maria Antonia, and soon, the sound of the organ filled the church, and she happily joined the choir above for the first time. Singing lightened her heart as it always did, and she forgot her worries. The service and sung litany enthralled her, and she barely noticed that Maria Antonia was stifling yawns and nodding off from time to time.

After Komplet, the final service of the day, the magistra noviciarum showed the two novices the cell they were to share during their novitiate. The spacious chamber they were assigned was more inviting than the confining white cubicles of the aspirants' dormitory. To be sure, each bed had a dense curtain for privacy, and Magistra Maria Cunigunde admonished them never to undress without closing it and preferably keep them drawn all night. The window overlooked a small orchard, and a large apple tree virtually stretched its branches across the windowsill. There were two chests, a washstand with a small mirror and a prayer stool for each, facing opposite corners with a simple crucifix above. On the occasion of a visitation in the seventeenth century, a zealous bishop had forbidden the use of mirrors as well as the wearing of gloves and fur wraps in the bitterly cold church, but a successor canceled the severe regulations. They had to dress for night services by the dim light of a small oil lamp and were indeed in need of mirrors to ensure that wimple and veil were properly draped.

Lay nuns had stocked the chests with linens and hose from their trousseaux. Columba knew that her little menagerie of carved animals from Transylvania was not among her things. Maria Henrica had told her that they would be given to poor village children. She wondered whether they would enjoy and handle them with as much care as she had. Her papa's devoted valet had carved them for her from the wood of a larch tree when she was but a small child confined to bed with a severe case of scarlet fever. The man was talented and did a beautiful job with the small figures. Columba stared at her neatly folded handkerchiefs in the top drawer, where she used to keep them, when a small bulge caught her eye and lifting a starched nightcap she found the tiniest member of her collection, a young deer curled up with its slender legs neatly folded below the body, its little head alertly raised. The artist had not forgotten the tiny indentations on the back of the deer to indicate the camouflage dots nature provides during the first few months of a fawn's life. Columba smiled and carefully hid the figure below her linens. Antonia saw the nightcap in her hand and said, "You're wondering why we're given those things that in secular life only old women wear? Because we're bald, that's why! My, do I look funny!"

Columba was appalled to see Antonia discard veil and wimple and laugh at her reflection in the mirror. Her round pink face below the white scalp with stiff little tufts of hair that had escaped the scissors looked pitiful, and Columba feared that the expression on her face mirrored her thoughts. Antonia chuckled.

"Dear me, I never thought much of my hair, but it was more flattering than this! I look awful, don't I? Good thing we have our veils, and looking at the bright side, I guess they could get real hot with hair piled up underneath. Poor you, losing those pretty curls!"

And noticing Columba's hesitation to remove her veils, she added casually, "Might as well get it over with! We'll have to get used to it like many other things."

However, down to earth and self-deprecating, Antonia was a sensitive human being, who rarely showed her own hurts and always considered the feelings of others. She gave Columba a hug, kissed her on both cheeks, and said lightly, "It's been a great day, but I'm dead tired, and all I want to do is sleep, and surely so do you! Don't you worry, I think it'll get easier with time, and I'm so glad I can share it all with you!" She pulled the muslin curtains around her bed, and Columba saw her shadowy figure remove the habit and slip into her nightshirt. She herself was not quite ready.

"Thank you, Josepha, dear," she finally said forgetting her friend's newly given name in the emotion of the moment. "You are a treasure, and I really don't know how I could have come this far without you! I too am grateful for us to be together and look forward—" she stopped and searched for words. About to continue, she realized that Antonia had blown out her candle and deep and even breathing from behind the curtain told her that her exhausted friend was asleep. Columba smiled to herself, undressed and blew out her candle before removing the wimple. Pale moonlight found its way through the branches of the apple tree into the room, and Columba stood by the open window looking into the garden, a silent prayer on her lips. She climbed into bed and left her curtains open to savor the cool night air. A little time passed before she could bring herself to feel her scalp. It was a strange experience to run her fingers over the stubble and intermittent little tufts of hair, and she wasn't sure she'd ever have the courage to look at herself in a mirror without cap or veil. Nature finally triumphed, and she fell into a fitful sleep. In her dreams, she saw Bernarda holding a pair of huge scissors, laughing loudly, and joined by a guffawing chorus of faceless choir women. Suddenly, they all stopped to whisper in unison, "Columba, the one who needs to be punished, punished, punished."

The whispers became a crescendo of voices that droned like a waterfall. She saw the stern face of the bishop before her, his right forefinger raised in admonishing gesture, then his face dissolved into the kindly features of Sister Agnes, her revered Vienna music teacher, who silenced the menacing whispers. "Sing to the glory of our Lord, Tessa. Raise your voice in His honor, and He will hear you!"

Columba woke with a start, convinced that Agnes was standing by her bed, but the room was dark and silent except for Antonia's breathing. "Bless you, Sister Agnes, that is what I will do always," she said to herself and went back to sleep, this time without dreams.

When the bell rang at a quarter past five for the prim, she felt rested and very hungry. Novices were dispensed from choir service during the night but participated in most of the other services. The first bell told them that they had a half-hour to wash and dress and fifteen minutes for quiet contemplation. Pouring water into her wash bowl, Columba bravely raised her eyes to the mirror and a look at herself. Candles were only used during the dark months, and the early dawn gave only dim light. Still Columba stared with shock at the gaunt face with its large dark eyes, longish nose, and wide mouth

reflected in her mirror, painfully conscious of how her locks had softened her features. She quickly washed her face and began to drape
the wimple.

"I can't cope with this thing, do help me arrange it," said
Antonia, struggling before her mirror. Columba gladly did, and the
girls enjoyed helping each other. They then knelt in silent prayer for
the first contemplation of the day until the second bell told them it
was time to head for church. Their room was on the second floor
of the main convent tract, only a short flight of stairs above ground
and directly below the cells of cloistered choir women. When they
reached the landing, they could hear the muffled footsteps in the
"cloister walk" above, through which choir women's cells directly
connected to the choir loft. Columba and Antonia hurried down the
stairs, crossed the well courtyard, and entered the dimly lit church
through the south portal. After the service, they went to the aspirants' quarters to assume their new responsibility of supervising and
were joined that day by Maria Henrica. Like choir women, novices
were not allowed breakfast and fasted until after High Mass, following which they would take their main meal. Columba saw Antonia
cast longing glances toward the baskets of freshly baked bread, and
that morning, she too counted the hours until they'd be allowed to
eat. The excited chatter of the young aspirants talking about the
previous day's ceremony and festivities mercifully distracted them.
Especially Helena's eyes glowed with admiration, and she could not
say enough about how beautiful Columba had looked, which earned
her a reprimand from Magistra Maria Henrica that such secular
comments belonged to the past and were no longer appropriate for
someone betrothed to Christ. Helena duly apologized, but Columba
gave her a secret smile and little wink of the eye. She and Antonia led
the aspirants in prayer before and after the meal, proudly conscious
of their new responsibility. They checked the girls' attires, adjusting
here and there, and led them into church for High Mass. At communion time, they waited until the last choir woman had received
the host until they stepped forward to kneel at the altar rail. Placing
the sacred wafer on their tongues, the Supremus repeated in Latin,
"May the body of our Lord Jesus Christ preserve your soul for life

everlasting. Amen." After the final rousing hallelujah, they eagerly went to their dining room and a hearty meal, and with the start of the aspirants' afternoon classes, their own recreation time began. Columba took a walk through the park, and Antonia settled down on a secluded bench with a book about the life of St. Scholastica, but the hearty meal, early rise, and summer heat soon overwhelmed her, and she dozed off. Columba walked briskly back and forth under the trees humming a tune she'd picked up from the village band the day before, lighthearted and filled with youthful energy. She barely noticed the other nuns strolling silently with breviary in hand until she heard the quiet but firm voice of Magistra Maria Cunigunde, "Maria Columba, it does not behoove a future choir woman to stride like a child or hum secular songs! Your first recreation time after your vows would more aptly be spent reading your breviary, surely you carry it with you?"

Columba blushed with embarrassment. "Please forgive me, Reverend Mother, I must have left it in church after High Mass," she said. "And I am sorry for walking too fast, but I'm so happy to be a novice, I feel like jumping with joy."

Maria Cunigunde was not amused. "The Lord wishes us to serve him with joy, but there are more appropriate ways of expression than to behave like an immature child, and humming in the park disturbs the concentration of your sisters in Christ. Now go find your breviary and remain in church until your next duty. And I am not fond of novices repeating transgressions, do you understand?"

"Yes, Reverend Mother," Columba answered. It was as if a dark cloud had settled over the bright summer day, and she dutifully returned to the pew to collect her novices' breviary. The church was cool and peaceful, but Columba could not concentrate on her prescribed prayers and, after a little while, rose to seek refuge at the foundress's altar. She looked up to meet the eyes of the Virgin.

"Why is it, oh Blessed Virgin, that I always need an image of you before me to connect in my prayers? Why can't I find you in the written word? When I was little and you were my precious secret, I could hear you whisper to me in the branches of trees or a murmuring brook. Now that I have dedicated myself to serving your Divine

Son, where are you, Holy Mother of God? Please help me to humbly accept criticism, but was it really so wicked to hum and walk fast?"

Was it just her imagination that made it seem as if there was a tinge of reproach in Mary's wistful eyes? Columba bowed her head over her folded hands. "Oh, Holy Mother, it's so hard to do everything right, but I promise I'll keep trying!"

Columba kept her promise, no matter how difficult at times, and the weeks and months of her novitiate passed without major incident, though it anguished her to find so little time for solitude in her beloved towers. Her consolation was studying music with Maria Carolina, who made no secret of her satisfaction with the progress of her pupil. Columba soon played the spinet well and was anxious to learn the much more difficult techniques of the organ. There had initially been opposition that a novice be allowed in the cloistered area, but the resolute Maria Carolina declared that her hands were becoming stiff with arthritis and someone had to be able to play the organ once she no longer could. The first time she entered the choir loft, Columba could not take her eyes off the magnificently carved pews for choir women, arranged in two rows at both sides of the organ. Those in the second row were elevated to allow everyone a clear view of the altar. She knew they had been replaced only a decade ago and that it had taken years to complete the work. Richly carved scrolls of oak leaves decorated the armrests, and seats and backs had exquisite inlaid designs of different color woods. Yet despite their baroque splendor the overall impression was pious and austere, and there were no cushions on which to kneel or sit. Columba looked at them longingly. *Oh, for the joy of occupying one of these and singing from the depth of my heart*, she thought. Mother Carolina read her expression.

"You will have ample time at all hours of the day and night to sit or stand or kneel in one of them," she said dryly. "Each choir woman has her assigned place, and they indeed instill a feeling of pride. We're grateful to our Most Reverend Mother Abbess for having commissioned them soon after she assumed office. They are not restful, but then one is not supposed to feel physically comfortable in the presence of the Lord! You will sing from one of these for many years to come summer and winter. Then it is often so cold that you'll see your breath. Sometimes, our choir has only a few voices because many sisters become ill or too hoarse to sing. That is why I welcome young and healthy women with resistance to the changes of season. But now I want you to stand beside me and listen carefully as I explain to you how this most intricate of all instruments functions so you can master it quickly."

The magistra noviciarum insisted that Columba's music lessons take place during her recreation time and that none of her regular duties be neglected. But the girl did not mind especially when fall arrived with inclement weather and outdoor recreation all but ended. She would have loved to pursue her singing studies also, but Maria Carolina decided that her voice was sufficiently trained for the chants, litanies, chorales, and hymns.

The novice year passed quickly. Solemn affirmation of final vows, profess, was set for September 15, 1748, the week after Foundress Day. Feast days were always preceded by strict fasting, which meant that after a sparse meal following High Mass on the sixth, only water was allowed 'til the next day. Returning to their cell from Komplet, Antonia stood by the window and longingly looked at the branches of the apple tree loaded with plump yellow fruit so close yet just out of reach.

"'Tis a shame." She sighed. "I can smell those apples, and I'm so hungry I'm about to faint! What I wouldn't give to munch on a couple of those!"

Columba joined her. "They don't trust us and had those close by picked," she mused. "You know, Antonia, back home at Zay-Ugrocz, there was a cherry tree close to the window of my room, and I'd jump from the windowsill onto it after the ayah had put me to bed, eat my fill of cherries, and climb right back into the room. Sometimes, the ayah would find cherry stains on my nightgown, and then she'd wail that cherry trees had brittle branches, and I could have fallen to my death, which obviously never happened. I used to climb trees all the time then, day or night!"

Antonia looked at her in amazement. "You really could do that, Columba? Oh, let's give it a try after it gets dark and they've all gone to bed and no one's looking out the window! If we just had a couple of those apples, wouldn't that be great!"

From one moment to the next, the two girls were no longer novices a week prior to becoming dignified choir women of the abbey of Göss. Instead, they'd turned into hungry teenagers anticipating an adventure without thinking of consequences. They decided on the strongest branch on which Columba would climb, quickly pick a few fruit within reach to throw to Antonia, who was to extend a towel for Columba to hold when jumping back onto the windowsill. It would take but a few minutes, and no one would ever find out about it. They almost forgot their hunger while waiting for the long dusk turn into darkness. Finally, it was night, and a pale half moon cast only a dim light over the garden. Columba donned her white nightgown and used the habit rope to hitch it up for leg freedom. She wore her sandals and at the last moment tossed off her nightcap so it would not get caught in the branches. With youthful agility, she eased from the window frame onto the nearest branch and began to reach for apples outlined against the sky, throwing them back to Antonia, who was a poor catcher and allowed some fall with a thump onto the floor. She was getting anxious and whispered urgently, "'Tis enough, Columba, come back! Please!"

But her friend had tasted freedom and was too exuberant to end this adventure so quickly. She was climbing higher when she carelessly stepped on a rotting branch that broke with a distinct noise. An experienced climber, she'd secured herself with her hands, but having reached the level of choir women's cells, she knew it was time for a hasty retreat. And sure enough, she saw a white figure appear behind a window that fortunately was closed. Columba moved like a cat in her rapid descent and, grasping the extended towel, jumped onto the sill, hoping that the choir woman above was unable to observe her without opening the window. Her feet had barely touched the floor when they heard piercing shrieks from above and the building came alive.

"Quick, get into bed!" gasped Antonia, collecting the apples and tossing them under her pillow. She closed the window and jumped into bed when she saw Columba's nightcap on the floor and retrieved it just as voices became audible in the hallway outside. Antonia pulled her sheets up to her chin and tightly closed her eyes, hoping it would all go away. But the door soon opened, and Maria Cunigunde, accompanied by Maria Henrica, entered.

"Is something the matter here?" the magistra noviciarum asked sternly raising her oil lamp. Antonia rubbed her eyes and pretended to be startled.

"Reverend Mother, what is it?" she asked with a stifled yawn. "Is someone ill?"

"No one is ill, but Maria Bernarda says she was awakened by a loud noise and, stepping to the window, saw a white ghost in the tree! Have you seen or heard anything?" She proceeded toward the window to check whether it was closed.

"No, Reverend Mother," said Antonia. "We've been asleep and—"

"Speaking of sleeping," said the magistra, "Columba does not appear to hear us even now! Is she always so hard to wake?" She stepped toward the bed, in which Columba had turned toward the wall with the sheet pulled over her head.

"Oh yes, Reverend Mother," whispered Antonia, "I always have to shake her. She never hears the morning bell." She almost choked on the last word, noticing that of one of Columba's heels was visible near the foot end of the bed.

Maria Henrica, who until then had remained silent, now said quietly but with authority, "Perhaps, Bernarda had a bad dream, for everything seems to be quiet and in order," and—putting her hand on Cunigunde's arm gently pulled her toward the door. "Let us return to our rest, dear sister. And, Antonia, remember to always keep your window closed tightly for night air is unhealthy to breathe."

The magistra noviciarum hesitated for a moment, her eyes still on the sleeping Columba, then—with a nod to Antonia—followed Henrica out the door, and the room was left in darkness.

The two girls were paralyzed with fear and barely dared to breathe. Both suddenly realized that this escapade had put their profess in jeopardy, for if discovered, they would have been severely punished and profess likely postponed. Antonia was quicker to retrieve her equipoise and began to munch on an apple. Hearing her bite into the fruit, Columba emerged from under her sheets.

"How on earth can you feel like eating," she whispered. "Good heavens, was that close! And where's my nightcap?"

"Right here." Antonia chuckled pulling it from under her pillow. "What worried me a lot more was that your sandal was showing! I have a dim feeling Mother Henrica spotted it and that's why she shooed Mother Cunigunde out the door still wondering how you could be so fast asleep! Come now, have an apple, you deserve it! I've never seen anyone come down a tree that fast, and if there's a funny side to all this, it's that dearest Bernarda will be seeing white ghosts in her dreams for a while!"

Columba was too shaken to see humor in the situation. They hid the apples in their drawers and resolved to eat them before laundry time so a lay nun placing fresh linens in the chests wouldn't find them. They checked for stains on Columba's nightgown and, finding none, settled down to sleep after Antonia had eaten a third apple. But Columba could not find rest and, with a heartfelt prayer, thanked the Virgin for preventing Bernarda from recognizing her. She knew her adversary would have been only too happy to see her openly humiliated. In retrospect, she could not fathom why she had so recklessly placed her future in jeopardy, knowing full well that her motivation had not been hunger but the adventure, daring to do something forbidden. With the danger passed, she recalled how wonderful it had felt up there in the crown of that tree, free as a bird, deliciously aware of being eighteen years young! She wondered whether Henrica had indeed noticed something awry and had protected her before Cunigunde could further question her deep slumber. Then she began to feel ashamed for behaving like a child. Well, if all went well, her novitiate would end in about a week, and then she'd finally be allowed to sing to her heart's content. Surely, she would no longer be tempted by silly adventures once she was a choir woman! Calm and confidence returned, and she finally fell asleep with a smile on her lips.

After High Mass and their festive meal the next day, choir women as usual distributed loaves of bread to the villagers at the main gate while Columba, Antonia, and the aspirants sang nearby. It was a happy occasion blessed by traditionally lovely weather, and the crowd cheered the two novices with shouts of "God be with you" to wish them well for their upcoming profess. Both girls sang from the depth of their hearts, grateful that this Foundress Day was a happy occasion instead of the disaster it easily could have become.

Two days later, they took their final examinations, and again, Columba was able to help the struggling Antonia. They had to know the dates and names of all abbesses of record together with their major accomplishments at Göss, as well as Latin Mass texts, psalms, and litanies. Then there were the rules of St. Benedict that governed their order, even though not all the latter were strictly followed at Göss, the most notable exception being the rule of poverty. Since their inception as canonesses, the choir women had never lived in poverty and always been able to preserve their comforts of good food and small luxuries. Indeed, St. Benedict's motto, "Ora et Labora," only applied to them in the form of their exhausting choir duty to sing and pray during seven services around the clock. Members of the abbess's court devoted much time to administrative work, education of aspirants, preparing and dispensing herbs and medicines to the sick from their pharmacy and running a small hospital besides their own infirmary.

And the choir women created remarkably intricate handicraft. Their lives were far from idle as they designed and produced exquisitely beautiful embroidered vestments and altar cloths or dedicated themselves to the project of decorating relics. During the baroque, many convents and particularly contemplative orders went to great expense to acquire bones of saints. Such relics might consist of almost complete skeletons that would be lovingly assembled and given a face of molded wax then clothed in intricately embroidered garments and enshrined in a glass casket for display at a side altar of the church. When only few bones of a particular saint could be obtained, they were wrapped in embroidered, often jewel-encrusted silk and paired with a small picture, relief carving or perhaps the decorated skull. Small parchment strips identified the martyr, and everything was placed under glass in appropriate frames or boxes. These were made of carved and gilded wood and produced by local craftsmen. Many choir women devoted years of recreation time to such a project and their creativity produced remarkable results.

All aspirants were taught embroidery, and the lessons intensified during the novitiate. Columba found needlework tedious and difficult. Her hands, so well-coordinated playing spinet or organ, were clumsy with the needle, and her stitches usually turned out irregular and far apart. This was one subject in which Antonia outdid her; the chubby girl preferred to sit still, and her short fingers were extremely skillful. She lacked talent for design but was able to accurately follow a pattern on a vestment or antependium. Columba knew she would have been in trouble had embroidery been an examination subject. All her hopes and dreams were oriented toward music, and she secretly desired to one day be appointed choir magistra.

A few days prior to profess, Maria Antonia called each of the novices to her office to discuss their personal funds held by the abbess and available from time to time for personal needs, even small luxuries. Antonia's yearly allowance in addition to the substantial sum of three thousand florins was generous. Columba's dowry was small and so was her yearly allowance since her share from the sale of Zay-Ugrocz had been consumed to pay for her board as aspirant. All funds had the stipulation that in the event of a choir woman's early demise or the unlikely event of expulsion, any remaining balance became the property of the abbey. Columba was painfully aware that her dowry was smaller than that of most others, although she knew that sometimes all dowry requirements were waved to allow for special circumstances.

Columba and Antonia solemnly professed their final vows on a gray and rainy day that dampened the traditional festivities enjoyed at such events, though celebration of a profess was not as extensive as that at investiture. One reason was lack of a spectacle since there were no radiant brides in princely gowns escorted into church. Instead, two somber young women already in their black Benedictine habit stepped before the altar to exchange white veils with black ones and their diamond rings of betrothal with the simple gold bands of choir women. They bore the seal of their heavenly bridegroom, IHS.

This time, the bishop of Admont conducted the ceremony, Seckau having sent word that His Excellency was ailing. Bishop Johannes Count Palffy was of Hungarian origin and, during the interview, had kinder words for Columba and commended her on her remarkable knowledge of Latin. He also spoke at length about the finality of the commitment.

"No one," he stressed, "feels content with a chosen life at all times, nor is our frail human mind always able to remain free of doubt or temptation, but during such times, sincerity and strength of commitment to the church and dedication to Christ must prevail. Remember then, my daughter, it will be during such times that you must find the Lord in your prayers, even when He seems unreachable. 'If today you hear His voice, harden not your heart!' reads the psalm. Through the mouth of your Supremus or your abbess, His voice shall demand obedience in things you do not understand or like, yet you must not harden your heart and joyfully comply! You must love your abbess and sisters in Christ, for the Lord Jesus said that next to loving God with all your soul, your foremost commandment is to love your neighbor like yourself! Do you understand me, my daughter Maria Columba, and are you resolved to this important commandment?"

Columba could not help thinking of Bernarda and impulsively said, "But what if one of my sisters does not love me, Your Excellency?"

The bishop's face darkened. "Maria Columba, I see you have not taken my words to heart, and I am disappointed. There is no one within these walls whose heart nurtures ill feeling! All of us find it easy to love some of our brothers or sisters more than others. It is easy to love those we like, but religious life is not meant to be easy! God demands obedience and sacrifice, and sacrifice means joyfully doing for Him that which is most difficult! When you solemnly promise total obedience before the altar, you also must resolve in your heart to obey His commandment of unconditional love! If you find yourself unable to do so, your vows are not sincere, and you are committing a grave sin! Is your heart pure and dedicated to do as I said?"

His voice had become stern, and Columba felt him searching her mind. She flushed with shame, and tears welled in her eyes.

"Yes, Your Excellency," she said in a barely audible voice. "I do love Christ with all my heart, and I shall always listen to His voice and obey!"

There was a long pause as if the bishop had expected to hear more and was dissatisfied with her answer. Finally, he rose.

"Very well then, Maria Columba, I accept the sincerity of your heart and trust you will become a dedicated and obedient choir woman. You may go now and, in quiet contemplation, prepare your heart and soul. Kneel to receive my blessing!"

The solemn profession of her vows became a more uplifting experience for Columba than investiture when the joy of wearing a beautiful robe and jewelry so abruptly had ended in the traumatic experience of having her hair cut. She'd become used to her baldness during the past year, though she still avoided looking in the mirror without her wimple. She'd even come to appreciate the practical aspect of having no hair, thinking of how hot and tight it would feel in summer to wear garments wrapped so tightly round a head of long hair. A lay nun performed the periodic cutting and was more adept and skillful at the task than Bernarda had been, leaving an evenly cropped head looking less grotesque. Still after removing her veils, Columba always quickly covered her head with the frilled nightcap.

A solemn High Mass was celebrated, and the choir voices resonated through the church that once again was crowded with dignitaries. Antonia's parents were absent; her father had written an emotional letter that the long journey was too arduous for her mother's poor health. Some of what he wrote was stricken, presumably by the prioress who perused all correspondence arriving or leaving the abbey.

"There's nothing wrong with Mama," commented Antonia dryly. "She's always been perfectly healthy, but no longer worried I might change my mind. It could well have been her instead of the prioress who struck some of Papa's words."

Columba received a brief message from Sigismunda, but the unctuous words in which her sister voiced admonitions as well as blessings sounded like coming from a stranger. Sigismunda briefly mentioned that Ferenc was absorbed in cataloguing and organizing the library of Melk and that she had little contact with Michael, who devoted himself to practical tasks.

"He's the only one who managed to remain close to nature," Columba mused. "The rest of us siblings spend our lives behind walls, in classrooms or libraries."

During the solemn service, her mind wandered back into childhood—riding with Papa, roaming woods, climbing trees—and that thought brought her back to reality. "Thank you, dear Lord," she silently prayed. "Thank you for not being found out the other night! Thank you for Maria Henrica's kind heart and for sparing me great shame!" Then she remembered the bitterly crying Helena clinging to her because she was about to lose her beloved mentor to cloister rules. Their time together would henceforth be rare and very formal as choir women and aspirants were not expected to mix casually. Columba could feel her little friend watching her from a pew.

"Soon, dearest Helena," she had said hugging the child. "Soon, you too will make your vows and then we'll be sisters in Christ forever!"

It was little consolation for the nine-year-old who had to wait a number of years, but Helena bravely swallowed her tears.

"I'll practice very hard, Maria Columba, so you can be proud when I join the choir! And I may still watch you in the park or even meet you in the tower?"

And Columba had nodded. "Of course, you may, Helena. You'll always be my darling little sister, and the Lord Jesus will guard our secret!"

Hearing her name brought her back to the ceremony.

"Maria Columba, step before me and place your hand upon this cross! Do you solemnly profess—"

Columba's voice, affirming her vows, was clear and steady, and her slender hand did not tremble when she received the golden "wedding ring." She watched the bishop place her betrothal ring upon the altar rail then knelt to receive the black veil of a choir woman and remained kneeling as the ritual was repeated for Antonia. When the two new choir women rose, the door of the sacristy opened, and the prioress and women of the court stepped forth to receive these newest members into their sisterhood and lead them up a secret stairway to the choir loft while the church erupted in a rousing hallelujah. The magnificently carved door that led from the loft to the cloister opened before them to reveal a waiting abbess.

"Maria Columba and Maria Antonia, you are now our sisters in Christ and are welcomed into the cloister that henceforth you never shall leave without your abbess's permission, as long as you shall live!"

She kissed each young woman on both cheeks, and the members of her court and the other women did likewise. Stepping over the threshold, Columba instinctively turned her head realizing that she would henceforth remain concealed from the nave of the church by the intricately beautiful wrought iron railing above the balustrade of the choir. It was designed to leave the altar visible through its white and gold edge but shield the nuns from view.

Now I've left the secular world forever, she thought.

This time, the two new choir women sat on each side of the abbess during the banquet in the refectory, where again a sumptuous and elaborate meal was served. The rule of silence was lifted and subdued yet animated voices filled the room. The rain had stopped, and Columba's eyes focused on the garden outside, where wet trees glistened in a tentative ray of sun. *There'll always be the cloister garden*, she thought, *and I'll be able to see mountains from the towers.*

The meal was followed by a litany invoking many saints to intercede on behalf of the two new choir women. Then they were escorted to their separate cells. They did not have adjoining rooms, though both were located on the third floor. Maria Henrica led Columba to the end of the long hallway and opened the heavy oak door to a spacious cell. It was furnished with austere but quality pieces: the bed she had slept in as novice, two dressers, a washstand with mirror, and a low privy commode. Rugs covered the scrubbed oak floor. A six-foot-high stove occupied one corner, the white base topped by green concave tiles to increase the heat surface after the fire, which was stoked from the hallway, had gone out. White muslin curtains framed a window facing the garden, which delighted Columba. Some cells overlooked courtyards, whereas she could see crowns of trees and mountain ridges in the distance. A simple crucifix hung on the white-washed wall above the bed. And amidst the austere surroundings a touch of color welcomed the new choir woman like a gentle gesture. In a niche above the prayer stool was a statue of the child Jesus. It was a painted wooden figure not of particular artistic quality, but the chubby face below the crown smiled with a naivete that belied the princely robes in which it was clothed. Columba gasped with delight when she recognized that the statue's frock and mantle were made of brocade from her bridal gown. It was beautifully sewn with gold lace lining sleeves and seam, and the rich green-and-gold material adapted well to the dimensions of the two-foot figure. One hand was raised in a blessing, the other clutched a globe. Innocent holiness with an aura of love and warmth, and at the same time, divine mystery radiated from the little statue. Columba turned to look at Maria Henrica and saw gentleness in the magistra's usually cool eyes.

"We all have a figure of the Divine Child in our cells, perhaps a small concession to our motherly instincts as women. But the clothes are always princely to prevent us from becoming too familiar with our Lord. Your gown was made into a canopy, and it was the Reverend Mother Abbess's idea to use remaining pieces for dressing the Child Jesus you would have in your cell. Your things have been placed into the chests, and you may remain here until vespers."

She prepared to leave then turned to Columba.

"I trust you will be content in your cell. We place our younger sisters on the third floor because it is easier to climb stairs at a your age. And, Maria Columba, it is better to look over trees than at their fruit." There was a slight pause before she continued, "Your little carved deer has made a young child very happy. May God be with you, Maria Columba, as you begin your life of choir woman in our abbey."

Henrica turned to leave, moving without sound as usual, but the metallic click of the closing door evoked the image of a jail door being shut in Columba. She shook her head. "You're silly, Columba, with seven choir duties a day, meals and the garden, I won't have much time feeling locked up."

She knelt to pray then stood at the window and watched the aspirants in the garden enjoy themselves. Losing the last little souvenir from childhood saddened her, but then she looked at her hand with the ring that wedded her to Christ and felt ashamed. *Brides of Christ have no use for toys,* she thought. Something crossed her mind, and she examined the corner of her mattress, into which she had secretly sewn the ayah's two coins, but the corner was limp and empty, and she recognized someone else's stitches closing the hole. Her nest egg, which for a few brief moments at the Bruck inn she thought might buy her freedom, was gone. Had one of the lay nuns taken the money when they moved her things? She dismissed the thought knowing them as dedicated, honest, and pious. Telling the magistra noviciarum about it would earn her a stern reproof since aspirants and novices were not allowed to have money in their possession. There was nothing Columba could do; she was now a cloistered nun with a small monthly stipend for personal needs.

She learned what happened the next day. Returning from morning services, she found lay nun Maria Aloysia making up her room. Columba had always liked the modest young woman and greeted her warmly, glad to hear that Aloysia would be taking care of cells on the third floor. She deferentially wished Columba well for her new status then hesitated.

"Yes, Aloysia, is there anything you want?" asked Columba.

"Oh, Rev'rend Mother, there is," stuttered the nun. "But I know not how to say it, an' I fear you be angry with me an' I's not to tell anyone."

Columba smiled. "No, Maria Aloysia, I won't tell. I know you are a good person, though I do not know what you promised and to whom, so I won't press you."

The friendly words encouraged the timid nun to continue. "After they's moved your bed, Rev'rend Mother," she said, "Maria Pelagia and I carry the mattress, an' she feels a hard sumpin' in the corner, an' when we put it down, she sees glitter through stitches that were stretched a bit. She pulls 'em apart and out fall two golden coins."

She hesitated and Columba held her breath.

"We know they's yours 'cause the mattress was new when you was a novice. An' Pelagia, she's a good nun, Reverend Mother, but she knows there's big trouble if Mother Magistra finds out an' Pelagia, she jus' learn her brother's only cow died calving, an' he got three little ones, and they's very poor. God forgive her, I pray, but she says to me the Lord sent this money to buy a young cow, and if she tells 'bout you, you'd just be punished. An' she makes me promise not to tell on her, an' I pray all night for God to tell me what to do, an' I think He tells me let you know what happen jus' so you won't think I took it. An' I can't bear you thinkin' ill of me, Rev'rend Mother, with you always so kind and friendly to a lowly person like me."

The words tumbled from Aloysia's mouth, her eyes filled with tears, and she covered her face with both hands waiting for Columba's reaction. She was too scared to see the relief in Columba's face about another narrow escape. Her guardian angel was surely watching out for her, or she might never have made profess! She walked over to the shaking nun, gently took her hands and said, "You have done exactly right, Maria Aloysia, and I thank you. I was wrong hiding the money I inherited from a faithful and loving person, and I know I would have been punished if found out. I am glad it will find good use and help Pelagia's family. Do not hold it against her, Maria Aloysia, the coins could not have found better use. And let us never talk about it again."

The little nun heaved a sigh of relief and hastily kissed Columba's hands. "Oh, thank you, Rev'rend Mother. God bless you, an' I's so glad I can listen to your voice ev'ry day!"

Columba thought that her first day as a choir woman was blessed.

The Choir Woman

Chapter 1

Columba and Antonia were dedicated and enthusiastic choir women and adjusting to their rigorous schedule bravely fought fatigue. But they were still in their teens, and the bell calling a half-hour before midnight was especially difficult to obey. This first Mass of the day was sung in its entirety, and Antonia mischievously thought that this was the only way to keep everyone awake. The young women fumbled in the dark to light their little oil lamps and hastily dressed to arrive at the cloister walk in time to head with their sisters for the choir loft. The immediately following "Laudes" was a lengthy hymn of praise, and by the time they were back in bed, it was half past one. They rose at a quarter past five for private contemplation in their cell before the six o'clock "prim" and litany to the saints of the day, both rituals to which they had adjusted during novitiate. The choir women then proceeded to the chapter hall for a commemoration of all past founders and benefactors of the abbey. They barely had time to finish their breviary before the bell again called at quarter past eight for the sung "Terz" and subsequent High Mass at nine that included a lengthy psalm. At ten o'clock, they assembled in the refectory for their main meal of the day, which they ate in silence listening to one from their midst reading from scripture. The women sat on wooden benches with their backs toward the wall and Tessa would steal glances out the windows, which were open during clement weather.

St. Benedict's rule forbade meat except for ailing clerics, but in 1624, a bishop intervened directly with the pope and obtained dispensation on two days of the week. The abbey owned fishing rights at various brooks and lakes and owned man-made ponds for farming trout and bass that were served on fast days. Crabs, snails, turtle, beaver, and even heron were allowed on meatless days because of their "relationship" with water.

Meals were plentiful and well prepared and seven or eight different types of food the rule for the main meal. There was always soup, two kinds of meat or fish, dumplings, cabbage, cauliflower or spinach, noodles, and a hearty dessert such as crepes or cake. Even the more frugal Friday meal included soup, fish, scrambled eggs, vegetables, and dessert. A goblet of wine was optional, and some of the women declined. On special feast days, the abbess and her court joined them in the refectory and various additional delicacies were served.

During the recreation period after the midday meal, the women were allowed to converse with one another, take walks, embroider, or do other handicraft. At noon, they were back in church to sing the "Non" and listen to a reading, followed by another recreation time that ended with the vespers at three o'clock. They devoted themselves to scriptures during a strict silence period until the evening meal at five. The last and seventh choir duty of the day was the sung "Komplet" and subsequent "Laurentian Litany," after which they retired for evening contemplation and examination of their conscience. Most cells were dark after nine o'clock to catch a few hours of sleep.

Lay nuns worked until late into the night in the laundry, kitchen, and bakery. They rose before dawn, and their only periods of physical rest were the times spent in prayer or at church services. Their workload increased with the arrival of the cold season in October when brisk winds blew from the mountains and days grew short. Heavy armfuls of wood had to be carried up long flights of stairs and stacked in the hallways outside each cell. The stoves were fired while the choir women sang the prim. After less than four hours of sleep since midnight Mass, the cold and tired women were happy to find a fire going in their cells, even though it would take hours until the tiles radiated heat. December usually brought bitterly cold weather when even the fur capes some of them owned failed to bring comfort. There were times when half the choir was ill or too hoarse to sing.

Young Columba was blessed with a healthy constitution and thrived on singing many hours each day despite lack of sleep. It was not all pleasure, though, because of the limited vocal ability or ear for music of several choir women and Columba often winced secretly. To make matters worse, the Galler sisters were among those with scant talent. Columba anxiously avoided criticizing Bernarda who, though young, commanded influence in the chapter due to her father's position as secular administrator of the Seckau Episcopate. Moreover, there were four Galler family members in the chapter, though the ailing Bernhardina had resigned her position as prioress.

Columba made every effort to be on good terms with all choir women and studiously avoided the Galler sisters. They were feared by many, and even Maria Henrica treated them with respect.

In her sixties, the now ailing abbess increasingly relied on Prioress Maria Ernestina and Sub-Prioress Maria Cajetana, who was unpopular because of her brusque manners. Prioress Ernestina suffered from painfully swollen legs and was frequently confined to bed. Fearful rumors circulated that Cajetana might succeed Antonia.

All members of the "court" exerted influence of one kind or another, and not surprisingly, politics flourished. Maria Henrica was the best educated and most artistically gifted of the choir women. She was very strict but well liked and enjoyed universal respect for her integrity and piety, as well as a sense of justice and prudence in her decisions.

Columba never told anyone about the torturous metal bracelet Henrica wore on her upper arm and often wondered whether any of the other sisters subjected themselves to similar suffering. She suspected some of them did. Friendship between the women was not encouraged, which made life for those without family ties lonesome. A natural consequence was the forming of "cliques" among siblings and close relatives. Maria Antonia did not belong to a clique either but enjoyed considerable insight into the situation; hence her early warning to Columba about Bernarda and her sisters. The idealistic Columba did not expect the powerful network of cliques, and the extent of political maneuvering was a blow to her enthusiasm. There had not been a profess at Göss for a number of years, and she and Antonia were the youngest members of the chapter, which meant they had neither seniority nor influence. Singing was a good example for this. Columba had by far the best voice and not only gave the choir depth but also carried others with her musicality. Soon, she found herself resented for just that reason. Maria Scholastica and her sister Leopoldina complained that Columba's voice was low and made it difficult for them to remain on key. Choir Magistra Maria Carolina appreciated Columba's talent and tried to mediate by explaining that each voice played an important part. Maria Philippina, in her fifties with a good and powerful voice, possessed exceptional penmanship and came to Carolina's aid. Philippina had devoted years to a project of painstakingly assembling and writing the choir's songbooks. The poor light in the church prompted her to write larger than the printed books, which was a great help and particularly appreciated by older women. Everyone acknowledged this labor of love and handled the books with great care to preserve them despite constant use. These books were not available to the two new choir women, and they often struggled to find the correct page in the regular ones. Both had good eyes so that at least deciphering the small print in the dim light was not too difficult. In her heart, Philippina knew that Columba had a much better voice than she did, though she would never have admitted it. Choir women have little opportunity for personal recognition among their sisters, and her vanity suffered no longer having the best voice in the choir. Philippina at one time had been prioress, a position from which she voluntarily resigned because she did not wish to be excused from choir duty. She preferred hymns to the Gregorian chant and aspired to succeed Carolina as choir mistress.

Chapter 2

Profession of final vows was the all-important step from novice to choir woman, but Göss and selected other abbeys had an additional ceremony referred to as the solemn blessing when a bishop bestowed upon choir women their "Velamen Sacrum." This "holy veil" was woven of finest, gossamer-thin black wool and easier to drape and more comfortable to wear than the original heavy one. No timetable or criteria existed as to when a choir woman would receive her solemn blessing, a ceremony unrelated to prestigious standing or holding office. It never coincided with an investiture, profess, or even visitation, so as not to distract from other candidates. Instead, it was conducted at intervals of several years and for women of varying seniority at the discretion of the highest-ranking bishop. As a symbol of religious prestige, choir women who had made profess a number of years ago were anxious to receive it. The Galler sisters belonged to this group, particularly Bernarda and Victoria, whose profess was in 1738, two years before their younger sister Eleonora. By 1750, there were twelve choir women without Velamen, including of course Columba and Antonia. A formal request by Abbess Maria Antonia would have carried much weight because members of her family had in the past held episcopates at Seckau and Lavant and even an archbishop of Salzburg had been among her relatives. In addition, two of Antonia's brothers were Benedictine monks at Admont and Kremsmunster and a sister nun at Frauenchiemsee. But Maria Antonia's health steadily declined, and by early summer of that year, she became bedridden. Abbesses were elected for life and did not resign because of poor health. Instead, her duties automatically passed to Prioress Maria Ernestina and Sub-Prioress Maria Cajetana. The sixty-five-year-old Antonia remained in full control of her mental abilities, but shortness of breath and severe pain from gout and arthritis weakened her to a point where even brief consultations with members of her court became extremely stressful. Prioress Maria Ernestina did not like making decisions, and many an important or controversial subject facing the abbey was postponed. The choir women diligently prayed for their abbess during each service, and when she felt better, they were occasionally allowed to visit her. Antonia was moved from her cell to a private room of the infirmary in the fall and patiently submitted herself to every procedure the magistra in charge deemed necessary, such as purges and bleedings, which weakened her only further. The Supremus visited daily to administer the sacraments and hear her confession, but her true condition was not known to anyone but members of the court, who continued the tradition of a place setting including food at table.

When the abbess did not appear at the Feast of Christ the King, the last Sunday of the church year before Advent, the choir women knew her condition must be very serious, and their prayers became ever more intense. At least three members of the chapter now prayed for her in the church and in her private chapel of St. Michael at all hours of the day and night. During one such occasion when Columba participated in the prayer watch, she overheard Bernarda and Sub-Prioress Cajetana have a whispered conversation on the subject of the Velamen Sacrum.

"How long is this going to continue?" asked Bernarda. "We should have received our sacred veil years ago if only the abbess had requested it! I'm tired of this heavy thing, it gives me a headache! By the way, will Ernestina succeed her and you become prioress?"

"Who knows?" was the answer. "Ernestina hasn't been feeling all that well either. You know that she's short of breath and her feet are always swollen, that's why she limps so badly. And you know there's not going to be a Velamen blessing unless the abbess personally requests it! Her relative, the bishop of Levant, wouldn't think of conducting the ceremony if she's too ill to attend."

At that moment, three choir women approached to assume the prayer watch and the conversation ended. Columba was appalled that a mere ceremony, however desired, was deemed important enough to fault the abbess on her deathbed.

A somber mood settled over the abbey. The four weeks of Advent were traditionally a season of fasting and abstinence in preparation for the birth of Christ. In oblation to the health of their abbess, the women went beyond precept and contended themselves with only a bowl of soup and piece of bread for their evening meal. It was a true sacrifice considering the hours they spent during the night in the cold church and the long fast between their supper at five and midday meal seventeen hours later. Eighteen-year-old Antonia especially suffered. But they all loved their abbess and firmly believed that sacrifice and intense prayer could relieve suffering and even restore health to their ailing Reverend Mother. Extra masses were read on Christmas Day, and before the midday meal, they visited Maria Antonia in small groups to receive her blessing. The abbess suffered intense pain yet had a gentle smile and kind word for each of her daughters. Columba and Antonia as the youngest members of the chapter were last to enter, and the exhausted abbess was barely able to speak; the two anxiously tried to read her parched lips.

"Antonia, my godchild," the abbess gasped, "pray for your mama and do not bear ill feeling toward her, for she does love you."

A long pause of labored breathing followed. Columba dipped a linen cloth into a bowl, gently moistened the abbess's lips, and was rewarded with a warm glance from the sunken eyes.

"Columba, my daughter, when you first came to my garden, you promised to seek calm in the hermit tower when—" the whisper trailed off.

"I do, Most Reverend Mother," said Columba, tears streaming down her face, and the abbess answered with a faint smile.

"You must leave now, our mother needs to rest," said the infirmary magistra and ushered them out.

Columba's tears continued to flow. "She's dying! I know she'll never speak to us again," she sobbed. "Oh, Antonia, I'm so afraid of what will happen to us if God calls her!"

"God will grant her a place in heaven." Antonia tried to console her friend. "Just as He will look after us, you'll see," she added realistically. "Come now, Columba, they're waiting to serve, and I'm so hungry I can hardly think! God alone knows what is best for her!"

The refectory was not the festive place it normally was at Christmas. Whispering choir women gathered in small groups, and the flickering candles in the chandeliers could not dispel the gloom and somber ambience of the gray winter day. The whole chapter traditionally dined together on this day, and the prioress was already seated next to the place setting for the abbess. As soon as Columba and Antonia entered, the choir women went to their seats, and Maria Ernestina rose with apparent difficulty.

"All-powerful and ever-living God," she prayed, "the eternal hope of all who believe in You, hear us as we ask Your divine comfort for our beloved Most Reverend Mother Maria Antonia! Restore her health that she may again walk among us and render her joyful thanks to You! We ask this through our Lord Jesus Christ, Your Son, who lives and reigns with You and the Holy Spirit, one God, forever and ever."

"Amen!" responded the choir women, and the lay nuns began serving the meal. The women spoke little. The day was cold with strong winds, and the two large tiled stoves of the refectory, though fired since dawn, could not render the large, high-ceiling room comfortable. The first course of hearty soup was most welcome to the women, who shivered from cold after the long fast and many hours spent in church. Roast capon, pheasant, and saddle of deer followed, together with winter vegetables, cranberry preserves, and a variety of condiments, as well as assorted cakes and sweetmeats for dessert. Everyone in the abbey and beyond ate well on Christmas Day, for Maria Antonia always made sure that no one within her extensive realm went hungry that time of year.

Columba was cold and hungry like everyone else yet could not enjoy the sumptuous meal. Her visit to the sickbed had convinced her that the abbess would not live much longer, and she feared an uncertain future. Would Maria Ernestina succeed or perhaps Cajetana? Columba recalled the overheard conversation and knew that Bernarda and Cajetana belonged to the same clique. She'd had no further incidents with the Galler sisters and kept her distance as best she could. Small gestures, though, revealed that their feelings toward her had not changed, perhaps with the exception of the kinder youngest sister Victoria. Columba had come to appreciate the far-reaching, if not absolute, powers of the abbess, and while Maria Antonia had never shown her special favors, she felt deep devotion and love for her.

Rumor had it that Maria Ernestina held her high office because of the large dowries she and her sister Aloysiy had brought, though the younger was of no consequence. Cajetana was a calculating and universally unpopular woman in her early forties. Either prioress or sub-prioress usually succeeded an abbess, and Columba was deeply worried about Cajetana's close relationship to cliques.

Everyone enjoyed more liberties and privileges on Christmas Day, and Columba went to the aspirants' quarters to visit Helena, now almost twelve. The girl's unabashed happiness to see her brought Columba close to tears. Choir women were not supposed to embrace anyone but each other and even that only on rare occasions and in a measured way. Helena flew into her arms, and Columba was equally glad to see her and hugged her tight. The child was frighteningly thin. Helena's face, though, was ever more beautiful with her large blue eyes, small straight nose, and a smile that could melt any heart.

"Oh, Tessa!" she exclaimed then quickly corrected herself, "Reverend Mother Maria Columba, I am so happy to see you, you bring such joy to my Christmas!"

Columba's eyes scanned the room, and she was glad that only aspirants were present who wouldn't report Helena's exuberance and her response. They had risen respectfully at her entrance, and Columba sat down to talk. A few new girls had arrived since her profess, all very young and excited to enjoy the delicacies of the day. Giving in to Helena's pleas, she went to the spinet in the corner to play Christmas carols, and everyone joined in the singing. She chatted with the children, encouraged them to talk about holiday customs at home, and shared traditions from Transylvania with them. She did not want to dampen their spirits and never mentioned the abbess, and when her recreation time drew to a close, she felt better for having spread joy. They begged her to come back soon, and Helena clung to her and shed a few tears, but she again reminded the girl that she'd soon be eligible for investiture and profess, after which they would always be together. There was a plate with sweetmeats, small cakes, dried fruit, and nuts on the table, and Columba noticed that while the others helped themselves from the goodies, Helena did not.

"You must eat more, my love," she told her. "You're so very thin!"

"It's because of the bad cough I've had since early December and I'm just never hungry!" was the answer.

Columba gently led her away from the others. "Helena," she said in a very serious tone, "you must force yourself to eat! Being a choir woman requires stamina and strength, which you will not have if you are weak and thin! If you're not strong enough, they may not allow you to become a novice, and then you have to wait even longer! Please, Helena, do it for me! Drink all the milk you can, make yourself eat, I know it will help your cough go away. Will you promise?"

"You know I'll do anything for you, Reverend Mother, especially when it will bring me closer to you!"

Columba smiled. "That's a good girl! Now go join the others and rejoice in the day our Lord was born!" She blew a kiss on Helena's forehead and hurried back.

Maria Antonia's condition changed little over the next few days. On New Year's Day, Columba took consolation in the readings from the Old Testament. "The Lord bless you and keep you! The Lord let His face shine upon you, and be gracious to you! The Lord look kindly upon you and give you peace!" She prayed with all her heart that His face shine upon Maria Antonia and grant her recovery. The choir women visited their abbess that afternoon to receive her blessings and found her slightly improved, propped up by large pillows to relieve the labored breathing.

"At this threshold of a New Year, may you gain in insight, my daughters, and like the shepherds and Mary, embrace God's presence within you," she said, pausing repeatedly for breath. But her voice was stronger than the week before, and Columba took heart. Yet during first Mass on January 3, at half past midnight, the bells of both abbey and parish church began to toll, and the choir women knew that their Reverend Mother had passed into eternity. A perceptible wave of anxiety descended upon the women as they continued their responses and litany. After the 'Ite, Missa Est ("go in peace, it is done"), they spontaneously fell to their knees.

From the high altar, the Supremus spoke in a grave voice, "It has pleased Almighty God to call His devoted daughter Maria Antonia, Countess Uberacker, thirty-eighth abbess of Göss and duchess of the realm, to His side. After receiving the last ointment and holy sacraments, she suffered a severe stroke, and her soul left what was mortal of her. Let us pray."

As word of the much-loved abbess's death spread the next morning, people gathered at the gate for admission to the parish church, where Maria Antonia's coffin had been placed with the insignia of her office displayed at her feet. It had snowed heavily the past few days, yet young and old from hamlet and farmhouses in the nearby mountains gathered to pay their respects.

Choir women, stiff and hoarse from frigid temperatures and continuous prayers, kept vigil in the abbey church and valiantly tried to suppress coughing. Columba and Antonia were about to return to their cells for a brief rest when the silent cortege headed by the parish priest and ministrants with incense vessels emerged from St. Andreas and headed toward their south portal. Antonia's eight administrative officers carried the casket on their shoulders and struggled through the deep snow. A path had been cleared a few hours earlier, but high winds effaced the effort. Columba and Antonia fell to their knees as the little procession passed.

Columba's relative Abbess Maria Johanna Countess Kollonitsch had ordered the ancient Crypt repaired in 1640 and designated it the place of last repose for choir women. The coffins initially were placed side by side in the crypt and adjoining alcoves and niches, but space grew scarce, and it became necessary to stack them. Church tradition prohibits funerals on feast days, and Maria Antonia joined her departed sisters on January 7, the day after epiphany.

Priests and other clergy from Leoben and adjacent hamlets braved the inclement weather to attend the funeral Mass.

"The Lord will open the gates of paradise to His faithful daughter, and she will return to that homeland where there is no death, only lasting joy!" the Supremus intoned, and an exhausted and shivering chapter of choir women paid their last respects at the open coffin. Maria Antonia looked at peace and her waxen face no longer showed the ravages of her suffering. Columba recalled how as a child she hid between the plants in the big hall at Zay-Ugrocz unable to tear herself away from her beloved papa. Then the ayah had died, and now death once again confronted her and took away her spiritual mother, leaving her saddened and depressed. "To you, O Lord, I lift my soul, relieve the troubles of my heart," she sang with the choir. "Relieve the troubles of my heart and bring me out of my distress." But neither the ancient psalm nor her strong faith could dispel her deep sorrow. She felt like a child facing an as yet unknown stepmother, afraid who she might be.

After Mass, the Supremus ceremoniously closed the coffin. Simple clasps in lieu of nails secured the lid. The choir women descended from the choir loft with burning candles in their hands and proceeded through a side door down steep, narrow steps into the crypt. Their chanted litany invoking a long list of saints to intercede for Maria Antonia filled the low vault with mournful sounds. It was the first time Columba entered the crypt that seven centuries earlier formed the basis of the abbey's first church, and she shivered in the cold, musty air. In the center, four slender columns supported a low, vaulted ceiling. The women formed a semicircle to await the casket and in the flickering light carefully averted their eyes from the east wall with its stacked coffins, some of them cracked or broken under the weight of those piled above.

Deacons precariously negotiated the coffin down the stairs, placed it near the others, and immediately withdrew. The simple wooden box bore no insignia signifying that all were equal in death before God. After litany and a Salve Regina, the Supremus blessed the casket one last time and ended the service with the words, "May our sister Maria Antonia, whom You blessed with life, enter into the everlasting peace and joy of Christ Your Son, who is Lord forever and ever!"

"Amen!" intoned the exhausted women and paused for a final moment of reflection before slowly ascending the steps and returning to their cloister, several of them ill and feverish from prolonged exposure to cold. A new chapter in the abbey chronicle was about to begin.

The election of an abbess was a formal procedure that by church law was conducted under the supervision of the area's senior bishop and an official government delegation. Each choir woman was entitled to cast her secret ballot, and simple majority decided on the person of the new Mother Superior. Formal office installation, called "Benediction," followed a few days later, officiated by the bishop and in the presence of secular officials including a representative of the crown and priests from surrounding parishes.

Snow and inclement weather made roads impassable, and it was weeks before messengers could even be dispatched to the monasteries of Admont, Seckau, and Lavant. Prioress Maria Ernestina was in charge during the interim, but the abbess's office and her seat at the table remained vacant. At the insistence of the Galler sisters, Ernestina added an urgent request to her message that the Velamen Sacrum be bestowed on eligible choir women at the occasion of the new abbess's Benediction. A snowy March further delayed coordination between the various officials whose presence was required, and it was April until the election date finally was set for Wednesday, May 19, 1751. Meanwhile, rumors throughout the abbey abounded and speculation about likely candidates shifted continuously. Prioress Maria Ernestina's deteriorating health thwarted the Galler sisters' intense efforts to promote her, and Maria Henrica emerged as a preferred candidate, favored by the younger choir women, who'd come to respect her during the fourteen years she had been magistra for aspirants. Others argued that office did not provide administrative experience and was inadequate preparation for the comprehensive duties of an abbess. Her supporters countered that her excellent education more than made up for lack of experience. Both Columba and Antonia hoped and prayed that the choice would fall on Henrica.

Spring finally arrived and preparations for the event intensified. Quarters in the guest wing were prepared for clergy as well as secular officials and their entourages. The abbess's cell, where candles burned continuously during the official three months mourning period, was freshly painted and refurbished with new curtains and rugs. The remaining accouterments were left to the discretion of the new occupant.

The senior bishop was Count Firmian from the Episcopate of Lavant in Carynthia, who would preside over the election process and officiate at the Benediction. He came a week prior to the set date and spoke privately with each choir woman about the importance of her vote. A few days later, secular officials from Graz, the abbey's steward Count Stubenberg as well as a delegation from the imperial court in Vienna arrived. Kitchens and bakery worked day and night to cater for the guests, and lay nuns barely found a moment's rest amidst all the activity. Vestments for priests, deacons, and ministrants had to be washed and pressed for the numerous daily masses.

On Election Day, the choir women followed their usual schedule through High Mass before assembling in the chapter hall. Bishop Firmian presided; also present were the Supremus as well as secular officials, for whom cloister rules were temporarily waived. They spoke at length about the importance of the pending vote, and Bishop Firmian invoked the Holy Spirit to guide the women's hearts and minds. Small vellum ballots were distributed, and a freshly sharpened goose quill and small inkwell placed before each woman.

"You are to clearly and legibly write down the name of the member of your chapter," said the bishop, "whom you freely choose to become your revered abbess and to whom you will pledge total obedience at Solemn Benediction. You will then fold the ballot and place it into the vessel that Count Eberstein will extend to each of you. Pray for God's guidance, sisters in Christ, for you have an important task to perform!"

Silence descended upon the large room with only the scratching of plumes audible. When each of the women indicated with an incline of her head that her choice had been made and ballot folded, Count Eberstein rose, took a silver bowl from the table, and paused before each woman to watch her deposit the folded vellum. Following tradition, they all waited with heads bowed in silent prayer. The count placed the bowl before the Supremus and resumed his seat. The Supremus slowly retrieved one ballot at a time, unfolded it, and—in a loud and distinct voice—read the name written on it before passing it on to the bishop and the other delegates to verify. Count Eberstein carefully recorded each vote in the chronic.

Forty-four choir women cast their vote, and when Maria Henrica's name had been called out twenty-four times, a slight gasp went through the refectorium. In the end, she received twenty-nine votes; Maria Cunigunde Countess Sturgkh, Court Kitchen Magistra, ten votes; Maria Xaveria Countess Welz, Sacristy Magistra, four votes; and the current prioress, Maria Ernestina, Countess Khevenhuller, just one. None was cast for Cajetana.

The bishop solemnly rose to his feet. "Maria Henrica, Countess Poppen of Stibelwitz, the full chapter of the abbey of Göss has duly elected you to become their thirty-ninth abbess. Will you accept their choice?"

Maria Henrica's face was wet with tears as she rose from her seat, walked to the center of the table, and knelt before Bishop Firmian. With a barely audible voice, she said, "I most humbly accept, Your Excellency, and beloved sisters in Christ. May God in His mercy grant me to be worthy of the great task conferred upon me."

Bishop Firmian took her hand. "Rise, my daughter Maria Henrica! Chapter of choir women of the abbey of Göss, I present to you your thirty-ninth abbess-elect. Step forward to greet your new Mother Superior!"

The choir women showed no emotion as they one by one stepped forward to embrace their new leader. Maria Henrica's tears continued to flow while she opened her arms to embrace each woman, no longer her sister but now her daughter, over whom she would exercise absolute authority for as long as she lived.

The next day after High Mass prior to the final blessing and dismissal, Bishop Firmian—who had been seated in a throne-like chair to the left of the sanctuary—stepped before the altar and announced, "My daughters, your Reverend Mother, the abbess-elect, has expressed a wish I shall be pleased to grant. There are twelve choir women, who have not yet been bestowed their Velamen Sacrum. Maria Henrica has requested that they receive this precious, ultimate insignia of their blessed state on the day of her Benediction as avowed brides of Christ. Maria Leopoldina, Maria Scholastica, Maria Bernarda, Maria Victoria, Maria Eleonora, Maria Caecilia, Maria Amalia, Maria Coelestina, Maria Gabriela, Maria Alexia, Maria Columba, and Maria Antonia—I command you to prepare your hearts and souls through fasting and prayer! This Sunday shall not only bring you a new Mother Abbess but also be a day of honor for each of you. After the new abbess's solemn Benediction, I shall call upon you to approach the altar so that I may bestow upon you this great blessing of our mother church!"

Palpable tension grasped the women on the choir loft at his words, and tension mounted with each name. The two youngest among the group, Columba and Antonia, were only in their third year since profess and did not dare hope to be included. When their names were announced, they grasped each other's hand in a joyful gesture of youthful exuberance. Bernarda noticed it and murmured to her sister Victoria loud enough for those close by to hear her words.

"I can't think why some are included that still lack adequate decorum for this honor!"

Maria Victoria made no reply, but the words hit Columba like a whip and dampened her joy. Antonia suppressed a giggle and winked at Columba.

"Won't she ever forget our differences of years ago?" Columba said when they walked in the cloister garden after their midday meal. "I try so hard to avoid her and she never misses an opportunity to say words that offend me!"

Antonia shrugged. She wanted to grasp her friend's hand but knew that choir women were not supposed to show signs of personal affection.

"Doesn't concern me one bit that she thinks I lack decorum! I felt like laughing in her face, but that would cost me my Velamen, and I don't want to give her that triumph. She's just sour grapes because she and Victoria made profess a dozen years ago and are still without it! And I think it's been eleven years for Coelestina, so they're all just jealous of us! Don't let it bother you, Columba dear, and remember that Bernarda will never change! Just don't give her a chance for a complaint."

Columba thought how mature and wise her barely nineteen-year-old friend was. She herself would soon see her twenty-first birthday and still struggled to control her temper, envying Antonia her easy-going, down-to-earth attitude.

"You're a treasure, Antonia! Please don't ever stop being my friend, I wouldn't know what to do without your good sense," she said gratefully.

"Nonsense! You're so much smarter and more talented than I am you just mustn't be so emotional and let everything bother you! Oh, listen now, the clock's striking twelve, we better hurry for Non. And then," she added rolling her blue eyes with an exasperated grimace, "spend our recreation time in meditation 'til Sunday. As if I hadn't had enough time already reflecting on my status as a choir woman! What bothers me most is the eternal fasting. Sometimes, I think I'm going to die from starvation. Only one frugal meal and bread and water for supper 'til Sunday, it's cruel. What would I do without Erentrudis in the kitchen! I'll smuggle something into your cell later when all is quiet."

Without waiting for an answer, Antonia led the way to cloisters and into church.

After the service, Antonia withdrew to her cell for meditation, and Columba headed for the reflection tower. She said a prayer of thanks for the pending honor then looked at Henrica's painting and wondered whether the new abbess, about to be bestowed with the highest honor a woman in religious life could hope to attain, still longed for her Silesian homeland. What was going through the mind of someone elected to such high office? Columba had voted for her and secretly hoped that the Galler sisters' influence would be curbed in the future. She had never overcome the humiliation of prostrating herself before Bernarda, nor the expression on the choir woman's face as she prepared to cut her hair at investiture. She'd also learned that as a convert without family influence and a small dowry, neither her musical talent, intelligence, nor even dedication sufficed to gain influence in the chapter. Columba was genuinely pious, did not regret taking her vows, and had adjusted well to her rigorous schedule. Yet internal politics and power plays among the women disappointed and dampened her enthusiasm. She'd expected that becoming a nun meant loving kindness and tolerance within the sisterhood, and her own greatest concern had been whether she would be able to love everyone equally. Instead, she felt that some of her sisters actively disliked her without knowing why. Columba did not have Antonia's mental indifference to shrug off personal attacks and felt helpless and inadequate. "Dear God"—she sighed—"why did you give me my musical ear? Perhaps if I sang off key like my sisters, they'd resent me less!" Yet in her heart, she knew that her love for singing had been a major motivation for becoming a choir woman and a major factor to cope with her life.

The ceremony on Sunday, May 23, 1751, remained engraved in the minds and hearts of everyone who witnessed it. The twelve candidates for the Velamen Sacrum escorted the abbess-elect into the church and remained near the altar throughout High Mass. For the first time, Maria Henrica's white wimple bore the two starched corners above the forehead, a traditional privilege of an abbess. The bishop presented her with the shepherd's staff and took her oath of dedication. In it, Maria Henrica promised not only to diligently administer the abbey's estates but also, like a true mother to love, admonish, and—if necessary—chastise her daughters-in-Christ, as well as lay down her life for them if the need arose. Then the court's envoy Duke Mellenberg bestowed on her the insignia of a duchess of the Realm and presented her with the keys, and Cadastral Register called "Urbar" as a formal sign of her authority over the abbey's landholdings. However, when Bishop Firmian moved to participate in the act by placing his hands upon her shoulders, he was gently but decidedly ushered aside by the duke. The gesture presaged a growing tension between clerical and secular officials of the time. The new abbess then received the solemn promise of total obedience from each choir woman and lay nun, as well as pledges of faithful service from all officials in the abbey's employ.

Maria Henrica looked pale and exhausted, only her voice taking the oath was strong and clear. After Benediction as abbess of Göss, she took her seat in a special chair next to the bishop who called for the twelve choir women to step forward. Each knelt to be handed a gossamer thin black veil of blessed consecration and retired to the sacristy, where they were assisted to replace their heavy woolen veil with the new Velamen Sacrum. Columba felt as if a weight had been lifted from her shoulders, and her heart rejoiced in the hope that this final symbol of her status would improve her standing within the chapter. The twelve choir women embraced and touched both cheeks of the other sisters in a symbolic kiss of peace and love before returning to the church for the final Te Deum. A cheering crowd in the courtyard joined into the rousing hymn. Maria Henrica and her newly blessed daughters were too deeply moved to join in the singing.

Chapter and distinguished guests assembled for a sumptuous banquet and the many visitors from far and near mixed with the local crowd to celebrate. Alms and small gifts were distributed among the common folk, whose festive mood was not curtailed by the fact that they would have to pay with a specially levied tax for the considerable costs incurred by the abbey for the travel expenses of secular and clerical emissaries and delegates.

An abundance of flowers decorated the refectorium. The garden magistra and her lay nuns had labored in the greenhouses for months to nurture blossoms that normally reached their bloom much later in the season. During early spring, families of abbey administrators had been commissioned to collect primula and gentian growing wild in the meadows. The flowers were placed into the icehouse for preservation. Maria Henrica was fond of alpine blossoms, and the innovative idea was intended as a special surprise that deeply touched the new abbess.

The rule of silence during meals was waived, yet conversation remained sparse and subdued. Bishop Firmian felt slighted by court representatives, who conversed among each other, but hesitated to address choir women. The new recipients of the Velamen were expected to humbly contemplate their new blessing, and those holding offices silently wondered about their future in a hierarchy entirely at the discretion of the new abbess. The guest of honor was deathly pale and apparently made a valiant effort to endure the banquet, but only those close to her noticed that she barely touched the food on her plate.

"She looks ill," Antonia whispered to Columba. "Do you think it's just the long ceremony or awe of her new responsibility?"

"I don't know," came the reply, "but we've never seen her lacking strength in the past. Perhaps, she just does not feel well today or fasted too much."

Columba remembered the horrible steel bracelet on Henrica's upper arm, a knowledge she had promised never to disclose. Could it be that the new abbess was subjecting her body to even more cruel suffering, perhaps flogging? Columba knew from studying the history of religious orders and particularly that of Göss that self-inflicted bodily punishment was not uncommon nor considered abnormal. She hoped that the slender Maria Henrica, for whom she felt great respect and affection, was not being too harsh on herself. An intelligent and healthy young woman like Columba found such cruel physical punishment for sins of the mind harsh and eccentric, though she had good reason to suspect that several choir women and lay nuns adhered to the practice.

Maria Henrica had not deliberately inflicted pain upon herself during the past days, nor was her inability to eat caused by stress. She had for some time suffered from what was then known simply as "stones"—in her case, gall bladder stones. She never consulted the infirmary magistra during her numerous violent attacks. Surgery, of course, was not an option at the time, but the magistra was well acquainted with herbal medicine and would have prescribed soothing teas or a tincture to ease the excruciating pain and induce sleep. Henrica's uncompromising piety did not allow for such remedies; she considered illness and pain as God-sent in just punishment and to purify the soul. She had just suffered an especially vicious attack that lasted well into Saturday night with some of the pain continuing through the ceremony. She also suffered unquenchable thirst but, because of fasting prior to communion, denied herself relief. The attack left her body severely weakened and exhausted, yet she'd told no one and thought of it as God testing her for the challenges and tasks ahead. At times, she followed the proceedings as if through a haze, and only her iron self-discipline and inner strength enabled her to speak the words of her oath clearly and distinctly. The banquet itself was sheer torture. The smell of the various foods made her feel nauseous, and all she could do to avoid offending those who had prepared the feast was to bring food close to her lips and pretend to eat. She hoped that guests and sisters appreciated the labor and diligence of the kitchen magistra and her helpers. A few small sips of wine made her feel slightly better and helped through the long ordeal. She silently prayed for the strength to walk away from the table and to avoid beginning her "reign" with a collapse. God heard her prayer, and she was able to stand during Bishop Firmian's closing prayer and albeit in a barely audible voice thank her guests for joining in her day of honor and wish them farewell and a safe journey home. Her sisters in Christ formally escorted her to her new cell, refurbished according to her wishes during the last few days, where she was expected to spend the time until midnight Mass in prayerful meditation. Henrica again thanked her daughters for their love and devotion and breathed a sigh of relief when the door finally closed, and she was alone. The conscientious woman fully intended to spend the next several hours on her knees asking God for inspired leadership, but her physical strength failed, and she staggered toward the bed. "Dear Lord, only a few minutes' rest." She sighed and collapsed onto the embroidered quilt, immediately overcome by a deep sleep. A dream took her back to her childhood home, Castle Stibelwitz near Troppau in Silesia, where, as little Baroness Barbara, she'd hidden with a book about medieval paintings behind heavy draperies and overheard her tutor talking to her parents, baron and baroness von Poppen.

"The young baroness is exceptionally intelligent and talented," the teacher said. "She learns easily and quickly, though what she enjoys most is to draw and paint. I am afraid I am no longer qualified to teach her in that respect and would suggest the services of an artist from Troppau to continue her education."

"That," the baron had answered harshly, "will never happen! Artists are but a step above gypsies and will not be tolerated in my household! Whatever gave you the idea that I would agree to have my young daughter tutored by an artist! You will continue to teach her languages, history, and literature as before but curb drawing lessons or replace them altogether with music! Surely, you agree with me, my dear wife, that painting pictures is not our daughter's future!"

Mama had agreed and the conversation marked the end of her artistic training, for young Barbara had no particular inclination toward music, though she mastered the basic skills required of young ladies her age. As to her other education, her father was proud of his only daughter's intelligence and hoped that while not beautiful, her elegant figure and keen mind would secure a good match when the time came. Family law prevented a female from inheriting landholdings, which would fall to a nephew, but the girl would be assured a substantial dowry and a suitable marriage seemed likely. Baroness Barbara had other ideas and on her thirteenth birthday revealed to her astounded parents that she had decided to take the veil, a decision from which she adamantly refused to be dissuaded. Baron Poppen knew his strong-willed daughter too well to force a showdown and began inquiries about convents exclusively open to daughters of the aristocracy. There were none in largely Protestant Northern Germany, and the choice fell upon the abbey of Göss. Both parents still nourished the hope that their strong-willed child's highly trained mind would find religious life too restrictive and monotonous. They were wrong. Barbara von Poppen entered Göss in 1723 at the age of fourteen as an aspirant, became a novice a couple of years later, and made profess six months before her seventeenth birthday. Abbess Maria Antonia appointed her magistra for aspirants at twenty-six, an important office because the abbey very much depended on educating candidates for choir women and making sure that even those who came only for education would end up taking vows. The aspirants liked and respected their magistra, as did most of her sisters in Christ, though some of the women were awed by her sharp intelligence and superior education.

Maria Henrica took a few moments to find her way back to reality when she awoke. Darkness and the persistent bell indicated that it was only thirty minutes until midnight and that she had slept almost eight hours. She no longer felt pain, only drained, as if reborn to new life, her life as abbess. She rose and smoothed her finely pleated "Flocke," which she had been too tired to remove expecting only a brief rest. She washed her face with cool water, adjusted wimple and veil, and knelt at her prie dieu where a small oil lamp shed dim light upon the life-size crucifix. Henrica asked forgiveness for succumbing to her body and resting so long. Lowering her head toward her folded hands, her eyes fell upon the abbess ring that Bishop Firmian had placed on her finger. Such rings always bore the abbess's personal coat of arms, a symbol of continuing link to aristocratic origin. The ring also served as seal below her signature on documents and contracts executed under her rule. Maria Henrica's coat of arms was divided by a diagonal line, one side showing a lion in full stride, the other six stripes. *Dear Papa,* she mused, *was it your coat of arms that caused me to dream of you? I wish you and Mama were still among the living to witness the great honor bestowed upon your daughter. Perhaps, you would have better understood the fervency of my vocation!*

The second bell called, and Maria Henrica shook off memories, said the Act of Contrition, and stepped from her cell to lead the silently waiting choir women into church. Mass for an abbess and her court was traditionally read in the Chapel of St. Michael, but on this her first full day in office, she had announced that she wished to join her chapter. Some of the women breathed a sigh of relief to see her face less strained and her step stronger.

Maria Henrica was to be abbess of Göss for almost three decades of a difficult and enigmatic period. Circumstances beyond her control forced her to face great administrative challenges. Empress Maria Theresa remained involved in wars with sovereigns attempting to wrestle power and territories from the Austrian realm, notwithstanding the fact that her Consort Franz of Loraine had been crowned German emperor. Such wars cut deeply into the treasury and exorbitant taxes were placed on the clergy, particularly wealthy convents and monasteries. Meeting these obligations forced Maria Henrica to sell landholdings in Carynthia for seventeen thousand florins. She chose that particular parcel because of its greater distance from the abbey. The State started to control and reserve approval of all financial transactions and additional regulations bestowed the crown with close scrutiny in all economic matters. All these rules were profoundly affecting the abbey.

Maria Theresa became empress when her husband Franz became Holy Roman Emperor, yet in the vast Habsburg realm, he remained Queen Consort and his wife ruled with ministers and generals appointed at her discretion. Franz was the first and only love of her life, and she bore him sixteen children, eleven of which reached adulthood. Their marriage was a very happy one, and when Franz suddenly succumbed to a heart attack while the couple was at Innsbruck to celebrate the engagement of a son, the forty-eight-year-old empress was devastated and went into deep mourning. Touching entries in her prayer book give evidence of her everlasting devotion and love for Franz. Affairs of State, however, did not permit prolonged wallowing in chagrin.

During her reign, Maria Theresa introduced numerous reforms, some of which were rather unpopular, such as the infamous "morality police" that had caught up with Sigismunda during her foray to the Trauttmansdorff Palace. Anxious for her people to lead virtuous lives, agents were sent to spy on the personal behavior of her subjects. The Viennese passionately objected, and the idea was abandoned shortly after its introduction.

Though deeply religious, the queen increasingly limited church power. She severely taxed religious institutions to replenish her forever-empty treasury, particularly wealthy convents and monasteries. Measures to audit and control the administration of religious institutions grew ever more intrusive after she appointed her son Joseph coregent in 1770. He'd been headstrong and difficult since childhood, and Maria Theresa often expressed the wish that her son's personality more resemble his popular late father.

Joseph visualized himself the great reformer and, in spite of his strictly Catholic upbringing, never was a pious man. He opined that wealthy contemplative orders were hoarding money and treasures that should benefit the state, causing him to issue ever more restrictive regulations. The prince was unfavorably disposed toward the clergy in general, and his string of decrees negatively affected monasteries and convents throughout the realm.

Investiture of novices eventually became subject to government consent, and the age for young women to make profess raised and strictly enforced, which was not previously done. This deprived the abbey of sorely needed income. Dowries were limited to 1,500 florins and any liquidation of assets, even withdrawal of cash funds deposited at banks or the calling of debts became subject to official approval. State-appointed stewards now controlled all aspects of the abbey's administration, no matter how trivial.

Maria Henrica sought refuge from her difficulties through artistic embellishment of her beloved church. She acquired paintings and sculptures and commissioned special works. The arrival or completion of each new piece of art was a source of great joy to her. She also involved herself in the design of new vestments, antependia, and display cases of relics. Unfortunately, however, she had a total disregard for internal politics. She could not bring herself to acknowledge and therefore failed to prevent or remedy dissent within her chapter. Her idealistic mind ignored the existence of such sentiments, sadly failing those who had placed high hopes in her rule and simultaneously playing into the hands of family cliques. Out of pity for the ailing prioress, she allowed Maria Ernestina to remain in office even though she had little confidence in her abilities. She did replace the sub-prioress by appointing Maria Caecilia, who had received her Velamen Sacrum at her Benediction. As her health further declined, Maria Ernestina relied almost completely on Caecilia's advice. And nothing was done to curb gossip and intrigue.

Another recipient of the Velamen Sacrum in 1751 was Maria Gabriela, Baroness Schaffmann, who had entered Göss in 1739 at age fifteen and made profess at seventeen. Two older cousins, Maria Michaela and Maria Theodora, already were choir women. Gabriela was a beautiful young woman with an oval face dominated by large gray eyes below a finely chiseled brow, a narrow aristocratic nose and small mouth with full, red lips. Intelligent and ambitious, she was intent on rising in the abbey's hierarchy and hungry for power and influence. She had a talent to endear herself to those she considered important and had won Maria Henrica's heart. The abbess's aesthetic mind had a weakness for beauty, and Gabriela certainly possessed that. She was not a mean person and in fact not particularly fond of the Galler sisters but understood very well that a connection with other groups of relatives increased her own influence. Such "teams" succeeded better in reaching goals, whatever these might be. As a result, the chapter became divided into two groups—those who belonged and those who did not. The latter were mostly pious individualists without inclination toward politics or intrigue. Choir women in offices realized that their positions depended on the goodwill of the "family block," led by Maria Gabriela who had Henrica's ear. In a system as regimented as the lives of these few dozen women, whose every hour of the day was subject to strict rules, favors gained importance, and punishment for inevitable transgressions was doubly painful. The magistra in charge of the kitchen, for instance, deftly placed better pieces of meat or other tidbits on certain plates to safeguard her position. The prioress had the authority to dispense from certain choir duty, which during long cold winter months accounted for better health. Some important decisions made by the court never reached the full chapter and resulted in additional power for those in the know. Neither Gabriela nor Bernarda held offices at that time, but their recognized influence with the abbess resulted in a variety of favors and caused them to be respected, if not feared.

Columba and Antonia never were part of the "in" group. Both earnestly strove to be good choir women in accordance with their different personalities. Antonia loved to eat, and it didn't take her long to notice that not all plates arriving at the refectory table from the kitchen had equal food. Breadbaskets were set on the table and side dishes passed, but fish, meat, and desserts were served in the kitchen and placed before each woman. Antonia still enjoyed Sister Erentrudis's devotion and special treats found their way to her cell at odd hours.

Antonia had nimble fingers and could embroider very well, especially with metallic thread, which was difficult to handle and demanded special skills. She lacked the talent of designing patterns or relic displays but could follow Henrica's intricate sketches precisely. She was very disappointed when such tasks were assigned to other less-skilled women while she was assigned work on simple embroideries for use in the parish church. However, her penchant for looking at the bright side rarely caused her to become disheartened, and she would shrug off prejudices. She told herself that simpler work needed less careful attention and was less strain on the eyes than fine gold stitches, even though her pride and sense of accomplishment suffered from being denied exercising her skill.

Columba, unfortunately, lacked such attitude. Henrica relieved Maria Carolina of her function as choir magistra and left her only with the office of sacristan, which was the maintenance and supervision of supplies for the church. The new choir magistra was Maria Philippina, whose ideas were not in concert with those of Columba, for whom music and singing remained the most important aspects of her life. Philippina understandably selected music more suitable for her own voice, even though, as magistra, she no longer sang as much as before. Columba was deeply disappointed, and when her protests and pleas found no response, she conceived an idea. Well trained in harmony and gifted with an excellent ear, she devoted herself to arranging chorales, responses, and even litanies in different keys for different voices. She showed her work to Carolina, who was very impressed and discussed it with the abbess. Maria Henrica recognized and appreciated artistic creativity in any subject and asked Philippina to rehearse this music with the choir. The result brought praises from the Supremus and everyone else who heard it but did not endear Columba to the choir magistra. And the musically untalented Bernarda used the situation to her advantage and complained that traditional tunes had been altered to please just one member of the choir, causing a deep division over the issue.

Columba grew very discouraged. Whenever possible, she now spent her recreation time in the hermit tower and avoided reflection, somehow dreading to confront Henrica's and her own painting. She had made no further effort with the brush because she was too depressed to try her hand in creativity. Withdrawn and moody, she was happy only when young Helena joined her for a brief chat in the tower. The alert child would watch for her heading in that direction then follow unobserved to cheer her beloved Columba with stories about things happening in the aspirants' lives. There were times when Columba felt an urge to tell Helena how disillusioned and depressed she was as choir woman. Perhaps, this lovely young girl would have a happier life with a family of her own! One day, Helena told her that her mama had died of consumption and, while talking, suffered a violent coughing attack. Columba realized that the abbey would be the best place for her because this frail body might not survive bearing children. Deep in her heart, she also knew that nothing could have dissuaded Helena from her vocation and that such an idea coming from a much-admired friend would only leave the girl confused. Helena's life centered on a passionate devotion to the Virgin Mary, and she reminded Columba of her own childhood, when the Mother of God had in her heart replaced her own. Helena counted the months and days until investiture and was bitterly disappointed when her vows were delayed because she became seriously ill. She finally reached the ambition of her life with her profess in 1758, and when Columba placed her kiss of peace and friendship on her cheek, she felt as if receiving a daughter into the family.

Chapter 3

Helena's profess in July 1758, however, was both a joyous and mournful day for the abbey and especially for Columba because one of the novices took her final vows virtually on her deathbed.

The abbey's steward was Count Stubenberg whose family estate was located only a few hours' journey from Göss. The subject of his request for an urgent audience the previous year caught Maria Henrica by surprise. His only daughter Theresa, he explained, was betrothed yet on her eighteenth birthday shortly before the wedding announced to the family that she had decided to become a choir woman. He'd granted permission only reluctantly but now demanded the girl's immediate acceptance and participation in an investiture scheduled only weeks later. To add weight to his request, he offered the generous dowry of a bridal gown encrusted with jewels that Theresa was to have worn at her secular wedding, a ring with large diamond and a thousand Florins in gold at investiture, to be followed by another two thousand florins at profess. He argued that his intelligent and well-educated daughter was already conversant in Latin and would easily catch up on lacking church knowledge during her novitiate. The abbess could not help but wonder about the undue urgency of the request and might have hesitated had the girl been younger, but eighteen was an age when a young woman was expected to possess sufficient maturity for this important decision. Moreover, Göss had just been encumbered with a new levy of taxes, and Maria Henrica was anxiously searching for a source of money. The ready cash was most welcome, and the valuable gown could be used for Henrica's latest project of a processional canopy. She accepted the count's conditions, and he delivered his daughter the very next day. The young countess had a thin face and small hands that seemed at odds with her somewhat shapeless body hidden under heavily pleated clothes. Large gray eyes dominated an unusual face with arched nose and small pale mouth, but a pleading, and at the same time, timid expression in those huge eyes endeared Theresa to the abbess and appealed to her protective instincts. Perhaps, the girl's reason was to escape a dreaded marriage, not an uncommon motivation to take the veil. She had a long private conversation with the candidate and only later recalled that Theresa had said very little and cleverly avoided answering many of the abbess's questions, time and again adamantly affirming her decision to become a nun. She was accepted and promised to devote herself to intense studies. The priest who usually taught aspirants was ailing at the time, and Columba, among the best educated and knowledgeable choir women in the abbey, was asked to spend a few hours each day with Theresa to tutor her for the pending exams. Columba liked the girl but soon noticed that all was not well with her pupil, who would sometimes excuse herself and hurry from the room to return pale and exhausted a little while later.

"Are you ill, Theresa?" Columba asked.

"Oh no, Reverend Mother," came the quick reply, "it's just that I have to cough violently at times and don't want anyone to listen. Now, about Pope Urban and the emperor."

Columba did not buy the excuse since a coughing spell rarely gave a person time to leave the room but did not press further. Theresa studied hard and did well in her examinations and interview with the bishop, who was aware that the abbess was most anxious not to lose the substantial dowry to another convent as Stubenberg had threatened in the event his daughter was not accepted. The empress's regulations were not yet in effect, and there was no regulatory or lawful obstacle barring Theresa's quick investiture. Her bridal gown was indeed magnificent, cut very full and heavily pleated, as was the white linen shirt she wore below when her hair was cut in the sacristy and she was invested with the nun's habit. Theresa never flinched as her dark tresses fell to the floor, and her voice was firm and clear when she spoke her vows.

The new novice very much kept to herself, and Columba learned from Helena, who had become Novice Maria Anna with Theresa and shared her cell, that her roommate was obsessed with privacy. Aspirants, novices, and—of course—choir women never saw one another completely undressed. The tiny oil lamp below the crucifix in the cells always remained burning and cast only the barest light so the young women could find the chamber pot stand during the night or the utensils to light the kerosene lamp when the bell called for services. Still Theresa, now novice Maria Agatha, insisted that Maria Anna turn toward the wall before she would remove her habit.

"It's as if she had something to hide," remarked Maria Anna, "and then there are times when it sounds as if she were vomiting. She's not well, I think, though she never complains."

Columba watched Agatha during recreation time in the garden and noticed that she never walked much and rather settled down on the nearest bench with her studies or a prayer book. When it seemed that the young woman had a decided limp and barely managed to reach the seat, Columba descended from her place in the tower and strolled over to her.

"Did you hurt your leg, Maria Agatha?" she asked. "Perhaps, you are not aware that Reverend Mother Maria Xaveria, the infirmary magistra, is very good at curing aches and pains. She's knowledgeable and has many medicines and tinctures in the pharmacy for injuries. Would you like to go see her?"

Agatha looked up, and there was naked fear in her wide gray eyes. "No!" she replied vehemently. "No! I am well! I did not injure my leg, and I am not in pain. I do not need the help of the magistra, and I don't know what makes you think so!"

She broke off and, from the expression on Columba's face, realized that she had overreacted.

"Forgive me please, Reverend Mother Columba, for speaking to you in such a tone," she said humbly then continued with forced casualness, "it's just that I don't know why people always think I'm sick when I am not! Perhaps, it is because I am so pale and short and only my nose keeps growing bigger," she added with a feeble attempt at humor.

Columba was not fooled but respected the abbey's tradition, according to which prying into another woman's health was considered intrusive. She said with a smile, "You have very nice features, dear Maria Agatha, and especially beautiful eyes. I was only concerned because you seemed tired. But then, there's much to study, and you've worked long hours. Perhaps, you should give yourself a little more rest, that is all. And remember, I will always be there to help you, whether it's translations or anything else that weighs on your mind."

The friendly, matter-of-fact words put Agatha at ease. "Thank you very much, Reverend Mother Columba! To tell the truth, I have struggled with this psalm, and if you could explain—"

Columba was glad to help, but her concerns were not abated, and she mentioned them to Maria Xaveria, but the magistra replied that the novice was old enough to ask for help if needed.

Maria Agatha's deportment changed little during the year of her novitiate, and only Columba's watchful eyes observed that she required ever more effort to cope with her duties. During the week preceding the profess, her face was white as linen, and her thin hands trembled when idle, though she would quickly clasp them together or hide her fingers. During her final interview with the bishop on Thursday, he was unexpectedly called away for a meeting with the abbess. Columba was waiting for Agatha in the courtyard to ask whether all had gone well. She saw the bishop leave and, when Agatha failed to appear, went looking for her. She found the young woman lying on the floor, her face in a pool of bloody vomit.

"Agatha!" Columba exclaimed and knelt beside her, but there was no reaction. Columba hurried outside and found three lay nuns busy pumping water in the well court. She summoned them, and together, they carried the limp body through the south tract to the infirmary, where only Maria Xaveria was present. The magistra dismissed the lay nuns and asked Columba to undress Agatha while she went to the pharmacy for medicine. Columba removed veil and Sturz then untied the belt. When she slipped her arm below the novice's back to pull the habit over her head, she discovered that Henrica's body was deformed and misshapen and that she was a hunchback. Removing the linen stockings revealed that one of her legs was grotesquely bent and shorter than the other. What enormous effort it must have taken the girl not to limp all the time, to hold herself straight and conceal the curved spine. So this was the reason for her voluminous, richly pleated garments! Worst of all, Agatha's apparent suffering from severe colic had caused her to faint. Columba gently washed the pale face, cleaned her mouth, and pulled the sheets up to the girl's chin while rubbing her pulse and speaking to her in a low voice. She was concentrating on the thin, cold hands when she felt Agatha's eyes on her and, noticing their fearful expression, smiled and placed a finger on her lips.

"Don't talk, Maria Agatha," she said. "You're in the infirmary, and the magistra has gone for medicine. How do you feel?"

The novice's parched lips struggled to form the words.

"I'm well, I would like"—and a few moments later—"Reverend Mother, who did?"

Columba smiled reassuringly. "I undressed and put you to bed, Maria Agatha, and your secret is safe with me but only if you lie still, take the medicine the magistra will bring, and obey her instructions! God is by your side, Agatha, and if you are not well enough by Sunday, I shall ask Reverend Mother Abbess whether perhaps you could confirm your vows here if that is what you wish to do! But you must rest now so that you do not lose more blood, do you understand?"

Agatha nodded weakly and obediently drank the bitter brew of herbs Xaveria brought.

"I wish you could stay and help, Maria Columba," said the magistra. "The lay nuns have all been assigned other work, and everyone is involved in preparations for Sunday. Surely, you'd rather be with the choir, but—"

"I shall be most happy to remain and help care for her, Mother Magistra," Columba volunteered. "Do not concern yourself, the choir will do quite well without me."

Xaveria missed the expression of relief on Agatha's pale features. The girl apparently feared not to be accepted into the chapter because her malformation had not been disclosed, meaning she had gained admission under false pretense. Columba wondered whether she hoped her condition to forever remain secret.

The bell rang for the evening meal. The magistra briefly returned with instructions for more medicine then left to join the abbess's table and promised to send a lay nun with food for Columba. When she was gone, Columba rolled up a small blanket and placed it below Henrica's neck and upper back to relieve the pressure on her curved spine. The tincture was taking effect, and the patient was drowsy. Dropping off to sleep, her thin fingers grasped Columba's hand as if seeking reassurance. By the time Erentrudis arrived with a tray, Agatha was in a deep slumber, her hand still in the choir woman's. Columba motioned the nun to place the meal on a bedside table and helped herself with her free hand not to disturb the girl. She knew that Agatha was seriously ill. The deformity was probably a birth defect, but the colic was serious, all the more so since she apparently had been suffering from it for some time. Had Agatha's prospective groom learned about his intended's condition and canceled the wedding, and did that induce the count to bring her to Göss? It was well known that Stubenberg was no great friend of the abbey in spite of being handsomely rewarded for his stewardship. He frequently vented his opinion that religious institutions accumulated too much wealth, which made the generous dowry he offered to give his daughter all the more remarkable. But the abbey was known for a reluctance to accept ailing candidates, especially crippled ones, which over time presented more problems than benefits. At least initial good physical constitution was almost mandatory for the exhausting choir duties. Would the abbess postpone Agatha's profess if she found out? Bishops visited Göss only at several years' intervals, and it would be a while before Agatha had another chance to affirm her vows. Besides, it was humiliating and depressing for a candidate to continue the status of novice beyond one year. Columba thought of Maria Anna, who had been made to postpone her investiture because of her ill health. She worried about the effects frequent fasting would have on her young friend's frail constitution. Anna likely was in recluse at this time praying for divine guidance as the great day drew near.

Columba turned from her plate, no longer hungry after a few bites. A warm summer evening settled over the abbey, and she opened the windows for more air, idly listening to muted sounds from the hamlet, cowbells in the distance, a barking dog beyond the walls. Birds quieted down, and the air was so still she could faintly hear the river. Droplets of blood appeared in a corner of Agatha's mouth, and she quickly wiped them away, just in time before the abbess entered. Columba rose and curtsied.

"God bless you, my daughter," Henrica said quietly. "Maria Xaveria tells me that you are willing to remain with our ill novice, and I dispense you from choir duty until her condition improves."

She stepped close to the bed and bent over the sleeping girl. "I wonder what has stricken her so suddenly and at such a time," she mused. "Do you believe it was caused by the emotions preparing for her profess?"

Columba shook her head. "I don't know, Reverend Mother Abbess. But even though she seems quite ill, she has told me that she is most anxious to proceed with her profess, and I humbly besiege you, Reverend Mother, to allow her to do so. It could cause a serious relapse if she were told that she had to wait another year or two. Perhaps, His Excellency could have her affirm her vows here in the infirmary? There's a voice in my heart telling me God wants this daughter to join our community!"

Columba's voice had turned into an urgent whisper, and the abbess cast her a surprised look.

"I see," she said. "I shall discuss this with His Excellency and consult the chronicle and profess rules whether there is a precedence in our abbey for such measure. For now, remain with her and pray for the Lord's guidance in this matter! Magistra Xaveria wishes you to know that she shall look in after recreation time." Maria Henrica inclined her head and left.

Agatha barely stirred during the next few hours. Xaveria came to administer more of the tincture, which caused the patient to gag in labored heaves that brought perspiration to her forehead.

"There is little we can do but allow her to rest," she said. "When the bell rings for midnight Mass, I shall have a lay nun relieve you, so you may attend the first Mass of the day. You seem to have a calming effect on her, and it would be good if you returned and stayed with her through the night, Maria Columba. If her condition deteriorates, you may ring the bell outside the door, and one of the nuns on watch in the infirmary will call me."

The night passed without incident. Columba returned at one o'clock to resume her watch, and the lay nun, who'd worked hard all day preparing for the festivities, gratefully withdrew. Columba barely felt fatigue. She watched the stars gradually fade with the breaking July dawn.

The tower clock chimed the fourth hour when Agatha opened her eyes and whispered, "I'm so thirsty, Reverend Mother!"

Columba rose to reach for a tin goblet with water, but before she could bring it to the girl's lips, another colic set in, and Agatha vomited large clots of blood. When it was over, she took a few sips of water and smiled gratefully as Columba washed her face with cool water and adjusted her pillow.

"Please sing for me, Reverend Mother, you have such a beautiful voice." She sighed and Columba sang softly to keep her voice from reaching beyond the room. She sang the Salve Regina, and it reminded her when as a little girl, she had intoned this, her only chant as quietly as she could in fear of being overheard. Agatha loved it, and her shining eyes were ample reward.

"You sound like an angel," she said during a pause. "I'll miss not hearing you anymore."

Columba started to say that there would be many instances for that in the future, but something in Agatha's face stopped her. The pale morning light brought realization that the girl might not recover. Her features had the unearthly whiteness Columba remembered on the face of the dying Abbess Antonia. Agatha's calm voice interrupted her musings.

"I believe that I am going to die, and I am not afraid, but I want to die a choir woman. And I hope God will forgive the lie my whole life has been."

She fell silent for a few moments then continued in a slightly stronger voice, "I was born a cripple, but no one but the midwife, my parents, and my ayah ever knew, not even my older brother, though he may have suspected something. They always dressed me in pleated clothes and forced me to walk tiptoe with my shorter leg, no matter how much it hurt. The midwife said that they made special shoes for children like me that had a thick sole for one foot, but my papa would not hear of it. He said it would grow out over time, but of course, it didn't."

Labored breathing forced her to stop, and Columba was concerned that talking would tire her too much, but the tortured girl apparently wanted to unburden her heart and continued a few moments later.

"When I was seventeen, Papa betrothed me to a titled widower in his forties, who saw me once and only consented because of a substantial dowry and Papa's promise to pay the large gambling debts he'd incurred."

Agatha stopped again, and Columba made her take a sip from a goblet with chamomile tea.

"You shouldn't really talk, dear sister, it will tire you," she urged but Agatha shook her head.

"I want someone to know my story, for I do not have much time left. Following the betrothal, I spent a year agonizing over my wedding. I pictured my bridegroom's face when he discovered my ugly disfigurement and how he would turn from me in disgust. I hated my father for arranging this marriage and my mother for allowing it. I could imagine my husband despising me for my ugliness and, once in control of the dowry, send me home in disgrace. In my desperation, I thought of an escape and, at the same time, punish my callous father. As you know, Reverend Mother, the counts of Stubenberg have for generations been stewards of Göss, though it's never been a cordial relationship. My father does not like the abbey because he thinks choir women enjoy too many luxuries without contributing to the world and he would never have consented to my becoming one. So on my eighteenth birthday and with the wedding only months away and the gown already made, I told him that unless I was accepted at Göss and he gave me a large dowry, I would let my betrothed know that I was crippled and afflicted with an incur-

313

able decease. And that was not a lie, for during the past few years, I have indeed suffered from colic, stomach pain and vomiting blood. I remained steadfast in spite of Papa's wrath and threats, the only time in my life I have ever stood up to him. He knew the abbess would not be anxious to have a member of the Stubenberg family within her walls and that only a large dowry could persuade her. It did and I derived wicked satisfaction watching him place the gold florins into a velvet bag and relinquish the jeweled gown meant to pay my husband's huge gambling debts. All through the past year, I'd hoped that coming here would bring me health, but it did not happen. Reverend Mother, you suspected something was wrong because you were the only one who cared and I'll be forever grateful that you did not give me away. I never confessed my deceit to a priest because God gave me this body and I do penance every hour of my life. And now it is too late."

The exhausted Agatha paused. Columba gently stroked her forehead. "Be still, child, and rest. God loves you and understands why you acted the way you did."

"But I'll only die in peace if I'm allowed to affirm my vows, and if I cannot stand before the bishop on Sunday, I know I won't live until there's another profess. Oh, Reverend Mother, please help me walk!"

She pushed the covers aside and tried to raise herself, but the effort made her grimace with pain, and she sank back onto her pillows. Columba leaned over her and spoke gently but firmly.

"Novice Maria Agatha, listen to me! You can say your final vows resting as you are now, and the bishop will hear them just as well. Our Lord Jesus had great compassion for the sick, and His eyes will be upon you when you affirm your vows as His bride. I only wish you'd confess your deceit! Remember that a priest has to die rather than reveal your secret. However, you have done penance by your suffering, and I trust that if you sincerely regret your sins, no fault will remain on your soul. Now let me help you prepare for when the Supremus or His Excellency may visit."

The tall and strong Columba more carried than led the girl to a privy stool, washed her face and hands in cool water, and settled her in an armchair while she straightened the bed anxious to forestall assistance by lay nuns, who might discover Agatha's secret. The fewer people knew about it, the better. The novice was embarrassed to be waited on by a choir woman but gratefully obeyed. She was resting when the magistra arrived with a lay nun to look after the patient. Columba told her that Agatha's physical needs had been taken care of and that chamomile tea appeared to calm her stomach. Xaveria mentioned bloodletting but abandoned the idea when Columba pointed to the patient's weakness and deathly pale features. The magistra was herself much involved in the festivities, and bloodletting was a long procedure that required her to be present for several hours. A lay nun came with the message that the abbess wished to see Columba and offered to remain in the sickroom with the sleeping Agatha. Columba hurried off to her cell to freshen up and went to the abbess's office. She found her in the presence of the bishop, Prioress Ernestina, Sub-Prioress Caecilia, and—to her surprise—Maria Gabriela, who held no office.

"Do come in, Maria Columba," said Henrica. "I've spoken to His Excellency, and he would, of course, prefer to see all novices in church for their final vows. How is our patient this morning?"

"Most anxious to actualize her vocation and make profess, Reverend Mother Abbess, but I fear unable to leave her bed without grave danger to her well-being and likely unable to stand for any length of time. In the name of our merciful Lord, I beg of you, Mother Abbess, and you, Your Excellency, to perform the ceremony at her sickbed this very day, tomorrow may be too late!"

Columba's anxiously pleading voice almost broke from emotion. There was a silence, then the abbess said evenly, "We have sent a message to her parents to inform them of their daughter's grave illness but have not received a reply. Count and Countess Stubenberg had not indicated that they would attend their daughter's profess, which I found surprising considering that they are only a short distance away. There does not seem a precedent in our abbey's chronic about a novice making profess in a state of serious illness. It appears that in the past the ceremony was simply postponed. What is your opinion, Excellency?"

The bishop of Admont was a friendly, rotund old man for whom the journey to Göss had been quite strenuous.

"I am your guest, Reverend Mother," he said, "and shall comply with your wishes. Church law does not require that final oaths be confirmed in church, the ceremony could take place anywhere, provided it is before a bishop and witnessed by the chapter."

He was expecting the abbess to make the decision when Maria Gabriela spoke up in her cool voice.

"Church law may not require it, but our tradition and our rules do! It is my understanding that Count Stubenberg has not yet paid the entire dowry as agreed. If we make an exception and allow Maria Agatha to make profess and she does not recover, we may never receive it! I suggest, Reverend Mother Abbess, that we postpone affirming her vows until we receive—"

Columba was aghast and deep emotions made her forget protocol.

"Maria Gabriela!" she cried out. "It is possible that Maria Agatha may become unconscious or even die any moment! She is aware of her condition and has begged me to plead for her, and I shall do so with every breath I have! It is her last wish and how can we deny her to die in peace over a few pieces of gold!"

"Two thousand florins are not 'a few pieces of gold,'" began Maria Gabriela, but a gesture from the abbess cut her short.

"Maria Columba," said Henrica, "I understand that you spent the night watching over our patient and are tired, wherefore, we shall forgive your outburst, which is unseemly for a choir woman. Maria Gabriela's point is valid, and it would be most unfortunate for our abbey if Count Stubenberg did not make good his promise. However, as brides of Christ united in loving sisterhood, we should not deny a novice what may be her last wish. The magistra for the infirm agrees with Columba that Maria Agatha is gravely ill and may well be on her deathbed. Therefore, Your Excellency," she addressed the bishop, "if you are willing, I propose that we have her carried to St. Michael's Chapel after High Mass for the solemn affirmation of her vows. The other novices will make profess tomorrow in church as planned. Maria Ernestina, will you kindly assemble the chapter in St.

Michael at ten o'clock? Maria Caecilia, please inform the magistra for the kitchen that our meal will be delayed until after Agatha's profess."

There was a pause then, "Dearest Maria Gabriela, kindly advise the choir magistra to arrange for song books brought to my chapel."

Henrica shifted her gaze to Columba and added with a faint smile, "I am sure you wish to sing for your new sister in Christ, Maria Columba, and assist Maria Xaveria with the arrangements to have Agatha brought to St. Michael's Chapel. She has made confession, and I trust her heart is pure and free from sin to receive her Savior."

Columba bowed and turned to leave when she looked up and met Gabriela's eyes. In them she saw an expression of such cold contempt that the thought flashed through her, *I have just made another implacable foe.* She tried to put it from her mind as she crossed the well courtyard and hurried down the long hallway toward the infirmary. Agatha's eyes lit up when she entered, her face one anxious question.

"She's vomited more blood, Reverend Mother," whispered the lay nun rising from her chair in a corner. Columba leaned over the bed and smiled her most encouraging smile.

"I have good news, Maria Agatha," she said. "A few more hours and you will become my beloved sister in Christ forever! We shall carry you to the abbess's private chapel, where you will receive your veil and solemnly affirm your vows! It will be very special, but you must force yourself to remain calm so as not to suffer another colic. The chapter will be present, and we will sing the responses and Te Deum for you today just as we shall tomorrow."

A faint glow of joy appeared on the narrow cheeks, and Agatha's pale lips parted in a smile.

"Mother Maria Columba, I owe this joy to you alone! May all saints in heaven pray for you!"

I need it, Columba thought, but aloud, she said to the lay nun, "Do go, Maria Gertraud, and have a stretcher prepared. Then call four of your strongest sisters to carry our novice to St. Michael Chapel after High Mass."

The nun hurried off as the Supremus entered carrying a chalice, accompanied by two young ministrants with oil to administer the last ointment. A shadow of fear crossed Agatha's face, but it passed, and she submitted to the traditional ceremony for the desperately ill. Columba made the responses, and the priest placed a host on the girl's parched lips. A litany for the ill and suffering was prayed, and when they had left, Columba gently helped Agatha dress in her habit and fresh wimple. Excitement and fever colored the thin cheeks and made her look healthier than she was. She tried sitting in a chair, but her stomach pains grew so severe she was forced to lie down. The nuns arrived with a stretcher, and Columba was happy to see Aloysia among them.

"Go to linen storage, Aloysia, and select the best embroidered cloths you can find! Tell them they're needed for a very special purpose! Then hurry back!"

Columba later often thought back to these hours when for the first time in her life she was in charge and recalled how she was consumed by the single purpose of helping Agatha fulfill her desire. Moving around the infirmary cell, issuing instructions to the lay nuns, she felt Agatha's eyes follow her every gesture. The girl refused, and Columba did not urge her to drink from a tincture to ease her pain because she understood her wish to remain fully alert.

Aloysia returned with an armful of linens, and a throw of blue velvet with gold fringes and tassels that Columba knew was used to cover tables for exhibiting artwork. She rewarded Aloysia with a grateful glance, and the women placed the stretcher on two chairs next to the bed. They covered the rough frame with embroidered linens, and Columba used pillows to cushion any expected jolts during transport. She gently slipped a sheet underneath Agatha's body to avoid direct contact with anyone else, and the women carefully pulled her onto the stretcher while Columba's arm supported her neck and back. Grateful for Columba's efforts to hide her deformity, Agatha never gave a sound and made sure that her feet did not show below the seam of her habit. Once on the stretcher, Columba supported her upper body with more pillows to minimize the impression of a desperately ill person. They covered her with the velvet throw, and the tassels almost reached the floor.

"My, the countess looks like a queen being carried to her coronation!" exclaimed a lay nun, and they all smiled.

"You are indeed a beautiful bride of Christ," said Columba, "who within the hour will trade her ring of betrothal with that of a choir woman wedded to Christ."

Agatha thoughtfully contemplated the large diamond on her finger.

"Reverend Mother Columba, I hear they've recently acquired a relic of St. Theresa. Will you request the Most Reverend Mother Abbess to have the stone of my betrothal ring used in the ornamentation? I don't want—"

"You will surely have an opportunity to ask her yourself, dear Agatha," Columba said quickly, "and I shall be happy to support you. You know that the wishes of those bringing the dowry are considered in selecting jewels for a new project. But now I hear the bell announcing consecration, High Mass will be over shortly, and we need to reach St. Michael's so we don't keep the bishop waiting. Sisters, be gentle and watch your every step!"

Lay nuns were accustomed to carrying heavy buckets of water or armfuls of wood, and the four women had no trouble with the stretcher's light load. Columba walked by its side, holding Agatha's hand and anxiously watching her face, but the girl made no sound, and only tiny beads of perspiration on her forehead indicated her discomfort, or was it fever? Columba wondered whether Agatha any longer felt much pain; her cheeks were burning feverishly now, and the expression of her large gray eyes was like in a trance. She seemed spiritually removed from her environ.

St. Michael's had always been the private chapel of abbesses. It was a two-story annex to the south tower of the church with access from the cloister. The chapel was on the upper level. The lower one, according to tradition, had been part of the abbey's oldest building. It is documented that the second story was added in the thirteenth century in early Gothic style that was never changed. The semicircular apses had tall, narrow windows with light falling upon a simple stone altar, the abbess's chair, and a few pews. Here the abbess and her court attended daily Mass, and ordinary choir women rarely entered.

A priest escorted them into the chapel and asked the sisters to rest the stretcher on a low rectangular pedestal that had been placed in the aisle before the altar and was covered with black cloth. *Dear God, it looks like a coffin*, thought Columba, hoping that Agatha wouldn't share her notion. The priest spoke quietly to the candidate, and Columba withdrew to kneel in a pew. She had always loved this chapel and never tired admiring the medieval frescoes that covered walls and archivolts, which culminated in the two distinct ceiling vaults. Each apex was adorned with a stone sculpture, one with the blessing hand of God and features believed to be that of the abbess who had commissioned the structure. The other showed a seraph with six wings, a stone in his raised right hand. Such seraphim were regarded as symbols of ultimate wisdom and love. The stone represented a glowing ember from the altar of God that had purified the lips of the Prophet Isaiah.

What Columba most loved were the frescoes. The tall, slender Gothic figures displayed none of the stiff, unearthly characteristics often typical of the style. Though constrained by architecture and outlined in black, these biblical figures and angels seemed to move across the walls. There was dynamic in their bodies and vivid gestures, conveying the artist's effort to create scenes observed in real life.

Behind the altar was a crucifixion scene showing Christ's body wreathing in agony on a low cross. The Apostle John's arms supported the collapsed Virgin, her heart pierced by a sword. A figure to the right held a plaque with the words "Vere filius dei erat iste" (This was indeed the Son of God). Below and much smaller in size to symbolize a mere human was a kneeling Abbess Herburgis in blue tunic, red cloak, and short blue veil, evidence that choir women at Göss in the thirteenth century still were canonesses and dressed as such. The remaining representations were in decided contrast to the despair of the crucifixion scene. They pictured the wedding of Mary's parents Joachim and Anna and episodes from the Old Testament. As usual, the frescoes cast their spell upon Columba, though she kept an anxious eye on Agatha, who lay motionless with eyes fixated on the altar. The slight shuffling of approaching steps broke the silence. The choir women entered to form a circle along the walls, and Columba rose to join them. Abbess Maria Henrica appeared, touched Agatha's cheek, and made the sign of the cross on the novice's forehead. Then she went to her chair, and members of her court filed into the pews. Everyone awaited the bishop, who was announced by ministrants ringing their little bells. Most of the ceremonial pomp and circumstance of a solemn profession of vows was eliminated to reduce the stress on the ailing novice or, Columba wondered, because the fasting chapter and clergy were anxious for their midday meal. While not as elaborate as the official banquet, the following day, it surely would be a special repast.

The choir opened the ceremony with a hymn, and the bishop spoke briefly about the dedication, humility, and unconditional obedience of life as a religious. He then asked Agatha whether her decision to become a bride of Christ was taken of her own free will and without undue influence or pressure by any person or event, which she affirmed in a clear and surprisingly strong voice. The abbess removed the diamond ring from the novice's finger and placed it on a velvet cushion next to the one bearing the seal of Christ. The bishop asked the candidate to solemnly affirm her preliminary vows taken at investiture, and again, she answered clearly and with fervor while her eyes never wavered from the cross on the altar. The bishop placed the gold ring on her finger, and Maria Henrica draped a choir woman's black veil around the candidate's head.

"Choir woman Maria Agatha, I welcome you into the chapter of the abbey of Göss," the bishop said gravely, "and I direct you to kiss your abbess's ring in affirmation of your loyalty and obedience!"

The abbess extended her hand and added with a gentle smile, "My daughter Maria Agatha, may your life as a bride of Christ be one of joyful dedication!"

Maria Agatha's voice was weak but clearly audible when she said, "My Most Reverend Mother Abbess, I have but one wish—that my sister in Christ Maria Columba, sing the Salve Regina?"

There was a brief silence when everyone held their breath since it was not customary for a candidate to speak other than professing her vows. Maria Henrica returned to her chair and, without looking at Agatha, said evenly, "I shall grant your wish, my daughter. Maria Columba, you may sing."

Columba was most surprised. She'd thought Agatha to be dozing when she'd sung this fervent prayer for mercy during the night and had not recited it before an audience since Vienna. Her compassion and piety came to the forefront as she sang the hauntingly melodious Gregorian chant she had so loved since childhood. "At te conspiramus, gementes et flentes, in hoc lacrimarum valle." (To you we plead, sighing and weeping in this valley of tears.) And once again, Columba's voice touched every heart in the room. There was an admiring smile on the lips of Maria Carolina, and several of the women bowed their heads to hide tears. Others looked straight ahead, but all were clearly moved. A Te Deum closed the ceremony, and four lay nuns stepped in to carry the stretcher, followed by Columba and the others with abbess and bishop closing the procession.

By the time Columba and the lay nuns reached the infirmary, the flush of excitement on Agatha's cheeks had changed to ghostly pallor. Her eyes were closed and her lips tightly pressed together. Columba noticed drops of blood seeping from her mouth. She removed the velvet throw and, when the stretcher was placed upon the chairs by the bed, put her arm under Theresa's shoulders to help her slide onto the bed, still covered by a sheet. The lay nuns offered to help undress her, but Columba dismissed them, and—having closed the door—held a bowl at Agatha's chin.

"All is well now, beloved sister in Christ, we are alone."

The girl relaxed her lips to release large lumps of clotted blood, and Columba thought of the self-discipline it must have taken to control the nausea. Now her body shook with hives as she vomited more blood, and Columba dried beads of perspiration from her forehead. When the attack had passed, Columba gently removed veil and habit and draped the garments over a chair. A small sound caused her to turn.

"My veil, please, Reverend Mother," Agatha whispered between chokes, and Columba understood. The new choir woman wanted to wear the emblem of her status, the black veil. Ailing nuns habitually removed it, though the wimple was always retained in the presence of others.

"Of course, dear Sister Maria Agatha," she said, using the formal address among choir women. "But you must not address me as Reverend Mother any longer, for I am now your sister! And as a sister, I must ask you to drink from the new medicine the magistra has prepared for you and then rest so you may get better!"

Maria Agatha smiled weakly and drank the bitter tincture that seemed to ease her pain, for her body relaxed and she closed her eyes. There was a slight knock at the door, and Aloysia entered with a plate of food for Columba, who had felt no hunger until then. However, lack of sleep and fasting since the previous afternoon began to take their toll on her body, and she ate from the roast fowl, vegetables, and fresh bread, withdrawing to a corner so the smell of food might not disturb the patient. When Aloysia came for the tray, Columba followed her into the hallway.

"Maria Aloysia, I'm aware that you have had a long day of hard work, but I have a favor to ask. I shall continue to watch with our ailing choir woman but want you close by so I can call on you for help. If you are assigned a task, return when it is completed. And see that it will be you bringing my evening meal. Will you do that?"

The pockmarked cheeks of the little nun flushed with pride. "I am most honored, Reverend Mother," she said, took the tray, and hurried off.

Columba sat in the armchair and leaned back her head. The food made her drowsy, and she dozed for a while, though she never really slept. The tension in the suffering girl's body seemed relaxed, and her breathing was even, but as the hours wore on, Columba sensed strength slowly draining from the frail body. She could not bring herself to touch her evening meal, and Aloysia removed a full tray. Columba asked her to assume the watch while she attended Komplet, aware that her continued absence from choir service might arouse suspicion. She prayed intently that Agatha would not wake up and be afraid she might have abandoned her, but there was no change upon her return. Aloysia asked permission to leave for cleaning duty in the kitchen, and Columba was aware that the nun would be punished if she failed to report. She knew that asking the tired woman to return later was a burden, but Aloysia was intelligent and trustworthy, and Columba had a sinking feeling she might need her during the night.

"Aloysia," she said, "I know you must be very tired. After you're done in the kitchen, do take a rest, but I would be grateful if you'd come back and be available during the night if I need you."

The nun was accustomed to simply being ordered around and was humbly grateful that Columba asked for her service as a favor. She curtsied.

"Oh, Rev'rend Mother, I's honored, and not a bit tired! I slept last night when you watched! And I'll sure hurry back!"

"But first, rest a while," Columba whispered and the nun left.

A short while later, the infirmary magistra came to check on her patient. The experienced old woman scrutinized Agatha's emaciated face and said, "She does not have much longer, Maria Columba, another day or two, no more. You've done right asking mother abbess for an early profess. Do you wish to be relieved by another choir woman so you can participate in the profess ceremony tomorrow? I understand that Novice Maria Anna is very anxious to have you present when she takes her final vows."

Columba thought of young Helena's devotion and affection through the years and the many times she had expressed the wish to hear Columba sing on her most solemn day. Her keen musical ear would easily discern the absence of her admired friend's voice in the choir. Maria Xaveria stood by the open window with her back turned as she spoke, unaware that Agatha had heard her words and was look-ing at Columba with large, anxiously pleading eyes. Columba calmly met her gaze and silently shook her head then said aloud, "I am very grateful for your kind consideration, dear Mother Magistra, but I have promised Sister Agatha that I would remain at her bedside until her condition improved. I would indeed love to hear Novice Maria Anna affirm her vows, but I believe that the ill need our help more in their suffering than the healthy in their joy, and I trust Maria Anna feels the same. Reverend Mother Abbess has graciously dispensed me from choir duty, and with your permission, I shall remain here. May I ask what your instructions are if the colic or pains return, Mother Magistra?"

Maria Xaveria briefly nodded agreement. "There is truly not much you can do, Sister Maria Columba. If she vomits more blood, have her drink as much chamomile tea as possible. It's no cure, but it will soothe. I can do nothing further, but God hears us, and I shall ask the Supremus at midnight Mass to say special prayers for our Sister Maria Agatha. You too pray for her, Maria Columba, and let us commend her soul to Christ!"

With a final glance at the apparently sleeping girl, the magistra left. When the sound of her steps on the stone floors in the corridor had faded, Agatha, her eyes still closed, said, "Dear sister in Christ, do you also believe that I am dying?"

Columba was deeply disturbed about Agatha overhearing the magistra's words about her condition. She thought for a moment then sat on the edge of the bed and took the girl's hands into hers.

"Agatha, I believe that where there is life, there also is hope. Therefore, as long as we have life, we must believe in preserving it. You are very ill and have suffered much, but you are young, and God loves you, be it as a choir woman serving Him in this abbey or by His side in blissful relief of suffering. I love you and shall pray to Him from the depth of my heart that you may remain within our midst for many years to come!"

Agatha's response was calm. "The magistra thinks I shall die soon. I fear God will punish me for deceiving the abbey about my condition. You are my only source of consolation, Sister Maria Columba, and I pray that God shed His blessings upon you for helping me die."

Her feverish eyes were full of fear of a different type from when she thought Columba would leave her bedside.

"When I was engaged to be married, Sister Columba, I often prayed God would let me die to spare me the shame and humiliation of a wedding night. Yet now when I may be near death, I am so afraid! Columba, will it hurt very much to die? And I shiver when I think of myself in a casket in the crypt with the other dead choir women! Help me, please help me, Columba, and do not let me die!"

Columba was deeply moved. She tried to think of an answer but could find no words. Then she remembered confiding her fear of final vows to Maria Henrica, and the magistra's words had been those spoken by the Prophet Isaiah as well as in the New Testament. She half spoke, half chanted them now for Agatha, "Be not afraid! I go before you always. Come, follow me, and I shall give you rest! If you stand before the power of hell and death is at your side, know that I am with you through it all! And you shall see the face of God and live!"

"The face of God," Agatha repeated slowly, "the face of God! It must be more beautiful than anyone can imagine. What do you believe His face is like, Sister Columba?"

"We do not know, sister, but loving Christ and following Him will lead you to see the face of God and will give you peace and rest."

The naked fear faded from the feverish eyes, and with a smile on her pale lips, she begged, "Thank you, dear sister, please chant those words again for me!"

And Columba repeated them over and over, her voice becoming softer until even breathing told her that Agatha was sleeping. Aloysia returned and Columba knew that the nun had not taken any rest. She settled down on a small, uncomfortable bench in the hallway and urged Columba to go get some sleep, but nothing would have induced her to leave. The warm summer dusk became night, and Columba lit a lamp and placed it on a table against the wall so it would not disturb her patient. When the bell called for midnight Mass, Agatha opened her eyes and tried to speak.

"The bell tolls for me," she whispered. "Please sing for me, sister, one more time."

"Be not afraid, for I go before you always," Columba sang with a choking voice, firmly holding Agatha's stiff cold hands in hers, "and I shall give you rest."

A strange light filled the huge gray eyes that stared at the stucco ceiling.

"I see the face of God!" She breathed and her hands became limp as she passed from this world. Columba leaned forward, tears streaming down her face.

"You shall live with Him and see His face forever," she said and gently placed her hand over the breaking eyes to close them.

The bell continued to toll, and Columba fell to her knees beside the bed.

"Almighty God of mercy, hear my prayer! May my Sister Maria Agatha, who was your daughter on earth, enter the kingdom of peace and light, where Your saints live in glory. I ask this through our Lord Jesus Christ, whose bride Agatha became today and who lives and reigns with you and the Holy Spirit, one God, forever and ever. Amen!"

"Amen!" echoed Sister Aloysia, who had quietly entered the room and knelt behind Columba. The two women remained on their knees as the bell fell silent announcing that the choir women had gathered for midnight Mass. Columba finally rose and motioned Aloysia, who was about to withdraw.

"Sister Aloysia, I need your help and your promise not to divulge to anyone what I will say to you."

The nun bowed her head in agreement, and Columba continued, "Choir woman Maria Agatha not only was very ill but since birth had suffered from a deformed body. No one knew about it until she disclosed it to me, and I promised her secrecy, for she could be denied her status because of deceit, which was not hers but her family's. I cannot keep this promise without your help. I want you to go wake the carpenter, have him deliver a coffin to the infirmary, and place it outside the door. He may question the hour, but if you tell him that I ask it, he will do so, and there are always coffins ready. Together, we shall then prepare our sister for final rest, so no one else need touch her body."

"Rev'rend Mother, I do what you ask," Aloysia said and left.

Columba sat by the side of the bed and looked at Agatha's face that no longer showed signs of suffering, only peaceful surrender to the dignity of death that gave her features a strange and unearthly beauty. She thought of the mental and physical pain of a child despised and unwanted by her parents because of her deformity and forced to disguise it. The betrothed young woman must have anticipated her wedding with utter horror! What immense courage she must have summoned to defy her proud father's wishes and enrage him with her demand to enter Göss, which he insisted she do pre-

327

tending to have a normal body. Each day of her life within these walls must have been one of fear about being found out, yet she had successfully kept her secret even through investiture; finally her collapse and very real chance to be rejected for profess! Columba was overcome with guilt for often bemoaning her own fate, the lack of affection from her mother, her papa's death, separation from her siblings, or rejection by some of the choir women.

"You have put me to shame, beloved Sister Maria Agatha, I should thank our Lord each hour of my life for being spared suffering such as yours! You truly deserved to receive the veil and become His bride, you earned it with the pain of your heart and body, and I know He will open His arms in heaven to receive you!"

Watching by her departed sister through the still night, Columba experienced feelings she'd never had before. She longed for death and envied Agatha, who had walked past its gates and found her peace. "I wish I could join you," she whispered, "for I'm still fearful of my future in this abbey." Then she remembered the words of Isaiah she had sung for Agatha, and her guilt returned. "I shall remember your courage in your hour of suffering and death, dear Sister, and I shall sacrifice my pain and fear to the Lord, who walks before me always."

Low voices and footsteps approached, and Columba heard Aloysia's voice.

"'Tis good, Master Berger, place it by the door, 'tis not 'til later they prepare the departed Rev'rend Mother."

There was a slight thump as the men put down the coffin, and a moment later, their steps faded on the stone floor as they walked away. Aloysia waited until all was quiet.

"I did as you say, Rev'rend Mother, jus' got the carpenter an' woke no other. Berger an' Jacob, his boy, jus' came home. They's been at the inn an' was in good spirits an' glad they's not have nothin' else to do," she added with a little smile.

The spruce wood boards of the casket were barely an inch thick, Columba was tall and strong, and Aloysia's arms were accustomed to heavy loads, which enabled the two women to place the coffin upon two chairs. Aloysia went to the cell that had been prepared for Agatha as choir woman and fetched a freshly starched wimple and the habit of fine black wool she would have worn for the first time on Sunday. Columba removed the black veil Agatha had insisted keeping as she lay on her deathbed then the bloodstained wimple still damp with perspiration. She gently washed the face and head with its unevenly cut thin hair and the clammy hands. Together, they dressed the body in the finely pleated Flocke. Columba wanted Agatha to rest softly, and they searched the infirmary for small pillows and covered them with the embroidered linen cloth from the stretcher. Columba carefully arranged the edges so the beautiful needlework lined the coffin with a delicate frill. Placing the body into the coffin was a challenge for the two women since rigor mortis had not yet set in, and though Agatha was light, her limp body was difficult to handle. When the task was complete, Columba tenderly arranged wimple and veil.

"Look, Rev'rend Mother," whispered Aloysia, "she looks like a saint!"

Columba nodded. "Let us pray for her, Sister Aloysia," and the two women knelt and recited the customary prayers and a litany. When dawn broke and the bell rang for the prim, Columba relegated the deathwatch to Aloysia and went to her cell for a fresh habit and veil. She was last to enter the choir empore, where she approached Maria Philippina and said quietly, "Our beloved Sister Maria Agatha has gone home to her Savior. Sister Aloysia is keeping watch. I have had her placed in a coffin to avoid distress amidst today's ceremonies and not diminish the joyful anticipation of our novices. Will you inform our Reverend Mother Abbess, Mother Magistra?"

If Philippina was surprised, it did not show. "I shall do so, Maria Columba. If you need rest, I will excuse you from prim for you are needed in the choir at High Mass."

"Thank you, Mother Magistra," Columba replied, "but I long to pray the litany for our Sister Agatha and shall also sing at High Mass in honor of our new sisters. I would beg, however, that Reverend Mother Abbess grant me dispensation from the banquet, for my heart grieves, and I would rather hold watch by our departed sister."

"I understand." Philippina nodded. "I shall speak to the abbess and have a priest sent to the infirmary. You may lead the litany in my absence. And may God bless you, my daughter, you have acted with prudence."

Columba went to her seat and intoned, "Maria, Mater Dolorosa." And the choir chanted in response, "We implore you, pray for us," followed by the traditional long list of saints, "Sancta Margareta, Sanctus Laurentius, Sancta Magdalena, Sanctus Chrysostomus, Sancta Agnes," each time answered by, "We implore you, pray for us!"

The church was still in semidarkness during this early morning ritual. Only a few candles on the choir loft and at side altars shed light until the summer dawn gradually reached through the stained glass windows. Columba's voice and the answering chorus eerily echoed from the dark walls. The litany comprised few notes, and the choir chanted them to perfection. When Columba reached Saint Agatha, emotion broke her voice, and several of the nuns, unaware of what had happened, thought, *She's praying hard for her.*

Maria Henrica had just ended her morning prayers in St. Michael's Chapel when Philippina brought the news, and the abbess immediately sent word to the Supremus. She decided not to announce the death until evening since this was to be a day of joyous celebration. The Supremus dispatched one of his priests to the infirmary, where Columba found him upon her return. He informed her of the abbess's decision to withhold Agatha's death news from the chapter at this time. Columba and Aloysia knelt by his side while he recited the prayers for the dead.

"Almighty God and Father, you have made the cross for us a sign of strength and marked us as yours in the sacrament of resurrection. Now that you have freed our beloved Sister Maria Agatha from this mortal life, unite her with your saints in heaven! We ask this through our Lord Jesus Christ, your Son," followed by the responsorial psalm, "Relieve the troubles of my heart, and bring me out of my distress." And the women responded to each verse, "To you, O Lord, I lift my soul!"

He sprinkled holy water over the casket to bless the body. After he left, an immense fatigue overcame Columba. For a long time, she looked at Agatha's peaceful face, less pale in the flickering candlelight. Aloysia gently tucked her sleeve.

"Rev'rend Mother, do rest, you need strength for your singin' an' 'tis almost time for High Mass."

Columba shook her head. "I can't leave her, she's afraid to be alone, she told me so!"

When she saw the worried look on the little nun's face, she smiled warily and added, "Oh, I know, Sister Aloysia. She's with God now! But I don't want her all alone in this room where she suffered so much! Do go find one of your sisters you can trust and ask her to watch by her while I am in church. I shall return after the ceremony."

Aloysia disappeared to return a short while later with Sister Erentrudis, barely able to walk because of a hurt ankle which excused her from kitchen work. Columba went to wash her face and, at the first strike of the bell, joined her sisters on the choir loft. Maria Carolina played the organ, and the women sang a rousing chorus as the Supremus Capellanus and the abbey priests led the procession of candidates into the church. The bishop, splendid in his vestments of embroidered gold brocade, entered from the sacristy, anteceded by the abbess and eight ministrants. Maria Columba's eyes sought Maria Anna. From her vintage on the choir loft, the four novices in their black habits and white veils were hard to tell apart, but Columba had known and loved the child and young girl Helena for so long she could have picked her from any group of nuns. She watched them take their places before the altar, and something within her wanted to cry out, "Helena, beloved child, give yourself more time before you profess your vows, you're too young." But then she recalled the radiant piety in Helena's eyes and knew that nothing could have deterred her. The girl was extremely anxious to become firmly wedded to Christ and continuously spoke of her ardent love for the Virgin. Columba knew then that anything she might have said would likely meet shocked surprise, confusion, and lack of understanding. And so she witnessed the four young women solemnly affirm their eternal vows and receive their veils and rings to become irrevocably elevated to the status of choir women.

Fanfares announced the conclusion of the ceremony, and the women assembled in the cloister walk to receive their new sisters in Christ with the traditional embrace and kiss of peace. When Maria

Anna embraced Columba, she whispered, "Dearest sister, I am so very happy and only pray I can be like you!" And Columba warmly returned the hug, feeling deeply ashamed. "God forgive my doubts and make me worthy of her thoughts," she silently prayed.

Yet when she later resumed her watch by Agatha's coffin, she felt lost and disconsolate and found no words to pray. What was wrong with her? She suddenly saw life ahead an unending sequence of masses and litanies amidst women who resented and disliked her! So troubled was her mind she forgot about cheerful Antonia and loving Anna. "If only I could join you, dear Agatha, and have it all behind me," she whispered. Moments later, a hand touched her shoulder. Columba never knew how long the abbess, who moved soundlessly, had stood behind her and perhaps overheard her words.

"My daughter Maria Columba, many a fear and despair are born of fatigue," the abbess said evenly. "Our Sister Maria Agatha sleeps in peace, and you have helped her find that peace. You will now retire to your cell and rest. I have ordered a continuous watch until the remains are taken to the crypt tomorrow afternoon. You are excused from choir duty until High Mass tomorrow. Now go with God!"

The quiet voice expressed a command, and Columba rose, bowed, and left the room. When she reached her cell, three days of suppressed fatigue finally overwhelmed her. She removed habit and veils, washed with cool water, and donned her nightgown. Too tired even to fetch a fresh nightcap from the chest, she collapsed on her bed and mercifully sank into dreamless slumber. Though a healthy woman in her early thirties, the emotional and physical strain of the past three days took their toll. She never heard the bell for vespers, midnight Mass, or prim and only opened her eyes when Maria Antonia gently shook her shoulder.

"Wake up, dear Sister Columba, time to get ready for High Mass! I knocked at your door when I didn't see you, but you never answered, so I came in to make sure you are all right. We've been told that Maria Agatha has gone home to the Lord, and I have missed you. We are laying her to rest after the midday meal today."

Columba sat up. "I'm grateful you woke me, Antonia! I must have slept very long, but I feel better and will join you in a few moments."

She dressed and, after brief meditation, said her morning prayers. The long rest had helped her physically and improved her mental outlook despite heavy summer rains and gray, misty air that had settled into the valley. During High Mass, she felt intense hunger and remembered that she had eaten very little for the last several days. Later in the refectory, she could hardly wait for prayers to end and the meal be served. It was considered unseemly to reach for the fragrant bread in the small baskets until each woman had a bowl of soup before her and it required all of Columba's self-control not to do so. Maria Anna was designated to read during the meal, and Columba noticed that her voice was hoarse and that she had to interrupt herself repeatedly for small bouts of coughing. She fervently hoped that it did not presage a recurrence of her illness. After the meal, she went to the infirmary to say her final farewell to Agatha since the casket would shortly be moved to the church for memorial service. Approaching, she saw two men through the open door standing by the coffin, one holding a small bucket of chalk and the other dipping a ladle in it to generously sprinkle the white substance over the body. Columba knew of the custom to cover bodies with chalk as a means to impede decay, but at that very moment, it seemed barbaric to see Agatha's face covered with chalk, and she shouted, "What on earth are you doing?"

The two men looked up, startled, and the older one said, "Just doin' what we's asked to do, Rev'rend Mother." Then replacing the ladle in the bucket, they took hold of the lid, and together, the two men shut the coffin and rotated the levers to tighten the lid. They briefly lifted their caps to show respect and left to make room for four deacons in white robes who entered with a stretcher on which they placed the casket.

"O, do wait for a moment," pleaded Columba and placed her hand on the lid. The men respectfully stopped.

"Goodbye, dear Sister Agatha," she whispered, "I hope to join you in the not too distant future."

She withdrew her hand, and the deacons took away the casket. Columba blew out the candles and replaced the crucifix to its niche in the wall.

The funeral Mass was read by the Supremus Capellanus, who spoke briefly about this new bride of Christ whom He had called from this world so soon. No one knew much about Maria Agatha, who'd arrived barely a year ago and kept mostly to herself. After the service, the choir women filed through the empty church to precede the casket down the steep steps into the crypt. Columba stood amidst her sisters in the cool semidarkness, and her eyes came to rest on the four slender columns supporting the center vault. She'd not paid much attention to them on previous occasions and now recalled what she'd read not long ago.

The four columns rested directly on the stone floor without pedestal and had no capital merging seamlessly into the low vaulted ceiling. Two were identical; the third was of spiral design like those in the church. The fourth column was distinctly different. It clearly consisted of two parts as if the stonemason had accidentally cut it too short then inserted a piece to make up the height. Two legends for this phenomenon existed. One told of the humble stone mason afraid to create perfect work purposely "mending" one column. But in a parallel case, where a similar "mended" column existed in a Nuremberg edifice, a different explanation was given. The story told of the devil and a priest making a bet, according to which Satan would, one by one, carry four stone columns from Italy across the Alps in the time it took the priest to celebrate Mass. As the devil approached with the fourth column, the anxious priest prematurely said concluding prayers. The devil, thinking he had lost the bet, angrily dropped the column onto the chapel, and it broke in half. A stonemason fitted the two pieces together and included them in the edifice to commemorate the event. Columba shook off her thoughts and joined her sisters in prayer while the coffin was placed next to that of Abbess Maria Antonia.

The Supremus intoned, "The Lord will open the gate of paradise to her, and she will return to that homeland where there is no death, only everlasting joy."

And with this brief ceremony, Maria Agatha departed the chapter of choir women as abruptly as she had arrived. Count Stubenberg incidentally never made good on his dowry pledge.

Chapter 4

Columba suffered a great deal during the following months. In many hours of prayer and meditation, she tried to reason with herself why the death of Maria Agatha had changed her outlook so decidedly but found no answers. At first, she thought her troubled mind-set derived only from witnessing the suffering and death of a sister, but she knew it went beyond, for in past years, she had mourned Abbess Maria Antonia as well as other choir women. The impulsive Columba was also a clear thinker with a sharp mind. Whenever possible, she retreated to the hermit tower and tried to ban the emotional aspect from determining what affected her so deeply. Was it the heart-rending story of a cruel father forcing a child and teenager to hide a painful disability until her agony finally made her rebel? Or a diffident mother who allowed such things to happen to a daughter out of shame of having born a crippled child, for which a ruthless husband likely blamed her? Had either parent been aware that their daughter's colic had deteriorated into bleeding stomach ulcers, probably aggravated by trauma? Was the prospect of a humiliating marriage simply the last straw for the girl?

Columba recalled watching Agatha walk with difficulty and how she had often abruptly excused herself during a lesson to later return pale and drawn. She reproached herself for not prying more deeply for the reason, not having made a better effort to win the novice's confidence. Yet if Agatha had confided in her, could she have done something to prevent the tragic outcome? Most likely not, given the strict rule that choir women were not to share confidences and personal struggles. These were to be shared with their father confessor during the weekly act of reconciliation, and Columba knew only too well how little practical advice was offered to cope with inner turmoil, other than a harsh penance and stern admonition to pray for strength and fortitude. Her unsettled state of mind had to have a deeper cause than losing a sister in Christ, no matter how dear, for it stood to reason that spending her life in a community of women of all ages she was bound to witness death many times over the years. Then she recalled pleading with the abbess to permit Agatha's early profess and making clear that the girl might not live to see the designated day. The abbess, her spiritual mother, had been hesitant to grant her wish and was apparently impressed by Maria Gabriela's heartless suggestion that such action might deprive the abbey of two thousand florins. What was the worth of all the money on earth before God compared to the pious wish of a dying novice? In the end, she had been able to sway the abbess's heart but would never forget the look of chilling enmity on Gabriela's face, nor her triumphant smile when it later became clear that her prediction of the count's default was correct. She also overheard a remark by Maria Henrica that perhaps Stubenberg could have been coaxed into paying by a threat to postpone the profess, which Agatha would not have lived to see. Since he would not travel a few hours to visit his daughter's deathbed, Columba doubted that he ever intended to make good on his dowry promise. It caused her to shudder. Perhaps, he even welcomed this unwanted daughter's death as a convenient solution to an embarrassing problem. She was ever more shocked when she heard he had made an albeit feeble demand for the return of the jewels sewn into Agatha's wedding dress, which was legitimately refused since she had been betrothed to Christ at her investiture. Much as she held him in contempt, Columba thought his materialistic attitude less despicable than that of choir women, whose life was supposedly dedicated to charity and Christian love and who even considered denying the deathbed wish of a sister because of money! How many times had they read the passages in which Christ speaks about loving one's neighbor and his words, "What you do to the least of my brothers that you do unto me!" Columba was not a saintly person, but she had a warm and generous heart and could never have hurt anyone with words such as Maria Bernarda had spoken to her in the past. She readily admitted that she tended to find faults with members of her sisterhood or privately considered one or the other unintelligent and lacking talent, especially in music, but she made brave efforts to hide her thoughts or at least voice her opinion without deliberately hurting others. She had repeatedly confessed her failure to love everyone equally and with her whole heart, and the Supremus always ordered her to extend special acts of kindness and charity toward certain sisters. Columba had to admit that she did not follow such orders when they concerned Bernarda or Gabriela.

She also watched with deep anxiety and apprehension that the abbess more and more fell under the influence of Gabriela, the Galler sisters, and others belonging to powerful families. Columba knew that Henrica suffered from "stones" that caused her severe pain and that this was the reason for her frequent absences from the chapter. Maria Ernestina, in turn, was plagued by shortness of breath and a weak heart. Sub-Prioress Maria Caecilia had lost influence, and it came as no surprise when after Ernestina's death in 1757, she was succeeded by Maria Philippina as prioress.

Another incident concerned Columba even more. Her first love without doubt was music, but she had been educated in the arts and admired the extraordinary medieval frescoes decorating the walls of St. Michael's. She was always fascinated by the way they differed from other works of the thirteenth century in theme as well as vivid execution. She thought of the figures as actors representing real life, and her vivid imagination let her hear the rustle of their mantels and veils. So she could not believe her ears one afternoon when the women were busy with embroidery work, while a February snowstorm was howling outside.

"The abbess," Gabriela said, "concurs with my opinion, that the frescoes in her personal chapel do not represent the spirit of our times, in which the New Testament takes precedence over the Old. I, for one, have suggested to conceal them, one option being to hang tapestries."

She looked round for approval then continued piously, "The frescoes distract from concentration and prayer! Also I have drawn

Reverend Mother Abbess's attention to the fact that they were most likely commissioned by Abbess Herburgis, who is shown in the colorful clothing of a canoness of which our abbey does not wish to be reminded."

Columba was aghast. "But they're beautiful works of art, Sister Maria Gabriela, and Herburgis's attire only follows the customs of her time! These frescoes have conveyed great joy to choir women through centuries, of which we would be deprived if they were hidden from view!"

Gabriela raised her eyebrows and said coolly, "I find it astonishing, dear Sister Maria Columba, that you prefer 'the joy' as you care to express it, of scenes from the Old Testament to holy simplicity that purifies the mind and promotes concentration in prayer! Be that as it may, our Most Reverend Mother Abbess tends to agree with me. As you are aware, she has not been well lately and does not concern herself with such decisions of minor importance at this time."

Columba lowered her face over her embroidery to hide the tears welling in her eyes as she thought of the frescoes hidden behind wall hangings or baroque paintings clashing with the Gothic architecture's simplicity. And to think of such an act as "of minor importance!" She felt akin to the figure of Mary below the cross, whose heart was pierced by a sword, then was ashamed to compare her chagrin to that of Christ's mourning mother. Equally disturbing was something else Gabriela's words revealed. The talented and highly artistic abbess, who had done much to beautify the church and appreciated the vivid colors and joyful representations of the worldlier baroque, had apparently succumbed to the influence of advisers without artistic understanding. Columba sadly took it as another harbinger of events to come and knew that her critical remark had further estranged her from one of the "powers behind the throne."

All was not sadness, though, in her life. Antonia's gay personality and happy banter with which she tried to lift her friend's spirits was always welcome. And she loved Maria Anna, whose beautiful soprano was the perfect counterbalance to her alto voice in the choir. Their closeness was frowned upon by some, though no one ever dared criticize power cliques uniting relatives. Columba and her two friends did not "belong" and knew they could not openly show their mutual affection. These conditions caused Columba to become increasingly restive, and minor confrontations between her and others of the choir increased in frequency and gravity. She did remain uncompromising in her dedication to the Gregorian chant and tended to be unreasonable in her arguments defending this form of music. She considered choir service and chant inseparable and contemptuously dismissed objections by the sisters that it put too much strain on their vocal cords because of the lower key. Some of the women began to call her "batty" and "cracked," and most thought her difficult to get along with.

In time, Columba became interested in an activity that intrigued her. The abbess had decided to use material and jewels from Agatha's bridal gown for embellishing a pieta and commissioned a special case from a master carpenter to enshrine the figure. She personally designed Mary's regal robe and crown as well as elegant flourishes and blossoms to decorate the frame and granted Columba's request to participate in executing the project. Though not particularly fond of embroidery, Columba found consolation for her sad memories of Agatha's suffering in the work and dedicated every stitch to the departed girl. She knew that some of the others were more skilled in this regard and bravely curbed her impatience and difficulty to sit still for long hours. She and Antonia reembroidered the heavy brocade with fine gold thread and sewed jewels into the pattern, slow and tedious work that needed dedication and patience. Columba was very proud when her efforts elicited praise from the abbess. She appreciated without envy that Antonia's fingers were more skillful and nimble, but she put her heart into the task, and the two women worked well together.

One hot summer afternoon, Columba had just completed a particularly difficult flourish in fine shadings of gold and silver thread that completed the Virgin's robe. The few women working on the pieta were most anxious to finish the project by August 15, the important feast of Mary's Assumption into heaven.

The windows of the large room where the women assembled for their handicrafts and embroideries during afternoon recreation were open, but no breeze brought relief from the stifling summer heat, only a scent of hay drying in the fields drifted in. Maria Scholastica read from writings of St. Benedict, and her voice droned on monotonously. Columba found the excited chirping of swallows darting to and from their nests below the eaves a welcome distraction. Even though summer habits were made of lighter wool, they were still uncomfortable on hot days. Columba sighed as she cut the thread and rubbed her moist fingers on a linen kerchief.

"I'm glad that's done," she said to Antonia in a low voice. "I think we can finish in time, don't you agree?"

Before Antonia could answer, Maria Gabriela said sharply, "There are those among us anxious to hear the words of the great saint who gave his name to our order, and we are asking that their wish be respected!"

She walked across the room and leaned over Antonia's shoulder. Gabriela was skilled at embroidery and critically wrinkled her brow.

"These stitches are too far apart," she said, pointing to Columba's work but addressing herself to Antonia. "You will have to correct them, Maria Antonia, or find a way to hide them. Such work is unworthy to adorn our heavenly Mother!"

Columba had learned to accept criticism and might have reacted differently had Gabriela addressed her and not discussed her work with Antonia as if she did not exist. As it happened, Gabriela's voice was deliberately sweet, and those not close enough to overhear the conversation had to assume she was having a pleasant exchange with Antonia. Perhaps, the tension of the hot afternoon and approaching thunderstorm contributed, but Antonia's effort to squeeze Columba's hand under the table failed to calm her temper and frustration.

"You're wrong," she said in a loud voice holding up the embroidery before Gabriela's face. "Look at it closely, Maria Gabriela! There's absolutely no space between those threads! Mother Abbess has commended me on this other flourish I did exactly the same way! Why is it that I can never do anything right in your eyes?"

Scholastica let the book drop onto her knees, and all eyes were directed toward them. Columba's face was flushed, her eyes large and angry. No one moved, and in the momentary silence, the chirping of the swallow chicks greeting their parents' arrival at the nest seemed overly loud. Antonia tugged Columba's sleeve and whispered, "Columba, please, I'll—"

But Columba brushed off her hand and carried on as agitated as before.

"No, Antonia, you won't! I will not allow you to redo my work because it is fine the way it is! Mother Abbess has said so herself! I just want to know what I have done to Gabriela that she tries to insult me!"

Gabriela was not easily excitable and able to exercise considerable self-control. She was well aware that talking over Columba's head to Antonia would irritate the sister she disliked, though she'd been unprepared for so passionate a reaction. She coolly pushed away the embroidery work and said with forced patience, "Dearest Sister Maria Columba, I cannot imagine why you are so agitated! I was discussing Antonia's work, and you decide to accuse me of not liking you! Besides," she added nonchalantly, "Reverend Mother Abbess told me you are only tolerated on this project because of your pity for that strange girl, who deliberately concealed her deformity and ill health! She must have known that she would never have been accepted in our abbey with those horrible bouts of colic. Perhaps, she even knew her father would never pay, which caused us considerable expense for her training and care and laying her to rest. Just think of the cost of a coffin nowadays!"

Columba could not believe her ears. Her voice was icy in its cold fury as she again held the embroidery before Gabriela's face.

"Are you telling me, sister, that this magnificent material and these precious jewels are not compensation enough for what little we could do for a loving young woman, who wished to dedicate herself to Christ? Would you really have postponed her profess in the face of death for lousy two thousand florins? Yes," she added, looking intently into Gabriela's eyes, "yes, I suppose you would have let her die. Your heart is really that cold!"

There was an audible gasp in the room, and Gabriela turned on her heel and left the room with dignified, measured steps. Columba stared after her for a few moments then sat down and angrily looked at her work, too upset to continue. Scholastica timidly picked up the book and resumed reading. Antonia squeezed Columba's hand and silently mouthed the words, "Go in the garden," but Columba shook her head, too proud to leave the battlefield to wagging tongues. The afternoon wore on, and the bell rang to signal the end of recreation time. The women put away their work and utensils and, without looking at Columba, headed for the cloisters and onto the choir loft. Gabriela appeared last and joined the choir as usual. Columba had trouble concentrating, her mind in turmoil over the undeserved insult. It never occurred to her that the other women, who only were aware of Gabriela's pleasant voice speaking to Antonia, were aghast at her angry and hostile reaction. To them, Gabriela had acted normal, Columba unjustifiably rude. The women led a quiet, uneventful life, and a quarrel always intrigued them, especially when one party was powerful and the other considered a bit "wacky" and without influence. At the conclusion of the service, when most women headed for the garden for a brief stroll before their evening meal, Columba noticed Gabriela whispering to several of her closest friends, and they all headed toward the abbess's quarters. She knew that Maria Henrica was suffering from another one of her painful attacks and had not left her cell for several days. She still felt justified in defending her position, and even the pained compassion in Maria Anna's large blue eyes gave her no cause for concern.

A lay nun intercepted her with a folded and sealed message, as she was about to enter the refectory for the evening meal. She whispered that it was from the abbess and was to be opened right away. Columba stepped into a window niche, broke the seal, and read, "It has been reported to me that you once again have conducted yourself inappropriately. You shall withdraw to your cell forthwith and not participate in any activity besides choir duty until you appear before me tomorrow after High Mass. Abbess Maria Henrica, Countess von Poppen."

Columba read the note several times over, failing to comprehend. What did Maria Gabriela tell the abbess and why was she, Columba, not given a chance to speak her part? Did the chapter dislike her that much that no one would speak up and disclose

Gabriela's insulting behavior? Missing the evening meal was the least of her punishments, her inner turmoil too great to be hungry. "The tower," was all she could think of, she'd find her equilibrium there in the quiet summer dusk, refreshed by a heavy thunderstorm that had cleared the atmosphere during vespers. She waited until the last choir woman had entered the refectory then walked through the cloister garden, where raindrops glistened in the evening sun. She hesitated at the reflection tower, not wanting to look at Henrica's or her own painting tonight! All she wanted was to find peace, and she walked along the wall to the hermit tower. Seated on the cool stone bench, she watched the river turn first gold then red in the setting sun and was reminded of the summer evening when she first arrived. The view did not calm or inspire her to pray as in the past. She tried to sing a favorite chant, a psalm, but could not control her voice. Over and over, she read the stern note and suddenly became aware that her visit to the tower violated Maria Henrica's order to withdraw to her cell. Tears rolled down her cheeks.

"Oh, dear God, why am I here? Why was I not born a peasant girl living a simple life in Transylvania among people with compassion and understanding for one another?"

There were no answers to such questions, and asking them was futile. Prayer, she thought, would help her regain equilibrium, and she went to her cell and spent hours on her knees before the crucifix, but neither the suffering Christ on His cross nor the benignly smiling Child Jesus brought solace. She recalled Brother Sebastian in Vienna when he spoke about the human heart and mind being prone to doubt and periods of depression and turmoil. He'd said it was the devil dwelling within the soul and that conquering him made one stronger and better. "But it isn't the devil who's attacking me," said her inner voice, "it's one of my sisters in Christ!" It had begun a good day, and she'd been proud to create something beautiful in memory of Agatha! Surely, the devil would not hide in the person of a choir woman to hurt her. And if that were so, why had not Gabriela fought the urge to speak her callous words? "Because she is just as prone to temptation as you are," her conscience answered, "and how otherwise would the devil approach you but in the person of someone you did not suspect?" Loving her sisters and forgiving their shortcomings and petty rivalries had caused Columba difficulty in the past. She'd left Transylvania a child, became a young adult in Vienna, and was now a woman. Columba was genuinely pious and so accustomed to her rigorously scheduled days that it would have been difficult for her to imagine any other life. She'd never been exposed to temptations of a sexual kind and was completely naïve in that respect; love of music so filled her mind that all other feelings were relegated into the background. Yet she was still young at heart and often tempted to give in to her tendency of playing a little joke on one or the other of her sisters, convinced they would fall into her trap, but had forced such thoughts to remain playful fantasy. She would dutifully confess them and once even caught a fleeting smile on a priest's face when she told him what she almost did. He gave her only a mild penance.

She finally undressed and washed her tired face before going to bed, aware that she had missed Komplet. There was a small mirror above the washstand, and Columba took it off the wall and carried it over to the oil lamp for a close look at her face. She usually avoided looking at her reflection without veil or nightcap because she had never totally resigned herself to the loss of her hair. The lay nuns were skilled in keeping it as short as possible, but Columba had neglected to have it done for some weeks. Her head was covered with tiny curls, but she hardly noticed them as she examined her features. She was surprised at the deep circles below unnaturally large eyes. *And my nose is getting longer all the time*, she thought. *I'm so ugly I never would have found a husband to take care of me anyway! Becoming a nun was the only option I had.*

It became a long night without sleep, and she welcomed the bell calling for midnight Mass and early prim. After the eight o'clock litany, she remained on the choir loft unable to return to her cell. After the long night, daylight had not alleviated what seemed a hopeless situation. She prayed then carefully selected the words with which she would present her side of the scene to the abbess. After thinking it through, she could barely wait for High Mass to end. Maria Anna was absent, and most of the sisters seemed to avoid her, but Antonia stayed close while they filed out, and Columba looked at her with questioning eyes. Antonia briefly squeezed her hand and answered by ever so slightly shaking her head to observe the strict rule of silence at that hour. The women headed for the refectory for their midday meal, and Columba directed her steps toward the abbess's office. She was hungry after her fast of twenty-four hours and once again carefully searched for the right words, for surely being a choir woman would allow her to present her side. She took a deep breath and knocked. Her heart sank when she heard a harsh, "You may enter," which as soon as Columba had closed the door behind her was followed by the stern command, "Kneel, Maria Columba!"

She knew that she was not permitted to address Maria Henrica without being spoken to first, and as she waited with bowed head, she felt like an aspirant again. When she finally raised her eyes to the pale woman in the large, elaborately carved chair befitting a duchess of the realm, she realized how ill Maria Henrica looked. Her skin had a sickly yellow tinge, and her hands grasped the armrests to support her stiffly upright position. Columba's heart went out to the woman for whom she had a deep and respectful affection, and she impulsively asked, "Most Reverend Mother Abbess, are you unwell? May I—"

"Be silent, Maria Columba!" said Maria Henrica. "If I am unwell, it is because I am deeply grieved about your conduct! You have once again without provocation offended a sister in Christ with inappropriate words and behavior. Other sisters have told me that Maria Gabriela engaged in an innocent discussion with Maria Antonia about embroidery work, yet you felt compelled to attack her with harsh words, as you have others in the past. What is it that causes you to forget your promise of love and affection to all and makes you act in such ways?"

Henrica paused with labored breath, her face slightly flushed by anger.

"Reverend Mother Abbess, if you ask Maria Antonia, she will—"

"I ordered you to be silent, Maria Columba. Reflecting on your lack of love and consideration was not a question!"

Columba stared at her in incredulity and fear. Would she not be given any chance to present her story when it was clear that no one but Antonia had actually overheard the conversation? Had she lost all goodwill from the abbess? A heavy silence descended on the dignified room with its beautiful antique furniture and heavy rugs, then Henrica spoke again, her tired and resigned voice sounding no less firm.

"I have given prayerful consideration through the night of what your punishment should be, which, according to our tradition, is decided by the prioress who deferred to me. If our community is to be meaningful, then love, mutual respect, and affection must rule. Outbreaks such as yours are apt to destroy this rule, and this I shall not allow. I have decided to be lenient one last time, Maria Columba, but I pray you mend your ways. You will fast on only water until after High Mass tomorrow. For one full week, you will spend your recreation hours on your knees in church praying for divine help and ask your father confessor tonight for a harsh penance. Your sisters are delaying their meal today to pray for your soul. Therefore, you will immediately proceed from here to the refectory to formally ask your loving Sister Maria Gabriela's forgiveness. During the meal, you will read to them passages from the rules of our revered St. Benedict regarding punishment of unruly religious persons."

There was another pause, and Columba tried to suppress tears of shock and anger and to swallow the lump in her throat. When she finally concluded, Henrica seemed exhausted.

"Yesterday, you have disobeyed my order to go to your cell and instead went to the hermit tower, breaking the vow of obedience. Therefore, I forbid you to walk in the gardens and approach either tower for four weeks. You may go to the refectory now, so your sisters need wait no longer."

Columba swallowed then whispered, "Thank you, Reverend Mother Abbess," and—rising slowly from her knees—approached to kiss the abbess's ring. But both Henrica's hands were grasping the armrests, indicating that Columba had not been forgiven. She bowed and, when the door closed behind her, leaned against the wall to collect herself. She felt like in a bad dream, weak and exhausted from hunger and lack of sleep. *Perhaps, it is just a dream*, she thought, *from which I will awake on the way to the refectory.* But when she reached the threshold and faced the assembled choir women standing in their places like a black wall of reproach, she knew it was reality from which there was no escape. Moving mechanically in small steps like an inanimate mannequin, she approached Gabriela and said in a monotone voice, "I ask forgiveness for what I said to you."

Gabriela seemed to have expected a more elaborate excuse, but when Columba fell silent, she said sweetly, "I have prayed to our heavenly bridegroom, and His grace has lightened my chagrin. May He shed His mercy on you, Sister Maria Columba."

Columba thought that she was indeed in desperate need of Christ's mercy in order to continue living in this community. She silently turned and headed toward the lector's chair, where the book of rules, which St. Benedict had proclaimed in the seventh century and a monk had written down after the saint's death, lay open. The appropriate passage was indicated with a bookmark, and Columba read aloud about punishments to be inflicted upon monks or nuns for transgressions of various kinds. Fasting and exercises of penance, such as prolonged kneeling and prayer, were recommended, as well as humiliation before the assembled chapter similar to what she had just been ordered to do. But the rules also stipulated floggings on the bare back in the presence of all sisters, even isolation in a separate cell amounting to virtual imprisonment. Columba felt a cold tingle down her spine. What type of punishment had the abbess considered when she said that she'd opted for leniency? Being flogged on her exposed back?

The meal seemed interminable and the scent of food a torture, but she continued stoically in a monotone voice until all rose for closing prayers. She went to church to examine her conscience for the special confession she had been ordered to make before vespers then returned to her cell for a drink of water. When she turned the corner of the corridor, she saw Antonia come out of her cell and disappear behind her own door. Columba found a small bundle tied in a linen kerchief on her nightstand with a thick slice of bread and hastily scribbled note, "It's all I could get, but know that you are loved. Anna is ill, she prays for you with all her heart." This simple act of kindness and love by which Antonia chanced severe punishment if caught and the news of Anna's suffering released Columba's tension, and she began to sob, overwhelmed by sorrow, humiliation, fatigue, and shame for indulging in her own troubles when dear Anna suffered. Calming down, she realized how very hungry she was and looked at the bread. She was under orders to fast, but were bread and water not a form of fasting? Columba was honest enough to admit to herself that she had perhaps overreacted to Gabriela's words but, like on previous occasions, was deeply hurt that she was always the one punished even when clearly provoked. She heartily bit into the bread, which tasted more delicious than cake and drank several goblets of water. After her sparse meal, she desperately wanted to visit Anna in the infirmary, sit by her bedside, hold her hand, and pray for her friend's health. Yet the abbess's firm command was to spend her recreation hours in church praying for her own soul, so she washed her tearstained face, smoothed her veil, and walked through the cloisters. The August sun was still hot, and the church felt comfortingly cool. She descended the spiral staircase leading to the nave, headed for the foundress's altar, and looked up to meet the Virgin's steady gaze, which today impressed her as kind and understanding, not reproachful as it had sometimes in the past. Columba prayed fervently, not for her soul and the faults of her heart as ordered but for Maria Anna. There was a slight rustle as Antonia came to kneel beside her and whispered, "Maria Anna is begging for a visit from you, and Mother Abbess has granted her request. Come with me, Columba."

When the two women stepped into the cloisters, Antonia said, "Anna is coughing blood and running a high fever. You're not relieved of choir duty altogether, and I'm told you are to have confession later, but you may spend until vespers at her bedside. She wishes to see no one but you."

"Antonia, how seriously ill is she?" Columba asked.

Her friend shrugged. "It's one of her serious bouts of consumption, but infirmary magistra has strong medicine, and she is young. They hope you will persuade her to take some nourishment that she has refused. And," she added with a rueful little smile, "there's something else. I presented your embroidery to sub-prioress, telling her that I redid your work, which I didn't, and she thought it was really

349

beautiful. May God forgive the lie, I'll confess it on Saturday, but I think you had indeed done extremely well, and Sister Agatha in heaven will know the truth! We don't have much time left until the fifteenth, and you're not allowed to join us. So I brought the veil and lace and what you need to complete it and hope you won't let me down and work on it while you're keeping watch with Anna. Will you help me, dear sister?"

Columba was deeply touched that Antonia understood how much it meant to her to complete this work in tribute to Agatha. It would have deeply grieved her to see it finished by someone else. She spontaneously hugged Antonia, took the small pouch with the materials from her, and said, "You are a saint, dearest sister, you've saved me from starvation of the body and now of the mind. How can I ever thank you enough?"

Antonia turned and quickly walked away to hide her own emotion.

Maria Anna's face was as white as the pillows propping her up to help her breathing. Her blue eyes were feverish, but the lovely face framed by the starched wimple was of almost transcendental beauty. *She looks like an angel,* thought Columba, quickly shaking off the foreboding thought.

"Oh, dear Sister Columba, I see that Mother Abbess has granted my wish! I'm so grateful," said Maria Anna, her words ending in a coughing spell, and Columba quickly took a linen cloth to wipe driblets of blood from the pale lips.

"You mustn't speak, beloved sister, it irritates the lungs! I too am so happy to be with you."

Magistra Xaveria entered. "Maria Anna is quite ill and will not improve unless she takes some nourishment, which I trust you will persuade her to, Maria Columba," she said, handing the choir woman a bowl of semolina cooked in milk and sweetened with honey. "She needs to gain strength and calm her stomach so it can retain the strong medicine I have prescribed. Mother Abbess gave permission for you to be with her between services, and I trust you will be of help. I shall return with the medicine in a little while."

She left and Columba took a spoon and said, "Maria Anna, you can only get well if you help along the way! Now be my good little sister and take a few spoonfuls!"

Anna smiled and obediently opened her mouth as Columba fed her like a child while cheerfully chatting about embroidery work and how important it was for Anna to fully recover by Assumption Day so her lovely voice could join with the choir in praise of Mary ascending to heaven. Anna was swallowing the last spoonful when Xaveria returned with a goblet of strong tincture. The magistra did not hide her satisfaction.

"You're a good sick nurse, Maria Columba," she said approvingly. "You've accomplished what I was not able to do. Now let me watch you drink this, Maria Anna, it tastes bitter, but it will calm your cough and make you sleep!"

Anna never took her eyes off Columba's face, nor did she grimace drinking the bitter concoction. When the goblet was empty, Columba gave her water to chase the aftertaste then fluffed her pillows and smoothed the sheets.

"Now you must rest, dear," she said. "I will be right by your side until vespers and will return before Komplet."

And the exhausted Anna slept while Columba opened the pouch and worked, meticulously and with invisible stitches attaching gold lace to the Virgin's veil. The patient slept through the vespers bell, and Columba left her under the watch of a trained lay nun. At the end of the service, Columba went to the old cross in the church apses that Maria Anna loved so much and knelt on the stone floor.

"Jesus, Lord and Savior," she prayed, "I kneel before you and cry out that your suffering redeem my sins. Send me the Holy Spirit to fill my heart with wisdom so I can comprehend the depth of my guilt! When I feel superior to others, have I nailed your hands and feet to the cross with my thoughts and scourged you with my pride? Does breaking my vow of obedience crown you once again with thorns? Yet I love you with all my heart, my Redeemer and bridegroom of my soul, and resolve to show my love by trying to better my heart and soul and become worthy of your forgiveness. Punish me, O my Lord, and I will humbly accept it, but I beg you, grant that my beloved Sister Maria Anna recover so she again may raise her voice in your praise. O Lord, have mercy on my soul!"

She rose and went to confession, humbly accusing herself of resentment and unkind thoughts toward some of her sisters. The Supremus was indisposed, and the younger monk representing him in the confessional surprised Columba with gentle admonition and a light penance. She returned to the cross, prayed her penance, and renewed her pious dedication.

"Dearest Jesus, you paid with every drop of your blood, every pain of your passion for the redemption of my sins. You accepted my shortcomings as if they were gifts and requited them with your grace. Mary, my beloved Mother, I weep for the pain I have caused you and your precious Son with my transgressions of thought and word. But your son did not suffer in vain, for I firmly resolve to become a better person. I only ask you, Mother in heaven, shed your grace upon your daughter Maria Anna. Amen."

Anna peacefully slept through Komplet, and the watching lay nun said that she had not opened her eyes during Columba's absences.

"Rev'rend Mother Antonia's been visitin'," she said. "An' she left this pouch with mo' embroid'ry work. Rev'rend Mother Magistra won't return, she says you send for me when you need help."

The nun withdrew and Columba opened the pouch to find a small sourdough cake studded with raisins. She resumed work on the veil, but when dusk fell, the oil lamp did not shed sufficient light for the delicate work, and Columba suddenly felt very tired. She leaned her head against the back of the chair and dozed until the bell awakened her for midnight Mass and, opening her eyes, saw Anna smiling at her.

"Thank you for being with me all this time, dear sister," she said. "I feel much better because of it. It is time for midnight Mass, but will you return when it is over? I know I'm selfish for you must be very tired, but your presence is such comfort to me."

Columba took one of Anna's white hands into hers. "Of course, I shall return! You have made me so happy by asking for me, and there is nothing I wish for more fervently than your quick recovery. I will pray for you then hurry back, and sister will prepare some food for you to eat. Now rest and God bless!" She made the sign of the cross on Anna's forehead and kissed her cheek.

Anna did recover within a week, largely because, as Magistra Xaveria grudgingly allowed, Columba's presence, the only one who could persuade her to eat and drink the bitter tinctures. When Anna left the infirmary to return to her cell, Columba again spent her recreation hours in church as the abbess had decreed. During her vigil at the sickbed, Columba had used every moment of daylight to complete the Virgin's veil. And when finally she was permitted to join her sisters again, she and Antonia spent every free moment to complete their work. The wooden shrine with its glass front had been delivered. The background for the pieta was a burst of brightly gilded rays carved from wood signifying heavenly glory. The figures of Virgin and Son were no great work of art, that of Christ too small in proportion and lacking detail, though its white stiffness conveyed a finality of death. The Virgin was holding one of her son's arms to her heart, and the lifeless fingers seemed to reach out as if trying to grasp something—was it life? Most touching was the expression of unspeakable grief on the Virgin's face, framed by a carved wimple similar to that of a nun. The embroidered fabric veil was draped over it with the gold lace caressing the cheeks. The two women tenderly dressed the figure in the exquisite gown and arranged folds and veil with loving patience then stiffened the materials by brushing them with a solution of starch and water. A gilded crown embellished with jewels from Agatha's dress was secured on the Virgin's head and the pieta placed into the shrine. They made final adjustments to a garland of silk leaves and flowers and attached the glass cover. The impression of the work was one of deep chagrin as well as regal splendor, symbols of death and glory. When Jesus was placed upon Mary's lap after being taken from the cross, she surely wore no princely clothes or crown as she held the stiff, lifeless body of her beloved son for the last time. Were the rays of an invisible, golden sun rising in the background a precursor of His resurrection, the splendor of the Virgin's gown one of coming joy and glory? And the crown on the obedient handmaiden's head a symbol that she would become Queen of heaven?

Columba and Antonia felt a great sense of accomplishment about their work. They received much praise, especially from those outside family cliques. The shrine was ceremoniously carried into the church on Assumption Day, traditionally celebrated with a special High Mass. The choir women, joined by a still pale but sufficiently recovered Anna, watched from their loft as the procession moved through the nave to the sanctuary and a waiting Supremus, who blessed the shrine prior to ceremoniously placing it on a side altar. The voices of the choir joined the organ in the rousing music of a Latin Mass. It was a happy day for Columba. She derived joy and a sense of accomplishment from work, which she usually was not fond of, Maria Anna seemed recovered and the music of this particular Mass was one of her favorites.

On this feast day the chapter assembled for a festive meal of many courses, presided over by the abbess making her first appearance in almost three weeks. Her face was still drawn and the color of parchment, but her demeanor and movements were strong and controlled. She personally addressed each choir woman at one time or other during the banquet, including Columba, for whom she had appreciative words about her work on the shrine. When the meal was over and the women left for their recreation time, Maria Henrica motioned Columba to her side and said evenly, "On this special day of our heavenly Mother's Assumption into heaven, I shall lift your penance. You may join your sisters for a walk in the park, but you may not visit the towers. Tomorrow, you will resume spending your recreation periods in contemplation of your conduct."

If Columba had hoped to see a glimmer of warmth or affection in Henrica's eyes, she was disappointed. She answered, "Thank you, Reverend Mother Abbess," bowed, and went into the park. Confinement to the indoors during the past weeks had been harsh punishment for her vigorous constitution and spending the next hour walking about brought relief. Yet Henrica's cool demeanor without sign of forgiveness discouraged and dampened her spirits. Would she ever be able to regain Henrica's good graces, which she felt she'd had both as aspirant and novice? She tried to console herself with music, the one bright aspect of her monastic life. If only her sisters would share her passion for the Gregorian chant more fervently!

In later years, Maria Barbara, Countess Wildenstein, became choir magistra. She was a strong woman with a ruddy complexion, a good ear for music, and a forceful voice that matched her personality. Maria Barbara spoke her mind and could rarely be persuaded to change it, irrespective of approval. She was in her sixties and came from a wealthy Styrian family. She and her younger sister Maria Amalia entered Göss as children seven and eight years old. Amalia was her opposite, small and thin and prone to colds associated with severe, chronic catarrh. She had a charming personality paired with a gentle and amiable manner, and everyone had liked the frail young woman. The sisters brought a generous dowry of several thousand Florins, large diamond rings, exquisite gowns and a yearly stipend. Amalia died at age twenty-six prior to Columba's arrival at Göss when one of her severe catarrhs turned into pneumonia. Some choir women still spoke about how deeply she was mourned at the time.

Maria Barbara had held various offices over the years, such as magistra for the gardens, the library and sacristan. She now dedicated herself with great vigor to the choir, but like her predecessor Philippina, her strength lay in rousing hymns that suited her voice and were less demanding than the Gregorian chant that under her leadership suffered another setback. Of course, the chanted litanies and responses at Mass remained, but the beauty of Gregorian music is revealed in psalms and longer segments of the Mass, not in brief responses or the invocation of saints. The trend deeply saddened Columba. Of course, she sang even hymns better than most others, but her love belonged to the chant, and she never ceased to advocate it, unfortunately not always in the most diplomatic way.

Individual notes in the Gregorian chant were held longer and the key was lower, making it more demanding on the vocal cords of women, which was why monks excelled in it. And the voices of many choir women, particularly during the cold and damp season, were already strained by the many daily hours of singing. It was therefore not surprising that Columba's efforts to promote the chant met with resentment. Abbess Maria Henrica decreed that each woman be excused from choir duty one day a week to "sleep the night," but it was only partial relief.

Columba's disenchantment with Göss increased over the years. Her mind rebelled against the repetitive conformity of her daily schedule, made bearable only because of her joy of singing. With advancing maturity, her active intelligence sought challenges, and she tried to find them in reading. Her speaking voice was well modulated, and she frequently volunteered to read to her sisters while they engaged in handicraft, which lost attraction for her once the memorial for Agatha was completed. Columba sensed that she was unpopular and began to feel isolated and suffered periods of deep melancholy during which even Antonia's cheerful banter or Anna's abiding affection failed to reach her closed mind. Life was but an endless cycle of services with saints or holy days anteceded by fasting and celebrated by more and even longer services. Then there were the cold winters that confined everyone indoors. Investitures and professions added new faces to the chapter without changing its milieu, and illness and death entailed processions to the crypt to escort sisters to their final resting place. Each time Columba descended to that place permeated with the musty odor of death and intoned the ancient prayers commending the soul of the departed sister to her Savior, her eyes focused on the lone spiral column, and she prayed for release from her torturous confinement. Would the flame of her prayer reach God? One day, she became aware that unlike those in the church, the crypt column's spirals did not transcend into Gothic ribs as they did in the church where the flames of prayer flowed toward the vaulted ceiling that symbolized heaven. Instead, the spirals in the crypt ended abruptly where a crumbling mortar revealed exposed, uneven stones. It seemed like a barrier between spiral and vault, a barrier her prayers could not surmount, a rejection of her hopes, the harsh verdict to bear her cross.

There also were times when she felt guilty about her discontent. She was in vigorous health with a strong constitution that withstood disrupted nights, lack of sleep, and bitterly cold winters. Many of her sisters were not so fortunate, yet most bore their afflictions with humble devotion and offered them to God as a willing sacrifice to gain better understanding of Christ's suffering. Maria Anna did so when undergoing excruciating attacks of cough and fever as her frail constitution slowly succumbed to the cruel and fairly common illness of consumption that had taken her mother's life at an early age and was nearly always terminal. Anna never complained, and her lovely soprano revealed no trace of the pain that singing often caused her. Her feverish eyes would glow with devotion to the Virgin, and Columba thought that she sounded like an angel.

One of the few choir women Columba liked and admired was Maria Constantia, Countess Welsersheimb, whose sister Catharina died of consumption. Constantia and her sister had never been part of a family group, and after her sister's death, she sought isolation from the community and shed many tears meditating on the sufferings of her heavenly bridegroom. Her heart was full of kindness and love. She sought out ways to humbly serve her sisters and never refused a favor. She had devoted herself entirely to her ill sister's care and only left her bedside to attend services. Lack of sleep and exhaustion caused a near collapse after Catharina's death, yet she refused to rest.

"My small tribulations and sorrows cannot compare to what my Savior suffered for me," she said when the prioress urged her to rest. And she was in dire need of rest, for she too appeared to be in the early stages of tuberculosis. On a spring evening when she felt particularly discontent and restive, Columba headed for the reflection tower. As she climbed the stairs, she heard a voice and, recognizing it as Maria Constantia's, held her step not to disturb the praying nun. She recognized the words of a psalm and the piety and devotion with which they were spoken touched her deeply.

"Again, a day has passed, that You, O Lord, have given. Let me thank You for the blessings Your love grants me with each passing hour. Though night descends upon me, I have no fear, for You are with me and Your hands protect the just and of goodwill. You are merciful toward the good, faithful toward the true, and like a shield, am I surrounded by Your grace."

A feeling of shame welled up in Columba. Constantia had lost a beloved sister and already showed signs of the same illness, likely facing the same slow and excruciating death. Yet here she was, thanking God for the blessings each hour brought! What strength of character to accept pain and suffering as a blessing! Columba did not think she possessed such fortitude. She never voluntarily inflicted physical pain upon herself as penance or to purify her mind. There were whispered rumors about choir women devoted to self-flagellation and the masochistic pleasure derived from the practice. Columba asked herself whether a merciful God would demand physical torture and why it would please Him that Abbess Henrica wore a bracelet with barbs penetrating the flesh, rendering her life a continuous agony. Columba desperately searched for answers to such questions and found none. The bishop's words at her investiture still rang in her ears. He'd said that a person dedicated to religious life was nearer and more precious to God. Did that include hypocrites who gave false witness such as Bernarda or Gabriela, and were they better in God's eyes than a selfless, loving soul like the ayah or her revered papa?

Columba rested her elbows on the rough bricks of a window and stood watching the season's first two blackbirds darting back and forth as they built their nest. They too were God's creatures, and what did He demand of them? "He gave you intelligence and a mind to distinguish between good and evil, whereas they only act on instinct," the voice within her answered. Suddenly, Constantia stood behind her.

"Is it you, Maria Columba, and did I take your place in the tower? I know how much you love coming here and the place does inspire meditation and prayer! But you look sad, dear sister, is there something I can help you with?"

Columba shook her head. "No, Maria Constantia, I came here to rest and overheard your prayers. How I wish I had such abiding devotion! The tower belongs to all of us, and I am glad you share my love for it. Your words have given me the answers I came to find, so let us return, it is time for vespers."

The two choir women walked side by side to yet another service. Columba continued to search for a purpose in her life, something meaningful to which she could devote herself since her love of music seemed so misplaced. She had very little contact with Sigismunda, though she thought of her often. Her sister appeared to be blissfully content with her life as an Ursuline nun teaching children. Columba's contemplative order limited charitable activities to distributing alms on special occasions or dispensation of medicines and herbs from the pharmacy. The education of aspirants and candidates for choir women was primarily in the hands of priests. Now that Columba no longer had the respect and affection of her abbess and two of the most influential choir women as adversaries, there was little chance she would ever be appointed to an office. Her hope to one day lead the choir or play the organ had been dashed with Maria Barbara's appointment. She thought that perhaps Xaveria would train her in the pharmacy or allow her to work in the infirmary, where she had felt competent caring for Agatha and occasionally for Anna. Magistra Xaveria had in the past appreciated her assistance and was an influential member of the abbess's court. Even this prospect fizzled when she learned that the abbess had agreed to accept a common-born candidate for that position. Margaretha Michaeler was the daughter of a physician serving a Catholic foundation for noble ladies at Hall in Tirol. He'd trained his only daughter in the arts of medicine and pharmacy, and she was said to be especially proficient in bleeding techniques, a skill Xaveria was hesitant to apply. When Margaretha aspired to become a nun, the bishop of Brixen suggested Göss and wrote an ardent letter of recommendation to Henrica, who consulted with Maria Xaveria. Both felt that although Margaretha would only bring the modest dowry of two hundred florins and was without aristocratic background, her skills in the art of healing would be of great value to the abbey that never sought the services of a male physician. Margaretha soon became Novice Maria Bonaventura and, a year later, choir woman. She was a dedicated and hardworking person and, for her time, commanded considerable medical knowledge. True, her education was one-sided, and she showed little interest in church history or Latin nor was she interested in the arts or sang well. But she was a pious woman wanting to serve God and her sisters with all her heart, and they overlooked her lack of refined manners they had been taught from the cradle. She was put in charge of the pharmacy and introduced new herbs and medicines for manifold ailments.

Maria Xaveria appreciated Bonaventura's skills without envy, and the lay nuns gladly worked under her guidance in the herb garden and the infirmary, proud that a young woman of common birth had attained the precious status of choir woman. Her arrival put an end to Columba's hopes of working in the pharmacy, and as her frustrations and sense of uselessness grew, so did her eccentricity and feelings to be disliked and misunderstood. Gabriela and Bernarda, in many subtle and not-so-subtle ways, contributed to the unfortunate situation by making it known that Columba was difficult and unwelcome in their sphere of power. Over time, many of her sisters felt that Columba was indeed difficult. She could be arrogant and openly critical of those lacking musical talent. The fact that she was intelligent and well-educated should have qualified her for holding office, but it was evident that she no longer was in the abbess's good graces. Antonia and Anna remained her faithful friends and so were a very few others, who genuinely believed in sisterly love and harbored no ambitions. Yet even meek and gentle choir women now and then felt hurt by Columba's abruptness or harsh criticism. Indeed, only Anna's admiration and affection consistently overlooked Columba's dark moods. Antonia in her own humorous way tried to engage her friend in positive thoughts yet often with little success. Columba no longer participated in handicrafts and even withdrew from reading to her sisters unless assigned this duty during meals. She spent all her recreation time in the hermit tower brooding about her failed life and nurturing resentment and anger toward Gabriela and Bernarda. And so it came as a terrible blow to her when an ailing Maria Henrica in 1764 appointed Maria Gabriela Prioress and assigned her many of her powers and privileges too burdensome for her. Maria Gabriela now held the abbey's most influential position, and though no one would openly admit it, all but her closest friends lived in fear of her, not in the least because it was the prioress who meted out punishment for transgressions.

Maria Henrica's health declined further and she felt overwhelmed by the ever-greater involvement of government and its numerous decrees and new laws. She was only too glad to relegate handling of most administrative duties to the coolly intelligent

Gabriela. But she did not stop there. Plagued by frequent attacks of her gall bladder stones, she also left most internal affairs to the discretion of her prioress. Maria Bernarda as magistra noviciarum exercised considerable influence with the prioress, but even she was careful not to contradict Gabriela. All this brought deep divisions to the chapter between those who were part of the power group and those who were not. Only a few women remained so devoted to their faith and religious exercises that they took little notice of what was going on. Columba unfortunately was outspoken and rarely suppressed her criticism, even when not called for. Antonia would jokingly say, "Columba, my dear, age did not bring you wisdom! There's nothing to be gained by making them angry but trouble! You and I will never hold office or exercise influence, and life is so much easier when you don't provoke them 'cause they leave you alone. Just turn a deaf ear."

"But I just can't!" Columba would passionately reply. "Some of the things they say or want us do are blatantly stupid! They must realize that we do not have to comply with their every whim! We are entitled to think and should be permitted to express ourselves! I'm sure that many sisters agree with me."

"Columba, my dear," was the answer, "they may well agree, but they will never say so. Gabriela is in charge, for as we all know, our ailing abbess has never been fond of the controversy that comes with governing. And I shudder to think that if dear Maria Henrica were to leave us, Gabriela might well become our new abbess."

Columba heatedly replied, "Never! Too many choir women dislike her, and she'd never get a majority of votes! They're afraid of her now because of the power of her appointed position, but it'll be different when it comes to a secret ballot."

"Well"—shrugged Antonia—"be that as it may, it's not wise to make enemies from whom you cannot escape. I wish you would follow my advice, your life would be so much easier. Remember how long it took until your last request to draw from your spending money came through, whereas others are quickly approved? Think about it, Columba, and listen to me, I mean well."

Columba unfortunately would not listen, and as tensions within the chapter grew from year to year, she was often blamed for them. Neither Maria Anna's fervent prayers to the Virgin or Maria Antonia's friendly advice could change her negative attitude and more and more plunged her into periods of deep melancholy.

In 1777, Abbess Maria Henrica was sixty-eight years old, emaciated from an illness of three decades and cruel self-castigation. She was indeed not the only one to follow this practice. A decree of 1625 issued during a visitation encouraged the introduction of "Ceremoniae Regularis etc.," meaning ceremonial self-punishment to "regulate" personal thoughts and feelings. Such practices had originated in the Orient and were alien to the older church. They were introduced and promoted by the religious intensity if not fanaticism of the new orders, especially the Jesuits, who strongly believed physical pain to be a prerequisite for suppressing and controlling the senses. A relatively mild though by no means gentle form of such self-punishment was the "Zilizium" (shirt of penance), a garment of rough and hairy flax, which some choir women and lay nuns wore underneath their habits against the bare skin and which caused an excruciating itch and even open sores. Donning a Zilizium in lieu of the smooth linen garment normally worn was especially popular during Lent, another practice Columba never followed. There were rumors that some lay nuns wore metal belts around their waist similar to Henrica's bracelet, even more torturous for them since hard work from dawn to dusk meant constant movement and deeply embedded the metal thorns into the flesh. Neither old age nor illness could induce some women to abandon self-torture. Maria Xaveria often met with blatant refusal to accept medicines for an illness that the patient regarded as inflicted by God to atone for sins. Along the same vein, Maria Henrica suffered terrible thirst in addition to the pain during her attacks of gall bladder stones yet steadfastly refused a drink of cool water. She was to celebrate her golden profess that year, a half century of choir woman status at Göss. Many guests were invited to this rare celebration, which was set for May 15, and planning started at the beginning of the year. Members of her court conceived the idea of writing and performing a humorous sketch for Henrica's entertainment, and the entire chapter participated in the writing and performance, a welcome change of venue during the dark and dreary winter months. Throughout spring, the women devised small surprises and pleasures for their abbess. On May 1, the arrival of spring weather was traditionally celebrated with May Poles that were—and to this day are—erected on village squares; the nuns placed two small versions decorated with personal little gifts and treats into Henrica's cell.

Cloister rules were suspended to allow secular guest participation at the festivities. The magistrae of the kitchens spent long hours in consultation with the abbey's vendors discussing exotic and unusual ingredients for the special menus. They designed treats of giant proportions to hide surprises. The garden magistra planted flowers and seeds in the greenhouse hotbeds that would come to bloom at the special date, and the carpenter was ordered to construct a triumphal arch covered with blossoms for the abbess's entrance to the refectory.

The choir women dedicated their recreation time to rehearsing a recently written Mass by the composer Joseph Hayden. Columba found it enchanting and caught in the spirit of baroque music devoted herself to studying it with an enthusiasm she'd not experienced in years. Choir Magistra Maria Barbara came down suddenly with severe chest pains, and the magistra sacristan's hands were too crippled by arthritis to play the new music. Columba could barely suppress her joy when called upon to play the organ and direct the choir until Barbara's recovery. She had not been allowed to play for years and had lost a little of her technique, but by spending every free moment in practice, she quickly mastered the task.

Columba was now forty-seven and cold winters as well as damp weather had rendered her hands somewhat stiff, but she would not listen to Anna and Antonia urging her to preserve her strength for the actual event. Anna had again been plagued by her illness that winter, a great concern to Columba as well as many of the other sisters, for everyone loved the sweet and gentle young woman. Her tuberculosis, known as consumption because of the terrible way it eventually consumed those it struck, weakened her frail body by constant fever typical for the illness. Her soprano voice, however, was still lovely, though she needed all her will power and strength to control her painful breathing, an effort she was able to hide from everyone but Columba. The two women would admonish one another to preserve their strength, knowing full well that such urgings were not heeded. Both loved music too much and were determined to give it their best.

On the day preceding the festivities, Maria Henrica asked the Supremus to read a special Mass for her choir women in St. Michael's Chapel. Columba always savored time spent in the chapel and still derived delight and inspiration from the medieval frescoes. She especially loved the beautiful message of the south wall with its four scenes from the Song of Solomon. Other than psalms monastic life of the baroque discouraged or even prohibited texts of the Old Testament because of certain sexually explicit passages. Solomon's Song, however, narrates the faithful and chaste love between bride and groom that withstands temptation and trial. Church fathers interpreted it as a symbol of divine love, the spiritual marriage between God and His church and consequently between God and every loving and devout human being. The choice of these scenes to decorate the walls of a chapel in an abbey for Benedictine nuns devoted to contemplation, prayer, and total dedication to Christ was no accident. Mathew's gospel expresses this same thought of mythical brides of Christ when he tells of virgins awaiting their bridegroom with burning lamps in their hands. And David's psalms point to the union between Christ and his devout community: "Hear O daughter! Forget your people and your father's house. Your King and Master desires your beauty, follow Him!" (Psalm 44:11–12).

One wall divided by a narrow Gothic window was decorated in four segments, distinctly framed by red lines, though here and there a figure's arm or halo reached beyond them as if defying limits. There were two brides of God—tall, slender women, one white, the other black. The dark face was referred to in a passage of the high song, "I am black yet beautiful, you daughters of Jerusalem! Do not stare at me for being black, for the sun has colored my skin!" God gave this woman beauty of heart to replace the beauty of her skin that toil and suffering had taken away.

In Columba's eyes, the two lower sections depicting other scenes from the song were most beautiful of all. The bride pointing a lance to the heart of the groom related to the passage, "You have wounded my heart, O my sister, my bride! You wounded my heart by a single glance, a bending of your neck." The bridegroom Christ speaks of the wound of love to His heart by His bride, an eternal spiritual wound that elicits eternal reciprocal love. The lance is her eye forever seeking God, the bent neck her total obedience.

Another section represented the wedding and crowning of the bride by the groom placing a crown upon her head presaging the Virgin Mary becoming Queen of heaven. The demeanor of the bride is one of great humility while her hands reach for the scepter presented to her as a symbol of heaven's eternal glory.

The north wall depicted the annunciation of the birth of Mary to Anna and Joachim, the conversion of Thomas laying his hand in the wound of Jesus, and figures of two unknown bishops. A Latin inscription on this wall dedicates the chapel to the Archangel Michael and stipulates the date as the ninth year of the episcopate of Bishop Wernhard of Seckau, who had granted a special indulgence in honor of the archangel and all other angels. This placed the origin of the frescoes into the late thirteenth century, when Abbess Herburgis, represented in the crucifixion scene, likely commissioned the work. Though painted well after the chapel's construction, the frescoes were in perfect harmony with the original architecture, and half a millennium later, the vivid red and blue colors, the bright gold of halos, and ornamental ribs were as beautiful as ever. They never failed to inspire Columba, who on the rare occasions she was admitted to the chapel strove to imprint each detail in her heart for consolation during times of depression.

On the eve of the abbess's Jubilee, the choir women assembled in her private chapel. The bishop held a sermon, and Henrica spoke briefly about her love for her daughters and her concern about their well-being. She looked healthier than usual, perhaps buoyed by the excitement of the pending celebrations, and later, the voices of the choir filled the small chapel. Columba was last to leave; she felt as if held by an invisible hand, a voice asking her to stay. Since choir women other than members of the court rarely entered St. Michael's, Columba felt almost this being a farewell. She slowly walked along the walls and studied each segment to discover a new detail. Then she felt a presence and turning saw Maria Gabriela standing by the entrance, her beautiful face barely aged through the years.

"You are needed in the refectory, Maria Columba," she said evenly. There was a question in her large blue eyes. "Or are you searching for something in particular?"

Columba shook her head. "No, Mother Prioress, it's only that the beauty of these frescoes always awes me. I was about to leave, for I know I have the reading assignment."

Maria Gabriela seemed to stiffen. "It surprises me that you find them so inspiring if that is what you are trying to express. I rather consider them a distraction."

Columba inclined her head and, without answering, walked by the prioress to take her place in the refectory.

The following day was filled with festivities. After early morning services, Maria Henrica received delegations from the various hamlets of the abbey's land holdings with gifts and best wishes from their communities. A throng of common folk waited outside the gate and later crowded the courtyard and the parish church. The bishop of Admont celebrated High Mass in the magnificently decorated abbey church, assisted by the Supremus, abbey cleric, and visiting priests. The abbess was seated next to the bishop on the same elaborate chair she had occupied during her installation twenty-six years earlier. The bishop's lengthy sermon praised her virtues, wisdom, and dedication to high office. Columba recalled how hopeful she had been in 1751, expecting Henrica to be as loving and understanding an abbess as her predecessor Maria Antonia had been. The late abbess had also suffered from various illnesses yet, even when confined to bed during the last six months of her life, always took active interest in the well-being of her daughters.

The choir expressed jubilation over the unique occasion and at the conclusion of the service visitors, clerics, and lay nuns joined in a rousing Te Deum. Choir women and guests lined the way to toss flower petals at Maria Henrica's feet as she led bishop and priests to the refectory for the banquet. In the center of the refectory was a huge wooden vase filled with flowers, and when everyone was seated, a young boy emerged from between the blossoms to convey the best wishes of the hamlet. During the meal, a giant pie in the shape of a pheasant was wheeled in to reveal a young girl dressed as a shepherdess, who recited yet another festive poem. Course after course of special delicacies was served. And six children dressed as angels blowing trumpets emerged from yet another huge cake!

Those holding important secular offices for the abbey, such as the local administrator, the granary master, brewer, fishery master, and so forth performed "field music." Servants and lay nuns recited poems or sang songs they had composed with love and dedication. And the abbess accepted everything with goodwill and motherly love.

Even the weather cooperated with bright sunshine, and it became a perfect day of joy and contentment. The festivities lasted for three days, and in the province's capital of Graz, the newspaper dedicated a whole page to a detailed report. It was as if special blessings were shed upon the abbey of Göss for what had been sowed during nearly eight centuries. Five years later, the strike of an imperial pen would abruptly end it.

The Prisoner

Chapter 1

Villagers and townspeople talked for months about the golden profess, for many the most splendid celebrations in their lifetime. For the very first time, common folk had joined priests, choir women and lay nuns, abbey officials and servants in the preparation and execution of an event. And while the fun and joy came first and foremost for lay people, choir women also experienced it as a singular break in their monotonous life, a mental and spiritual challenge. Carrying off everything perfectly after months of planning and preparations filled them with a sense of accomplishment, the reward for successfully executing something important and exciting. Afterward, the abbey resumed its quiet routine, and only the lay nuns heaved a secret sigh of relief from months of crushing travail.

June and July of that year brought relentlessly hot days without cooling rains. The heat was even more stressful than cold winters because even nights were without respite. The heavy folds of the albeit lighter summer habits worn over linen shirts, not to speak of a heavy Zilizium, left the women very uncomfortable. Fans were considered frivolous, and some magistrae even frowned upon open windows. On a particularly steaming day in late July, a tense Columba was reading to her sisters busy with handicraft when Prioress Maria Gabriela appeared and walked from table to table to inspect progress and express praise or offer criticism and advice. Columba paused and reached for a drink of water to moisten her throat when Maria Gabriela said pleasantly, "Beloved sisters, our Reverend Mother Abbess has a wonderful surprise for us! When next you will visit her chapel, you will find it greatly changed and much more beautiful. It will only be another two or three days until the work is completed."

"What kind of work?" asked Antonia. "Is it being cleaned?"

"Indeed, it is," was the reply, "though not of dust and grime but of undue distraction from pious meditation!"

Columba had a sinking feeling, and her voice was apprehensive.

"What are you telling us, Mother Prioress?"

Gabriela ignored the question and, without looking at her, addressed herself to all the sisters.

"As you are aware, our Mother Abbess commands a most refined taste for the arts. Together, we have come to the conclusion that the medieval figures covering the walls of her chapel are no longer relevant or appropriate for our time. I have mentioned in the past that I find the bright colors and themes from the Old Testament irrelevant and distracting during prayer, for which simple austerity is more conducive. Since they cannot be erased, we decided to cover the frescoes with whitewash. You will appreciate that this requires several layers of paint and may have noticed painters in the well courtyard for the past few weeks. The work is not yet complete, but—"

Columba rose from her seat, her face ashen, her voice deadly quiet.

"Are you saying, Maria Gabriela, that you are about to cover magnificent art of centuries past with whitewash because you can't concentrate when abbesses and choir women have done so through the ages? Are you—"

"Sister Maria Columba, do seat yourself, continue with your reading and do not offer advice to our mother abbess about meditation and prayer. I find your remark highly inappropriate!"

Seated nearby, Maria Anna reached over and grasped Columba's sleeve in an effort to pull her back on her seat.

"Please, dearest sister," she whispered urgently. "Please—"

But Columba's eyes were burning in her pale face, and she would not listen. Forgotten were the scenes of the past that got her in so much trouble, forgotten humiliating and harsh punishments incurred. Shaking off Anna's hand, she gathered her skirts and, without another word, hurried from the room.

"I trust she's going to her cell to cool off," Maria Gabriela said with a chuckle. "Continue with your work, sisters. And, Maria Anna, you're near the lector seat, do continue with the reading. I need to return to mother abbess, we have important matters to discuss."

Anna was filled with fear and premonition and could barely control her voice as she continued, "And Saint Catherine would not be intimidated, for her heart overflowed with her love for Christ."

Columba was not headed for her cell. In haste unbecoming a choir woman, she ran down the stairs, across the well courtyard and up the steps toward the vestibule of St. Michael. Disregarding convention and spurred on by the smell of chalk, she reached the threshold of the chapel. What she saw confirmed her worst fears. Two of the walls already presented themselves in bright white all the way up to the stone seraphim and the blessing hand of God at the vault's crown. On a ladder behind the altar was one man, another standing nearby, both busy brushing a second layer over the crucifixion scene that could still by discerned underneath the first coat of whitewash. Columba, beside herself, rushed toward them.

"Out!" She screamed. "Get out!"

She grasped the ladder and kicked over the bucket of paint with her foot, spilling white liquid across the stone tiles. The man climbed down hastily.

"Rev'rend Mother," he stuttered, "we's here 'cause Mother Prioress ordered us do the work and we's almost done!"

"Go away! Get out!" Columba was so excited her voice broke. "Don't you understand that you have destroyed a priceless work of art?"

His blank look lacked understanding for her excitement, and he made no effort to stop her as she reached for brushes and bags of chalk and threw them in the direction of the door.

"Take those things and leave and never come back!"

One of the bags burst open landing at the feet of the magistra sacristan on the threshold and left a layer of white dust on her skirts.

"What is going on here? Maria Columba, what in heaven's name—"

"Look what these men have done, Mother Magistra!" Columba screamed. "They've destroyed the abbey's oldest and most precious art!"

The magistra quickly took charge. "Pray control yourself, dear sister!" she said with authority and to the men, "You may leave and return tomorrow at the regular time. Do not concern yourself with your tools, it shall be taken care of."

The men left as quickly as they could, and when their steps had faded, the magistra turned to face the shaking Columba.

"If there is an explanation for this scene, I cannot think of it. I am shocked and dismayed at your lack of dignity and shall find it difficult to describe your demeanor to our Reverend Mother Abbess. I ask you to retire to your cell forthwith and remain there until summoned. You are relieved from choir duty!"

Columba stood by the semi-concealed crucifixion scene, too shocked to comprehend the extent of what had happened. She turned toward the wall and lovingly passed her hand over the barely visible, damp figures, bowed to kiss the feet of the crucified Christ. Her lips white from wet paint she looked at the magistra and left the chapel with stiff little steps. The magistra shook her head and reached for the bell pull. She ordered the entering lay nun to clean the chapel floor.

Columba later could not remember how she got back to her cell, nor did she pay attention to Aloysia pumping water from the courtyard well. The little nun's eyes followed her in worried surprise for she did not remember seeing Columba so detached, when in the past she always had a smile and friendly word for her. "Dear Lord, I pray Mother Columba is not in trouble again," she said to herself lifting the heavy bucket to carry down the long hallways to the kitchen.

In her cell, Columba sat down on the chair by the window and stared into the park. Had she lost her mind, or was everyone else insane? How could Maria Henrica, likely the most artistically inclined of all the abbesses Göss ever had, authorize the destruction of timeless beauty? Could it be that the abbess did not know about it and the zealous prioress and her circle had ordered the work to demonstrate their hypocritical piety? Perhaps, when Maria Henrica found out, the fresh whitewash could be removed and the frescoes saved! She'd pray for it! And kneeling at her prie-dieu, she poured her sorrow into fervent words asking God to save St. Michael's beautiful frescoes. Columba would never know that God heard her prayer, though more than a century would pass until the very existence of frescoes beneath layers of chalk was discovered and restoration began. And only twentieth century technology finally developed the procedure of carefully removing layer upon layer of white paint to bring the magnificent figures back to life and restore to the joy of future generations what false sense of pious austerity tried to destroy.

Hearing the bell call for vespers, she automatically rose to head for the choir then recalled the magistra's firm order to await word in her cell. *What will they do to me this time*, she wondered, *have me fast 'til I starve to death to get be rid of me? Or humble and degrade me once again by forcing me to apologize, but to whom? To Maria Henrica because I object to her foolish destruction of art, or to Maria Gabriela, who surely influenced the decision, for speaking up? Never!* This time, she knew she was right and the person responsible for this despicable deed should suffer the punishment!

The afternoon wore on. The bell called for supper, and silence settled over the abbey while the choir women assembled for their evening meal. Finally, there was a timid knock and Aloysia's voice.

"May I enter, Rev'rend Mother?"

The little nun seemed grief-stricken by the message she came to deliver. It summoned Columba to the Great Chapter Hall when the clock of the parish church tower struck seven and present herself before the assembled choir women. If the content had not conveyed the gravity of the message, the lay nun's face did. In almost three decades as choir woman, Columba did not recall anyone ever cited before the chapter in the Great Hall. Were they going to expel her? *Then I shall walk away with my head held high and exist as a pauper on my stipend, preferable to living among women bent on destroying beauty in the name of God!* She was still anything but calm but thought through her situation. This time, she would insist on explaining and making Maria Henrica understand why she had lost her temper and composure, which she admittedly had. She'd offer to forego recreation money from her personal fund for the rest of her life if it was used to remove the ugly paint and she prayed that her offer be accepted.

When the clock struck a quarter off seven, she washed her face with cool water, smoothed her habit, and—a few minutes later— walked to the chapter room, waiting outside the heavy oak door for the chime. The Great Chapter Hall was the largest room of the abbey and rarely used except for occasions such as electing a new abbess or discussing major decisions when the advice and consent of all choir women was sought. It was a beautiful room with white and gilded moldings, heavy wainscoting, and an intricate stucco ceiling. The tall windows were closed and the air stifling hot after many hot days. Abbess Maria Henrica was seated on a slightly elevated chair, flanked by the magistrae of her court. The rest of the women sat to each side, and Columba noticed that most of her sisters studiously avoided meeting her eyes. Only Maria Anna, her lovely thin face sickly pale, stared at her with an imploring look as if begging her to submit to whatever awaited her. Columba tried to look assured but felt disheartened when she saw even Antonia lowering her eyes to her folded hands. *They look like a court of the inquisition*, Columba thought. After a prolonged silence that oppressively lingered in the room, Maria Henrica spoke with a voice so low that Columba could barely understand her words.

"Maria Columba, you have once again severely transgressed the limits of behavior befitting a choir woman. Not only did you rudely insult the prioress, you then saw fit to disgrace yourself in a most disgusting way before ordinary workmen doing their duty. Unless witnessed by the magistra sacristan, I would have found it difficult to believe such demeanor by one of our choir women expected to serve God and her sisters in Christ in love and devotion. Our community cannot survive if such actions continue, and I have consulted with the full chapter regarding a fitting punishment that would prevent incidents like these in the future. Fasting and prayer have failed to bend your stubborn mind in the past, and although it grieves me and all your sisters deeply, your punishment this time must be harsh."

She paused. Had the speech exhausted her, or was she hesitant to pronounce the verdict? Columba waited, physically aware of the tension hanging over the room. Then Maria Henrica spoke again, her voice hoarse but clearly audible in the hushed silence.

"It has been many years since corporal punishment was inflicted upon a choir woman in this abbey, Maria Columba, but my court and most sisters agree that in your case, it is the only choice left to us. You will therefore remove yourself to the adjoining room, where you will don a shirt of penance. You will then prostrate yourself before this chapter and, on your exposed back, receive one stroke of the whip from each of your sisters. You will thank each one for administering justice and helping you to find Christ. Do you understand me?"

All blood seemed to drain from Columba's heart at Henrica's words then rushed to her head, and her cheeks turned a bright red. Her dark eyes flashed as she made a step forward and cried, "No! Never! How can you whip me for trying to save art that glorifies our Lord and His Holy Mother, art that has inspired generations of choir women and would in all future if you had not ordered it destroyed! Solomon's High Song, is it not the perfect symbol of the marriage between Our Lord Jesus and His church? Of each one of us becoming His bride? How can it be called a distraction and no longer valid in our time? How can you justify—"

Prioress Maria Gabriela raised her hand. "Enough!" she said in a loud and commanding tone. "Enough! How dare you question an order by our most Reverend Mother Abbess, to whom you vowed total obedience! How dare you have the arrogance to consider your judgment superior to that of our Mother Abbess, who is infinitely superior to you! You are a disgrace to our chapter, a disgrace to the annals of our abbey, and unworthy to be called a bride of Christ the Savior! Unworthy of the mild punishment pronounced upon you! Reverend Mother Abbess, I move to—"

Maria Henrica gently placed a hand on the prioress's arm, and Gabriela hesitantly fell silent. Another heavy quiescence descended upon the room, then the abbess spoke, and there was a connotation of pleading in her voice.

"Choir woman Maria Columba, submit yourself to the punishment I have pronounced, and your transgression will be forgiven."

Columba's cheeks remained flushed, her jaw firmly set. For an instant, she met the pleading eyes of Anna who, with hands folded in prayer, silently mouthed, "Please!" but to no avail. Frustration and built-up resentment, the Hungarian noblewoman's pride and temper, suppressed during decades of obedient monastic life, took the upper hand.

"No!" she said in a voice of suppressed fury. "No, I will not submit to your punishment, Reverend Mother Abbess, for I have done nothing wrong! All I ask is that you take my entire funds to pay for having the paint washed off! As an artist, Mother Abbess, can you not see that irreplaceable art is being destroyed? Do you not understand—" her voice broke in a choking sob.

Gabriela spoke again, "Dear sisters, Columba proves herself unworthy to be among us. Let us therefore confine her to the camera correctionis until she repents and asks forgiveness of Mother Abbess and our chapter and humbly submits to punishment!"

Without waiting for the abbess's consent, a dozen women approached Columba, firmly seized both of her arms and began to pull her toward the door. Maria Henrica suddenly looked immensely tired. She had not uttered another word, and only Maria Anna's suppressed weeping was audible in the embarrassed silence. When the group reached the door, Gabriela said, "Wait!" She stepped from her seat at the side of the abbess, approached Columba, and—with a sweep of her hand—removed the Velamen Sacrum from the choir woman's head.

"You are not worthy to be a bride of our Lord," she said.

"And you," Columba answered through clenched teeth, "are a bride of evil!"

The women quickly pulled Columba from the room, down a long flight of stairs and to the end of a long hallway to the "penitence cell." They pushed Columba inside and bolted the door.

Chapter 2

No choir woman had occupied the "camera correctionis" for years, and even lay nuns were rarely confined there except for a few days. The room was partially below grade with one small window high up on the wall facing a courtyard. There was a narrow bed with a sack of straw in lieu of a mattress in one corner, a washstand with bowl and pitcher, and a chamber pot on the lower shelf, a chair and prayer stool below a tall cross bare of Christ's body. On a shelf were a couple of sheets, a pillow and folded blanket, a tin goblet, and a Bible. The window had apparently remained closed for a long time, and the cell was musty and humid, its gloomy ambiance heightened as dusk fell. The choir women's footsteps faded on the hallway's stone floor, and only oppressive silence remained. Columba was still trembling from excitement and found the air hard to breathe, so she climbed onto the chair and tried to open the window, but it was apparently painted shut, and her efforts failed. *I'll suffocate here by morning*, she thought. She reached for the pitcher to pour water into the goblet, but it was empty. Overcome by anxiety, she broke into a sweat and wiped her brow. She knew that no one would answer her call and pulled a sheet and the pillow from the shelf to lie on the bed that was too short for her height. She was exhausted yet not for one moment regretted her actions or words spoken. She recalled a decree by the empress governing monastery life, which prohibited lengthy confinement amounting to imprisonment of monks or nuns. In cases where a religious institution considered one of their own incorrigible, that person could be expelled and his or her vows declared forfeited. *They'll find a way to rid themselves of my presence,* she thought, *and I will gladly leave, for no secular world could be worse than this!* As darkness fell, she slept but woke abruptly when a light shone into her eyes. She'd had a nightmare of being made to scrape the frescoes off the chapel walls, and it took her a moment to recognize Aloysia's pockmarked face. A small oil lamp in one hand, the nun stood beside the bed, a finger on her lips.

She carefully placed the light on the floor and whispered, "Rev'rend Mother, I bring water an' a little bread, 'twas all I can get, but you got to be thirsty and 'tis so hot in here."

Columba rose herself on her elbows and smiled gratefully.

"Thank you, Aloysia, you are a treasure! I only wish I could open the window, but it is painted shut, and I do not know how long I can exist here without some fresh air."

Aloysia placed the pitcher of water she had brought and the chunk of bread wrapped into a kerchief on the dresser and climbed onto the chair, but she was too short to reach the window. When she slowly climbed down, Columba became aware that the little nun had aged through years of hard work. *She must be about sixty*, she thought. Aloysia sadly shook her head.

"'Tis painted shut all right, and I can't do nothin' 'bout it," she said. "I try to think of somethin', though. For now, how's it if I leave the door open? 'Tis cooler in the hallway, an' I keep watch for someone coming, but all's quiet. An' keep this here light on the floor, Rev'rend Mother, an' blow it out when you hear the bell for midnight Mass."

"What is the hour?" Columba asked, having missed the tower chimes.

"'Tis almost the eleventh hour, Rev'rend Mother. I go now an' watch by the end of the hall. I say to my sisters that I's gone prayin' 'til Mass. An' while watchin', I pray that God love you an' that all be well, an' when the first bell calls, I come bolt the door."

The hallway air brought welcome relief, and Columba eagerly drank several goblets of water and ate the bread, which she gathered Aloysia had saved from her own modest ration. She felt calmer and more relaxed breathing cooler air. She removed her robes and properly made up her modest bed with sheets and blanket. She extinguished the oil lamp and hid it under her bed then lay down and was asleep when the nun returned to bolt the door, which she did after listening to Columba's even breathing.

"Dear Jesus, forgive what I do," she prayed, "but you say to us, 'What you do to the least of my brothers, that you do unto me' an' I can't bear see her suffer.'"

Columba never heard the midnight bell but by habit awoke at the time of the first morning service. The cool light of dawn brought awareness of the indignity to be imprisoned like a common offender. She'd complain to the bishop on the occasion of his next visit and fully expected to return to her cell, if not immediately, then certainly within the next couple of days. They would not dare keep her confined like this for any length of time!

The abbey's familiar morning sounds did not reach this remote cell, and all remained ominously quiet. She said her customary morning prayers kneeling before the cross, washed her face, and began to read in the Bible. She could faintly hear the various bells and, with some effort, made out the chimes of the parish church, though she knew the time of day by the calls for service. Shortly after ten o'clock when High Mass was over, footsteps approached, the door was unbolted, and one of the lay nuns she barely knew entered with a large pitcher of water and a small loaf of sourdough bread. She inclined her head in greeting but appeared under orders not to speak, silently making up the bed and attending to the chamber pot. When she had left, Columba eagerly drank the cool fresh well water and ate the bread.

The hours stretched interminably, and Columba wondered how long she could bear being confined like that without turning insane. In late afternoon, steps again approached, and Antonia entered. She carefully closed the door behind her, and the two women embraced.

"Columba, my dear sister, I bring food Erentrudis procured, for I hear you are to have only bread and water and one can't live on that." And she pulled a small bundle with cheese, a piece of ham, and a little raisin cake from her pocket.

"I also have a message from Mother Abbess she gave me when I asked permission to visit you. Prioress Gabriela objected but was overruled. Mother Henrica seems in poor health again, perhaps from the stress, but she said again if you submit to the punishment and admit to your wrongs, you may return to us, and she will forgive you. Columba, please come to reason! You know Gabriela will never allow the abbess to give in, and moreover, it's the prioress's prerogative to decide punishments! Many of us love and respect you and will not strike you hard, believe me! We're all afraid that we too could find ourselves in your position one day. But you must give in, my beloved sister, because you cannot win this struggle!"

Her voice was one of pleading urgency, but Columba shook her head.

"Never, Maria Antonia, never! You, a countess, would you allow yourself to be whipped on your bare back like a common thief? Surely, you would never submit to such indignity!"

"If it got me off bread and water and out of this smelly place, I suppose I would," came the realistic answer. "Oh, do think about what I said, Columba, and don't be obstinate! You're breaking your vow of obedience to Mother Abbess, and you know that is a serious offense. You must give in and relent, do it for the love of Christ, for the Holy Virgin, and for us, the sisters who love you! Worrying about you brought on Maria Anna's fever again, though she sends her abiding love. And I love you too and will try to return when I can. I'll tell Erentrudis that I'm especially hungry these days and ask her to find ways of getting me treats. You know that Kitchen Magistra Coletta is among your friends, so if all else fails, I'll speak to her. And now I must leave, God be with you, Maria Columba, I pray He may bring you to reason!"

When she was gone, Columba carefully thought over Antonia's words, but nothing could change her mind. She remembered having to prostrate herself before Bernarda, and it had not improved their relationship and did not induce the other woman to like her better. The contrary, rather! Bernarda continued provoking her in subtle ways, and Gabriela would do likewise. She imagined the look of triumph in the prioress's eyes when it was her turn to swing the whip. No member of the chapter would ever respect her again! Most of all, she felt completely justified in her outrage over the destruction of the frescoes. Perhaps, she should have found a way to approach Maria Henrica in private and appeal to her artistic vein. Was it too late already, and could the white paint no longer be removed without destroying the frescoes? Hot tears of anger filled Columba's eyes when she thought of the irreplaceable art. The question occurred to her whether the abbess, even if she wanted to, could release her without placing her authority in question. Still the empress's decree limited confinement amounting to virtual imprisonment to a few days. But then would anyone know about how she was being treated? Cold fear crept into her heart at the prospect of spending the rest of her days in this damp room, so sticky in summer and surely terribly cold in winter. There was no tiled stove or other means of heating in the cell. Columba's heart sank, and she fell to her knees before the cross, resting her forehead against the wood. Once again, the words of the Prophet Isaiah and Luke's gospel came to mind: "You shall cross the barren desert, but you shall not die of thirst. If you pass through raging waters in the sea you shall not drown. If you walk amid the burning flames you shall not be harmed. If you stand before the power of hell and death is at your side, know that I am with you through it all! Be not afraid! I go before you always, come follow me, and I will give you rest!"

She had looked up the prophet's further words that Henrica had not mentioned and spoke them aloud, "And if wicked tongues insult and hate you, all because of me, blessed, blessed are you!" The psalm had brought peace to Maria Agatha in her hour of death and would surely guide her through this ordeal! Columba's faith in God had not wavered, only her confidence in the rules of St. Benedict, which prescribed and condoned flogging as punishment for disobedience.

Days passed without a message from the abbess or a visit from any member of the chapter, and Columba gathered they were forbidden to see her. A lay nun came twice a day with bread and water, made up her bed, and took care of the chamber pot. Columba had always been kind and friendly with the lay nuns and never treated them haughtily like some other sisters. Over the years, she had come to know many of them quite well, though she always had a special affection for the intelligent Aloysia, her very first link with Göss.

It followed that the lay nuns in turn liked Columba and admired her voice in the choir. One of them was Maria Floriana, a taciturn woman about Columba's age, who had vowed not to speak except as needed for her work. She came from a prosperous peasant family in Upper Austria, where she had worked in the fields and stables until her parents died and her brother and his wife inherited the farm. Left without a home, the local priest referred her to Göss, where she became one of the hardest working lay nuns. Yet no matter how strenuous and long her day, she always fulfilled her vow of praying three stations of the cross each day, an obligation that deprived her of much-needed sleep. Floriana looked older than her years, but she was tall and strong with a constant serious expression on her taciturn face. She had an oddly hoarse voice totally unsuited for singing, and her greatest joy was listening to the choir and especially to Columba's unique alto, which she easily distinguished from other voices. Floriana never shared her silent admiration for Columba with anyone, whereas Aloysia's devotion to Columba was common knowledge. Therefore, it was not surprising that during the next few weeks, the little nun was assigned duties keeping her away from the camera correctionis.

News of the scene in the chapel and the dramatic exchange in the chapter room quickly spread throughout the abbey and became the subject of intense, though carefully guarded discussions among choir women and lay nuns. When Magistra Coletta said on a very busy morning about a week later that a lay nun should fetch a small loaf of bread from the pantry and take it to Columba's cell together with a fresh pitcher of water, Floriana volunteered. The magistra agreed, knowing that this particular nun would not engage in conversation with the prisoner. Floriana took a kerchief, went to the pantry, and tied the bread, a small round of cheese, and a sausage into a bundle and filled her pitcher at the well. She knocked respectfully, removed the bolt, and entered the cell, where she was immediately struck by the hot, stale air in the musty room. Columba was seated on the chair near the far wall from where she could see a bit of sky. Floriana respectfully curtseyed to the choir woman and placed the water and the bundle with food on the dresser.

"Thank you, Maria Floriana," Columba said with a smile then sighed. "O how I wish there was a way to open the window, the air is so hard to breathe, but the frame seems painted shut!"

Floriana gave the window a hard look. She put the tin goblet in her pocket, pulled over the washstand, gathered her skirts, and—with little effort—climbed onto it. She slipped the rim of the goblet under a corner of the window and using it as leverage broke the seal of the paint. A moment later, she was able to open both panes of the small window allowing the cool morning air to come in. Columba got up to stand below the window and breathed deeply.

"O Floriana, God bless you! I can't tell you how grateful I am. Thank you ever so much!"

The nun nodded, and the trace of a smile softened her serious face. She looked at the choir woman who had not had a change of linen in days. Without her Velamen Sacrum, the exposed white wimple clearly lacked freshness, and its starched crispness was wilted from perspiration.

"The Rev'rend Mother need change her linen," Floriana said evenly then went about tidying the cell. She left with another curtsey and went straight to Columba's cell, where she collected a fresh shirt, stockings, wimple, and the heavy black veil Columba wore prior to receiving her Velamen. She also took a fine towel and toilet utensils including the little mirror, Columba's breviary, and one of the volumes from the bookshelf. Floriana could neither read nor write, but she figured that a book would bring the confined choir woman a little diversion. She knew she was expected at work in the kitchen but first returned to a profoundly grateful Columba who, after a change of linen, felt much better, not in the least due to the veil. It was heavier and more cumbersome than the Velamen but, as choir woman, perceived being without a veil an embarrassment and personal affront.

The heavy volume was about Early and Medieval Christian art that Columba had borrowed from the library, making it a perfect choice. Lack of exercise was another hardship, and she prayed her daily breviary pacing the cell. At forty-seven, Columba was still fond of physical activity and used recreation time for brisk walks in the cloister garden during all seasons. Floriana left the window a tad open, making it inconspicuous.

Pacing the cell had Columba feel like a caged animal, but it helped her circulation, and she felt better when she settled down on her chair by the window to peruse the book. It was written in Latin and contained original drawings and sketches. Extensive descriptions of frescoes from old churches bitterly reminded her of her situation, even more painful because the ones depicted in the drawings were not as special, elegant, and moving as those whose loss she mourned. Still the book helped pass the time, and she heard the tower clock strike the noon hour. The chimes were more audible because of the open window, and at times, she thought she could make out faint voices coming from the archway of the well courtyard through which the choir women passed from garden to cloisters. She longed for the reflection tower with its pleasant cross ventilation even on the hottest day. Would she enjoy its peace and tranquility again in the near future?

Floriana had never attended school, and her education solely consisted of religious instruction by the parish priest of the village where she had attended church on Sundays. She would have had a chance for more learning had she been able to sing in the choir but, because of her hoarse voice, was dropped from the priest's classes. She had difficulty expressing herself but possessed good common sense and an excellent memory that enabled her to remember Sunday readings or sermons almost verbatim. To enter the novitiate for lay nuns at Göss, a young woman had to be healthy and willing to do hard work day in and day out, for they were little more than servants. Of course, they received instructions prior to taking their final vows, though the ability to read and write was not a requirement and few of them actually possessed that skill. They learned their prayers by heart and, through daily services, picked up basic Latin. Some of them were gossips and keenly interested in the lives of their mistresses, the choir women. They knew they were not supposed to discuss, let alone criticize them, and would be punished harshly if overheard or reported to their magistra. Floriana was known for her taciturn ways and vow of keeping silent except when necessary at work, so her sisters sometimes treated her as if she were deaf. It followed that even though she made no effort and considered gossip a sin against the ninth commandment, she overheard several versions of why choir woman Maria Columba had been sent to the camera correctionis. Floriana had often swept or washed the floors or replaced the altar antependium in St. Michael's and was well acquainted with its interior. Her heart related to the unadorned message of the figures in the frescoes better than to the sophisticated baroque paintings of the church. Columba's chagrin therefore elicited her empathy, not for artistic reasons, which were beyond her comprehension, but simply for losing something religious that spoke to the heart. She became painfully aware of it when she was given the task of cleaning up after the painters had completed their job. The whole incident still reverberated through the abbey. No one could remember a choir woman ever being deprived of free movement within the cloister. Entering St. Michael's with her bucket and brooms, Floriana was stunned by its stark whiteness and, for a while, stood motionless to contemplate the new appearance. "Don't like it, 'tis dead and cold," she finally muttered with a frown and instantly became aware that she had infringed against her self-imposed vow of silence. She would punish herself for such lapses with a small whip she carried on her belt, and she pulled it now, mercilessly striking her legs three times for each word that had escaped her. The cruel deed done she set about her work, unable to keep tears from rolling down her narrow cheeks, not so much because of the burning pain on her calves, but the thought of never again seeing the "pictures," as she referred to them. She'd been especially fond of the Mater Dolorosa in the crucifixion scene with her heart pierced by a lance; that scene years ago had inspired her vow of silence. "I will always remember your pain, Holy Virgin," she silently prayed and, having finished her work, remained before the empty wall to say a rosary.

The magistra, who came to inspect the cleaning, interrupted her, "Why are you standing there staring at the wall when there's much work to do, Floriana? You should have been done a while ago for I need you to clean the vestibule. Idleness is sinful, you should know, and won't be tolerated!"

Floriana humbly bowed her head and picked up her utensils to follow the magistra who kept on talking how the devil was always waiting to put evil thoughts into lazy minds. The nun did what she was asked to do but could not get Columba out of her mind and the dear price she was paying for defending the chapel's decorations. Floriana did not claim the right to have an opinion about who was right or wrong in this case, and she would never have dared to be disobedient or insubordinate, no matter what the circumstances. But since no lay nun had actually witnessed the scene in the chapel and what took place later in the chapter hall, common sense told her that none of the versions she overheard might be the real and whole truth. And so her sympathies remained with Columba, whose voice in the choir she sadly missed, and she resolved to do all she could to make her life more bearable. She stayed close to the magistra in charge of the choir women's kitchen when the evening meal was served in the refectory and indeed was again asked to take bread and water to the prisoner. This time, she added a piece of cold pheasant left over from the midday repast to the bundle as well as a handful of cherries. She was about to include but had to leave behind a small cake when the magistra walked into the pantry and asked her to hurry. Maria Coletta suspected that there was more in Floriana's bundle than bread, but she let it pass. Coletta was a Countess Althan from Gent in the Netherlands and five years younger than Columba, with whom she shared not being native Austrian. The two were temperamental and intellectual antipodes but had always been on friendly terms. Coletta was an intelligent, strictly down-to-earth practical person, which earned her being appointed magistra secretary with duties to closely assist the prioress in administrative matters. She found Maria Gabriela very difficult to please and requested taking over the kitchen for choir women when that post became open. She understood Columba's feelings toward Gabriela, though not her eccentricity and temperament to turn a difference of opinion into a heated argument. Still she was sorry that the sister had to pay so dearly for her passionate beliefs.

Floriana's concerns for Columba went beyond food; she knew the choir woman's penchant for brisk walks in the garden and figured that the enforced idleness was an additional punishment. She kept thinking of a solution and, by the time she delivered the food to the correction cell that evening, had devised a plan. She again found Columba sitting in her chair trying to glimpse a bit of sky. Floriana set the food on the little table by the bed as nicely as she knew how and remained standing with arms folded across her chest. Columba saw the meat and cherries and smiled.

"Thank you for your kindness, Sister Maria Floriana. I think you are taking it upon yourself to bring me food other than bread and water, and I am very grateful, but I do not wish you to incur trouble because of me. Promise me you will not do anything that may cause you to be punished! I am strong, and I can bear what is being done to me. Do you understand, sister?"

The nun nodded. "Yes, Rev'rend Mother."

There was a pause, and Columba, aware of the nun's vow of silence, perceived that she needed to be prompted for something she wanted to say.

"Do tell me what is on your mind, Sister Floriana," she queried.

With an obvious effort, the nun said, "Me, I pray three ros'ries in church after first Mass each night. Afore I do, I take the bolt off, an' Rev'rend Mother can walk in the garden, if she wishes, then after I finish come put back the bolt. The moon's in second quarter, an' it's not all dark an' not too bright either."

It was one of the longest speeches Floriana had ever made, and Columba was deeply touched. She knew that following midnight Mass all choir women were likely to settle down as quickly as possible for a few hours of sleep before the prim. The idea delighted her, and she could hardly wait. She thanked Floriana from the depth of her heart and anticipation had her enjoy the simple but tasty meal even more. After days without physical exercise, Columba had barely dozed when the bell called for the first Mass of the day. She closed her eyes and vividly imagined the choir women file through the cloisters to the choir empore, where her seat remained vacant. She could almost see the sleepy young ministrant, who sometimes had to reach twice until his hand found the bell pull announcing the priest's entry as the choir sang the "Entrate." Her heart ached. If only last week, or whenever the dreadful project of painting the chapel had begun, had never taken place! Columba had been a choir woman for too long not to miss the strong and soothing powers her faith and the daily routine exerted. She sighed. Perhaps, she should indeed have joined a charitable or teaching order instead of a contemplative one! But the prospect of living in the company of aristocratic women and singing for hours each day had been so enticing to an immature girl. She and her siblings lived a life of strict discipline in Vienna, but Kollonitsch had always been just, and she had no comprehension what it meant to be under the absolute power of a few women who did not like and even despised her. Columba still had respect and even affection for Maria Henrica and was convinced that the ailing abbess had fallen under the controlling influence of Gabriela, Bernarda, and others in their group.

The bell announced consecration of the host, and Columba reverently knelt; she had not received communion for days and sorely missed the cherished ritual. A short time later, she heard light footsteps in the hallway and the slight grating of the bolt being removed. She knew she had to allow a few more minutes until the abbey fell totally quiet, and she counted them off pacing the small room on tiptoe to avoid any sound. Praying three rosaries would take Floriana about three quarters of an hour, which gave her thirty minutes in the garden. She slowly pushed open the door. The hallway was dark and quiet, but with her eyes adjusted to the darkness, she swiftly moved toward the door leading into the well courtyard. The floors above her cell were used for storage and workshops such as sewing rooms, where lay nuns made habits and pillowcases, stitched hems for table clothes and bed linens and did the mending. There were no cells or dormitories in the building, only the infirmary at the other end of the tract.

The heavy door squeaked, and Columba froze for a few seconds, but when all remained quiet, she slipped across the courtyard and walked through the arched passage by the west wall of the church into the park. She knew that she could be observed from windows of the tract where the choir women's cells were located, but a young moon cast only dim light, and she hoped her sisters to be asleep.

Columba resisted the temptation of visiting a tower; there would not be much of a view at this hour, and what she needed was not contemplation but exercise for her stiff limbs. Columba knew the brick-paved paths between trees and flowerbeds well, followed their winding pattern, and enjoyed a swift walk. It occurred to her that she was less likely to be observed in the lower garden, and she decided to head there for the brief time she had left, but haste did not induce her to become careless, and she closely watched each step. It brought back memories when as young Tessa she had accompanied her papa hunting in the Transylvania woods and he taught her to walk without noise by avoiding dry twigs or stones so that deer might not be forewarned. The fond memory put a smile on her face.

Moments later, she thanked God for her caution; she had just rounded the corner of the building to descend the brick steps toward the lower garden when the sound of a small cough, little more than clearing the throat, made her freeze in her tracks. She strained her eyes in the dark, and when the pale moon reappeared between clouds, she made out a choir woman seated on a stone bench and silhouetted against the pale night sky. As the figure moved her head, she could distinguish the two starched corners of the wimple identifying the abbess. Why did Maria Henrica not visit her own garden on the opposite side of the abbey if she longed for the outdoors at night? For a moment, Columba was tempted to approach her and humbly present her case without interference from the prioress or anyone else. Surely, the chance of finding the abbess alone was a rare opportunity! But she resisted the impulse because no matter what the reaction, it would likely expose Floriana, who'd face severe punishment for setting the prisoner free and Columba was too conscientious to let that happen. But what should she do? Instinctively, she pulled her black veil tightly to her face to conceal the white wimple, noticing how clearly Maria Henrica's was visible in the dark. She noiselessly stepped behind a rosebush to watch if someone followed to meet the abbess, but all remained quiet. She was considering a careful retreat when Henrica rose and walked directly toward her. Her step was slow and tired, and both her hands were pressed to the side of her body as if in pain. It was too late to leave, and feeling her heart beat hard against her ribs, Columba was aware that the bush did not conceal her completely. She bowed her head to hide her face and hardly dared to breathe as Henrica approached. Just then heavy clouds moved in front of the moon, and it turned very dark. She could hear Henrica's labored breathing, and time stood still when the abbess hesitated just a few feet away. Had she seen her, or was she catching her breath?

After what seemed an eternity, she more felt than heard Henrica move on and finally dared breathe again when she heard the abbess open a gate to the tract in which her apartments were located. She saw light come on in the window and waited until it was extinguished a short time later. The clock struck the half-hour, and Columba knew that she had only minutes until Floriana ended her prayers and returned to bolt the door. She did not want to deprive the tired woman of her hard-earned sleep and give her concern about a vacant cell. She moved swiftly but cautiously with the veil pulled tightly around her face, hoping that the moon remained behind clouds. She reached the passage and the gate to her tract, but fear seized her when the door handle would not give. Had someone checked on her, found her cell empty, and locked the access door? There was another entrance to this tract, but it could only be reached by a lengthy detour through the church, where lay nuns often prayed during the night. Then she remembered that her cell faced this side of the building and walking close to the wall spotted her open window. Surely, it would have been closed if someone had discovered her absence. She sat on the windowsill, lowered her legs into the room, then turned onto her stomach and carefully pushed herself inside. Her strong hands firmly grasped the frame as she let her body slide down the inside wall then let go and dropped several feet to the floor with a loud thump. She landed safely and breathed a sigh of relief. The whitewashed wall had stained her habit, but that could wait until tomorrow. She checked the door, and it was still unbolted. Minutes later, she heard footsteps, and Floriana appeared to see if Columba had returned. Coming from the church, she was unaware of the locked door, and Columba kept quiet so as not to worry her.

When she had gone, Columba removed her veils and habit and sat on the side of her bed for a long time, too shaken to rest. Did

Maria Henrica see her? And if so, why didn't she confront her? She finally concluded that her temporary escape had remained undetected and settled down for a few hours of fitful sleep.

Chapter 3

The next morning, a different lay nun appeared with a jug of water and to make up the cell. She responded to Columba's greeting with only a silent curtsey. However, the same nun returned after High Mass with food for the midday meal similar to what was served in the refectory. There was soup, fowl with cranberry sauce, cabbage, bread, and a slice of cake layered with peach. The nun silently placed the food on the small table by the bed, bowed, and left. Eating was not as important to Columba as to some other choir women, particularly Antonia, but after several days of cold food, she savored the hearty meal.

Columba had become a loner over the years and did not miss the company of others. She was fond of Antonia and enjoyed listening to her cheerful banter, though their closeness had suffered a little over time because of Columba's eccentricity. She still had the greatest affection for Maria Anna, prayed fervently each day for her health, and cherished their common love for music and singing.

Columba was encouraged by the drastic change in her food and anxiously awaited a visit from Antonia with news and perhaps a message from the abbess about a pending release, but the day passed with agonizing slowness, and no choir woman visited. She spent her time reading in the art book, pacing the floor and praying. The total idleness was increasingly difficult to bear, even though like her sisters, she had often wished for a respite from rigorous choir schedule. Saints' feasts or other church holidays that brought rest to ordinary folk were more strenuous for choir women and dreaded by many because of prior fasting and longer services. Still her present predicament's worst aspect was confinement in the small damp cell, and the lack of exercise brought on a nervous stress bordering claustrophobia. If only they had confined her to her own cell with its large window and view of the mountain ridge, of trees, and the sound of birds singing! At present, the only way to catch a tiny glimpse of a tree and piece of sky was from just one spot. How much longer was her torture going to last?

The same nun delivered her evening meal of bread, butter, cheese, sausage, and milk and again silently tended to the room. Columba had spent the day in excited anticipation of a visit and, encouraged by the better food, hoped for word from the abbess, but when dusk turned into night, she felt tired and went to bed. She vaguely heard the bell toll for midnight Mass but did not wake until a light shone into her eyes. She was lying on her side facing the table by her bed and found herself looking at a brightly burning oil lamp. For a few moments, she thought she had failed to extinguish her own when she became acutely aware of a presence and sat up with a start to see Maria Henrica standing in the middle of the room and regarding her with an expression of exasperated sympathy. Columba was not sure whether she was seeing an apparition, but a slight movement by the abbess convinced her otherwise. She rose from the bed, instinctively reached for her veil to cover her head then bowed respectfully. Maria Henrica took a seat on the room's only chair and said, "I see that someone brought your veil and assume it to be the same person who removed the bolt from your door the other night. Why did you not make your presence known to me in the garden, Maria Columba? I have always considered you courageous. It seems to me the person helping you is more so than you are."

When Columba remained silent, Henrica continued, "I can respect that you do not wish to disclose her name and that nothing would induce you to do so. That is not why I have come. Are you willing to submit to the punishment I have inflicted upon you and return to chapter?"

Columba kept her head bowed while the abbess spoke but now looked up and squarely met Henrica's eyes. With a low voice hoarse with emotion, she firmly and distinctly said, "Most Reverend

Mother Abbess, I deeply regret the chagrin I have caused you, but I shall never allow myself to be whipped like a common criminal, as God is my witness, never!"

"God is witness that you have broken your solemn vow of obedience, which our Holy Order of St. Benedict considers a most serious offense," Maria Henrica replied sternly. "Very well, Maria Columba, you shall remain confined until you come to your senses. As your Mother Superior, I am, however, responsible for your spiritual needs, and a priest shall visit you from time to time to hear your confession and administer the sacraments. On special days you may attend Mass, though not in the community of your sisters, only from the nave." There was a pause before she added, "It saddens my heart, Maria Columba, that you cannot find it in yourself to sacrifice your vain pride to Christ, your heavenly bridegroom, and that the talents and abilities He bestowed upon you have been for naught. But the Lord, our God, gave us all free will, which separates us from the beasts and allows us to choose between good and evil. I pray you may come to understand your grave offense. Farewell, Columba, I shall await word that you have conquered your pride and are prepared to submit to just punishment."

She rose and the two women stood eye to eye, and during these few moments of silence, each perceived that the other would never give in. Columba did not bow when Henrica turned to leave. *She still moves without a sound*, she thought idly when the door closed behind the abbess and she could neither hear the bolt or Henrica's fading footsteps. She stood still for a few minutes then removed her veil and sat down on her bed. Henrica had not taken the lamp she'd brought with her. It was elegant, made of brass, and shed brighter light than her primitive one did. Was it a small gesture of goodwill or just an oversight? There'd been a time when Columba thought she knew Maria Henrica quite well, but that seemed no longer the case, and in her mind, she attributed the change to Maria Gabriela's influence, without considering that she also had undergone a mental and psychological metamorphosis over the years. Columba had been headstrong, proud, and outspoken all her life, not a good combination for a choir woman bound by vows of obedience and humility.

In spite of what the abbess had said, Columba was convinced that news of her confinement sooner or later would come to the attention of a secular official and that the empress's rules against such methods of punishment would be enforced. For the time being, that did not appear to be the case.

Her circumstances improved slightly with better food and additional items from her cell, such as linens and sheets. A lay nun now came several times a day to attend to her hygienic needs and even brought hot water for washing. Columba no longer nurtured illusions that she would leave her cell any time soon and designed a schedule, to which she clung rigorously. She remained concerned about whether Floriana had been identified as an accomplice and punished for her disobedience. She would never know, for it was many weeks before she saw her again and when she did, the nun silently shook her head in answer to her question.

On the Friday following the abbess's visit, there was a strong knock at her door and the Supremus Capellanus entered, not unexpected in view of Henrica's words. Pater Benedict of Springenfels hailed from the abbey of Admont, like his predecessors during the past century and a half. He was a stern but wise man in his sixties who, unbeknownst to Columba, shared her disappointment about the loss of the frescoes. When the abbess had discussed her plans with him, he acceded that in the spirit of the time themes from Solomon's Song might no longer be considered desirable decorations for a chapel but suggested they be covered with tapestries or other suitable wall hangings. This presented practical difficulties because the frescoes followed the Gothic architecture and covered narrow, vaulted spaces between windows and near the ceiling. His ideas were vigorously opposed by Maria Gabriela, who wanted them forever removed from the sight of future generations of choir women. The Supremus's function was to guide the abbess spiritually, which meant considerable influence, but he also depended on the goodwill of the ruling abbess. As Maria Henrica's father confessor and witness to her frequent sickbeds, he was well aware of her poor state of health. He was also astute and harbored little doubt that Gabriela was being groomed as the next abbess. He was therefore not inclined to deprive himself of the prioress's goodwill because of some old frescoes, whose true value he did not appreciate.

Columba greeted the Supremus with the respect choir women and nuns accorded to priests and invited him to take a seat on her only chair. He declined, asked her to kneel beside him before the cross, and led her in the traditional psalm of penitence.

"From the depth do I cry unto Thee O Lord hear my prayer! O may in grace receive Thine ear the voice of my distress! If Thou would not forgive our sins, O Lord, whoever dared to stand before Thine eyes? But then I know that Thou art merciful, and confidence has given me Thine Law. Yes, in His word do I entrust myself and to the Lord I turn my hoping soul. From early dawn into the night, His people turn their hope to Him, for full of mercy is the Lord and infinite the measure of salvation. It is He who shall redeem His people from all their sins!"

"Are you ready to make a good confession, my daughter?" he asked after a few moments of silent prayer, and when she answered, "Yes, Father Supremus," he sat in the chair, and Columba knelt before him. She openly and frankly confessed her frustration about the frescoes, her anger against the prioress, and her refusal to submit to what she thought was undeserved and unjust punishment and humiliation. The priest knew what had happened through conversations with the abbess and agreed with Maria Henrica's position, but he was anxious to save Columba's soul and see the choir woman reconciled with her chapter. Yet he was also in contact with the secular world and understood the embarrassment for the abbey if it became known they were imprisoning a choir woman, particularly the niece of an influential cardinal. He asked Columba to do her act of contrition, express her sorrow for having offended God, and firmly resolve to avoid all occasion of sin. He granted her absolution since the church does not deem it mandatory that the penitent regret sins, only the resolve and honest effort not to commit them again. Columba did not hesitate to make that resolve. How could she offend anyone from her prison cell? The Supremus ordered her to say ten rosaries kneeling on the bare floor by the cross, then blessed her, and left with the words:

"A lay nun will come in time to escort you to midnight Mass, where you shall remain in the nave below the choir empore, out of view from the chapter. It is where you shall receive communion after Mass. I pray that God may enlighten your soul and that our Savior's love fill your heart with humility and obedience."

Columba dutifully said her penitence. Praying ten rosaries requires well over two hours, and her body ached when she finally rose from the hard floor. Yet her heart was light and almost joyful, filled with hope that the priest's visit had been a harbinger of change; perhaps a way could be found to solve the dilemma by sending her to another convent? Being a nun was the only way of life she knew and, at age forty-seven, her only option of a secure existence. Confinement to the back of the nave was humiliating for a member of the chapter, though. This was the abbey church, and as a choir woman, she had earned the unique privilege of occupying a seat on the choir loft, away from other members of the congregation.

During the third week of her confinement, she experienced a special joy. Initially, she mistook the gentle knock at the door for the lay nun collecting the utensils of her midday meal, but to her immense surprise, Maria Anna entered. Columba rushed to greet her visitor with tears of joy. The two women embraced tenderly, and Columba led Anna to the chair, seating herself on the bed. Her initial happy excitement quickly gave way to anxious concern. Maria Anna's body had felt painfully emaciated in the embrace. The blue eyes in the pale face were unnaturally large and feverishly red.

"Anna, dearest sister, please tell me that you have recovered? I know that you have been ill, and I've prayed with all my heart that you may be spared more suffering! To see you is the greatest gift I could receive!"

A gentle smile spread radiant beauty over Maria Anna's features as she answered, "It is such for me also, dear Sister Columba, I have longed so much to see you, and when Mother Abbess visited me in the infirmary a few days ago and asked if I had a wish, I begged for this visit. She granted it from the goodness of her heart."

A violent coughing spell interrupted her, and Columba saw with dread that the linen kerchief she held to her mouth became stained with blood. She quickly poured water into a goblet, and Anna drank slowly.

"It is nothing," she said when she had caught her breath. "You know that I've had this silly cough ever since I was a child. I lay my pain at the feet of the Virgin, who suffered more than I could ever bear. I only wish my condition would not interfere with my singing, but it does. And your voice is sadly absent from our choir, Maria Columba, but it is your presence that I miss the most."

There was a pause during which only Anna's labored breathing could be heard. Columba reached for her friend's hand and tried not to let her face mirror her deep concern. She began to chat lightheartedly about her days and that she was given good food and personal things from her cell. She could not deceive the sensitive Anna, who wanted to know whether there was anything she could do for her.

"O Anna, I trust that means that you will visit with me again soon?" Columba exclaimed.

Anna nodded. "Yes, dear sister, Reverend Mother Abbess has given me permission to visit you once a week and to ask you about things that help lighten your solitude," she said after the slightest of hesitation, and it was clear she had meant to say "imprisonment." Columba pointed to the heavy volume by her bed.

"Reading does help pass the time," she said, "and I've enjoyed reading up on art. Before all this happened, I was studying the writings of church father Augustine but would rather stay with art or perhaps history for a while. I will be ready for new material by the time of your next visit and would be grateful if you would select something for me from the library."

Anna promised to do so, and the two women chatted until the relentless bell signaled the end of recreation time.

Anna and Antonia were the only choir women visiting Columba and the single interruption in the monotony of her life. She did not know whether they were the only ones granted permission or because no one else asked to see her, though the two went to great length to describe the concern of several of the sisters. They also spoke about a growing unpopularity of the prioress and the Galler sisters with the exception of the youngest, who suffered from a painful lung ailment and was not expected to live much longer.

Columba always looked forward to her weekly attendance of midnight Mass, to which a lay nun escorted her. She desperately missed not being allowed to join in the singing but took comfort in kneeling close to her favorite altar of St. Catherine. And over time, she noticed that lay sisters usually sitting in the center of the nave began to move closer to her. At first, only one or two then more and more would respectfully curtsey to Columba and attend Mass in adjoining pews. Columba interpreted it as a sign of empathy and compassion. Still her frustration and resentment increased with the passing of time, and though she counted the hours between seeing Antonia and Anna, she tended to make their visits less than pleasant if in a poor mood. During long hours of brooding over her fate, Columba became obsessed with certain aspects of the Benedictine rule or traditions at Göss, which she would make the subject of the conversation and bitter critique. Anna always listened patiently, but Antonia interrupted her when she engaged in one of her angry tirades and sought to cheer her with talk about small incidents of current daily life. Her well-meant efforts met with little success.

As days grew shorter and the hours of darkness longer, Columba suffered from sleeplessness induced by lack of physical exercise and mental stress. The physical restrictions were a very painful aspect of her confinement. Many choir women at Göss were no strangers to periods of depression furthered by long periods of forced silence yet took comfort in living in a community where everyone was subjected to difficult exercises of self-control. However limited their change of scenery, they could move around and not be confined within a tiny cell, converse with one another during certain hours of the day and savor the brief hours of sleep their rigorous schedule permitted. Columba had become something of a recluse in recent years and rarely looked for conversation, but she'd put her heart and soul into singing and express joy or chagrin in music. One gray November afternoon, she told Anna how terrible she felt about being excluded from singing.

"Why don't you sing in your cell after Mass and repeat all the responses and parts of the liturgy?" she suggested.

Columba confessed that she had not sung a single note since her imprisonment, as she referred to it and sometimes thought she might have lost her voice.

"But that can't be!" exclaimed Anna and began to recite a psalm in which sections of the choir were assigned different passages. Anna's soprano was lovely as ever despite her illness, and Columba's initial resistance crumbled at the loving insistence of her friend. Soon, the two voices, so different yet perfectly complementing each other, filled the small room, and the magic power of music lifted their spirits. With the window closed since the onset of cool and damp weather, they never heard the bell calling for vespers, and when the tower clock struck the hour, Anna rose with a start.

"O Columba, my dear," she exclaimed, "see what your beautiful voice does to me? I'm late for litany and will be reprimanded for sure! Let me hurry off, but not until you promise that you will sing whenever your heart is sad! Will you do that for me, dear sister?"

Columba thought that her heart was always sad and filled with grief, but she did not want to burden her loving friend.

"I will do so, Anna, and think of you while singing. But now do hasten, you can go directly to the church from this tract! I'll count the hours until your next visit."

The two women embraced, and Anna hurried off. When the door closed behind her, Columba sank onto her chair and buried her face in her hands. After a brief hour of joy, her predicament appeared all the more hopeless with silence and early dusk permeating her cell. A sudden rage filled her, and she jumped to her feet, grasped the cross with both hands, and—in desperate frustration—beat her forehead against it, oblivious of the pain.

"I can't," she screamed, "I can't bear it anymore! Help me, O God, help me! How could this happen to me! Please, dear God—" her voice broke into sobs that shook her body until all strength left her, and she sank to the floor. The passionate outbreak released the tension, and after a while, she began to shiver on the cold planks yet could not gather enough strength to move. Then she noticed dark stains on her hands and, with the room in almost complete darkness, wondered what they were until she felt something warm dripping from her brow. She could feel a bruise on her forehead where apparently her skin broke beating her head against the wood. She pressed her kerchief to her head and tiredly felt her way to the chair, too exhausted to light the oil lamp or find water to wash. That was how Floriana found her when she arrived with supper. The nun carried a small lantern and did not notice anything amiss until she had lit Columba's lamp, thinking that the choir woman was resting in the dark cell. When Floriana saw the blood on Columba's face and her stained wimple, she exclaimed in distress, "Rev'rend Mother! The blood! Are you ill?"

Columba tried to smile and shook her head. "No, Sister Floriana, I fell in the dark, I could not find the lamp."

Floriana quickly soaked a towel in the wash basin and gently began to clean Columba's face and hands. She took a fresh linen kerchief from the dresser, moistened and shook it to cool further, then placed it over the bruise and guided the choir woman's hand to hold it in place. With a mother's tenderness, she gently removed both veils from Columba's head, who was too tired to worry whether anyone saw that her hair had grown back. Floriana's skilled hands quickly wound a fresh wimple over the short curls and replaced the black veil. She could feel Columba's shoulders shiver and thought that in this cold, damp place the heavy wool of the ordinary veil provided more comfort than the gossamer thin Velamen Sacrum. The two women did not exchange another word, and when Floriana placed the bread, butter, cheese, and milk on the table, Columba sadly shook her head indicating that she did not wish to eat. The nun thought for a minute then picked up the bucket and soiled linens and left. Columba just sat holding the cloth to her forehead when Floriana returned with a small iron vessel of glowing embers and two pitchers, one with fresh water, the other filled with wine. Most choir women drank wine with their main meal, but Columba had not been brought any since her confinement. She hadn't really missed it, but when Floriana held the tin goblet to her lips, she drank and it warmed her and made her feel better. She did not ask whence it came, nor did she care whether Floriana had just taken it or had been authorized by the magistra in charge of the wine cellars. The nun spread a piece of crusty sourdough bread with butter, placed a thick slice of cheese on it, and—with respectful insistence—made Columba take a few bites. And she refused to leave until she'd helped Columba undress and go to bed with a fresh compress on her forehead. Exhausted from her breakdown and lulled by the wine, Columba lay back on her pillow, and her lids became heavy. Floriana waited until she was asleep, placed the tripod with the coals in close but safe distance from the bed, and covered it with a grill to prevent sparks. She extinguished the lamp but left her little lantern so Columba would not find herself in total darkness.

Thereafter, Floriana came twice each day with glowing embers from the kitchen, and Magistra Coletta did not object or mention it to anyone. She felt that as a member of the court, she did not need permission for this act of kindness even though she was not part of a "power circle." Coletta and other outsiders shared a growing embarrassment over Columba's isolation in the camera correctionis, or "prison cell" as it was called, which everyone knew had no tiled stove and was bound to be cold and damp this time of year. The red-hot embers in the small kettle radiated heat to only a small area without adequately warming the high-ceilinged room. On nights when a shivering Columba returned from midnight Mass to a cell almost as cold as the frigid church, Floriana would make another trip to the dark kitchen to retrieve two heavy bricks she'd earlier placed on the stovetop. Wrapped in flannel, they'd at least warm the bed.

It became a long, sad winter, and for the first time in her life, Columba suffered severe arthritic pain in hands and knees. *I'm getting old*, she thought, *perhaps I'll become sick and die*. It seemed a welcome option to these short gray days and long nights, one as dreary and hopeless as the other. Anna again fell ill in December and was unable to visit and Antonia secretly dreaded her times with the morose and unreceptive Columba.

On Christmas Eve after vigil vespers, Columba thought she heard a familiar light step outside. During her months of silence, she had learned to identify those approaching her cell by the rhythm of their step, and she held her breath in hopeful anticipation. A moment later, Anna stood in the doorway, looking ever more pale and thin than before, a large bundle in her arms and a smile on her lovely face. Columba pealed from the blankets in which she wrapped herself in the daytime and hurried to embrace her. The two women shed a few tears of joy then sat together on the bed. After a frugal midday meal, Christmas vigil was observed by strict fasting until after High Mass on Christmas Day, which was especially hard on Columba, who needed every ounce of energy to fight the cold. But seeing her dear friend warmed her heart and allowed her to briefly forget her misery. Anna was shocked about the dampness and frigid temperature in the cell and silently resolved to help. She placed the bundle in Columba's arms.

"I have asked Mother Abbess, and she granted permission because it's Christmas," she said happily. "Our Lord was born tonight when His light began to shine and bring joy and salvation to the world and to you also, dear sister in Christ!"

Columba removed the cloth to reveal the statue of the Child Christ she had found in her cell after her profess. For a few moments, she stared wordlessly at the figure in its regal clothes and crown. Why did the smile on the painted face seem so artificial and the splendid finery of the clothes like mockery of her suffering? The profoundly pious Anna did not read her thoughts and attributed her silence to speechless surprise. Columba loved her too much to reveal what went through her mind and looked up with a smile.

"What a lovely thought, Maria Anna, it will bring joy to my days," she said.

When Anna had left, she placed the statue on her dresser and contemplated it for a long time. She had enjoyed its symbolic innocence through the years, the subtle appeal to motherly instincts, and the solidarity with the Virgin it gave the women. She had offered prayers of thanks to it on good days and brought her darker moments to the suffering Christ on the cross. Now her whole life was dark and without hope, and she could not think of anything for which she felt grateful. The bare cross was like a symbol that even the suffering Lord had left her. Columba no longer submitted to bouts of passionate tears, her mind and heart were hardened, and her body focused on surviving the bitter winter in her cold prison. Her immediate and greatest challenge was to cope with the long, hungry hours until the next meal.

On Christmas Night just before midnight Mass, Floriana brought heated bricks for Columba's bed and pulled a fur cape from under her cloak that she placed round the choir woman's shoulders. Columba was startled.

"Sister Floriana, what is this? Who gave it to you?"

The nun silently shook her head. "For you to keep Rev'rend Mother," was all she would say and motioned that she was ready to escort her to church.

Several wealthy choir women owned fur capes to wear for choir duty in winter. At visitation a century earlier, a bishop had forbidden them to wear furs and gloves, but his orders were never followed. Abbesses understood that such small luxuries saved the women from becoming too ill to sing. The cape obviously belonged to a member of the chapter since no lay nun owned anything that valuable. But who had sent it? Columba would never know that following her visit earlier on Christmas Eve, Maria Anna had gone from cell to cell to appeal to her sisters. She gladly would have given up her own if she'd had one, but knowing that some choir women possessed more than one fur, she hoped to move the heart of a compassionate choir woman. She found an unlikely candidate—Maria Victoria, the Galler sister near death in the infirmary. Maria Anna visited with her, and Victoria confided that she secretly prayed for Bernarda's soul, knowing that her sisters and Gabriela bore much of the responsibility for Columba's predicament. She asked about Columba, and when Anna told how much her friend suffered from the cold, she did not hesitate to send Anna to her cell and fetch one of her two capes, saying that God wanted her to help a sister in distress. Her only condition was that Anna not reveal the donor, for a good deed everyone knew about no longer could be considered as such. Maria Victoria Countess Galler died of her lung ailment early the following year.

The gesture was of immense help to Columba and likely prevented serious illness. She used the cape at night for additional cover and wore it all day long, turning the fur to the inside. It was made of fox skins, and the long hair afforded extra warmth. Yet more than giving her physical comfort, the gift was a message that there were sisters besides Anna and Antonia who wished her well and had not forgotten her. She knew she was liked by most lay nuns, some of which went out of their way to provide her with small comforts, especially Floriana and Aloysia, who did everything in their power not to allow the iron kettle get cold and often brought little treats. During the worst days of January and February of that severe winter, Columba only left her bed for physical needs and the weekly midnight Mass. This total lack of exercise brought on insomnia, want of appetite, and depression. She barely ate anything but hot soup and drank chamomile tea and became very thin; days and nights followed one another monotonously like a path never reaching its destination. Columba began to lose track of time.

Strong southerly winds originating at the Adriatic Sea swept across the Alps in March and caused the weather to turn unusually warm. These air currents often gave people attuned to cold weather severe headaches but never had affected Columba in the past. Hearing the gusts of wind howl between abbey walls and through courtyards, she thought it might be yet another snowstorm. When Floriana brought the midday meal, the nun climbed onto the chair to open the window, and a gush of warm air blew into the room. It was balsam for Columba's lungs to find relief from the stale air of the musty cell that had not been properly ventilated in months. She immediately got out of bed, wrapped the cape around her body, and looked for a glimpse of blue sky. The taciturn nun's eyes lit up when she saw Columba smile.

"Sister Floriana, what day is it?"

"'Tis today the thirteenth day of March, Rev'rend Mother, and jus' three weeks to Easter! There's some choir women ill 'cause of warm winds blowing, but they's good for airin' out this cell."

"You're so right, Maria Floriana, and I'll eat sitting by the table today. Why, all of a sudden, I even have an appetite! What did you bring me, sister?"

"Pickled beef an' beet puree an' carrots, Rev'rend Mother. The cellar don't give much this time o' year, but there's hefty broth an' also a goblet o' wine."

The nun was relieved to see Columba less apathetic and glum and to hear her talk and even smile.

"Sister Floriana, three weeks before Easter means we're in Lent, when wine and meat are not served. Surely, everyone in the abbey is fasting!"

Floriana shook her head. "Today's Sunday Gaetare, Rev'rend Mother, when the priest's wearin' pink 'stead of Lenten purple. He says 'tis 'rose color,' though," she added with a sly smile. "An' Reverend Mother's fasted all winter, not jus' Lent! Can't be a sin gettin' back a little strength, an' wine's good for that."

Columba drank the red wine and indeed felt better. Later, she walked to her dresser, pulled out the small mirror, and removed her nightcap to stare at her image. She saw a haggard face with sunken dark eyes and narrow pale lips, framed by matted hair streaked with gray, which had grown long during the over six months of her confinement, but the curls were stiff from neglect. Floriana had washed her face and hands each day, but Columba realized that she had not washed her whole body since the onset of the bitter cold when she began staying in bed all day. She felt grimy and uncomfortable and decided she had to do so without delay. The water on her washstand was cool, but she felt such urgency she could not wait another moment and, taking off all her clothes, began to scrub herself from head to toe. When she ran out of water with her hair still soapy, she used all her drinking water for rinsing. She'd scrubbed herself so hard she felt warm and pleasantly tingling, even though the spring air had not warmed her room all that much. Bright rays of sun fell through the open window and donning a fresh linen shirt, and her flocke instead of the crumpled habit, she moved the chair so the sun would dry her hair. She knew it should have been cut months ago, but the sub-prioress, who reminded choir women and nuns of their frequent haircuts, apparently had forgotten the prisoner. *And I won't remind her until it's good and warm again*, Columba thought. The women had no need for combs and didn't own any, but she managed to separate the short wet strands with her fingers and shook them until they were dry and curly. A different person was reflected in her mirror this time. Scrubbing her skin and drinking a glass of wine had given her face color, and the thick curls softened the gaunt lines.

"I don't even look like a choir woman now," she said to herself. "Is it that perhaps at heart I no longer am one?" It made her chuckle. "Perhaps, I should never have become a nun but a monk instead! With my hard face and deep voice, I could have passed for a boy, and who'd ever know? I don't think men are as mean as women toward each other! I bet they left Ferenc pretty much to himself and never told him he was worth less because he grew up protestant. And monks are dedicated to the Gregorian chant and wouldn't worry about Solomon's Song being unsuitable for the religious." She again picked up the mirror and grinned at her image. "Perhaps, you are indeed beyond eccentric and about to become mad, Columba!" The thought frightened her, she resolved to strive for a more positive outlook, and the better attitude lifted her spirits.

Chapter 4

T he mild weather persisted, an early spring followed the severe winter, and life in her cell grew more bearable. Her joints and especially knees and hands still ached with arthritis and rheumatism, and Floriana brought oil derived from beaver tails from the pharmacy. Rubbing it into her skin relieved some of the pain, and the lay nun's gentle massage contributed to make her feel better.

The pharmacy was an all-important segment of the abbey's daily life. Herbs, tinctures, and ointments were used to treat pain and a variety of diseases and afflictions and were the sum total of medical treatment the choir women received. The only other forms of treatment were bloodletting and the purge, arbitrarily administered for any ailment.

The current magistra of the infirmary was Maria Amalia, Countess Konigsacker, born in Vienna and close in age to Columba. She'd been among the twelve choir women who received their Velamen Sacrum in 1751. Maria Amalia was the daughter of a medium-level court official and not a loquacious person. Raised in a household of strict discipline, she learned to control her feelings at an early age, especially a hot temper. Though never confidants, Columba and Amalia respected and liked one another. The magistra lacked empathy for what she considered Columba's want of self-discipline that in her opinion was a basic requirement for religious life. But Amalia had a good heart and easily guessed the recipient when Floriana asked for beaver oil. A few days later, she took it upon herself to visit Columba. Maria Amalia was of short and wiry stature with a long face and unusually large hands. She was strong for a woman her size and often amazed her sisters with the tenacity and persistence with which she cared for her patients. She had a high forehead and intense black eyes below prematurely gray, bushy eyebrows, a short straight nose, and a long chin. The stern, even hard expression of her unusual face changed when Amalia broke into one of her rare smiles. Her mouth was well shaped, and she had exceptionally beautiful teeth, rare for women her age at that time, yet that was not the sole reason of this transformation. When she smiled, her whole face radiated kindness and reassurance, and she conveyed confidence and a sense of well-being. Amalia cared deeply about those entrusted to her care and devoted every waking hour not in church to her patients, often having her food sent to the infirmary so she could remain with a sister in need. She'd worried about Columba's health during the long dark winter. Like most choir women, she had never seen the camera correctionis and imagined it not too different from ordinary cells. Abbess Henrica was in her care at the time with another severe attack of gallbladder stones, but Amalia did not ask permission for the visit, simply considering it within her authority to visit the sick. Floriana's request for the oil revealed that Columba was in need.

Her first impression was one of shock about the choir woman's gauntness and listless demeanor that signaled depression, but her face showed no concern when she greeted Columba in her usual way without wasting words as if her visit were nothing out if the ordinary. Seeing a new face surprised and pleased Columba, who was in one of her defensive moods that day. She offered her visitor the chair and sat on the side of her bed, and the two women shared a few minutes of silence. Amalia unabashedly scrutinized the room, and what she saw shocked and embarrassed her. As a member of the chapter and magistra for the ailing, she felt a shared responsibility for what she considered punishment too harsh for the transgression. She had not condoned Columba's behavior and concurred that she'd been out of order and conducted herself inappropriately no matter how disturbed about the frescoes. They had all pledged allegiance and total obedience to their abbess, and if the abbess decided to paint her personal chapel—or anything else for that matter—no choir woman had the right to protest such action. Still, imprisonment over many months and through the cold winter in a tiny, below-grade, unheated, and damp cell with only one small window and lack of ventilation was simply inhuman to her. Amalia concluded her silent scrutiny of the cell and fixed her intense gaze at Columba's face.

"Floriana asked for beaver oil," she said. "Do your joints give you pain?"

"Both my hands and knees do," said Columba, showing her swollen knuckles. "It's been rather cold in here this winter." Her voice trailed off.

"What you need is gloves," said Amalia, intentionally not picking up on the comment about the cell. "I'll send you some, and I want you to wear them at night, in bed, after you've rubbed your hands with the oil. Can't do much for the knees, they hurt most of us, it's the kneeling in the cold church. How's your health otherwise? And by that, I also mean your spirits?"

"Ask Prioress Gabriela how she'd feel being jailed in a disgusting, humid place filled with putrid smell! Everyone says I'm deranged, and there are times when I think I've been sent well on the way to madness! Perhaps, that is the goal she has in mind for me!"

Columba's voice was calm but dripping with contempt, and her tired eyes were flashing. Amalia shook her head.

"I won't," she said dryly. "I know better than to provoke her, and you should have realized that. None of us can win a battle with the prioress, not even our abbess. And yes, Maria Columba, the word is that you're a bit off your head, you always were. But I don't think you're mad at all—a bit batty, perhaps, but aren't we all?"

Amalia finished with one of her radiant smiles that charmed Columba, who couldn't suppress a chuckle.

"Maria Amalia," she said sadly, "you're good with medicines and herbs, but there's no tea or tincture that can bring me comfort or cure my melancholy, except one called 'freedom' and your shelves don't stock that. What I need is brisk walks, hear the birds sing, feel the sun on my face, see a field in bloom! Can you prescribe that?"

Her voice again was tired and apathetic, and the hopelessness of her tone touched Amalia's heart.

"No," she answered. "No, I can't give you that, Maria Columba, there is only one person in the world who can, and that is you! Dear sister, you know that it is within your power to put an end to your misery by submitting to your punishment. Perhaps, it is true that the prioress wants you confined, but Mother Abbess does not, I am sure. She is in the infirmary again and very ill with another attack of her stones. Columba, this is in confidence, and God forgive me for saying it, but I have watched her getting weaker over time, and she refuses medicines that might help because she thinks that God has willed her suffering. I'm afraid she will not be among us much longer, and with her, our chapter will lose a loving and kind heart such as I do not see beating in another breast."

It was a long speech for the taciturn choir woman, and it had a deep effect on Columba, who'd come to think of Maria Henrica as a permanent institution. If she were to die, who was most likely to become abbess? The frightening realization struck her that she might not ever gain her freedom if it were Gabriela! Columba's only hope was the fact that the prioress was not popular. Yet what were the choices? She looked up and met Amalia's compassionate gaze.

"Maria Amalia," she said almost in a whisper, "would you allow yourself to be whipped upon your bare back by Gabriela?"

Amalia hesitated then answered in an equally low voice, "I truly do not know, dear sister, but then it wouldn't happen because I would not call her a 'bride of evil.'"

There was another silence before Amalia rose resolutely, smoothed her habit, and said in an attempt of cheerfulness, "I need to leave now but will visit again. And do tell Floriana to let me know if there's anything you need from the pharmacy. God bless you, Maria Columba, may He show you the way toward ending this, for the chapter will gladly see you back."

She hesitated at the door and asked, "I shall not conceal my visit from our Mother Abbess. Do you have a message for her, Maria Columba?"

Columba stared at her. "Tell Maria Henrica that I pray her pains may ease, Sister Maria Amalia," she whispered hoarsely.

The choir woman nodded briefly and left. Alone, Columba fell back on her bed and stared at the ceiling. She mentally went through every word of the conversation, her memory sharpened by the long solitude.

"I pray God may comfort you, Maria Henrica, and that He deliver me from this prison," she said aloud.

Amalia slowly walked back to the infirmary. Maria Henrica was resting in the very same room in which Agatha had died over twenty years ago. Bonaventura rose from a chair by the abbess's bed.

"Our Reverend Mother Abbess has been sleeping, I believe her pains have eased a little," the tall, square-built choir woman said in a low voice.

Henrica opened her eyes. "Please leave us for a little while, Maria Bonaventura," she said, "I need to speak to Maria Amalia."

Bonaventura curtseyed and quietly closed the door behind her. Amalia approached the bed, took the goblet with chamomile tea from the table, and said, "Reverend Mother Abbess, pray take a few sips of this tea, it will—"

Henrica's eyes focused on the goblet, and Amalia saw her longing for a soothing drink, but the abbess shifted her gaze to the large crucifix on the opposite wall and weakly shook her head.

"Our Lord does not send us pain we cannot endure," she whispered, "and He knows I can cope with mine. It is not my pain I wish to talk about, Maria Amalia, but your visit to Columba, for that is where you have been, is it not?"

The effort broke her voice, and Amalia took a moist linen kerchief and dabbed at the parched lips.

"Yes, Reverend Mother Abbess," she said, "that is where I have been. I learned that our sister is suffering from rheumatism, and as magistra of the infirmary, I feel it is my duty to—"

A slight gesture by the abbess stopped her. "Do not explain or excuse yourself, Maria Amalia, it is indeed your duty to help your sisters. How did you find my daughter Maria Columba?"

The choir woman hesitated for a moment. Should she spare the ailing abbess a description of the lamentable conditions she'd found? Henrica had guessed where she was without being told, and Amalia realized that the desperately ill woman would know the truth even if she were to hide it from her. And so she described Columba's emaciated gauntness due to lack of appetite and fresh air, as well as her melancholy and apparent hopelessness. The abbess listened with closed eyes, her face expressionless. Only when Amalia vividly described the deplorable condition of the cell, a quiver of emotion crossed her features, and a small wince escaped the dry lips.

"But," she said hoarsely, "does she not know that it would all end if only—"

"She does," answered Amalia, a little harsher than intended. "But I do not believe—"

Again, a gesture cut her off. Then Henrica spoke again, "Do what you can to bring her relief from pain, Maria Amalia, the warm season will also help make things better. And before your next visit, go to my cell where in the lowest drawer of my dresser you will find my painting utensils. There's parchment and brushes and various paints and crayons. Take them to Columba and tell her to express her pain and loneliness in art. I know it will help her."

Another exhausted pause followed.

"There is no need to discuss this with anyone, Maria Amalia, nor is there need to conceal anything, for no one will ask. The utensils are my own and have not been used by anyone but me. And tell my daughter Columba that I bless her."

The magistra nodded. "I shall do as you say, Reverend Mother Abbess," she said. "What you ask me to do will ease our sister's loneliness, I know. But you must rest now and preserve your strength for the visit of Father Supremus later."

She gently fluffed the pillows and smoothed the covers then withdrew to a chair in the far corner to pray her breviary while Henrica lapsed into a light slumber. Pater Benedict arrived, and Amalia withdrew. He heard the abbess's confession and placed the host on her tongue. Henrica's mouth was so dry she had trouble swallowing, and the priest silently filled a silver goblet with water and held it to her lips. Henrica could not speak, but her eyes silently pleaded with the Supremus, who shook his head.

"Mother Abbess," he said firmly, "I command you to drink!" And she dutifully took a few sips. "All of it, the whole goblet," said the priest. "You have a God-given duty to preserve your strength for your daughters in Christ, the chapter God has appointed you to lead. You have no right to allow yourself to die from thirst!"

And I hope you live many more years, Maria Henrica, he thought, for he too feared Maria Gabriela.

Henrica drank and the cool water was balsam to her parched throat and dehydrated body. During attacks, she was invariably plagued by a terrible thirst, and refusing water was a cruel punishment she inflicted upon herself. The Supremus wondered for what real or imagined sins the abbess resorted to such irrational denial of her body's basic needs. He suspected but was not certain that she practiced additional self-torture. Amalia knew about her spiked bracelet, but Henrica had sworn her to secrecy as she had Columba many years ago. A week later, the abbess recovered sufficiently to return to her chapter.

Amalia went to the abbess's cell the next day to retrieve the painting utensils from the dresser. She'd never painted but knew that colors were mixed with water and she had an ample supply of small bowls in her pharmacy. She placed everything into a wooden box and headed toward the camera correctionis to find Columba sitting in the only place from where she could glimpse a few treetops reaching into a blue spring sky dotted with puffy white clouds. She watched them race in and out of her limited field of vision, chased by a strong spring breeze. Her back was toward the door, and she only wore her white wimple loosely draped over her head with a few dark locks showing at the edges. She did not move when Amalia entered after a brief knock, and the choir woman placed the box on the table by the bed then turned to face her.

"God be with you, sister," she said. "I bring you blessings from our Reverend Mother Abbess and a gift she believes will bring you pleasure."

Columba slowly averted her eyes from the sky and stared at Amalia with a strange expression on her face.

"If her gift is my freedom, it would indeed bring me pleasure," she said in a caustic voice. "If it is whatever's contained in that box,

I doubt that I want it! And as for her blessing, ask her to bless this room, and perhaps, it will freshen the air I'm forced to breathe!" A bitter laugh followed her words.

Amalia did not lose her composure. "The abbess asked me to bring you her own personal painting utensils. As you well know, she is an accomplished artist and apparently thinks you may enjoy painting. One of our sisters told me some time ago that you did a landscape in the hermit tower that was quite nice. Perhaps, it would help you pass time to try your hand at—"

Columba rose and, looking squarely into Amalia's eyes, said angrily, "And did our Reverend Mother also send me a motif or model to paint? Should it be that damp, moldy corner over there? Or perhaps a rushing cloud I glimpse for a few moments? Is that what she wants me to paint?" She laughed contemptuously then went on, "Tell our esteemed abbess that this damp prison has no frescoes to paint over, only walls covered with mildew and mould! I would not know what to paint!"

She covered her face with her hands, and her shoulders shook with dry sobs. Amalia waited silently, and finally, Columba dropped her hands, and her face bore an expression of infinite sadness.

"I beg your forgiveness, Maria Amalia," she whispered. "I am very wrong to direct my anger at you, who have never been anything but kind to me. But I am so desperate that there are times when I don't know what I think or do."

Her voice trailed off. Amalia took Columba's hands into hers.

"You did not offend me, dear sister, and Reverend Mother Abbess only wanted to help. I know you have talent, and artists don't always need a model! Use your mind, your imagination, Maria Columba! Paint whatever you recall from your childhood, from our church, from our lives! Paint a tree, a child, a chair, or whatever but express yourself and I believe it will lighten your heart! And do not dismiss blessings, sister, for we all need them every day of our lives."

Her words pacified Columba, and she nodded with a wan smile. Amalia smiled too, lightly kissed her cheek, and left. Columba sat on her bed and, with unseeing eyes, stared at the wooden box. Muted noises of abbey activities drifted through the open window, she could hear the well pump and now and then the twitter of a bird. She thought of her long-ago conversation with Maria Henrica when the then magistra confessed her homesickness and encouraged her to paint whatever moved her heart, expecting it to be a childhood scene. Instead, she had decided on the view from the tower, and the details became indelibly impressed in her mind. Almost a year had gone by since her last visit to the place, and she idly wondered whether it remained unchanged. This was early spring, and the meadows would soon be emerald green, dotted with golden primulas and deep blue gentian, and the weeping willow branches that touched the waves of the river would be covered with tiny chartreuse leaves. She'd trade years of her life for an hour of savoring that view, but there was no one to accept her offer, and her thoughts returned to the reason of her predicament, the frescoes. During the times she had been allowed to spend at St. Michael's Chapel, she had rarely averted her eyes from the walls, and their beauty was forever engraved in her mind. As if commanded by a force beyond her control, Columba reached for the box and opened it. On top was carefully trimmed parchment paper and below a selection of charcoal crayons, various brushes, palette, and about a dozen tiny wood boxes filled with powder to mix the colors in the little cups Amalia had provided. She reached for paper and crayon and, without thinking, began to draw the figure of the dark-faced bride from Solomon's Song. Was it because of the rejection the young woman due to her black face and hands had suffered by her peers that prompted Columba to draw her?

"Nigra sum, sed formosa!" (I am black but beautiful.) Solomon had her exclaim to the daughters of Jerusalem, who unlike her did not work the fields and preserved their white skin. "My face may resemble the color of cedar wood or the rugs of the King, my sufferings suppress erotic attraction, but my heart has remained pure and beautiful," she said. Columba could well relate to this thought, and her artistic eye had always been attracted to this figure draped in magnificent robes and the way her left hand pulled them toward her body in a defensively protective gesture. She was taller and even more slender than the others, another kinship she felt. This bride's halo reached beyond the frame to flow into the architecture of the window, and a stylized desert plant symbolized the hot sun. Columba left out the halo and replaced the cactus with a little spruce tree. She completed her sketch without raising her eyes and when done knew that it was accurate in most details except the intentional changes. With grim intensity, she used several layers of coal to portray face and hands as black as she could, leaving only fine white lines to indicate the features of the face and details of the hand that grasped the cloak. She held the drawing up for her own critical evaluation and a bitter smile curled her lips.

"Abbess Herburgis," she said aloud, "the artist you commissioned to decorate your personal chapel would have been satisfied with my copy, but did you anticipate that it could one day be the only vestige of his genius?"

Sudden rage overcame her, and she tore her drawing in shreds. "But that shall not be!" she cried. "Henrica and Gabriela, only God will know of your crime!"

She shook with anger, and her heart was bitter.

"And God alone will know that you have driven this choir woman to such madness that she converses with herself," she added sarcastically.

The black bride was to be among those saved by twentieth century techniques. Some frescoes shall remain forever lost due to architectural changes, dilettantism in earlier recovery efforts, and climatic adversity, but what is visible today is as much alive in its timeless beauty of form and grace as ever.

Columba never again tried to draw a fresco from memory, yet Henrica's gift had not been in vain. Painting was to fill many hours of her enforced solitude. The themes and motifs of her gouaches were mostly landscapes, some imaginary, some from her memory. She tried her hand at her Transylvania family home and a view toward the Alford Plain that she'd loved so much, the rooftops of Vienna, flowers or birds, but never religious themes. Her skill improved and helped pass many hours otherwise spent in idle desperation and misery.

Throughout the summer, Columba tried her best to ban the thought of another winter in prison from her thoughts. She did not know that choir women Amalia and Coletta had joined Anna and

Antonia in their repeated petitions to move Columba to better quarters. Abbey rules prescribed that their pleas be addressed to Maria Gabriela where they fell on deaf ears. The punishment and chastising of choir women and lay nuns was at the discretion of the prioress and others also felt Gabriela's heavy hand, though Columba was the only one confined over a long period of time. The choir woman was out of control and mad, the prioress reasoned, and confining her was in the interest and for the protection of the whole chapter.

Chapter 5

Abbess Maria Henrica was well aware of the circumstances, but her health continued to deteriorate rapidly, and in September, another serious attack with complications again confined her to the infirmary. She would not leave it again. Constant agonizing pain rendered her unable to make even the most basic decisions, and the able and ambitious Prioress Maria Gabriela assumed full charge in all but name. As was customary, Maria Henrica's place at the table of her court was set at each meal and the food later distributed among beggars at the gate. A vigil of prayers for her recovery was held in the church by both choir women and lay nuns. Henrica also began to suffer from congestive heart failure, and even if Maria Amalia had possessed a medicine for her afflictions, Maria Henrica would have refused it. Unless insisted upon and supervised by the Supremus, she continued to decline water to quench her burning thirst since no one had given her Redeemer to drink when His pain must have been infinitely more excruciating than hers. Cooler fall weather brought her slight relief, but without doubt, her days were numbered.

During the late evening of November 1, All Saints' Day, Maria Amalia feared that the end might be near. The abbess had received communion and was resting, her upper body propped by pillows to ease her labored breathing. The abbey was dark and quiet after Komplet, and only Amalia kept watch. Henrica opened her eyes and motioned the magistra to come closer then whispered in a barely audible voice, "Maria Amalia, go fetch my daughter Columba, I wish to see her."

"Reverend Mother Abbess," said the magistra, "I have sent away the lay nun until midnight and cannot leave your bedside! I shall ask for her to be brought here in the morning."

The abbess weakly shook her head.

"No," she said, "I want to see her now! And I want no one else to know. Go, my daughter, I beg you." Her voice failed her.

"Yes, Mother Abbess, I shall do as you say," said Amalia, took a lantern, and hurried across the courtyard and down the long hall to the camera correctionis. Columba had extinguished her lamp to find sleep after a particularly despondent day when Amalia deftly removed the bolt and entered. Columba was still awake and sat up in bed to see who the unexpected visitor might be. Amalia was momentarily taken by surprise when she saw the prisoner's full head of dark, slightly graying curls that had not been cut in over a year. Columba made no effort to reach for her wimple and silently regarded the magistra. Antonia and Anna had talked about the abbess's poor health, and for a moment, she expected to learn of her death.

"Maria Columba," said the magistra in an exigent voice, "our Reverend Mother Abbess wishes to see you and asked me to escort you to her bedside in the infirmary. Do dress quickly and come with me. She is alone. I fear to leave her side and only came upon her insistence. I shall wait in the corridor until you are ready."

Columba kept staring at her without a move, and Amalia hesitated with her hand on the door.

"Maria Columba," she said in a hoarse whisper, "are you refusing obedience to your Mother Superior and deny a dying bride of Christ her wish? Surely—"

Columba made a slight gesture as if waking from a dream.

"I shall be ready in a few moments," she said dispassionately. "You may return to the abbess's bedside and be assured that I shall make my way to the infirmary without an effort to escape!"

The magistra ignored the irony and left without a further word. For a moment, Columba had indeed been unsure whether to follow the summons, offended by the phrase that she was to be "escorted," but compassion won. While Henrica's orders had led to her confinement, she sensed that it was Gabriela's pressure that kept her there because an aging and ailing Henrica no longer had the stamina to oppose her headstrong and persistent prioress.

She quickly dressed and arranged her veils. On her way to the door, she halted at the cross. "O my God, help me quell the bitterness in my heart and be kind to Your daughter who may soon stand before Thee," she prayed then picked up the lantern Amalia had left and, without haste, walked the short distance to the infirmary. The magistra was standing by the bed with a goblet, but Henrica's large feverish eyes focused on the entering choir woman.

"Please leave us alone, Maria Amalia," the abbess whispered and the choir woman left, closing the door behind her. Columba approached the bed, and when Henrica weakly raised her hand, she bowed and kissed the ring, her steady gaze never leaving the abbess's eyes. The deterioration in Henrica's appearance since Columba had last seen her was so striking that she instantly realized she had been summoned to a deathbed. The two women regarded each other silently, then Henrica said with a faint smile, "What are you painting these days, my daughter?"

The question caught Columba by surprise. "Why, whatever comes to mind, Reverend Mother, my surroundings offer little inspiration," she answered returning Henrica's smile. "And I am indeed grateful, Reverend Mother Abbess, for sending me your utensils, they have helped pass the time."

"Good," said the abbess. There was a pause, then Henrica spoke again, struggling physically and emotionally with each word, "Columba, I do not have much time left. I welcome death, not to end my pain but because I so long to see my Savior. And I ask you to grant me a wish, something only you can do for me."

She halted to steady her labored breath, and Columba's eyes hardened in anticipation of the demand to submit to punishment. But that was not on the dying woman's mind. When she could again speak, Henrica continued, "You have spent much time in the hermit tower and know my Silesian landscape. Much as I have tried, I can no longer recall what I have longed to see all these years. I want you to paint it for me, Maria Columba, as you remember it, and I want it placed in my casket when I'm laid to rest. I know you can do it, Columba, and I beg you."

Henrica was desperately struggling for breath, and her eyes were full of agony. Columba reached to support her upper body helping her to sit up. For a few agonizing moments, she thought that the abbess was about to pass on in her arms, but Henrica finally breathed easier, and Columba gently eased her back onto the pillows.

"Yes, Reverend Mother," she said softly, "I do remember your fields and poplar trees and wide horizon, and I shall paint your landscape. I'm honored that you think I'm able to—"

Henrica smiled wanly. "I know you can, Columba, but you must hurry. I want to see it all one last time before I die. Good night and God bless you, my daughter."

She closed her eyes and seemed to drift into sleep. Columba looked at the emaciated, deathly pale features of the abbess and found no hatred or contempt in her heart, only pity. She took a deep breath, and her lips moved in a silent farewell.

"Godspeed, Mother Henrica," she mouthed and left the sickroom. A lay nun she had not seen before kept watch outside the door and regarded her curiously. Amalia appeared in the dimly lit hall, and Columba said quietly, "I believe Mother Abbess is resting, Mother Magistra. I shall find my own way back to the camera." And her head held high she walked away, aware that there were footsteps following her. She never looked back but had hardly reached her cell when someone replaced the bolt.

A pale sun broke through the clouds as the bells tolled for All Souls' Day next morning. Columba assembled her painting paraphernalia and for a long time stared at the wall that with the onset of the damp season was again covered with a layer of mould. Her imagination intensified by solitude she mentally transposed herself to the hermit tower to envision Henrica's landscape, and with each passing minute, the details became clearer. When she thought she saw it all before her, she reached for paper and crayon and, with quick, sure strokes, outlined the basic composition. It needed few corrections, and two days later, the work was complete. She sent Aloysia with a message to Maria Amalia asking permission to see the abbess so that she could deliver what Henrica had requested. The lay nun she had seen in the infirmary hall appeared that evening with a note from Amalia. "The prioress does not wish you to leave the camera correctionis. I am not aware of any request the abbess has made and ask you to hand whatever it is to Sister Margaretha. I shall personally hand it to our Reverend Mother."

Columba looked at the neatly written words and suppressed the wave of resentment bordering on rage that welled up in her, too proud to display her emotions in front of the lay nun, who she sensed was watching closely. Undoubtedly, it was she who informed the prioress of her visit to the infirmary. Perhaps, Gabriela had stationed her there to report what went on in the sickroom. She waited until she had composed herself sufficiently then turned toward the table, where her painting, carefully rolled in a thin linen kerchief, awaited delivery. She took a piece of wax, softened it over her oil lamp and sealed the fold, then pressed her ring into the center to leave her seal. She turned to the nun and said calmly, "I wish you to deliver this to Magistra Maria Amalia personally, do you understand?"

"Yes, Rev'rend Mother." The nun nodded and left.

Columba did not see Amalia during the next few weeks, and even Antonia and Anna did not visit. The Supremus relegated one of the monks to hear her weekly confession. Anyone she asked about the abbess's condition was tightlipped and would only say that there had been little change. Columba knew that continuous tolling of the bells would have told her if the abbess had died.

The second half of November brought a snowstorm with heavy winds, and a huge drift accumulated in front of Columba's window, leaving her cell in virtual darkness. The dim light of her kerosene lamp did not suffice to read during the day for any length of time and inability to distinguish shades of color on her palette put an end even to painting. As a small benefit, the snowdrift provided a bit of insulation from wind and cold. *Perhaps*, she thought, *I've just become accustomed to cold.* But the kettle that Aloysia or Floriana faithfully replenished twice a day with embers from the kitchen seemed a little more effective. Columba's ankles swelled from inactivity, and once again, she spent most of her time in bed. She suffered from insomnia, and the endless hours of dim light again caused her to lose track of time. Then one night, she heard a scraping noise outside her window and initially attributed it to the wind or a small animal that had found its way within abbey walls. When she awoke after a rare period of sleep, a wan ray of wintry sun brightened the wall by the cross. Columba saw that the window was clear of snow and welcomed the daylight. Had there been a sudden thaw? Not likely, since even a drastic change of weather would have required several days to melt away the huge drift. She resolved to ask Floriana, whom she expected to come and tidy her cell. The light gave her a mental lift and prompted her to rise and briskly go through a ritual of washing and changing linens. The embers had long gone out, and the cell was very cold. She wrapped herself in the fur cape and moved the chair to take advantage of the sun, weak as it was. Perhaps, Floriana was ill, but someone certainly would come to bring her midday meal after High Mass. Finally, Aloysia entered with a heavy kettle of embers and the basket with her food.

"O my," said the little nun after her usual respectful greeting, "'tis sure chilly in here! Rev'rend Mother, quickly eat this hot soup afore it turn cold, an' I stoke the fire."

She placed the food on the table and went about setting up the kettle and straightening the cell.

"Sister Aloysia," asked Columba, "is Floriana sick? I missed her this morning! And say, what happened to the snowdrift outside my window? I couldn't believe all that lovely sunlight when I awoke!"

Aloysia stopped in her activity and cast a hesitant look at Columba. "I's so sorry, Rev'rend Mother, but I been ordered to help in the kitchen this mornin' an' can't—"

The choir woman knew that the nun avoided telling her the truth and said, "Sister Aloysia, you and I have known one another too long for such talk! Just tell me what prevented Floriana from coming?"

Aloysia sighed and averted her eyes. "Las' night," she finally said, "when First Mass was over an' Floriana, she finish' her three rosaries as she always do, she starts diggin' with a bucket at the drift that cover your window, so's you have a little daylight. An' Rev'rend

Mother Prioress, she been visitin' the abbess after Mass, an' when she goes to her cell, she sees what Floriana's doin, an' she gets very angry."

A flash of anger welled up in Columba, but she asked calmly, "And, Sister Aloysia, what happened to Sister Floriana?"

The nun still would not look at her. "She been punished, Rev'rend Mother, an' she won't come to your cell for a while. But I did see her, an' she says to me, an' you know, Rev'rend Mother, she don't talk much, but she says 'tis worth you seein' a bit o'sun an' able t' read or paint a pretty picture, like you been doin'."

After a pause, during which Columba was too moved to speak, Aloysia continued, "Floriana, she tell me she pray ev'ry day to hear you sing again, Rev'rend Mother, 'cause you sing like an angel."

Columba was unable to answer. She'd lost her appetite and just stared at her food. When Aloysia had gone, she rose abruptly and threw herself at the foot of the cross, grasping it with both hands.

"Hear me, O Christ!" she cried. "Did you not say that what is done to the least of your brothers that is done unto you? Answer me! Am I not among the very least of your children, locked away in damp darkness? And when a kind soul takes pity and tries to ease my misery, one who calls herself your bride makes her suffer for it! Answer me! Where is your justice, where your mercy toward those in need?"

Columba's voice broke, and leaning her forehead against the wood, she began to cry. She would never know the nature of Floriana's punishment and did not see her for weeks.

A few days later, Magistra Coletta visited. In charge of the chapter kitchen and the library, she brought a new volume about the history of Vienna the abbey had recently acquired. There was also a small loaf of bread studded with nuts and dried fruit as traditionally baked for the last Sunday of the church year, the Feast of Christ the King, which that year had been the previous Sunday, November 22.

"I thought you would be interested in the history of Vienna since I believe you lived there for a while, Maria Columba," she said. "I came here from the Netherlands and have never been to that city. And since we're about to enter Advent fasting, this nourishing bread will give you strength. This will be an especially trying time for all of us, for our beloved Mother Abbess is gravely ill and fighting death."

Coletta continued relating insignificant news, but Columba sensed there was something else she wanted to communicate. She asked about Anna and Antonia, and Coletta averted her eyes when she said that they were both involved in continuous prayers for the abbess that went on day and night in the church. Columba finally asked, point-blank, "Sister Maria Coletta, is there something you wish to tell me?"

After a moment's hesitation, the choir woman replied, "Yes, there is, Maria Columba. Amalia tells me that our Mother Abbess has asked to see you, but Mother Prioress believes it would upset her too much. She learned about your visit on All Souls' Day and has forbidden Amalia to visit you. She wishes us to visit Mother Abbess only in her presence and spends much of her time by her bedside. Amalia feels obligated to our abbess's wish and says you should be ready to come quickly when she sends for you at an unusual hour when she is alone with her."

Columba stared at her then said, "Tell my Sister Maria Amalia that I shall be ready whenever asked."

The two women silently embraced, and Coletta left. Columba guessed that Antonia and Anna had been assigned additional prayer duty to prevent them from coming to see her, and she hoped that the cold church would not further endanger Anna's fragile health.

By then, Columba's feelings toward Gabriela and Bernarda bordered on hatred. She felt less harsh toward Maria Henrica, and when Amalia rushed into her cell in the early morning hours of December 3, the feast of St. Barbara, she was ready.

"Do hurry, sister," the magistra said, "and pull your veil low so you may not be recognized. There's no one holding watch by the abbess, but she wishes to see you, and there's little time left."

Frozen snow crunched under their hurried steps as they crossed the courtyard under a pale moon and entered the infirmary tract. To avoid attention, Amalia had come without a lantern. She'd left the door to Henrica's sickroom open, and its light guided the women down the long, dark hallway. Columba expected the abbess to look worse than the previous month yet was shocked at her appearance and instantly knew that the end was near. Henrica's face had a bluish color, and her eyes were deeply sunken into their sockets, only the mouth gasping for breath was a feverish red. Her wimple with the two stiffly starched "abbess corners" had slipped back toward the pillow to reveal part of her head with thin white wisps of hair glistening with perspiration. Her bony hands grasped a large mother-of-pearl rosary. She was staring at the door as if expecting someone but only recognized Columba when she stepped close and spoke, "I greet you in the name of our Lord, Most Reverend Mother!"

The abbess struggled with each word and paused frequently.

"Columba," she gasped, "your painting is beautiful, a gift. Amalia—she promised to place it in my coffin. My home, Silesia, I still long." Her voice trailed off. She closed her eyes, and Columba reached for a linen kerchief to wipe the sweat off her brow. Amalia placed a hand on her arm.

"Mother Abbess does not allow us to dry her forehead, she considers it giving in to lascivious sensuality," she whispered.

Columba looked at her incredulously then proceeded to gently pat the driblets off Henrica's face. When she reached for the goblet to offer her drink, Amalia's voice grew urgent.

"Don't, Maria Columba! She endures her terrible thirst to honor our Savior and will only accept water when the Supremus insists that she take a few drops. You must respect her wishes!"

Columba nodded and dipped a corner of the kerchief into water to moisten Henrica's lips. The abbess had lapsed into slumber, and for a few minutes, only her labored breathing filled the room.

"She's mercifully resting," said Amalia. "Perhaps, you should return to your cell, I'll replace the bolt later."

Henrica opened her eyes and motioned the magistra to leave the room. She reluctantly obeyed, clearly under orders by the prioress not to allow anyone to be alone with the dying woman.

"Columba," whispered the abbess, "I cannot help you, but officials come for the election. They will hear about you, the empress—" her strength left her as she struggled with each word. Columba stared at her, waiting. "The decree," Maria Henrica began again near the end of her strength, "does not allow long confinement, they will free you." Then after another pause, she said, "Pray for me, my daughter, I have always loved you."

Two tears rolled down her sunken cheeks, and for a moment, Columba idly wondered that the emaciated and dehydrated abbess still had tears to shed. Apparently, Maria Henrica had communicated what she had summoned her for, and Columba gently kissed the ring that dangled loosely on the thin finger.

"Reverend Mother, may you die in peace." She rose and walked from the sickroom without looking back. "I believe she's resting," she said to the waiting Amalia in the dark hall. "Do not concern yourself about me, Mother Magistra, I shall find my way back, and you may replace the bolt on my door later. There's nowhere to escape," she added sarcastically.

Columba did not immediately return to her cell but went into the church. She expected to find choir women holding vigil for their abbess, but they'd be kneeling near the sanctuary. The heavy door swung silently in its hinges, and Columba slipped into the nave without a sound and went to the foundress's altar below the choir loft. She was unsure whether she intended to pray for Henrica or simply longed to visit the image she had always loved. The flickering light of a few votive candles left the upper part of the painting in darkness. The face of the Virgin and the supplicant figure of St. Catherine were both shrouded in darkness. The lower part, however, and especially the figures of the kneeling Foundress Adala, her son Bishop Aribo and daughter Kunigunde seemed strangely alive. Aribo gazed into the distance, but the two women looked directly at the beholder, and Columba felt as if they welcomed her like a visitor they had missed. Both faces bore a serious expression, but in her emotional turmoil coming from the deathbed of the woman who'd been her spiritual mother for thirty-five years, they appeared kind and understanding. "Bear with me and have patience, my daughter." She imagined Abbess Kunigunde saying, "Your troubles shall soon be over." Columba felt like having a dialogue across centuries. She did not know how long she'd knelt there when she felt a gentle tug at her sleeve; it was Maria Anna placing a finger over her lips and motioning her to follow. Columba rose and the two choir women silently withdrew into the shadows.

"You must leave, Columba," Anna whispered. "Gabriela will be here any moment."

She gave her a silent hug, and when her lips touched Columba's cheek in a sisterly kiss, they felt dry and feverishly hot. Anna pulled away and walked through the nave, deliberately making her steps to be heard to conceal any sound Columba's retreat might cause.

Her cell was still unbolted. She was too disturbed by the night's events to rest and sat staring into her little oil lamp until she heard the bell call for prim. The winter dawn was still hours away, and Columba time and again considered the abbess's words. She was well aware of the official decree prohibiting extended confinement of religious persons and even the rule of St. Benedict provided for the "dismissal" into the secular world for "incorrigibles." Returning to the chapter and resuming life as before did not seem feasible, but would they let her go? And if so, what would she do? Judging from the obstacles Gabriela had brought up in the past when seeking just access to her funds, Columba doubted whether she'd receive anything if she were dismissed! Could the officials overseeing the election process overrule Gabriela?

Abbess Maria Henrica, Countess Poppen, died during the morning hours of December 4, 1778, and the somber toll of the abbey's bells heralded her death to the community. Huge snowdrifts and bitterly cold weather prevented the news from spreading beyond the immediate area, and only people from the hamlet and surrounding farms were able to join abbey employees for the memorial Mass in the parish church to pay their respects to Maria Henrica.

When Amalia visited the next day, Columba asked to attend the chapter's private Mass and be permitted to escort the abbess to the crypt, but the magistra sadly shook her head.

"I already approached Reverend Mother Prioress about it, and she felt that your presence after so long an absence would be a distraction for the sisters on this somber occasion. She does not know about your farewell to our beloved Mother Abbess, Maria Columba. I came to tell you that I placed your painting underneath her Sturz to rest upon her heart—a heart that may have never left Silesia. No one but you and I are aware of this, and I invoke your reticence. I thought you wanted to know, for while you caused her much chagrin, your labor of love brought her joy as she lay close to death. Whenever I was alone with her, she'd hold the picture in her hands and gaze at it longingly. Pray for her and for your soul, Maria Columba, as she is praying for us now in the face of God and her Redeemer."

Amalia was about to leave then stopped with her hand on the door.

"My Sister Columba, I do not know what lies ahead for us all, and I pray fervently for the future of our beloved abbey. If Prioress Maria Gabriela is elected abbess, some of us will go through difficult times, but life of the religious was never meant to be easy. The prioress does not wish you well, Maria Columba. Trust in God and let us not be so presumptuous as to judge the wisdom of His decisions."

Gabriela's refusal to allow Columba's presence when the abbess was laid to rest was an ominous sign of both an unforgiving mind and the determination to keep the "disgraced" choir woman out of the eyes and hopefully the mind of her sisters. Gabriela was well aware that only very few had asked to visit Columba during the eighteen months of her imprisonment and had no desire to promote feelings of sympathy for her. Choir women not belonging to the court could not do so without her permission, and Gabriela had no intention to widen the circle. Antonia had been Columba's friend for many years, but her realistic and practical nature told her that in the interest of her own peaceful life in the abbey it was unwise to press her luck and persuade others to follow her example. She'd also grown somewhat exasperated with Columba's frequent angry ranting. Only the devoted Anna persisted and, when refused under some pretext, continued to beg until the prioress reluctantly assented. It was difficult to refuse Maria Anna anything. She was universally liked for her gentle nature and unfailing kindness and had everyone's compassion for her cruel illness, which progressed with relentless severity. No matter how bad Columba's disposition, Anna listened patiently and always found loving words of consolation. There were times when Columba did not fully appreciate the patience of her faithful friend and persisted in voicing a long list of complaints about things Anna could do nothing about. She would even reproach her for not visiting more often, but Anna never revealed how difficult it was to come as often as she did.

Chapter 6

Columba spent the second winter of her confinement in anxious anticipation and desperate hunger for news. She only stayed in bed on the coldest days, and though there was much snow, temperatures were less severe than usual. The real difference in her condition, however, was purely mental. The previous winter had been one of depressed hopelessness, knowing that her only chance of escaping her predicament was to submit herself to the imposed punishment.

Henrica's death dramatically changed the situation. A new abbess could overrule a previous verdict as long as it did not concern matters of faith or the church. If Gabriela was elected, Columba's fate was sealed, except for the hope the dying abbess's words had created. The election of an abbess always took place under the supervision of a bishop and in the presence of a court official. Columba could be physically prevented from casting her ballot, but could they conceal her very existence? Was it possible that official knowledge about the empress's decree against forced confinement could bring about her release? A release to what? A return to life within the chapter under the eyes of powerful cliques that despised her meant perpetual fear that even the smallest transgression would entail new punishment! Columba knew she could not stand such an existence and decided to ask any official she might meet for release from her vows or at least transfer to a convent or abbey of another order. Indeed, she now felt disdain for the Rule of St. Benedict.

Periods of hope were followed by gray and melancholic winter days when she was convinced that her confinement would be kept secret and prevent the secular officials from becoming aware of her existence. These were the worst times when life was but an endless string of despair and misery. Maria Gabriela was just six years older than Columba and of vigorous health. If elected abbess, she would likely outlive many others her age. Prayer was no consolation, and the weekly ritual of confession and communion failed to bring her peace. She found it more and more difficult to believe in mercy and justice, though on days when she was in a better frame of mind, she knew that injustice among men was no reflection on Christ and His teachings.

She anxiously questioned Anna and Antonia about the mood within the chapter, and both assured her that Gabriela's election was by no means assured since she was feared and disliked by those outside her influential group. Some women would pay her lip service, afraid that if she did become their Mother Superior, they would never be forgiven. Antonia, so well-versed to know about secrets, had no doubt that Gabriela faced considerable opposition.

"Our best hope is the fact that ballots are cast in secret," she'd say, "that should encourage the timid among us to vote their conscience."

During March, the official date for the election was set for Thursday, April 29, 1779. It was to occur under the auspices of the bishop of Seckau, Joseph II Philip, and in the presence of two delegates from the archbishopric of Salzburg, namely the influential and widely respected priests Albert von Moelk and Johann Michael Bonicke, both no strangers to the abbey. The name of the court observer had not yet been announced.

The date became an obsession with Columba, who felt that her life would take a dramatic turn on that day, and she began to count each new dawn. She continuously rehearsed in her mind what she would say during an anticipated interview. The only way she could vent her impatience was to endlessly pace her small cell, and the exercise made her feel better. Lent came and went with its frugal meals then Easter. Once again, she gratefully breathed fresh air when weather conditions permitted her window to be opened. Antonia and Anna kept her informed of changing moods in the chapter and the vigorous efforts by the prioress and the Galler sisters to garner enough votes to ensure Gabriela's election.

April brought sudden rains that caused the last patches of snow to disappear, but they also increased the dampness in Columba's cell, and there were days when even the clothes on her body did not feel dry. It caused her joints to ache and knees to swell, but her spirits remained high as the magic date approached. Twenty-eight years had passed since the election of a new abbess, and the chapter had grown by a substantial number of new choir women under Maria Henrica. Especially the younger ones were anxious to see a more contemporary and vigorous Mother Superior at the helm. Columba could sense the anticipation and increased activity as the important day drew near. In the solitude of her cell, she heard various noises indicating the extensive preparations for the expected guests, and little Aloysia looked just a bit more tired and harassed when she tidied Columba's room, though she never complained.

The clerics arrived on the evening of April 27, and after High Mass the following day, the choir women assembled in the chapter hall for a "preliminary examination" and to receive directives about the procedures of the balloting. Bishop Joseph spoke at length about the great responsibility each and every choir women had in the election. He then asked whether to the best of their knowledge all members of the chapter considered themselves fully capable of making an informed decision, which the prioress affirmed. It was then that Anna raised her hand and requested permission to speak. She was suffering another serious attack of fever and coughing and had spent the previous week in the infirmary. Magistra Amalia thought she was too ill to leave her sickbed and hesitated giving permission for her to leave, but Anna was persistent and cited her solemn duty to participate in the election of a new abbess. It was a privilege no one could deny her, and Amalia reluctantly consented. Now Anna's eyes were large and feverish, and there were two bright red circles on her high cheekbones, so typical for tuberculosis. Her mouth was pale and dry, but her voice strong and clear addressing the bishop.

"Your Excellency," she said, "one member of our chapter is not present. It is choir woman Maria Columba, Countess Trauttmansdorff, who has been confined to the camera correctionis on the lower level of the storage tract since the summer of 1777."

Anna's words were followed by an embarrassed silence that was broken when Prioress Gabriela's said hastily, "Excellency, there are good and important reasons for choir woman Maria Columba's absence. Our beloved late abbess found herself compelled to confine this member of our chapter because of her violent outbreaks of temper, refusal to obey her vows, and general madness. Most Reverend Mother Maria Henrica believed this confinement to be for the choir woman's own good and protection. A priest and members of the chapter visit her regularly and her accommodation and food do not lack anything other members of the chapter enjoy. It breaks my heart to say, but Maria Columba is indeed of a deranged mind and cannot be tolerated in our midst. She is not capable to participate in this election. I respectfully request, Your Excellency, to proceed with your instructions about tomorrow's election."

Bishop Joseph looked around the room and noticed that many of the choir women did not meet his gaze and kept their eyes downcast. He could sense an atmosphere of embarrassment and distress.

"Very well," he said, "we shall continue, but I believe Father Bonicke and Father Moelk will concur in my desire to personally speak with choir woman Maria Columba and determine her state of mind so that we may properly present the situation to the secular officials."

Maria Gabriela bit her lip but said nothing, and Anna breathed a sigh of relief, praying that they would find Columba in a calm mood and that her dear friend would refrain from indulging in one of her violent outbursts.

The meeting was immediately followed by the midday meal. Following tradition, the bishop would speak privately to each member of the chapter about the election during the afternoon and answer any questions or reservations they might care to voice. However, as soon as prayers following the meal were said, Bishop Joseph addressed Maria Anna.

"Sister, will you kindly announce our visit to choir woman Maria Columba and tell her that I, together with Father Moelk and Father Bonicke, wish to speak to her within the hour in private," he added pointedly, noticing that the prioress was about to protest. Anna hurried off, and Gabriela made one more effort to gain time.

"Perhaps tomorrow after the election would be a better time, Excellency? Our sisters are anxiously waiting to speak with you today, and there are thirty-two of us."

But the bishop shook his head. "I know you mean well, Mother Prioress, but we are here for all members of the chapter, even those who are not well."

Anna was breathless when she arrived at Columba's door and struggled to remove the heavy bolt. She found her friend sitting by the table, staring idly at her folded hands and filled with emotions that spanned the gamut between expectation and hopelessness. Her wimple was loosely draped over her head, and she was without her Sturz. Anna had to rest a moment to catch her breath, but Columba immediately gathered that her friend brought important news.

"O dearest Maria Columba," Anna finally gasped, "do quickly prepare yourself to receive Bishop Joseph and the two fathers from Salzburg! They wish to speak to you very shortly, and despite Gabriela's protest—" she stopped as the door opened abruptly, and the Magistra Parlatorium, who arranged and supervised visits by secular relatives to the cloister, entered.

She regarded the choir woman without her black veil and Sturz with obvious disapproval and said coolly, "Maria Columba, do forthwith dress appropriately and follow me to the parlatorium, where His Excellency, Bishop Joseph of Seckau, and two priests from Salzburg have graciously seen fit to see you. But hurry, they have little time to devote to you, considering—"

Columba slowly rose from her seat.

"Reverend Mother Magistra," she said haughtily, "I know how to properly attire for visitors. Perhaps, you are not aware how rare they have been. Be assured that they will not find fault with my habit." She paused for a moment then continued with growing sarcasm, "But I shall not leave the cell to which I have been confined for the past twenty months and trust my visitors will agree to see me here! Perhaps, you might have a few chairs brought, for hardly is it appropriate for priests to sit on a choir woman's bed!"

The magistra's face turned red with indignation, but something in Columba's demeanor convinced her that she could not be induced to change her mind.

"Very well," she said curtly. "But be aware, Maria Columba, that you are committing yet another breach of your vows by refusing to obey the wishes of Mother Prioress, who we all hope and pray will become our new abbess!"

"Perhaps tomorrow but she does not hold that office today," Columba said coldly, and the magistra turned abruptly and left.

Anna had watched the exchange uncomfortably.

"Beloved sister," she pleaded, "I beg you to be compliant and calm with the bishop! Perhaps, he will help you, but there's also Father Bonicke, who's a close advisor to the archbishop of Salzburg. We hear that he commands great power and influence and may speak for your cause! Please do not give them reason to think that you are difficult, dearest sister!"

Anna was not sure whether Columba heard her plea, for her friend was staring fixedly at the wall. After a few moments, she spoke, "I want them to see the disgraceful conditions of my prison! How would they ever believe my words, the words of someone called deranged, sitting in the parlatorium! I shall enlighten them how Christ's love is practiced within these walls, and they shall see the cruelty and inhumanity of my punishment with their own eyes!"

Anna had retrieved a fresh wimple from the dresser, but Columba appeared oblivious to her friends' busy hands arranging it around her face. Anna also found the Sturz, wiped it down with a dampened kerchief, and slipped it over Columba's head, followed by the black veil. She was barely done when there was a knock, and several lay nuns arrived with three chairs. These were elegantly carved and adorned with velvet cushions. Columba regarded them sarcastically, her eyes drifting to the stiff and modest wooden seat with which she'd had to make do. Then a sudden panic gripped her.

"O Anna, what am I going to say to them? How can I face a bishop and two priests, all on Gabriela's side and biased against me? I never expected it to happen this way, I thought—"

Anna took her hand. "Do not let your heart be troubled, dear sister! You must stay calm and convince them of your innocence but, most importantly, dispel the charge that you are confined because you're a threat to your sisters! You must—"

Columba abruptly withdrew her hand and took a step back. "What are you saying, Anna? I am accused of being a danger to my sisters? Is that what Bernarda and Gabriela have told the bishop? You know that is a lie, I have never, ever threatened anyone, and I refuse to be traduced in such a way!"

Anna realized her mistake in revealing Gabriela's charge and again tried to calm her friend, but it was too late. There was a brief, forceful knock, the door opened, and Bishop Joseph entered, followed by the two priests. Father Moelk was a youngish, small-boned theologian with pale features that seemed incapable of showing emotion, whereas the much older Father Bonicke had a kind pink face and shiny tonsure encircled by white ringlets. Bishop Joseph was tall, an able and ambitious man in his late forties, who presently coveted a transfer from the old and famous but rather remote abbey of Seckau to a more influential post. His gray eyes cast a cool and searching look at the two women, who obviously were involved in impassioned conversation. Both curtseyed and Anna retreated hastily.

Columba gestured toward the three chairs, and the priests sat down. Bishop Joseph and Father Moelk silently scrutinized the gaunt woman with the hauntingly large eyes darting from face-to-face, and only Father Bonicke paid attention to the condition of the narrow cell. He noticed the grayish-green mold on the stark walls and the sparseness and extreme modesty of the worn furnishings that seemed barely adequate for a lay nun. The bishop's hand reposed on the richly carved armrest of his seat, and to bridge the silence, he said casually, "A beautiful chair and worthy of your abbey, my daughter."

It was intended as a neutral remark but struck the wrong cord in this particular circumstance, and a frustrated Columba could not resist the perceived challenge.

"Yes, Your Excellency," she said a little too forceful. "It was brought here moments before your arrival to save you from having to sit on my bed! This here has been the only chair at my disposal since my imprisonment twenty months ago. As you can see, it is very uncomfortable, yet I must use it for reading, painting, or anything else I do other than sleeping!"

Father Moelk's eyes narrowed, but Bishop Joseph's expression did not change.

"You should not look at your temporary confinement as imprisonment, my daughter, for it is nothing of the kind. You are suffering from mental depression, an illness that is best treated by solitude and meditation."

"Your Excellency," said Columba coldly, "it is difficult to meditate in an unheated, damp cell with mildew-covered walls, where during winter, my hands are so stiff I cannot even fold them in prayer! And my solitude is of little benefit when I can hardly breathe for lack of ventilation on hot summer days!"

The bishop shifted uncomfortably in his seat. "Choir woman Maria Columba, your Mother Prioress has told me that you broke your vow of obedience by refusing to submit to just punishment for improper conduct. Prior to becoming a novice and during your novitiate, you were clearly instructed in the rules of the Holy Order of St. Benedict, which stipulate obedience as one of three binding vows you took and affirmed. There can be no excuse for breaking this vow, yet you did so by refusing to submit to just punishment. Your stubborn behavior has brought great sorrow to your sisters in Christ that all love you dearly and—"

Columba laughed bitterly. "Your Excellency," she said in a contemptuous voice, "most of my 'loving sisters' have despised me because I was born a Protestant and converted to Catholicism after my widowed mother abandoned us children and sent us to Vienna into the guardianship of my uncle, Cardinal Kollonitsch. I did not object to my conversion or to religious life! I wanted to sing to the glory of our Lord all the days of my life, but too many of my 'loving sisters' would not allow me to! They cannot master the most beautiful of all forms of ecclesiastic music, the Gregorian chant, which had been practiced in this abbey for centuries! This envy has all but removed the chant from the repertoire of our choir. And the same loving sisters have agonized, harassed, and tormented me with petty

441

criticism and made a mockery of the 'sisterly love' we promise one another when we enter the chapter! Your Excellency, I can no longer live in their midst! All but two or three of my sisters have totally abandoned me, I suspect because they fear revenge from the powerful family cliques that rule this abbey! I ask, Your Excellency, in the name of Christ's mercy to transfer me to a community where I can live in peace instead of being imprisoned in this cold and damp crypt! Your Excellency and Reverend Fathers, please help me!"

Columba could not continue and covered her face with her hands. The priests exchanged glances, and Father Moelk spoke with a dry, dispassionate voice suited for a learned discussion of theology but bound to frustrate a desperate woman in need of understanding and compassion.

"Choir woman Maria Columba, the saintly father of our Holy Order prescribed very specific penalties for subverting a religious community with outbreaks of rage and transgressions such as yours. Such punishment includes a diet of bread and water consumed while sitting on the floor, prostration before the chapter, flogging, and—as a final resort—separation from the community by confinement to a cell. And in your case—"

Columba raised her face and stared into Moelk's cold gray eyes. "Father, you failed to include the ultimate punishment, which I would gladly choose instead of having those who hate me strike my naked body with whips. It is release into the secular world. The rules of St. Benedict do provide for it. Perhaps, you should read them again."

The priests perceived that the last sentence was spoken from utter frustration yet considered her words unwise and of little help to her cause. She realized her mistake when she saw Moelk's face color with suppressed anger and the bishop's expression change from earnestness to indignation.

"Maria Columba," he said, "I must ask you to control yourself. This conversation serves no purpose if you regress to groundless accusations and bouts of ill temper, which are precisely why you are incarcerated—confined," he corrected himself. "The vows you have taken and affirmed are forever, and you cannot be released from obligations you have undertaken of your own free will. And what would you do if you were expelled? Beg for food and shelter, and disgrace your noble status as a choir woman and your aristocratic heritage? Answer me!"

Columba knew she had gone too far with her criticism of Father Moelk, but she was not beaten and said in a calmer voice, "Seven years ago, Empress Maria Theresa officially decreed that members of religious orders are not to be confined to a cell like prisoners for lengthy periods of time. And if restricted briefly, confinement should equal the conditions to which they were accustomed as members in good standing. Excellency, please feel these damp walls, look at the only window difficult to open and so high it barely allows me to see the tiniest segment of sky! Every piece of my furnishings is penurious, and there is no stove for heat during winter. They bring a small kettle with embers from the kitchen on the coldest days, from which I have to keep my distance so as not to burn alive. My few friends in the chapter have to beg for permission to visit me, and their request is often denied! One of the lay nuns was banned from serving my cell because of a simple act of kindness she extended to me. I am not even permitted to attend Mass on high feasts, only once a week at midnight! Your Excellency, does all this not prove that I am imprisoned like a common thief?"

Again, Columba could not continue, and her body shook with sobs. At that moment, the bell announced vespers. The quickness with which Bishop Joseph rose showed his relief about ending the interview.

"My daughter," he said, "do calm yourself. I must take leave now having promised the chapter to speak during the service. I shall weigh your words and the impression I have gained, and I ask you to pray for your health and your soul as well as for tomorrow's election process. Now kneel to receive my blessing."

Without raising her eyes, Columba let her body slide from the chair to kneel on the floor. Bishop Joseph made the sign of the cross above her head and murmured a Latin blessing then turned without another word and left the room, followed by Father Moelk. The door closed behind them, and when Columba did not hear the familiar rasping of the bolt, she looked up to meet Father Bonicke's eyes, who had remained seated. They regarded one another for a few long moments, then the priest rose, gently helped her get up, and led her toward the comfortable chair the bishop had occupied. He spoke for the first time since entering the room.

"Be calm, Maria Columba, all is not lost if you remain composed and control your emotions, and yes, I can understand how difficult this must be for you! But when we enter religious life, we must be prepared to subordinate ourselves to our vows and to sacrifice our lives on an altar of love to our Redeemer. You have done so for many years, Maria Columba, and I know in my heart that you still are able to. I do not believe that you have lost your mind, and I promise that I will try to help you, but I cannot succeed if you do not contribute your share! You must convince others that you are not mentally deranged, only depressed and frustrated with your conditions. Will you promise me, my daughter, that you will use your willpower to comply with what I said?"

He reached Columba's mind and appealed to her intelligence. She wiped the tears from her eyes and said gratefully, "Yes, Father. Forgive me, but I do not know your name."

He smiled. "I am Father Bonicke, advisor to the archbishop of Salzburg. I cannot open this door and set you free, Maria Columba, but I am confident that I can improve your circumstances and perhaps even more than that."

The bell sounded again, and the priest rose. "I must leave you now, Maria Columba, but I shall not forget you. God be with you, and may He have mercy on us all!"

After vespers, Bishop Joseph briefly met with each choir woman in private.

Such conversations would normally be limited to the pending election, but the bishop made a point of specifically asking each woman her opinion about Columba. He was a perceptive man and easily detected those who supported Gabriela and considered Columba deranged and in need of isolated confinement. Others referred to her as eccentric, at times difficult to get along with, perhaps overly devoted to music and the Gregorian chant in particular, but certainly not mad or dangerous. Magistrae Amalia and Coletta expressed deep concern about the physical conditions of Columba's confinement and pleaded for a change of venue. Antonia and Anna said that Columba's punishment was extremely harsh for her offense. Her outbreak of temper about the effaced frescoes had been passionate, but there were others who also mourned the loss of art that had graced St. Michael's for centuries. Anna went further by openly voicing her fear of Maria Gabriela, the Galler sisters, and certain members of the court who intimidated and even traduced others, inflicted harsh punishments, randomly withheld allowances, or frequently prevented choir women from recreation in the park.

"If Prioress Maria Gabriela is elected abbess," Anna said, "we may end up with additional Columbas in the future."

It was clear to Bishop Joseph that the apparently seriously ill Anna was deeply devoted to Columba and had to be regarded a less than reliable witness. However, each of the choir women or magistrae who had visited Columba considered the state of her cell deplorable and unworthy. Later, the bishop met with Fathers Moelk and Bonicke to seek out their opinion. Moelk had paid no attention to the condition of the camera correctionis and only spoke about Columba's undue criticism of Benedictine rules and his indignation over what he considered a personal affront. Father Bonicke had a different attitude. He did not deny that Columba was high-strung, eccentric, and probably too outspoken for a religious but was of the opinion that most women would act strangely after twenty months of solitary confinement under such deplorable conditions. After all, Columba not only was of aristocratic origin and had been separated from her family at an early and impressionable age, but also she was the grandniece of a late cardinal. Moreover, it might be questionable whether she took her vows to follow a genuine vocation or for lack of choice. Moreover, inquiries he made revealed that lay nun Maria Floriana had been severely punished and banned from serving the confined choir woman because of a simple act of kindness that caused no harm to anyone. Her offense was that she removed a snowdrift that almost completely blocked light from the cell's only window and had done so in her spare time. Prioress Gabriela considered that a grave offense and sentenced her to a month of only bread and water and carrying firewood to a whole tract of cells, which was extremely hard work that twice caused the middle-aged woman to collapse from exhaustion. He strongly pleaded for Columba's transfer to another convent or abbey and most importantly for an immediate improvement of conditions, warning that if word were to reach secular authorities it would entail an embarrassing official investigation. Bishop Joseph agreed to take up Columba's case with church authorities after his return to Seckau and to immediately press for an improvement of her living conditions.

Chapter 7

The following day, April 29, 1779, Maria Gabriela Baroness Schaffmann was elected to become the fortieth abbess of Göss by a majority of one vote. Bishop Joseph suggested to the abbess-elect that as a gesture of goodwill on this important occasion, Columba be assigned a new cell above grade comparable to that of other choir women and to have it furnished with the her personal belongings. He added that they all shared responsibility for Columba's soul, wherefore she should be allowed to regularly attend midnight Mass and a twice-weekly walk in the park, perhaps at a time during which other choir woman attended services. Flushed with the triumph of attaining the highest position she could ever hope to fill, yet painfully aware of the nominal majority of only one vote, the stressed Gabriela agreed to issue the necessary directives after the festivities. She argued that at this time all hands were engaged with preparations for her formal installation and the celebratory banquet. Bishop Joseph, however, insisted arrangements be made forthwith and that lay nun Floriana again be allowed to serve the confined choir woman. Gabriela adroitly concealed her indignation and realized that she had little choice but to comply with the bishop's wishes, albeit made in the form of a request. She discussed the matter with Maria Coletta, and they agreed on a vacant room on the third floor of the infirmary tract, the abbess-elect being adamant that Columba not be confined adjacent to other choir women. Preoccupied with details of the pending festivities for her Benediction, Gabriela asked no further questions, except directing that only Floriana and Aloysia do the necessary work and that no other help could be spared. Coletta knew that any objection would be fruitless and went to find the two lay nuns. She knew it was a tough order to ask of two middle-aged women already overworked, but when Aloysia and Floriana learned the purpose of their assignment, they were more than willing to drop what they were doing in favor of the new task.

Columba spent the day in nervous anticipation of the election result. The lay nun who brought her midday meal curtly professed not to know anything, and Columba resigned herself to wait. She could hear frantic activities throughout the abbey and passed her time pacing the tiny cell like a caged animal. Finally, hasty footsteps approached, the door opened, and there stood Aloysia and Floriana, smiling and flushed with excitement, and for a brief moment, Columba thought that someone other than Gabriela had won.

"Rev'rend Mother, we come to say your new cell's all ready an' waitin' for you!" said Aloysia, thinking that Columba already knew about the move.

Floriana placed a tray with the evening meal on the table and added, "Soon, as Rev'rend Mother's done eatin', please come see an' say if we done good."

Columba stared at them. "I do not know what you are talking about," she said. "Tell me quick, who is the new abbess?"

"O that," answered Aloysia. "'Tis Rev'rend Mother Prioress they choose an' jus' one vote extra she got, I's told," and when seeing Columba's face fall, she quickly added, "But we's been busy fixin' a fresh place for you, Rev'rend Mother, by order of the bishop! 'Tis o'er by the infirmary with a big window, an' there's trees an' mountains you see! An' 'tis dry an' bright wi' lot o'light too! An' Floriana an' me, we take all the Rev'rend Mother's things o'er there, an'—"

Floriana had silently watched Columba's face and put her hand on Aloysia's arm.

"You talk much," she said dryly. "Rev'rend Mother will say if she's satisfied."

She turned to Columba, and her taciturn face looked happier than the choir woman had ever seen it.

"'Tis me an' Aloysia who's goin' to serve the Rev'rend Mother from now, an' I's glad 'cause I miss Rev'rend Mother."

Columba was so touched she could not speak. She put her arms round both nuns and whispered hoarsely, "Thank you, thank you, Sister Floriana and Sister Aloysia. I can't wait to see! No, I don't want to eat, I want to move right now, and I beg you take me there."

The practical Floriana picked up Columba's meal and said, "No reason Rev'rend Mother can't eat in th' new cell. 'Tis here is good food 'cause of the 'lection!" And the three women went on their way.

The bishop and priests had joined the chapter in the refectory for a festive evening meal, and peace and quiet settled over the abbey that spring afternoon. The two nuns could hardly keep pace with Columba as they hurried across the courtyard to the infirmary tract. Aloysia led the way down the familiar hallway and up the stairs to an open door. Rays of a setting sun fell through the open window filling the spacious room with a golden light, and Columba felt like entering heaven. There was her bed, her dressers, her chair, her rugs, and other familiar things, but she only had eyes for the window and approached it as if in trance. It overlooked the park, and above the crowns of trees in their first tender leaves of spring, she could see the tiled steeple of the hermit tower and the mountain ridge beyond. Columba stood with her hands resting on the windowsill, and tears rolled down her gaunt cheeks. During the few times she had left her cell, it had been evening or nighttime, and her eyes had not feasted on nature in almost two years. The two lay nuns exchanged glances and left quietly to fetch the choir woman's personal things from the camera correctionis. They returned with linens and the little statue of the Child Christ to find Columba at precisely the same spot. Only long after they had left, she tore herself from the window to scrutinize her new abode. It was a spacious room, and the first thing she looked for and saw was a tiled stove in the corner. Her privy commode replaced the disgraceful chamber pot she'd been forced to use, spare habits hung neatly on a rack, and her other modest luxuries such as silver flatware and china cups for hot chocolate and tea were on a shelf. This had to be a first step toward freedom! Her heart was filled with joy, and she relegated the bitter disappointment about Gabriela's election to the background for the time being. She knew that Aloysia and Floriana must have worked very hard to prepare the cell in so short a time, and though she would have arranged some things differently, she decided to show her appreciation by leaving everything the way they placed it. The crucifix from her cell was there also, but Columba knelt before the open window, her eyes raised to the golden sky as she offered a devout prayer of thanksgiving. And she stayed close to the window all the following days, even placing her plate on the wide sill when eating. A favorite psalm echoed in her heart: "I look to the hills, from whence cometh my strength."

Then a terrible thought struck her. What if this was but a temporary reprieve likely to be reversed as soon as the bishop left and the new abbess was safely installed in power? Columba knew the cogent authority wielded by this office only too well and just as her past circumstances had remained a secret of the abbey, so most likely would a future one. Overcome with fear, she went to find her painting utensils and driven by desperate compulsion began to draw the view from her new cell. As soon as the sketch was completed, she aligned the little cups and mixed the colors. She was working with frantic concentration, and this was how Bishop Joseph and Father Moelk found her when they visited on the eve of their departure to satisfy themselves of her improved quarters. Columba was so involved in her project, so anxious to complete it before a possible return to her former prison, that she barely paid attention to them, thereby unwittingly confirming doubts about her accountability, at least in Father Moelk's mind. Bishop Joseph made a serious effort to convince her that her sisters bore her no ill will and admired her good voice and that the new abbess was deeply concerned about her well-being. Perhaps, the interview would have gone better had he not added the last remark, for it made Columba stare at him incredulously, then erupt in loud and hysterical laughter that lasted several minutes and left her oblivious of the bishop's efforts to silence her. Father Moelk was particularly shocked. As a theologian, who since entering religious life had devoted himself solely to spiritual bookwork, he lacked empathy or even basic understanding of human emotions, especially those of women. He was most anxious to escape the embarrassing and uncomfortable presence of what to him was a deranged choir woman, who earlier had dared to express dislike and even contempt for the Holy Order of St. Benedict. Bishop Joseph too was taken aback by the hysterical outbreak that was bound to convey a strange impression on anyone lacking empathy for the mental state prolonged solitary confinement causes. When the two clerics later discussed the scene with Father Bonicke, this kind and down-to-earth priest managed to persuade the bishop that the reason was the overwrought nerves of an eccentric but by no means mad choir woman. Maria Columba, he insisted, desperately needed help from quarters other than the abbey.

Chapter 8

M aria Gabriela von Schaffmann's Benediction was a triumphant affair. Members of the chapter who feared her suppressed their apprehensions and joined in the festivities.

Bishop Joseph II Philip of Seckau did not forget the unexpected
and, to him, bizarre episode at the occasion of Gabriela's election.
Immediately upon his return to Seckau, he addressed a detailed
account of the events witnessed during his sojourn at Göss to the
archbishop of Salzburg. The report has survived two centuries and
describes his impressions of the confined Maria Columba, as well as
the differing opinions various choir women expressed under questioning. No one had opined that Columba had lost her mind or
was totally irrational. Instead, the consensus seemed that Columba
was eccentric, obstinate, and unreasonable. Bishop Joseph carefully
avoided second-guessing the judgment of the late Abbess Maria
Henrica to have her confined. The report mentioned that she apparently had many adversaries in the chapter but also several "friends"
who shared her apprehension vis-à-vis powerful family cliques. He
recounted his and the two fathers' personal interview, during which
the choir woman at times had been quite reasonable and intelligent,
at others belligerent and irrational. He described her as consumed
by antipathy toward most of her sisters, filled with deep-seated aristocratic pride and dissatisfied with life as a religious including general disdain for convent life. Combined with a hot temper and high-
strung nerves, such feelings had apparently unsettled and somewhat
deranged her mind, which led to her confinement. Bishop Joseph
neglected to mention the deplorable conditions under which he had

found the choir woman, aware that nothing would be gained by accusing the late abbess. Instead, he went on to say that he and the two fathers deemed her accommodations commensurate with those of regular choir women, who he stated regularly visited their confined sister.

Bishop Joseph seemed honestly intent on improving Columba's lot by making her detention known to religious and secular authorities. Alas, his efforts came to an abrupt end when barely three weeks later, he was appointed bishop of the important Diocese Brixen in the province of Tyrol, which removed the abbey of Göss from his sphere of influence.

Father Bonicke, on the other hand, did not forget Columba. As soon as Seckau's new bishop, Count Adam von Arco, was installed, he appraised him in a detailed report of Columba's case. It stated that he and other members of the election commission had found the choir woman in a small room below grade where walls and floor were covered with mould and mildew. She appeared to be quite reasonable in speech and manner and acknowledged that the reason for her confinement was an outbreak of temper during an artistic dispute. She also appeared deeply distressed that her abiding devotion to the Gregorian chant was no longer cherished. There had been disagreements with the prioress about her personal funds, which she felt were withheld out of sheer malice and spite. Her mental and physical health had suffered greatly in the cold and damp cell, and she sometimes did not see any of her sisters for weeks at a time. Bonicke stressed that Columba had neither complained about her difficult fate as an adolescent or her life as a choir woman, but it was clear that she'd prefer any place on earth to living at Göss. He urgently requested a transfer to another convent or abbey so that an innocent human being "whose conversion and persuasion to religious life might not pass close scrutiny would not die imprisoned and in despair."

It redounded upon the honor and credit of two enlightened clerics, Father Bonicke and Bishop von Arco, both of whom seriously tried to intervene on Columba's behalf and it was not their fault that their efforts remained fruitless. Secular authorities refused a transfer of the "crazy and with a raving madness" inflicted Columba to a suggested convent in South Tyrol.

Bonicke did not give up. He approached Sigismunda and persuaded her to join in a petition to the court in Vienna, citing the disgraceful and degrading circumstances of Columba's confinement. This led to an official investigation that landed in the hands of Count Stubenberg, the steward of Göss. He had no intention of creating a hostile relationship with the new abbess, who quickly succeeded in establishing a reputation of implacable tenaciousness. Stubenberg reported to Vienna that Columba was indeed irrational to a degree that necessitated her separation from the chapter and that the conditions of her confinement were entirely comfortable. It was not known whether his depiction of the circumstances was based on an interview with the prisoner or Abbess Maria Gabriela and her newly appointed Prioress Maria Bernarda. Columba remained confined, though under much improved conditions. In a final effort, Bishop Arco instructed the recently installed new parish priest of nearby Leoben to visit Columba at least once a month in order to grant her some contact with the world outside abbey walls.

Empress Maria Theresa died in 1780 at age sixty-three and was succeeded by her eldest son, Emperor Joseph II, who considered the wealth of abbeys, convents, and monasteries deprivations to the state. He imposed additional regulations and restrictions upon religious orders, and such circumstances likely persuaded Abbess Gabriela and Prioress Bernarda not to subject an already powerless prisoner to more hardships. Since the abbey had to provide periodic documentation of the private funds of all members of the chapter, she was careful to leave those in the Trauttmansdorff account untouched. Columba, who had no use for money, was not concerned about such matters. Even though her physical environment was greatly improved, she was still a prisoner, her mental health was deteriorating, and her melancholy was exacerbated by the physical decline of Maria Anna. As the year 1780 drew to an end, Anna's tuberculosis threatened to win the battle the frail woman had bravely fought for so many years. She was now the only member of the chapter who visited Columba regularly and continued to listen to her tearful outbreaks or impassioned tirades with unfailing patience and love. Though Anna was well liked by all, her constant coughing began to annoy some women. Tuberculosis was a fairly common illness, and many a choir woman had died from it over the years. That it was also highly contagious was not fully appreciated, but the symptoms were stressful and uncomfortable for the patient's milieu. And so some of her sisters breathed a sigh of relief when shortly after Christmas, Anna again entered the infirmary, and Maria Coletta indicated that she did not expect her to recover sufficiently to return.

Columba learned of Anna's acute illness through Aloysia and sent a message to the abbess pleading that she be allowed to spend time with her dying friend. Gabriela did not respond, but Maria Coletta, aware of the closeness of the two women, took it upon herself to ask Columba that she spend nights with Anna, which relieved her and Bonaventura from keeping watch round the clock. The turn of the year brought heavy snowfall and bitterly cold temperatures, and Coletta knew that there was no risk in the unsupervised visits, for there was no place to which the prisoner might escape.

During these long winter nights of early 1781, the two women became closer than ever before. Columba was grateful for the opportunity to show her appreciation for Anna's lifelong love and devotion by trying to anticipate her every wish and doing whatever she could to ease her friend's suffering. She anxiously waited each evening until after Komplet when Coletta would fetch her and instruct and advise her about Anna's care during the night. Columba was well aware that Anna was on her deathbed and that if her condition worsened during the night, there was nothing Coletta or Bonaventura could do if summoned. Speaking was exhausting for Anna and brought on new bouts of coughing, and Columba, so accustomed to solitude, was happy to entertain her friend with stories from her childhood or read to her. As Anna grew weaker, she was content to just lay still clasping Columba's hand in her thin fingers. She no longer had the strength to say a rosary, and knowing her friend's devotion to the Virgin Mary, Columba would pray it aloud for her, rewarded by Anna's blissful smile. When the end finally drew near, a merciful

God eased Anna's suffering and allowed her to spend her final days in semiconsciousness.

During a howling storm the night of February 12, Anna's feverish eyes were fully alert, and she whispered, "Dearest sister, please sing to me."

Columba had not sung a single note for so long and was taken aback, torn between a mental block against singing and doubts whether she was still in control of her voice. Anna noticed the hesitation and guessed the reason. She smiled her endearing smile.

"Please, one last time."

And Columba began, hesitant at first but more assured with each note. She sang what came to mind, Latin chants and psalms and captivated by the radiant expression in Anna's beautiful blue eyes she experienced a happiness and peace not felt in years. Anna's thin hand relaxed in hers, and without averting her gaze from her friend's face, Columba sensed life draining from the emaciated body. She knew that death was near and that Anna was not afraid to embrace it. The pale lips tried to form a word, and Columba bent to listen.

"Love," they seemed to say and, "Regina," as Anna's eyes shifted to a statue of Mary. It sounded as if Anna was greeting the Virgin, and Columba sang the beloved prayer while the abbey church softly tolled the third hour of February 12, barely audible through the falling snow. Sometime during Columba's chant, Anna made her last breath. Columba gently placed her hand over the dead eyes then fell to her knees and rested her forehead on her friend's hand.

"Sleep in peace, my beloved nightingale. I will not sing again until I join you, and oh, how I long to be with you right now," she whispered.

She recited a Latin rosary, her eyes dry and her heart at peace. The only person who had loved her for almost forty years had gone to where there was no more pain.

When Maria Coletta entered the infirmary before dawn, Columba informed her of Anna's peaceful death. She did not ask permission to attend the memorial Mass or accompany the casket to the crypt. The knowledge of comforting her friend in her final hour was more important than paying last respects.

Columba's depression and melancholy further increased during the following months, and there were days when she would not respond to being addressed by lay nuns or the occasional choir woman who came visiting. Antonia, still in good health and indomitable spirits, was prompted by guilt vis-à-vis her long-time friend and visited again yet often felt rejected. There were times when she was not sure whether Columba paid any attention at all when she talked about life within the chapter or rumors from the secular world.

When the minimum age for profess was raised to 24 years and dowries limited to 1,500 florins, Göss had no new candidates for either choir women or lay nuns. Word spread that because of exorbitant fees and taxes levied by the government, living conditions in the abbey had grown very frugal. No investiture or profess took place after Gabriela's Benediction.

When news of certain deplorable circumstances prevailing in a monastery in Lower Austria reached Emperor Joseph, he asked his provincial governments for a review and recommendations concerning all religious institutions, with special emphasis on contemplative orders. Unfortunately, the review of Göss was placed in the hands of a subaltern official by the name of Plockhner, who reported that this abbey could be dissolved without regret or negative impact on the area because the choir women lived only for themselves and contributed nothing to public welfare. Their educational facility presently listed just ten aspirants, of which only three could be considered "pupils." Needless to say, the fact that the abbey owned huge landholdings and substantial assets in cash and precious objects caused the mouth of many a secular official, including that of the emperor, to water.

When Abbess Maria Gabriela learned that Göss might be in imminent danger of dissolution, she addressed a lengthy epistle to the emperor, in which she pleaded "at the feet of Your Gracious Majesty" for continued existence. She stressed the importance of the abbey's hospice and free dispensation of herbs and medicines to the public and reasoned that the small number of students was due to the relatively new institution of secular schools for young women. She went so far as to offer opening a public school for girls. Her letter ended up in the hands of Plockhner, whose reaction was dictated by greed and envy and therefore predictable. He dismissed the importance of the pharmacy, insisted that the hospice could be taken over by lay people, and called the offer to start a regular school an excuse made too late.

These were times of great anxiety for Göss, and Antonia tried to share the chapter's fears with Columba yet met with little response. What could be worse than being confined to a cell and pronounced of unsound mind by an abbess and sisters who after promising love in fact despised her?

She rarely left her chair by the window these days, staring at the small piece of the world within her view, watching the trees bend in the wind, listening to leaves rustle and drop in the fall so she could see more of the hermitage tower. She regularly attended midnight Mass but was never granted the privilege of walking in the park. Columba read little during that year but spent many hours drawing or painting. The parish priest from Leoben visited her once a month and in effect took over her spiritual guidance from the abbey clerics, but he too frequently met with a total lack of response, which he ascribed to Columba's "feeble" mind.

As the fateful year of 1782 dawned, Columba learned that the infirmary had another seriously ill patient, Maria Eleonora, the second of the Galler sisters. She'd been magistra sacristan but resigned due to ill health. She died of congestive heart failure on March 12, 1782, and Bernarda, the only surviving Countess Galler, would later often think that a merciful God had spared her sister the cruel fate that awaited the choir women of Göss.

Chapter 9

March 21 was St. Benedict Day, and in 1782, the usual special High Mass was to be celebrated on that day. The choir women were on their way to church when the abbess received word of the arrival of official visitors. The district administrator and Steward Wolf von Stubenberg presented an official Order of Cloister Entry. They demanded to address the assembled choir women in the chapter hall without delay. A terrible premonition overcame Gabriela, but she calmly complied, and during the ensuing meeting, all choir women displayed most admirable self-discipline and exemplary conduct in the face of extreme duress. Accompanied by several officials and without preliminaries, Count Stubenberg proceeded to read the emperor's official decree of the "Dissolution of the Abbey of Göss," which not only deprived choir women and lay nuns of a roof over their head but of their means of existence. They were ordered to leave the abbey within six weeks. Abbess, prioress, and those holding office were instructed to declare under oath and certify by their signature that they would faithfully and honestly disclose all landholdings and chattel, moneys, and any and all precious items in their possession. They were to hide nothing, be entirely truthful about what they owned, and denounce anyone who did not obey. The women had to cease wearing a habit in favor of regular clothes and were to live entirely on their own. For the remainder of their stay at the abbey, Gabriela would receive one florin per day for sustenance, the others thirty farthings. They were to take with them only their personal belongings, no cash or valuables.

A stunned silence followed the announcement until a composed and collected Maria Gabriela spoke, "God placed our fate into the hands of our monarch, to whose wishes we bow and devotedly obey the decree of Joseph's scepter. However, if we were granted permission to continue our current existence, we would submit to whatever work our monarch deemed fit!"

The count maintained a stony silence, and Gabriela with tears in her eyes pleaded for the state to provide for her and her sisters in Christ so they be saved from starving in abject poverty. Stubenberg replied that the state was to requisition all assets owned by the abbey but would pay a living allowance of five hundred florins a year for the abbess and two hundred florins to each choir woman for the remainder of their lives. A choir woman joining another order within the realm would receive a yearly stipend of 150 florins, and those wishing to return to a country outside Austria would be granted a one-time allowance of 150 florins.

When the door closed behind the commission, a spontaneous outcry of pain rose from every mouth. The choir women were sufficiently familiar with the finances required to run their abbey to understand that the quoted amounts were a pittance and barely sufficient to keep them alive. Most of them faced the cruel injustice of owning personal cash funds from their families that generated considerably more than two hundred florins a year, as well as personal trusts or inheritances, all which were now forfeited to the state. Their shock was all the more profound as it came without warning and included the cruel deadline of only six weeks.

At that moment, the abbey church bells tolled for High Mass in honor of their order's founder St. Benedict, and like marionettes, the women rose in unison and stiffly walked through the cloisters to their choir seats. They sang their responses with the usual devotion but inwardly cringed at the psalmist words of the day recited from the altar. "Do not concern and agitate yourself about the man blissfully walking the path of the unjust!" They humbly and with heavy hearts entrusted their fate to God, a fate that not only was greatly unjust but also would constitute the irretrievable demise of the province's most venerable foundation, together with the livelihood of numerous people.

Many a tear was shed and little spoken during the festive meal of the day, the last of its kind served ending a tradition of close to eight centuries. The women were mercifully unaware at the time that most of the treasures accumulated and created during the abbey's existence were destined to be squandered, plundered or even destroyed.

Columba stood by her window and stared at the patches of late snow and few blades of new grass venturing into the cold March air. An aging Aloysia had earlier started a fire in her tiled stove, and she was comfortable. There were days when she lost all sense of time and barely took notice of the parish church clock chiming the hours; on others, she kept close watch and, in her mind, pictured her sisters heading for service and choir duty. Aloysia had mentioned that today was the feast of St. Benedict, and Columba idly wondered about the menu for this Sunday during Lent. She heard the clock strike the ninth hour and wondered why the abbey bell did not call for High Mass. She was unaware of the commotion caused by the secular visitors and knew that there was no ailing choir woman or nun presently in the infirmary, whose sudden death might account for a delay of the service. Columba watched a first robin's anxious quest for food on the still largely frozen grounds, and it occurred to her that she was hungry. A late start of High Mass, which on feast days was followed by a special litany, meant a later meal, and she resolved to question Floriana about the reason. Footsteps approached, and when the nun in her usual deliberate manner opened the door and greeted her respectfully, Columba said, "Mass was late today, Maria Floriana, was it not? The bells did not toll until nearly—" she saw the expression on Floriana's face and stopped abruptly. "What happened? Is something wrong?"

The taciturn woman put down the dishes and began setting the table.

"I don't rightly know, Rev'rend Mother," she said. "That is, I been told, but don't unnerstand." There was a pause then continued, "Sev'ral important officials from the government came, an' they talk to the Rev'rend Mothers in the chapter. Then they come o'er to us nuns, an' there's a bunch o' us workin' in the kitchen, an one o'them with a big hat, he say our abbey now belong to all th'people an' we's to leave in a few weeks' time, an' to tell the o'er sisters an' that Rev'rend Mother Abbess is goin' to s'plain."

Columba could not believe what she heard and was sure that the elderly nun had misunderstood. She had heard of tightened regulations but had paid no attention. It likely was just another special tax or rule the government saw fit to impose, she told herself. But the deeply disturbed demeanor of the normally imperturbable Floriana left her restive, and she hoped that if something really important had happened, Antonia would visit on this feast day when a longer recreation time was granted.

And Antonia indeed came just after vespers, which surprised Columba because of the silence rule between that service and the evening meal at five o'clock. Antonia's cheerful, round face was pale and her eyes red from tears. In deference to the rule, Columba waited for her to speak.

"Sister Maria Columba," Antonia said in a strange voice, "our life as we know it has come to an end. Six weeks from now, there will no longer be an abbey, or a chapter, or even lay nuns. The emperor has ordered us to live among common people, and we will not even be allowed to wear our habit anymore! And all we get—"

If Antonia expected Columba to react like her other sisters, she was mistaken. The gaunt woman in her worn, shabby habit turned abruptly toward the window and flung open both panes. She pulled off veil and wimple, revealing her head of graying curls, and shouted into the early spring dusk, "Hear me, you trees and mountains! I'm free! They no longer can imprison me! I can live again! I can go home to Transylvania, home to Zay-Ugrocz! I can visit your grave, Papa! I can—"

The portly little choir woman pulled her back and put her arms around her friend of many years.

"Columba, calm yourself! None of us know as yet what we are going to do, and everything is commotion and unrest! And you cannot leave the country because if you do, you will receive nothing! All our personal funds are forfeited and belong to the state now! Besides, you don't know whether anyone of your family is alive anymore. I suppose you'll get two hundred florins per year like the rest of us, and that's awfully little, Columba, hardly enough to exist. Right now, we are all very confused and do not know what will happen next, except we'll all have to work very hard on the inventory the officials have ordered us to submit. I will visit you whenever I can and tell you what goes on. And, Columba, I must go now. Silence rules have been lifted because there is much to discuss. Pray, Maria Columba, pray as hard as you can, pray as we all do, for God's help in this terrible tribulation!"

She briefly hugged Columba, more than ever convinced that her friend's mind had become impaired during her long confinement.

Columba stared after her in silence, and when Antonia's steps had faded in the hall, she again turned toward the window and looked up at the few stars twinkling between clouds.

"God in heaven," she said in a hard and sarcastic voice, "I thank you for the emperor's decree! For whatever awaits me, nothing could be crueler than what I have endured in these hallowed walls! Amen!"

Columba's patience was put to a hard test during the following weeks. Antonia's account of the situation had her expect that the door of her cell would open once and for all, and she would enjoy freedom of movement, at least within the abbey. Instead, nothing changed. Floriana and Aloysia were too confused and disturbed to be of help, neither one fully grasping the situation. A week went by without Antonia or anyone else visiting. Still Columba's mental disposition changed dramatically. Hope and dreams concerning her future replaced melancholy and depression. She did not suddenly become the person she had once been, but she grew alert and busily imagined scenarios of a future life. They were not focused on her Vienna relatives, who had wanted no part of her as a healthy and intelligent child and would certainly not welcome an elderly woman pronounced mentally deranged and sufficiently dangerous to be incarcerated for years. A couple of years ago, there'd been talk of a possible relocation to a convent in Tyrol. She would have gone willingly and done her best to adjust, for any place was preferable to Göss. But now there would be freedom! Freedom from unconditional obedience, freedom from despised women like Bernarda and Gabriela! According to Antonia, it likely meant a life of poverty, but

Columba cared little about food, and doing without the delicacies of the abbey's menu was of minor importance. For years, she had existed in an unheated room with mildew-covered walls and stagnant air, sleeping on a paillasse like a common peasant. She was willing to do so again if only she were free to open her door each day and walk through it!

She decided to make use of her solitude. Antonia had mentioned that each woman would be allowed to take her personal belongings, and Columba set about drawing up a meticulous inventory of her possessions. Some of her linens had been replaced, but her two habits were the same she'd owned that fateful August day almost five years ago, and both were shabby. There was still the finely pleated flocke for special occasions that Columba had rarely touched. Antonia had said that they would have to wear regular clothes, and though she did not know whether she'd have funds to buy anything new, she could barely wait to rid herself of the threadbare habits. She noted down the beloved fur cape that had been such a comfort, a black coat, a dozen shirts, ten pairs of stockings, and seven linen nightcaps that—because of her full head of hair—had remained in the drawer except for cold winter nights. She counted almost five dozen hand-kerchiefs, three towels, and the bathrobe dating back to the time when she had made the customary weekly visit to the bathhouse. Columba included three pillows in her list, a blanket and quilt, bed sheets, pillow covers, and the green bed curtains commonly used in the wintertime.

She next sorted her pewter plates and silver drinking goblet, flatware, and blue china cups for coffee and hot chocolate, a delicacy she had not enjoyed in years. Her furniture consisted of three chests of drawer, one armoire, the privy seat, table, chair, and three small trunks with handicraft items made over the years, several throw rugs, white window curtains, and somewhere in an abbey storeroom should still be her large footlocker. There was also the bronze lantern Abbess Henrica left in her cell that night so long ago, as well as a couple of tin candlesticks and three scissors. Also from Henrica was the little wooden box with the painting utensils, and she was surprised to discover that she'd painted no less than twenty-seven gouaches. Columba spent days compiling her inventory and carefully recorded each item. The task kept her busy, and when Antonia visited almost two weeks later, it was Columba who calmed her distressed friend.

"I will go back to South Tyrol," Antonia said listlessly. "I have a message from my brother, and he has offered me to live in his household, though I gather from the tone of his letter that his wife is not too happy about it. I'm surprised he was able to get her to agree at all, perhaps he feels a bit guilty about my being hauled off to a convent to preserve his inheritance. But I just couldn't stay here where I have few friends. Most sisters belong to the abbess's circle and will live with her!"

Antonia's round face was pale, and for the first time, Columba noticed deep lines on her friend's forehead and at the corners of her mouth. Gone were her cheerful disposition and happy outlook.

"We are all working very hard to help the magistrae compile records," Antonia continued. "There is so much to do, and it seems impossible to have it all done in the little over four weeks until the deadline. The state wants a record of every precious item and every florin, every piece of furniture or work of art in the whole abbey! We still feel obligated to cloister rules, so Reverend Mother Abbess asked the granary master to find us modest accommodations. We now take turns doing choir duty so more of us can help with chores."

Antonia stared disconsolately at her hands then looked up and asked, "What are you going to do, Maria Columba? I did ask my brother whether I could bring you since we've been friends since the time we were both aspirants, and I offered to share a room, but he refused. Looks like I have to be grateful that he will take me in! I really did try to help you, but—"

Columba took Antonia's hands. "I am and always will be grateful for your friendship, Maria Antonia, and I understand! Without you and dear Maria Anna, I do not know how I could have survived through the years! I so fondly think of the fun that we had together when we were young and careless! Remember the night just before profess when I climbed the apple tree and surely would have been discovered without your maneuvers to distract attention?"

The memory brought a smile to Antonia's pale lips, and the two women chatted about happier times with Columba trying to cheer up her friend and Antonia inwardly marveling about the calmness of her normally tense and depressed sister in Christ. And this in spite of the fact that her future was the most uncertain of all the choir women! She could not comprehend that the simple prospect of no longer being confined within four walls was more than sufficient compensation for uncertainty. A few weeks later, Count Wolf von Stubenberg ended Columba's uncertain state.

When he announced his visit, she reluctantly donned her flocke because she did not wish to face a secular aristocrat in shabby clothes. She was unsure of the relationship between the current abbey steward and Maria Agatha and assumed that he was the late choir woman's younger brother. She was correct, and his resemblance to Agatha was unmistakable, though he apparently suffered none of her afflictions. Stubenberg was about Columba's height and held himself very erect. He greeted her respectfully and sat on a small stool, indicating for her to occupy the only comfortable chair available.

Count and choir woman regarded each other in silence for a few minutes before he spoke with sincerity.

"Reverend Mother, it is my understanding that you were very kind to my late sister, who died here shortly after becoming a choir woman. My source tells me that without your intervention with the abbess about an early profess, she would have died a novice and without fulfilling her dream. I am also told that you did not leave her bedside and made her last hours easier, if one can say that about dying. For this, I wish to thank you and pray the Lord may reward you. I am several years younger than my late sister and did not become aware of these circumstances until very recently."

Columba inclined her head and resisted commenting on the cruelty of the late count, who she ardently hoped was suffering just punishment in purgatory for the treatment he'd accorded his unfortunate daughter. Stubenberg paused briefly then continued.

"I trust you are aware of the dissolution of Göss and the terms under which choir women may choose between joining an existing order or release from their vows and life in the secular world supported by a stipend from the state's religious fund. Abbess Maria Gabriela and the prioress adamantly insist that you are not well and unable to fend for yourself."

Columba was about to speak, but the count raised his hand. "Please allow me to continue, Reverend Mother. I have interviewed several choir women and lay nuns who are of a different opinion. Therefore, I have taken your case into my own hands and presented it to the authorities administering the religious fund in the hope of negotiating more favorable terms for you than those allotted to your former sisters, who I feel did you great injustice. However, until Maria Gabriela and the other choir women are released from their vows and have left, the abbess has sole jurisdiction, and my request for your early release from confinement was declined. I must therefore ask you to be patient."

A bitter smile curled Columba's lips. Despite all the upsetting events of the past weeks negating eight centuries of tradition, Gabriela remained intent to deny her the small favor of free movement within abbey walls! The count watched her face and guessed her thoughts.

"I am aware that asking for patience after five years of confinement must seem unreasonable to you, Reverend Mother," he said, "but please understand my position. I am at this time not entitled to contradict the abbess in matters concerning her chapter."

Columba's smile lost its sarcasm, and she spontaneously extended her hand.

"Count Stubenberg, I am very grateful for your efforts on my behalf! I only feel that since it is unlikely I could escape without means of support, I wish I were permitted to walk in the garden! And I want you to know how much I appreciate that you want to help me, as long as it does not entail transfer to another convent! I refuse to submit to a hierarchy similar to one that had me imprisoned for half a decade because I objected to the willful destruction of works of art!"

And Columba briefly described her chagrin about the loss of the frescoes. The count listened intently and found nothing unreasonable or indicative of mental illness in Columba's behavior, which strengthened his resolve to achieve an equitable solution to her problem. The prioress had strongly hinted that Columba was dangerous and her continued confinement and separation from the chapter imperative, but Antonia and especially lay nuns had described her as only eccentric and depressed. Count Stubenberg was more ambivalent toward religious institutions than his father had been, and when his mother had revealed why his sister wished to become a nun, he understood the reasons for her decision. It was not until much later that he learned of the personal initiative and courage of a not very popular choir woman to fulfill the dying girl's wish, and he thought it indicative of the cruel harshness that prevailed within these walls. Was it possible that then Prioress Gabriela held Columba responsible for an interference that deprived the abbey of his sister's substantial dowry? If so, Columba had suffered enough, and he was ever more resolved to make up for it in some small measure by negotiating better living conditions for her!

Chapter 10

A strange, almost surreal atmosphere settled over the abbey. A number of choir women and lay nuns, as well as three novices, opted to enter other convents. The ten aspirants, most of them children, were returned to their parents. Less than a half dozen choir women now sang the seven daily services because the others were needed to assist the abbess in collecting the data she was obligated to submit to the authorities. Most lay nuns could neither read nor write and remained limited to manual tasks. The drastic reduction in funds for running expenses necessitated simple meals, mostly prepared from dry goods stored through the winter. The early season of the year yielded no garden produce or even fish, and the meager allowance did not allow purchase of meat. No one complained. It was Lenten season, and they knew in their hearts that their future would never again include the rich table of the past. Of course, there was no longer a separate court table or kitchen, and Gabriela and the magistrae henceforth dined with the rest of the chapter.

None of the frantic activity reached Columba, but she could sense it. The infirmary had no patients, and Magistra Coletta and her assistant Bonaventura devoted themselves to other tasks. No one but Antonia found time to visit, and even she was so busy she could only drop in briefly to appraise her friend of the evolving situation. Most of the remaining choir women decided to live out their lives close to their beloved abbey, trusting in the help and charity of the people who had never found a deaf ear at their gate in times of need. Antonia reported that an extremely modest cottage had been located for Gabriela, Bernarda, and a close group of women in the hope that sharing a household would stretch their meager allowance.

The original deadline of early May could not be met, and Count Stubenberg who, better than greedy bureaucrats, understood the enormity of the inventory task, demonstrated his consideration by extending it. Abbess Gabriela and Prioress Bernarda finally submitted their official inventory during the third week of June. It consisted of net cash funds amounting to 301,000 florins and silver and precious objects estimated at 20,000 florins. Total landholdings comprised over 2,000 pieces of real estate of varying acreage that were home to 1,400 persons, as well as a substantial nearby farm that had supplied the abbey with meat, eggs, and dairy products.

On Sunday, June 20, 1782, the full chapter assembled after High Mass for their last meal in the refectory. It was frugal, but few of the women were inclined toward eating. After a prayer of thanksgiving, Maria Gabriela presented her flock with the final entry into the abbey chronic she had written that morning. It read:

"The fortieth and last abbess was Gabriela Baroness von Schaffmann. Was elected on April 29, 1779. In 1782, we were dissolved. Amen."

After church services early next morning, Maria Gabriela led a procession of women past the gate tower of the abbey and across the little bridge over the old moat. Not one of them had set foot outside the walls since their entry to Göss decades earlier. Columba stood below the arch of the well courtyard and watched them leave. The tall gaunt woman in her flocke looked like a dark angel of revenge, watching those who had taken away her freedom pass with lowered heads in a slow and sad column. In accordance with the imperial decree, they wore random, shabby secondhand clothes acquired through lay nuns. Gabriela's eyes were red from tears when she raised them to meet Columba's cold and hostile gaze. She stopped for a moment and raised her hand with the sign of the cross as if blessing her, but Columba did not bow or even incline her head. Bernarda took Gabriela's arm, and the choir women continued on their way. Antonia was among the last. She had said farewell to Columba the evening before and now briefly halted to wave goodbye, tears rolling down her pale face, whose round cheeks had become hollow during the past months. Columba waved back then turned on her heel and walked through the well courtyard past the south portal of the church into the park. It was the first day on which she could enjoy free movement within abbey confines because there no longer was an abbess of Göss. Only Floriana was to remain with her until her fate was decided. The nun had asked earlier if she wished to step from her cell. Watching her former sisters' exodus happened by chance.

It was warm and sunny on this first day of summer, and Columba felt somewhat unreal. From her window, she'd listened to the birds singing, but it felt different to be surrounded by happy chirping, and she quickened her step toward the lower garden. By the time she reached the arched entry through the old wall and the brick steps, she was out of breath and painfully aware of her lack of exercise. Mentally, she had made this walk countless times over the past five years, and the image of the beautifully manicured little park was engraved in her mind. What she now saw was very different. Tall weeds choked the irises, once the pride of the magistra for the gardens, the rose bushes were past their first bloom, but without faded ones being cut, there were few new buds. The grass reached her knees and almost covered the brick path winding past small benches that invited quiet contemplation. Columba stared at the neglected flowerbeds that no one had found time to tend since snow had melted, turned swiftly, and headed south toward the abbess garden. Visiting it had always been a rare privilege for women not belonging to the court. The little gate sadly hung on one hinge and stepping though it, Columba recalled the very first time she'd seen this garden when Abbess Antonia had asked to see aspirant Marie Therese von Trauttmansdorff. To her distress, the scene there was equally sad. The wooden trellises along the wall and the loggias had not received their annual coat of fresh white paint; winter storms had knocked down some, which left the creeping plants to wind along the ground for want of support. Here too weeds choked the perennials, and no new flowers had been planted. Columba had paid scant attention to Antonia's lament that the daunting task of the inventory, and preparations for leaving demanded the entire time of both choir women and lay nuns, and the sad state of the gardens now made it evident. She strolled toward the gazebo with her pleated wool skirts collecting fluffy seeds of faded dandelions. The abbess's carved chair had been removed, but Columba sat on a little swing to rest and reflect upon her situation. According to Count Stubenberg, the authorities had not reached a decision about her future, and until such time, she was permitted to reside in her cell, attended by Floriana. Secular employees of the abbey supervising the various departments—such as the granary, brewery, or land administration—had all left, but a number of villagers still manned workshops and offices. A couple of village women would provide food for her and Floriana. Stubenberg was very solicitous and repeatedly assured Columba that the state was anxious to make up for the injustice of her long confinement that clearly infringed upon the imperial decree that forbade confinement. Columba was impatient to leave, but watching the sad procession of her sisters and the despised abbess and prioress changed her outlook. Why, it was as if she had the whole abbey to herself! Plain food was of no concern to her; the important part was that her door was open at all hours, and she thought of asking Floriana to have the locksmith remove the bolt so no one could keep her from leaving her cell at any hour of day or night. Seated in the cool shade of the gazebo and surrounded pretty however neglected scenery, she felt peaceful and relaxed for the first time in years. She was idly listening to the faint noises of life outside the walls when voices attracted her attention. Presently, two young boys appeared in the garden and looked around curiously.

"'Tis here's as good a firewood as I seen," said the older one, leading the way toward the wall trellises and starting to pull down those closest to him. The other accorded the same treatment to the graceful carved railings between two sections of the garden, and in a few minutes, the two lads produced a heap of splintered wood. They broke the thin, dry boards across their knees and bundled them with strings pulled from their pockets. Columba could not believe her eyes. What were they doing here? She had anticipated that the abbey would perhaps be used for offices of the local government or converted into housing for families, but this was sheer vandalism! Surely, these thieves had no business being here. They had not been aware of her sitting in the shadows, and when she approached them, the sound of breaking wood drowned her steps. Her voice had the authority of an aristocrat speaking to a trespassing inferior when she said sharply, "How dare you break what is not yours and steal it like common thieves, which is what you appear to be! Why, I shall report you to the authorities! What are your names?"

The two startled lads stared at the tall black figure that had appeared from nowhere. The younger one, a boy in his early teens, seemed frightened and made the sign of the cross as if faced with an unholy apparition. After a brief moment, the older one gave a sly grin.

"My, my," he said in a jeering tone, "they done leave one o'them behind! 'Tis no more yo' place, nun, but ours now an' you got nothin' t'say no mo' here! An' so th' mayor says, hear?"

When a stunned Columba just stared at him, his voice became louder, and he continued with impudence, "You deaf, nun? 'Tis ours now, us people own th' place, hear?"

There were hurried footsteps, and from the corner of her eye, Columba saw Floriana approach as quickly as her arthritic legs would permit. Columba's arrogant stare remained fixed on the older one, who became uneasy in his newfound insolence vis-à-vis a figure that traditionally commanded respect and deference. Floriana lost no time to send the two lads on their way, telling them to take their wood and leave forthwith and hearing their own dialect spoken with authority by an older woman produced the desired effect. The two boys picked up their bundles and left but not before the older one made a sneering gesture toward Columba and mumbled a curse under his breath. As soon as they disappeared through the gate, Columba turned to the nun.

"Floriana, these were thieves and you let them go without getting their names! We must report what they did to Count Stubenberg to prevent it from happening again!"

The nun sadly shook her head. "No, Rev'rend Mother, 'tis no good. I been told the gate of our dear abbey's now open to one an' all, an' people's comin' and takin' what they want, an' th' authorities allows it! An' them boys is jus' th' beginnin'!"

"You mean to tell me," asked Columba incredulously, "that the rabble has permission to plunder the abbey? It can't be! Why, Count Stubenberg said he would visit me this afternoon, and I shall discuss this with him!"

Seeing Floriana's sad face, she was concerned that the faithful woman felt criticized and hastily added, "But I'm grateful that you intervened, Maria Floriana! You seemed to have more authority, and I was uncomfortable because of his insolence."

Alas, the count bore out the nun's words. Most of the items the choir women had meticulously laid out on tables in the chapter hall—such as silver refectory candelabra, flatware, and items from the treasure chest—had been "requisitioned" by officials, but the abbey had indeed been opened to the people. The authorities, Stubenberg said, intended to turn a blind eye toward those wishing to take things that, according to the mayor of Göss, "had enriched idle nuns through the labors of common folk." It was conveniently forgotten that the abbey's wealth derived mostly from personal fortunes of choir women. No one working for the abbey's landholdings had ever gone hungry, and in times of need, such as drought or flood, abbesses had readily forgiven taxes, levy, or dues and instead opened granary and storerooms to the hungry. Columba was to witness what lust of plundering can do to otherwise decent people.

A few days later, Stubenberg introduced a dignified elderly man to Columba. He was Anton Baron von Schafersfeld, a retired court judge from Graz, who had been asked to assist in some legal ramifications of dissolving the abbey. When Stubenberg informed him of Columba's tragic circumstances, the judge requested a meeting and quickly won her trust. He was a tall, authoritative figure with a mane of white hair and bushy eyebrows, but his piercing blue eyes were kind and so was his quiet, gentle voice that reminded her of her father's. She did not know that he had a middle-aged, retarded daughter, and when learning of the forcefully restrained, "feeble-minded" choir woman, he expressed a wish to meet her. Lifelong experience with persons from all streets of life immediately convinced him that Columba was anything but feeble-minded, eccentric perhaps, and difficult to deal with, but not mad. His inquiry had revealed that the state intended to transfer Columba to the Spanish Asylum in Vienna, which was in effect an asylum for the deranged. There'd been a time when authorities threatened this fate for his daughter, even though she had never hurt anyone. He visited a similar institution in Graz and moved heaven and earth to avoid this fate for his child. Meeting Columba left him equally determined to save her from becoming incarcerated in an even worse prison such as the Spanish Asylum.

He again visited Columba a few days later and promised to devote his best efforts toward securing satisfactory living arrangements for her. His words gave her confidence, and she began looking toward her future with anticipation.

The following weeks became a difficult test. Columba had been a choir woman and part of the abbey of Göss for too long not to have affection and devotion to the place. There'd been times when she hated these walls, but her feelings had been more directed toward her sisters and the restrictions they placed on her, not the institution of the church or even the locale of the abbey. Her highly developed sense for the arts suffered as she watched wanton damage done to irreplaceable treasures. Doors and gates remained unlocked, access to most areas was unrestricted, and word quickly spread that things were there for the taking. Spurred by curiosity to see a cloistered world hitherto obscure, people arrived in droves while the lone choir woman watched in dismay. Objects were hauled off that could hardly be of use to these individuals yet were irreplaceable to the church. Among these were vestments and antependia, lovingly embroidered by diligent choir women through the ages, illuminated volumes grabbed by people who could neither read nor write but took a fancy to the fine pictures, as well as delicate furniture of no use in a peasant household. Precious inlaid chests and trunks were taken to serve as tool chests and feed containers. It was a miracle that the magnificent thirteenth century "Göss vestments" were saved and are to this day on display in a Vienna museum.

And the pillaging mob would not stop at the church doors. Concealed by the railings of the choir loft, Columba sat in her old pew one day when she heard loud voices from the nave. She'd been amply warned and remained quiet, though it took all the self-control she could master not to interfere with the motley bunch of people helping themselves freely from the side altars to anything not firmly attached, such as statuettes, candelabra, and even relic boxes. She could hear the sound of wood breaking and clinking of metal. Did these people have no shame, no respect for what they had revered all their lives? She watched a man walk up the center aisle to inspect the main altar for something to steel. A bright ray of sun fell through a window, and her eye caught a glitter. In the sack over the man's shoulder was a partially concealed sterling silver angel that had graced the altar of St. Sebastian. The head and one raised arm were clearly visible, and Columba felt as if the cherub extended his little hand for help. When all was quiet, she walked through the nave, and the devastation by the vandals brought back bitter memories of her ill-fated attempt to save the frescoes of St. Michael's. The thought kept her from shedding tears. Imprisonment had transformed the frescoes into the most precious and irreplaceable treasures of the abbey against which all else paled. Her disdain toward those who had so mercilessly punished her for wanting to save a work of art was boundless and overwhelmed any good memories. She no longer harbored positive feelings toward any of her former sisters in Christ, nor did she experience her once genuine piousness and abiding devotion toward the Virgin Mary. Even her great love of music was banished into the background. Masses were no longer said in the abbey church, and when sounds of the organ playing in the parish church drifted through the summer stillness, she'd quickly walk to the farthest corner of the park with hands over her ears. Her gaunt, black figure was observed wandering aimlessly through gardens and courtyards during those weeks, and many a superstitious villager made the sign of the cross at her sight, thinking they had seen the ghost of Foundress Adala.

One day, she almost inadvertently found herself climbing the stairs of the hermit tower. When she reached the small circular chamber, her eyes fell upon her picture of the north view, and looking out the arched window, she noticed that much had changed. The large barn on the meadow below had disappeared and the weeping willows been cut down. The road along the riverbank seemed improved and protected by a stone wall. But the wooded mountains on the horizon were there, and it was still a beautiful view, perhaps not as peaceful and picturesque as before, but Columba savored it. Then she recalled the reason for her painting and turned to look at Henrica's Silesian landscape. She was too well educated in the arts and too honest not to appreciate that it was done with more skill and greater talent than her own, but it was not that realization that raised her ire. Here was the work of a woman, who had allowed a narrow-minded and ambitious person to prevail upon her and agree to willful destruction of timeless beauty.

"If the Song of Solomon did not survive, why should your barren landscape, Henrica!" she cried, picking up a piece of brick that had crumbled from the wall and, with all her strength, scratched it back and forth across the faded painting. She did not stop until only faint traces of color remained. Exhausted, Columba dropped onto the stone seat and wept hysterically for her broken life, the loss of all once dear to her, the loss of music in her heart. Columba never again returned to the hermit tower.

A month later, Count Stubenberg informed her that she was to leave the abbey within a few days. The authorities still had not come to a final decision on her future, but Judge Schafersfeld and his family were opening their home to her. Count Stubenberg provided his own carriage for the journey. Columba had permission to bring all her personal belongings, but her request for Floriana to remain with her was denied, not by the judge but the state.

Faithful Floriana packed Columba's things, and since the new regulations decreed that former nuns no longer wear habits outside abbey walls, Count Stubenberg purchased clothes for both women. The simple brown dress of fine-quality material was very different in style from what women had worn four decades earlier and felt strange to wear, but Columba was so anxious to leave Göss that she cared little about clothes. Count Stubenberg had given her five gold florins from his own funds to help cover unforeseen expenses, and Columba gave three to Floriana, making her promise not to donate the money to either the church or the poor but to use it for her own livelihood. When the two women embraced for the last time, Columba found it difficult to part from this faithful, devoted soul.

It was shortly after sunrise on August 21, 1782—almost to the day thirty-eight years after her arrival at Göss—when Marie Therese Countess von Trauttmansdorff, released from her Benedictine vows, walked through the abbey gate a dignified, elegant figure, every ounce an aristocrat. A lackey assisted her into Stubenberg's carriage, and the coachman shouted a brief commend. The sound of hooves and wheels on the cobblestones reminded her of the day when she and Sigismunda had left the cardinal's palace in the Vienna dawn to head for Göss. Countess Trauttmansdorff never looked back.

Epilogue

C ount Stubenberg kept his word and his testimony that she was too ill for the journey to Vienna persuaded authorities to abandon efforts to transfer "the demented nun Columba von Trauttmansdorff" as she was referred to in documents, to the Spanish Asylum at Vienna. Her sister Sigismunda lived in Vienna at that time, but the two maintained little contact over the years, and the teaching Ursulines were exempt from the emperor's dissolution decree. The religious fund finally agreed to a payment of four hundred florins per year for Columba's living expenses, twice the sum granted her former sisters. However, she was not considered fit to live on her own, and Columba gratefully accepted the judge's hospitality. She spent a year with his family and was content there despite returning bouts of depression and melancholy. It was not known why the authorities in the end declined permission for her to remain in the Schafersfeld home. Stubenberg induced Sigismunda to make a detailed petition stressing the importance for her sister's mental health to remain with people she knew and trusted, but it was in vain.

In July 1783, Columba was placed in the care of a woman named Maria Abholzer, who lived in a small apartment in downtown Graz, which deprived Columba of the garden at the judge's house she'd so enjoyed. Aware that objections would be futile, she became ever more apathetic and despondent.

Count Stubenberg never forgot his debt of gratitude and remained in regular contact. He visited her from time to time bringing books or painting utensils. Through him, Columba also learned the fate of some of her former sisters. Most of them wished to live in the shadow of their beloved abbey, but their petty pension condemned them to a life in abject poverty.

Maria Abholzer provided for Columba's physical needs as contracted. The two women, however, never established an intellectual or even societal relationship, not to speak of friendship. Spiritual kinship or perhaps just kindness of the heart had led Columba to feel much closer to Aloysia and Floriana, albeit both had less formal education than Frau Abholzer, and there were days when Columba barely uttered a word. She would sit by her window and stare into the street below; at other times, she would read or paint.

A decade passed. Her hair became white, and contrary to custom, she wore it short, her thick curls softly framing a pale, elegant face with large dark eyes. She still carried herself tall and straight, a gaunt and regal figure.

Then one day, a new tenant moved into the apartment below. Maria mentioned that it was a single woman who taught at home, and Columba acknowledged the information without paying much attention. It was summer, and sitting by her window, a few days later, she heard music. True to the promise she'd made her dying friend Maria Anna, she had never again sung or even listened to music and never asked to accompany her caretaker to church on Sundays. Someone was playing the pianoforte, an expensive instrument that had steadily replaced the spinet over the past decades. When the music stopped, she could hear voices of a woman and a child and gathered that the new tenant was a music teacher speaking with her student. Then the child played, and Columba, who had been about to close the window since music touched a raw nerve, changed her mind. There was something infinitely engaging in listening to a child play, and she knew that the young girl was talented and commanded good touch and interpretation.

Other pupils would come and go, and Columba's fine ear could easily tell them apart. On a day when she again had enjoyed listening to the girl, she saw a small but distinguished carriage arrive and watched an elderly woman in a plain gray dress enter the house. Columba stepped into the hall and stood at the stop of the long flight of stairs separating the two floors. Through the open door, she could hear the older woman talking to the teacher while a blond child of about eight stood waiting outside. She looked up and, far from being frightened by the tall silent figure in the dark dress, smiled charmingly.

"Good day, gracious lady," she said with a polite curtsey, using the term common for addressing middle-class women. "I hope that I did not play too loud? My mama always complains that I do!"

Columba shook her head and broke into one of her rare smiles. "No," she answered, "you play very well, and I enjoyed listening. Have you been studying the piano for a long time?"

The pretty little face turned serious. "No, gracious lady, but I've been wanting to ever since I can remember! My mama says I'm still too young and my hands are too small, but I try very hard, and Madame Hauser, my teacher, says I do well!"

Columba had slowly descended the flight of stairs and now stood towering over the child that looked up at her with large blue eyes that painfully reminded her of a very young Maria Anna.

"What is your name, child?" she asked and felt another stab at her heart when the child answered, "I'm Anna Elisabeth von Gelberg, and my papa died a short time ago."

The governess emerged from the apartment followed by the teacher, a middle-aged woman with stern features. Both stared at the dark-clad lady with the short white curls, who did not wear the frilly little cap customary for older women. The teacher recovered first, but the concerned expression on her face revealed that she'd been appraised of a mentally ill woman living upstairs. With the innocence of a child, Anna Elisabeth easily bridged the awkward silence.

"Do you like music, gracious lady?" she persisted, charming the reticent Columba, who for years had excluded all music from her heart.

"Yes, Anna," she said, unconsciously leaving off the second name. "Yes, I love music very much and would like to listen to you play."

She spoke with simple dignity and perfect reason, and the two women relaxed and joined the conversation, during which it was agreed that Columba would be invited to attend Anna Elisabeth's next lesson. She did so and many more thereafter, and a close affection developed between her and the child, who reminded her so much of the late Maria Anna. The relationship was the only ray of sun during Columba's last years. Her health declined rapidly as the turn of the century drew near, and she frequently suffered from shortness of breath and fatigue, for which there were no known remedies. Anna Elisabeth adored her, would sit for hours by her chair, and the two chatted about their shared love of music. Anna's Mama had remarried and seemed content to allow the young girl time in the company of the former nun.

Marie Therese von Trauttmansdorff died of congestive heart failure on February 6, 1801, her thin fingers resting in the soft hands of a blossoming young girl, who a decade later took her solemn vows to become a Benedictine nun.

Maria Gabriela, the fortieth and last abbess of Göss, died of the same ailment six months later on September 15, 1801. After her death, she was praised as a model of mildness and gentle disposition, but the fact remains that during Abbess Henrica's illness, it had entirely been in her power as prioress to provide Columba with acceptable living conditions, which she chose not to do. Improved circumstances for the unfortunate prisoner were solely due to Father Bonicke's efforts. And Abbess Gabriela undoubtedly was aware that Benedictine rules provided for a dismissal into the secular world for those that could or would not adapt to religious life. She made no such move, nor did she in any way support Bonicke's efforts for a transfer to another convent. Was it out of fear that internal conditions at Göss would become public knowledge? We'll never know, but a humane and compassionate attitude toward Columba would have set a worthier memorial for the fortieth abbess of Göss than kind words chiseled in stone.

Few of the treasures of Göss survived the abbey's dissolution. The emperor's official reason for his action had been the welfare of the area's common people, but in the end, only those who plundered and stole and desecrated derived benefits. Records testified that pearls and jewels taken from relics and altars were sold for a pittance to a Polish merchant or showed up on the necks and wrists of wives of local officials entrusted with managing the items the abbey submitted. Nary a single volume from the extensive library survived, only one solid gold monstrance and chalice did. Some statues and paintings later appeared in surrounding churches, and a few carvings found their way into a local museum.

In 1786, Emperor Joseph decreed the establishment of the Bishopric Leoben. The first and, as it turned out, only Bishop of Leoben was Alexander Francis Joseph Count Engel zu Wagrain, who took up residence in the abbey. The grossly neglected church of St. Andrew was demolished during his tenure with the exception of the tall clock tower that stands to this day. The abbey church of St. Mary and St. Margaret was designated St. Andrew and transferred to the parish.

When Napoleon's Army swept through Austria in 1797, French soldiers were quartered in the abbey, which caused further damage to the buildings already in need of maintenance. Bonaparte himself spent a few days within abbey walls to sign the Preliminary Peace of Leoben, and it was said that he treated the bishop with respect.

Financial difficulties plagued the diocese from the outset, and when Bishop Engel died after a long illness in 1804, Emperor Joseph's successor Franz decided not to appoint another bishop and Göss and Leoben again became part of the diocese of Seckau. The once proud abbey was almost entirely left to the elements and continued to deteriorate. In 1860, Max Kober purchased the complex with the exception of the church and founded a brewery, which in effect continued an existing tradition, since fifteenth century records testify of beer being brewed at the abbey. Kober's "Gosser Brauerei" (brewery of Göss) was singularly successful and, in 1888, sold for one million florins.

During the twentieth century, two World Wars, depressions, and deflation brought various ups and downs and economic difficulties, but today, the Göss brewery is Austria's largest and its product available in many countries, including the United States.

Sources

"Hinter Klostermauern" (Behind Convent Walls) by Austrian historian Hannes P. Naschenweng. This booklet, acquired during a tour of the former abbey, devotes a brief chapter to the life of Countess Trauttmansdorff, which inspired me to research and write this story. It also describes convent rules, schedules, names and dates of abbesses during the 17th and 18th century, and provides other information I used. H. P. Naschenweng appears to be a primary authority on the Abbey of Göss.

"Stift Göss", Geschichte und Kunst (Abbey of Göss, History and Art) With contributions by Professor Dr. Heinrich Appelt, Dr. Herwig Exner, Dr. Walter Modrijan snd Dr. Inge Woisetschlager-Mayer

Studies and information concerning the history of the Benedictine Order, published by the Bavarian Benedictine Academy, Volume 103 (1992) and Volume 108 (1997), containing names and dates of choir women, bishops, ceremonies etc., including brief excerpts of sermons.

A newspaper article, which appeared on 22 August 1937 in the "Grazer Volksblatt", titled "Columba von Trautmannsdorf (sic), Choir Woman at Göss", written by Father Karl Bracher, and subtitled "A documented effort to save the honor of the Abbey of Göss". This article indeed represents an 'effort' and is contradicted by various authentic documents.

About the Author

Eleanor Cripps was born in Vienna, Austria, and educated at Leoben in the Province of Styria, close to where this story took place. A job opportunity brought her to South Africa at an early age. where she worked for five years in a consulting office for mining and metallurgy. Within months after returning to Europe, she went to Burma (now Myanmar) as trilingual secretary for an international team of engineers setting the first steelworks in Southeast Asia into operation; she also served there as official Delegate of the German Trade Information Service.

After a short stay back in Austria she emigrated to the United States with little money and no job. It involved hard work and many adjustments, but Eleanor has always considered it the best decision she ever made and is proud to be an American citizen.She and her husband live in beautiful Virginia and have made Falls Church their home. When a class reunion brought her back to Leoben, a guided tour through what today remains of the Abbey of Goss inspired her to research and write the story of choir woman Maria Columba.